of the organization, the author finds yet another type of bureaucracy which he labels "professional bureaucracy." By defining the ways in which this particular structure differs from the classical model of bureaucracy, Professor Smigel makes a significant contribution to the growing literature on complex organizations. His detailed study of what happens to lawyers in a bureaucratic situation is of vast import to occupational sociology and to the sociology of the law.

ABOUT THE AUTHOR

Professor Erwin O. Smigel is chairman of the Department of Sociology and Anthropology at Washington Square College, New York University. He is former editor of *Social Problems* and is currently an associate editor of *Social Problems* and *Estudios Sociologia*. Dr. Smigel has presented papers at international meetings, including the Second World Congress of Sociology at Liege and the Third International Congress on Criminology at London. Author of numerous articles on the sociology of work, he has also recently edited a volume entitled *Work and Leisure: A Contemporary Social Problem.*

THE WALL STREET LAWYER

ERWIN O. SMIGEL

THE

Wall Street Lawyer

Professional Organization Man?

THE FREE PRESS OF GLENCOE

COLLIER-MACMILLAN LIMITED, LONDON

Second Printing April 1964

Copyright © 1964 by The Free Press of Glencoe
A Division of The Macmillan Company

Printed in the United States of America

For information, address:
The Free Press of Glencoe
A Division of The Macmillan Company,
The Crowell-Collier Publishing Company
60 Fifth Avenue, New York, N.Y. 10011

DESIGNED BY ANDOR BRAUN

Library of Congress Catalog Card Number: 64–16968
Collier-Macmillan Canada, Ltd., Toronto, Ontario

To My Parents

PREFACE

The Wall Street Lawyer is not only a study of a unique and important type of attorney but also an examination of his work organization (the large law firm) and the impact this organization has on him and, ultimately, on the client and the law. Although no sociology of law can be considered complete without an understanding of the legal practitioner, one must also consider the milieu within which the practitioner works. This context leads us equally into the areas of the sociology of professions and of complex organizations. The law firms studied range in size from 50 to 125 lawyers, most of whom were salaried, often with double that number of nonprofessional employees.

The concept bureaucracy is usually used in connection with giant organizations; even the largest of the law offices is relatively small in comparison and this raises the question of whether they may properly be called bureaucratic. Bureaucracy, of course, is not used here in the popular, derogatory sense, but rather as described by Max Weber. The major characteristics of bureaucracy he found (as listed by Peter M. Blau in *Bureaucracy in Modern Society*) were used to determine the answer to the question. Briefly, they are: a division of labor, a defined system of hierarchy of authority, a consistent system of abstract rules, impersonal detachment of the official in interpersonal relationships, hiring and promotion based on technical qualifications.

The examination of the Wall Street law firms revealed that these offices do manifest these characteristics. This finding is not unexpected, since it is probably true that all formal organizations contain elements of bureaucracy. In fact, except for the ideal type, bureaucracy must be placed on a continuum. Richard H. Hall, in the July 1963 *American Journal of Sociology* goes a step further and contends that not only must bureaucracy be placed on a continuum but each element in bureaucracy can be arranged on such a gradation. Therefore there are not only degrees of bureaucracy but also variations in intensity of its constituent elements. The large law firms can be judged bureaucratic then, even though they do not have all the bureaucratic elements in the same degree as one would find in government agencies or in military organizations or in giant corporations.

Most of this book is written on three levels—from well-documented evidence, where the points made seem conclusive, to material that is believed to be true but for a variety of reasons is not as well-documented, and finally, to speculation based more on insight and intuition than on the scientific analysis of the collected data. Direct quotations from respondents are often used as evidence. Unless a selected quotation is preceded by a modifier, it expresses my opinion that the respondent's statement is, for the most part, consonant with reality, or objectively represents the stated evaluations of a sizable portion of the sample. Some of the composite pictures may be irritating to some lawyers, when elements of that picture do not fit their firm. Still, such a presentation is often necessary to insure anonymity; furthermore, where there are only small differences between organizations, the overview in fact presents a more accurate account of the whole.

Many people have helped me with this book and I would like to express in print my gratitude to them. My appreciation goes first to the many lawyers in my sample who gave generously of their most priceless commodity—time. Special thanks are extended to sociologists Louis Kriesberg, Karl Schuessler, Dietrich Rueschemeyer, and Jerome J. Carlin, who read the entire manuscript in its early drafts and gave unstintingly of their advice. David Riesman, Marvin Bressler, and Amitai Etzioni are among those who examined parts of this volume and their suggestions were most helpful. The comments of lawyers who read these pages were especially valuable, among them Louis Auchincloss, Jay H. Topkis, and Bernard Robbins. George Turner and Justice Samuel J. Silverman were generously helpful in opening the doors of the Wall Street Law firms. Among the many graduate students who helped with the statistics and with the tedious job of checking and rechecking references are William Simon, Martin Goldman, Paul Montagna, and Heather Strange. Wholehearted appreciation is due to my father, Dr. Joseph O. Smigel, to Ursula Wolff, and Jane Shipton for their editorial advice on the early drafts, and to Martha Crossen for her diligent and creative final editing.

Indiana and New York Universities through their special research funds provided sufficient sums to make this study possible; the University of Chicago Law School, in appointing me a Senior Fellow in Law and the Behavioral Sciences for a period of a year, allowed not only uninterrupted time to work on the collected data but also the opportunity to talk to Dean Edward H. Levi (now Provost of the University of Chicago) and his staff, to my fellow Fellows, especially Howard Mann, and to colleagues Fred L. Strodtbeck, Anselm L. Strauss, and Edward Shils, who provided stimulation and encouragement.

Portions of this book first appeared in somewhat different form in articles and are used here with the kind permission of the publishers: "Interviewing a Legal Elite: The Wall Street Lawyer," 64, *American Journal of Sociology*, September, 1958. "The Impact of Recruitment on the Organization of the Large Law Firm," 25, *American Sociological Review*, February, 1960. "Professional Bureaucracy and the Large Wall Street Law Firms," 2, *Estudios de Sociologia*, 1962.

Erwin O. Smigel

New York, November 3, 1963

CONTENTS

	Preface	*vii*
ONE	The Large Law Firm In American Society	*1*
TWO	Sample, Method, and Techniques	*17*
THREE	The Recruitment of Wall Street Lawyers	*36*
FOUR	The Selecting-out Process and Resultant Career Patterns	*72*
FIVE	The Selecting-out Process: Past and Present	*113*
SIX	Work of the Wall Street Lawyer	*141*
SEVEN	Differences in the Practice of Law: A Glance at Various Types of Large and Small Firms	*171*
EIGHT	Organization of the Large Law Firm	*205*
NINE	The Success of the Organization: Rationale	*249*
TEN	Strains and Dilemmas	*292*
ELEVEN	The Professional Organization Man?	*311*
TWELVE	Realities and Possibilities	*341*
	Index	*359*

THE WALL STREET LAWYER

ONE

THE LARGE LAW FIRM

IN AMERICAN SOCIETY

THE demands of the industrial revolution and the social invention of the corporation, with its ability to amass capital, have been primary factors in the increasing development of large-scale organizations.[1] How the social structure of these organizations—with their reliance on increased specialization, and their demands for teamwork—is affecting the individual in his work role (and in his self-concept) has been for some time a matter of concern to sociologists and other social scientists.

Team-play is hardly a new requirement for mankind, although the phrase may have gathered special meanings in recent times, some of these pejorative. The individual being socialized into any society must learn not only the rights and privileges afforded him but also the restrictions placed on him if he is not to come into conflict with society. What is new is the tremendous increase in the division of labor with its concomitant growth in the demand for team-play and the relatively greater number of people who are now working in large-scale organizations and in a larger variety of them than formerly. This is the issue which now engages many sociologists: with increased specialization, and therefore increased dependence upon the resources of the large organization, the individual necessarily finds his personal sphere of independent action narrowed. How does this affect him personally? How does it—or does it—alter his attitude towards his society? Robert K. Merton[2] has hypothesized that bureaucracy, through its demands for limited responsibility concerning a limited problem, makes for a narrowing of perception of larger issues. This, together with the desire for reward, makes the bureaucratic "worker" afraid to take a stand for fear of being wrong. Eventually, these workers become "methodical, prudent, and disciplined"—in a word, conformist. Whyte[3] argues that this conformity tends to become generalized—that the "worker" conforms not only in the plant but in his life outside the work group as well. His life in the family and community analogously takes on the same conforming tendencies.

Most of the speculation concerning the socializing processes of large-scale organizations has referred to civil servants and to employees (including executives) of large industrial plants. Recently, however, the focus has begun to shift to professionals:[4] scientists, engineers, physicians, and, with this volume, lawyers. Some of the factors which helped create large-scale industrial organizations are also affecting the professions; perhaps most dramatically in the case of the scientists, who have been leaving academic research for salaried jobs in industry in increasing numbers.[5] Another, and independent, factor operates for an increase of specialization among the professional groups—the proliferation of knowledge, which makes it more and more difficult for a single individual simply to learn enough chemistry or medicine to make him perform with competence in all situations. Thus, we are now seeing the development of work units which contain elements of the production line and of bureaucratic structure. Business firms set up "research and development" units which employ scientists and engineers on a salaried basis. Physicians who have specialized in different branches of medicine set up private clinics for more competent care of the "whole" person than the general practitioner can presumably offer.

As our society has grown increasingly complex, the legal tools for social control have indeed increased beyond the possible total comprehension of a single individual. And the lawyers, like the scientists, have increasingly, although on a much smaller scale, met the problem by specializing within large law firms.

Much of the published literature on "big" organizations supports the charge that bureaucracy breeds conformity and stifles creativity. The charge is a serious one, for it implies the fostering of mediocrity and, eventually, stagnation perhaps even on a national level. When we turn to the practice and formulation of law, the implication is peculiarly disturbing. We boast of being a nation not of men, but of laws. If the men who help to shape our laws are shaped in the direction of conformity, we are threatened with the loss of that capacity for innovation which may well be essential for the continuing growth and adaptation of a society.

The nature of the research problem for the social scientist who is studying lawyers in large law firms has a number of characteristics which make it distinct from studies of professional people who work in industry. Scientists in industry, for example, work for nonprofessionals—the businessmen. Lawyers in large law firms are apt to be either partners or associates (employees) who work for partners. The salaried lawyers described in this book work for lawyers, whereas the scientists work for businessmen who cannot be expected to know them as well as their colleagues would. Furthermore, whereas scientists are expected to work in teams, the practice of law is thought of as among the last of the "free" professions. The public expectation that the lawyer will function as an independent practitioner may threaten his prestige or authority if he becomes a team man. The thought of a lawyer as a salaried person is obnoxious to some while this same thought about the scientist is not, since precedent for the scientist was established by his presence in academia. The very fact, however, that lawyers historically and statistically did and do practice as solo or small-firm attorneys gives the sociologist an ideal opportunity to compare the "free" lawyer with the member of the "law factory."

The popular issue of personal freedom is vital in this study, for it raises a number of central questions: do lawyers in large organizations "overconform" and become methodical, prudent, and disciplined beyond the need of their profession? If the answer is "yes," how does this affect their creativity? Will they be able to find solutions to problems where precedent (so important to the lawyer) does not exist? Will they be able to answer the client's professional needs? The controversy over these queries revolves around whether the professional person can be sufficiently free despite the demands of the organization (requirements of team-play, the insistence of conformity to organizational norms, etc.) to use the benefits of teamwork to give a client the service he needs. The problem differs somewhat for the various types of lawyers in this investigation because some are employees and some are employers.

The problems of the conflicts between nonprofessional employees and their organization are greater for attorneys, since there is a substantial possibility that the values of the profession may be in conflict with those of the organization. An attempt will be made to evaluate the degree to which lawyers in large law organizations are successful in their fight for professional independence, while taking advantage of the benefit which the "team" offers the client.

On a broader basis, what is the significance of the development of the large law firm for society? This is difficult to measure—and it is outside the scope of this study. It is not, however, a subject on which it is difficult to find written opinion, although the opinions conflict. And no one doubts that the impact of the Wall Street lawyer on our society is significant.

Spokesman for Big Business —

The large law offices are indisputably the spokesman for big business—hence the term "Wall Street lawyer." (Although the law firms represent corporations, they cannot by law incorporate themselves.) According to a leading legal historian, James Willard Hurst, the lawyer became a familiar figure on boards of directors after 1880.

> First, the railroad general counsel, and then the lawyer for the investment banker led the way into this new role as corporation director. Dos Passos observed in 1907 that: "The lawyer boldly enters into the business end of his client's transaction—he sells him prudence and experience, sometimes even usurping the client's discretion and judgment." The reach and detail of new social

regulation, the higher stakes, and the wider range of interests which must be reckoned with in guiding affairs—all these emphasized the lawyer's planning function. Also they put a premium on the hardheaded objectivity of the policy advisor; more and more this was what the client's interests demanded rather than the zealous partisanship of an advocate. Clients were no longer satisfied to put to their lawyers a statement of facts on which to obtain an "opinion." They wanted the lawyer to share the responsibility of deciding what were the determining facts in their situation, to bear part of the weight of fixing policy in the light of the facts so assessed.[6]

However a controversy exists over the wisdom of accepting positions on their clients' boards of directors (because such intimacy might affect the lawyer's professional decisions), still, many leading Wall Street lawyers are active members of their clients' corporations. Edward S. S. Sunderland (Davis Polk Wardwell Sunderland & Kiendl), for example, is a director and member of the executive committee of the Illinois Central and a trustee of the United States Trust Company. Arthur H. Dean (Sullivan & Cromwell) is a director of the American Agricultural Chemical Company, American Banknote Company, Bank of New York, Mexican Light and Power Company, Ltd., Solvay American Corporation, and American Metal Climax, Inc. In the latter corporation he has also been a member of the executive, finance, and compensation committees.

The lawyers' position on boards of directors and their indispensable legal advice give attorneys increased opportunity (some lawyers regard it as a forced necessity) to take part in the business decisions and policy-making of their clients. Since many of their clients are the giant corporations, their decisions have an important effect on the country. In their role as spokesmen, advisors, and often policy-makers for big business,[7] these lawyers become part of what C. Wright Mills called the "power elite."

As advice givers these attorneys also may serve, as Martin Mayer[8] points out, as the conscience of big business. This is part of their job. Justice Charles Edward Wyzanski, Jr., writes: "The modern lawyer almost invariably advises his client upon not only what is permissible but also what is desirable. And it is in the public interest that the lawyer should regard himself as more than predictor of legal consequences. His duty to society as well as to his client involves many relevant social, economic and philosophic considerations."[9]

Lawyers often use their positions as advisors to guide their clients into what they believe to be proper and moral legal positions. The opinion letter (a document in which the law firm says that in its judgment "such-and-such" is the law or within the law) in itself tends to induce the client to take conservative business positions and perhaps to increase his economic conscience in terms of a broader distribution of profits. It often gives advice on laws not yet written, what Adolf Berle calls "inchoate law."[10] This means that the lawyer tells his client there is no law preventing a certain behavior; nevertheless, if he does "such-and-such," his action will ensure that such a law will be enacted. The lawyer then, as the conscience of the businessman, is saying: "So far as the law goes, you can do this—but you must not."

The histories of law firms cite anecdotes which illustrate this function of the lawyer. The late William Nelson Cromwell is credited, for example, with persuading one of his clients to give full disclosure of information in the company's annual report,[11] an innovation at that time. Now people dealing with the giant corporations have come to rely on the trustworthiness of the corporations' statements when they have been formulated by respected outside counsel. The Wall Street lawyers advise people who control other people's money. They stand in for the beneficiaries and must take this responsibility seriously.

In his book *Corporation Lawyer: Saint or Sinner?* Beryl Harold Levy devotes an entire chapter to the creative corporation lawyer. His feelings on the subject are so strong that he is able to proclaim a Cromwell or a Cravath just as intellectually bold as a John Marshall in the building of American society. They were particularly creative when it came to business needs. They helped make possible the growth of corporations "by bold counsel and by invention of new forms of credit, financing and control."[12] The holding company was one such device. The collapsible corporation, designed to minimize tax consequences, another. In fact,

Levy finds, "Our contemporary credit-industrial economy of abundance could not have been fashioned without the brilliant imagination of the daring corporation lawyers of the 19th century who forged one device after another to lead the way, pressing far beyond existing law."[13]

The problem of determining the effect the large law firms have on the law is the difficult one. Professor Harry Pratter of Indiana University's law school writes in response to a query on this topic:

> If you start with the premise that law is "made" at all in the judicial process, then it is the result of a cooperative process in which clients, lawyers, judges, legal writers all play a part. In this sense all lawyers and all law firms, small or large, who participate in litigation, help make the law, by new arguments, new analogies, new insights, new use of precedent, etc. It can even be said that it is the job of the lawyer to educate the judge, to help him see the precedents in a new way.[14]

To the extent that large law firms are more capable than others, handle more important cases than others, to the extent that they are more imaginative and more influential, they may play a particularly significant role in this process—especially in the area of business law. Eventually, the practices suggested by the lawyers may become part of the mores and accepted business practices of the community and so indirectly affect the law or its formulation.

Since much of their work deals with the grey area of the law (an area where no one really knows what the law is), the large firms' capacity to direct substantial portions of their energies toward research on a subject and to turn their most creative minds to working on the meaning of that research make it possible for them to formulate new definitions of the law. While there is only hearsay on the subject, judges are said to know which firms are the most creative, which have done the most research. It is said that they begin to rely on those firms' well-documented briefs before handing down their decisions.

The financial position of the law firms and their clients enables these large offices to appeal a case all the way to the Supreme

Court of the United States, leaving the weight of their arguments through the court system. Former Justice Bruce Bromley, of Cravath, Swaine & Moore, was able to take the *Esquire* case, in which the Postmaster General attempted to deprive (in what was considered a form of censorship) the magazine of its second-class mailing privileges, to the Supreme Court. The Cravath firm, which argued forty-three cases before the United States Supreme Court between 1928 and 1944,[15] was partly responsible for the demise of the NRA. Because of its steel clients, the Cravath firm cooperated with the counsel for the Kosher poultry dealers (Schecter) who had been convicted of disobeying the code for the live poultry industry. A Cravath lawyer made the main argument before the Court.[16]

Lawyers also "make" laws in other ways. They influence legislators. In fact, a few Wall Street lawyers, such as Senator Case of New Jersey (Simpson Thacher & Bartlett), were elected to legislatures. They lobby. They draft model statutes and uniform laws. So that Swaine writes: "In the early months of NRA the Cravath firm prepared codes for the steel and several other industries, and in the ensuing two years it advised in the operation of those and many other codes."[17] They testify before legislative committees. With the help of clients, and to serve their clients' interests, they "invent" new business forms and techniques which often call for the enactment of new legislation to counter these social inventions.

Public Services —

In a sense more directly affecting the public, the large law firms are also influential, in that they provide recruiting centers for government service. This is especially true in periods of emergency. According to Arthur Dean, these large partnerships offer "an exceptional opportunity to acquire a liberal education in modern government and society. Such partnerships are likely in the future, as they have in the past, to prepare and offer for public service men exceptionally qualified to serve. The very nature of such a partnership permits a man to do more, not less civic work, and permits him, as a true officer of the court and a responsible citizen, more readily to enter public service for various

periods and to serve society to his full professional capacity."[18]
Firms like Donovan Leisure Newton & Irvine and Simpson
Thacher & Bartlett encourage their lawyers to participate in poli-
tics, in government, and in professional activities. Few, however,
are active in grass-root politics; Senator Case is one, Justice J.
Edward Lumbard, Jr. (Donovan's firm) of the United States
Court of Appeals is another. Former Justice Simon J. Rifkind
(Paul, Weiss, Rifkind, Wharton & Garrison) helped manage
Mayor Wagner's (New York City) campaign for that office. R.
Burdel Bixby[19] (Dewey's firm) was very active in Governor Rocke-
feller's bid for the 1960 Presidential nomination. The late Gen-
eral Donovan, noted for his management of the OSS and his
World War I record, ran for Governor of New York. Others, like
Dewey, Willkie, Davis, and Stevenson, who have been very
important in government, all have or had important posts in large
law firms.

The list of those who have been appointed to high public
office is almost endless. Some, like John T. Cahill, senior partner
in the firm of Cahill, Gordon, Reindel & Ohl, seem to commute
between government public service and the law firm. They are
constantly shuttling between Washington and Wall Street. Cahill
started his legal career as an associate in the firm of Cotton &
Franklin. Four years later he left to become Second Assistant
Attorney General of New York. He returned to practice in 1933
as a partner in Cotton & Franklin, stayed for three years, then
spent a year as Special Assistant to the District Attorney of New
York County. He came back to the firm for two years, left again
in 1939 to become United States District Attorney, Southern
District, for three years, and then returned as head of his present
firm.

Among those internationally known are Dean Acheson (Covington & Burling—a large Washington, D.C., law office) and the
late John Foster Dulles (Sullivan & Cromwell) who served different administrations as controversial Secretaries of State. Dulles
later further involved one of his former partners, Arthur Dean,
in international affairs by making him Special Deputy to the
Secretary of State with the rank of Ambassador, and sent him to
Korea where he carried on the Panmunjom negotiations in 1953.

Most recently he served the government as spokesman for the
United States in the atomic disarmament conferences after returning to head Sullivan & Cromwell. President Eisenhower appointed
John Marshall Harlan (Root, Ballantine, Harlan, Bushby &
Palmer) Associate Justice of the United States Supreme Court,
and Herbert Brownell (Lord, Day & Lord) Attorney General of
the United States. President Kennedy too continued the practice
of "raiding" the large law firms. This practice led Adlai Stevenson, back in public service as Ambassador to the United Nations,
to remark: "I regret that I have but one law firm to give to my
country."

The Wall Street lawyers' influence on the law and the nation
cannot be measured just by their official services for the government or for their clients. They have been influential in some of
the major bar associations. And the bar associations have had
some influence on the nation—in the appointment of federal
judges, for example. Whitney North Seymour (Simpson Thacher
& Bartlett), has been president of both the Association of the Bar
of the City of New York and the American Bar Association.

Important "Do-gooding" Activities —

Wall Street lawyers also play important roles in the charity and
cultural affairs of the city and the nation. As one respondent put
it: "You will find a Wall Street lawyer in practically every good
work in New York, and you'll find that the boards rely on them
to a great extent." These men, with their excellent legal training
and technical skill, donate part of their time to guiding important
voluntary organizations. In this way, too, they can exert a considerable force in our society. Each of the large firms takes care
of the legal work of one or more charities and many partners are
on the boards of directors of such organizations. Martin Mayer
finds that the partners in these law offices have a fascination with
art and play a role in its development in this nation. He reports
that "Wall Street lawyers are, or recently have been, Chairman
of the Board of the Metropolitan Museum and Secretary of the
Morgan Library; Chairman of the Executive Committee of the
Metropolitan Opera; Chairman of Cooper Union and President
of the Grolier Club (book collecting); Secretary of the Whitney

Museum (modern American art); and President of the New York Public Library."[20]

International Affairs —

The influence of the Wall Street lawyer does not stop at our borders. It spreads throughout the world. Cromwell was instrumental in the drafting of a treaty (Hay-Herran), parts of which still define United States rights to the Canal Zone. John McCloy ruled a nation when he became High Commissioner for Germany after World War II. Swaine writes of him: "Probably no civilian other than the President himself had so direct a part in World War II military affairs and military decisions as did McCloy."[21] Under Kennedy, Roswell L. Gilpatric (Cravath, Swaine & Moore) was Deputy Secretary of Defense, and under President Truman he was Assistant Secretary of the Air Force and then Undersecretary of the Air Force. In World War II many held high positions in the services and influenced our military policy. Wright (Shearman & Sterling & Wright—now renamed Shearman & Sterling), for example, was a general. In World War II, Arthur Dean reports, 37 out of 75 Sullivan & Cromwell lawyers were in uniform.[22] And an analysis of the Cravath firm through its history up to 1946 reveals that 50 per cent (231 out of 462) of their lawyers had been in uniform,[23] some of them in posts of importance. Individual members of the large law firms affect international affairs not only through their activities for the government but also as counselors to American businessmen who deal with foreign governments. Cromwell helped bring the canal to Panama.[24] And the Cravath firm in 1929 worked on the Roumanian Stabilization Loan which involved one hundred million dollars. Swaine feels that:

> Probably the Cravath firm has never handled a more complicated issue. The bonds were the direct obligation of the Kingdom of Roumania Monopolies Institute, created for the purpose by the Roumanian Parliament, and were guaranteed by the Kingdom. All the monopolies operated by the Kingdom were irrevocably vested in the Institute. The monetary laws were amended to revalue the leu; the charter of the National Bank of Roumania was

amended; and a program of monetary stabilization and economic development enacted into law. The various new laws, all the basic documents (executed in French and English), the bankers' contracts and the prospectuses for the different countries (each affected by the law of the country concerned and usually in language other than English) were prepared under Cravath supervision.[25]

Large law firms have been involved in preparing foreign stock issues for brokerage houses, in oil acquisitions in foreign countries, and in protecting American interests abroad. Before the United States entered World War II the British Government, for example, retained the Cravath firm to supervise admiralty suits to prevent the escape of German and Italian ships from American ports.[26] Finland also secured the services of the Cravath firm, and that firm organized the Finnish-American Trading Corporation as "a vehicle through which the Export-Import Bank might make loans."[27] The list of foreign legal activities these firms are and were involved with could continue "endlessly." The law firms leave their mark in the international arena both as middlemen for powerful institutions and as creative bodies.

On Balance —

Over a hundred years ago De Toqueville saw the lawyer in America as the aristocracy of this country. Today only a handful of lawyers fit this description, and prominent among these is the Wall Street lawyer. The combination of important roles these men play—lawyer, businessman, governmental representative, public benefactor—makes the Wall Street attorney a man to be reckoned with. If C. Wright Mills is to be believed, they are indeed part of this nation's aristocracy—but it is a somewhat sinister aristocracy. Mills points out:

> The inner core of the power elite also includes men of the higher legal and financial type from the great law factories and investment firms, who are almost professional go-betweens of economic, political and military affairs, and who thus act to unify the power elite. The corporation lawyer and the investment banker perform

the functions of the "go-between" effectively and powerfully. By the nature of their work, they transcend the narrower milieu of any one industry, and accordingly are in a position to speak and act for the corporate world or at least sizable sectors of it. The corporation lawyer is a key link between the economic and military and political areas; the investment banker is a key organizer and unifier of the corporate world and a person well versed in spending the huge amounts of money the American military establishment now squanders. When you get a lawyer who handles the legal work of investment bankers you get a key member of the power elite.[28]

Despite his attempt to secure anonymity, the Wall Street lawyer is a controversial figure, and any effort to evaluate his position in society meets with the bias inherent in value judgments. Many authors (C. W. Mills, Ferdinand Lundberg, A. A. Berle, for example) writing in the Thirties or on data from that period find that large law firms breed organization men, narrow specialists, pawns of big business, or sinister power figures. A. A. Berle feels strongly that:

The law firms become virtually an annex to some group of financial promoters, manipulators or industrialists; and such firms have dominated the organized profession, although they have contributed little of thought, less of philosophy and nothing at all of responsibility or idealism. What they have contributed, however, is the creation of a legal framework for the new economic system, built largely around the modern corporation.[29]

Some of what these critics say is true. There would be no difficulty finding examples to fit the descriptions offered. Yet, to be objective we should examine the Wall Street lawyer's place in society in terms of the rules as they are played at the time the "game" is in progress, that is, not necessarily what the reader or the author would want of them, or what some of these lawyers want of themselves,[30] but in terms of the main task they have consented to take on—lawyer to big business.

The important role these men play in our society makes what

happens to them of general concern. Specifically, what this study attempts to do is determine the degree to which their individuality may be—or is—affected by membership in a large organization; whether the "free" nature of the profession is threatened by the growth of the large law firm. To do this it was necessary to study who the Wall Street lawyers are, find out their social backgrounds, where they went to school, how they were recruited, which of them stay with the large offices, which of them leave. In other words, to provide a portrait of the Wall Street lawyer.

To understand these attorneys and what happens to them it was also necessary to study the organization in which they work. Certain basic questions concerning their work group were asked. For example, how is the legal work assigned? What are the informal and formal organizational rules? What is the meaning for the organization of external professional rules? Also, the importance of size and location of large law firms and what results the difficulties of recruitment have on the structure of these firms are discussed.

It is hoped that the findings of this study will throw some light on what happens to professional people who work in a bureaucratic situation and concomitantly on what happens to their dependent clients. Answers to these questions could have major social implications, given the increasing number of professional people who work in complex organizations and given the special importance of the Wall Street lawyer for our society.

NOTES

1. Wilbert E. Moore, *Industrial Relations and the Social Order* (New York: Macmillan, 1951), pp. 17, 42.

2. Robert K. Merton, "Bureaucratic Structure and Personality," *Social Forces*, 18 (May 1940), 560–568.

3. William H. Whyte, Jr., *The Organization Man* (New York: Simon and Schuster, 1956).

4. For example, William Kornhauser, with the assistance of Warren O. Hagstrom, *Scientists in Industry: Conflict and Accommodation* (Berkeley and Los Angeles: University of California Press, 1962); Simon Marcson, *The Scientist in American Industry: Some Organizational Determinants in Manpower Utilization* (New York: Harper & Row, 1960).

5. Kornhauser, *op. cit.*, pp. 4–5.

6. James Willard Hurst, *The Growth of American Law* (Boston: Little, Brown, 1950), p. 342.

7. And sometimes the lawyer becomes the head of a corporation. Irving S. Olds, intermittently a partner in White & Case since 1917, was director and member of the executive committee of the United States Steel Corporation.

8. Martin Mayer, "Keepers of the Business Conscience: The Wall Street Lawyer—Part II," *Harper's*, 212 (February 1962), 50.

9. As quoted in Beryl Harold Levy, *Corporation Lawyer: Saint or Sinner?* (Philadelphia and New York: Chilton, 1961), p. 105.

10. Adolf A. Berle, Jr., *Power without Property* (New York: Harcourt, Brace & World, 1959), pp. 113–116.

11. Levy, *op. cit.*, p. 45.

12. *Ibid.*, p. 47.

13. *Ibid.*, p. 26.

14. Personal communication.

15. Robert T. Swaine, *The Cravath Firm and Its Predecessors* (New York: Ad Press, 1946 & 1948, privately printed), Vol. II, p. 696.

16. *Ibid.*, p. 557.

17. *Ibid.*, p. 556.

18. Arthur Dean, *William Nelson Cromwell 1854–1948: An American Pioneer in Corporation, Comparative and International Law* (New York: Ad Press, 1957), p. 86.

19. Theodore H. White, *The Making of the President 1960* (New York: Atheneum, 1961), p. 71.

20. Martin Mayer, "The Wall Street Lawyers: Part I—The Elite Corps of American Business," *Harper's*, 212 (January 1956), 32.

21. Swaine, *op. cit.*, p. 654.

22. Dean, *op. cit.*, p. 50.

23. Swaine, *op. cit.*, Vols. I, II, III.

24. Dean, *op. cit.*, p. 120.

25. Swaine, *op. cit.*, Vol. II, pp. 505–506.

26. *Ibid.*, p. 670.

27. *Ibid.*, p. 672.

28. C. Wright Mills, *The Power Elite* (New York: Oxford University Press, 1956), p. 289.

29. Adolf A. Berle, Jr., *Encyclopaedia of the Social Sciences* (New York: Macmillan, 1948), Vol. 9, p. 341.

30. A number of the lawyers interviewed expressed their discontent with their legal practice, and some indicated that some day they would practice a different kind of law. Frankfurter, in Harlan B. Phillips' *Felix Frankfurter Reminisces* (New York: Reynal, 1960), pp. 218–219, talks about Joseph P. Cotton, who was Undersecretary of State under President Hoover and had been a member of two large law firms. Frankfurter reports: "Cotton was a gifted fellow, an attractive fellow, and he made a great deal of money in what he called the 'green goods business' meaning

that he was legal adviser to big financial interests in affairs that ran into the millions, and therefore, the lawyers' fees were correspondingly large. . . . He also had scholarly interests and had a hankering for public affairs. He was very critical of the work he was doing and, on the whole, despised his rich clients. He squared his conscience by charging them more heavily, and since he was very good anyhow, that made them respect him more and more."

TWO

SAMPLE, METHOD,

AND TECHINQUES

IN order to study a social group, we must observe its individual members—in this case, the attorneys and other functionaries who make up the complex organization of the large law firm. But in order to observe these individuals, the social scientist must first get his subjects to stand still long enough for him to study them. This proved a particular problem because the subjects of this exploration were high-priced, in the main conservative, busy attorneys, and many of them had little faith or interest in sociology. The method of study and the samples selected eventually evolved partially out of a consideration of the difficulties involved in gaining cooperation from this legal elite and in interviewing them once they had consented to cooperate. This chapter will detail both the difficulties and their resolution, but it also serves the auxiliary purpose of offering insight and information about the Wall Street lawyer himself.

PREVIOUS EXPERIENCE

I HAD previously been engaged in a research problem involving law professors, attorneys practicing in a small Midwest-

ern town, and law students.[1] This experience proved to be, for the
most part, inadequate preparation for the investigation of the big-
city, large-firm lawyer. I encountered no trouble, for example, in
obtaining cooperation from the law students or the practicing
small-town lawyer except in one instance where the respondent refused to answer questions which dealt with ethics and civil liberties. Law professors provided a somewhat better preparation, in
that they were questioning and demanded further detail about
each query asked of them. Unlike the Wall Street lawyer, however,
the law professors were easily approachable (partially, perhaps,
because they were colleagues) and willing to give their time to
the project.

DIFFICULTIES IN OBTAINING INTERVIEWS

AT the outset the lawyers in this study, although polite, were
distant and seemingly unapproachable. They offered a number of
reasons for their disinclination to participate in the inquiry.

Professional Ethics —

The most common reason arose out of professional ethics—the
fear that the "privileged" nature of the attorney–client relationship might be violated. Strengthening this ethical canon is the
conservatism of the Wall Street lawyer and the desire for anonymity for himself and his client. These lawyers are perhaps even
more secretive than most advocates, for their giant corporate
clients, who are constantly in the public eye, want no notoriety
attached to their law firm.

Taboo Topics —

Too, the lawyers were reluctant to grant interviews because I was
requesting some information generally considered taboo. The taboo
areas dealt mainly with partnership agreements, finances in general, and the affairs of clients. Many lawyers felt that questions on
these topics were not "nice." This attitude made it difficult to
obtain interviews; even when the interviews were granted, the
attitude made interviewing more difficult. Roger B. Siddal, a

lawyer who was concerned with some of the same taboo topics, sent out questionnaires to two hundred law firms. Only forty-two filled out the questionnaires. He writes:

> The reason that so many of my questionnaires were unanswered is that in most of the large law offices in the United States today the partnership arrangements are considered top secret; they are matters which are only discussed among the partners when extreme privacy is assured . . . However much faith they might have in my integrity and discretion and however highly they might appraise the value of my study it would just go against the grain for many of these senior partners, acting individually or as a group, to disclose the details of their partnership arrangements to anyone unless it was absolutely necessary.[2]

They Are Part of an Organization —

Many attorneys who were willing to talk about themselves were at first reluctant to discuss their offices. They were either members (partners) of a firm and strongly felt a team responsibility, or they were employees (associates) and were not sure how much the firm wanted them to reveal and how such revelations might affect them. Some associates had to be convinced that I would not apprise "management" of the information disclosed. Associates were generally more willing than partners to be respondents.

The Right to Probe into the Profession —

In general, the older and more conservative lawyers felt that nothing worth while could come from a study of their law firms. They thought of their organizations in much the same manner as clergymen think of the church—as an institution that should not be studied. They resented the "prying into private affairs" and felt that such prying was not, or should not be, the function of scientific investigation. Among young lawyers, however, a good proportion had majored in the social sciences while at college and had been brought up in the age of Gallup and Kinsey; they accepted the process as both normal and legitimate. These younger people, though, did not control the partnerships and could do little to influence a firm toward deciding to participate.

A number of external factors seemed to reinforce some lawyers' feeling that an outsider had no right to probe into their affairs. Just as this investigation started, Martin Mayer's series on the Wall Street lawyer appeared in *Harper's Magazine*.[3] Almost all the lawyers interviewed had read or heard of the articles, and many felt that they were unfair. Older lawyers, stimulated perhaps by these essays, recalled another series of reports which appeared in the same magazine in the late Thirties.[4] They still seemed to bristle over these ancient analyses of the Wall Street law firms, which had labeled them "law factories." Many lawyers also mentioned the University of Chicago Law School's Jury Project. Researchers engaged in this study had tapped a jury room (with permission, although not from the jurors) as one means of obtaining information on how a jury decides a case. Some lawyers thought this behavior reprehensible and used it as a reason for refusing an interview or for being careful about what they revealed when questioned. Fortunately, these incidents were forgotten as the situations faded and as the Wall Street legal community gained confidence in me and recognized my investigation as a bona fide one. There was a cumulative aspect attached to this newly attained confidence, for confidence brought success and success begot success.

Of Time and Money —

One major practical factor a firm had to consider before allowing me to interview its lawyers was the loss of time and money involved. These lawyers are extremely busy. They often work at night and during weekends. The time spent on a legal matter[5] is an important item in calculating a client's bill. They charge from twelve dollars an hour for the rawest recruit to sixty dollars, or in some cases over a hundred dollars an hour for the experienced partner. Time to them means either money or the equivalent in night work. Some lawyers say that time is all they have to sell. For the associate, who works for more than one partner and who may be caught between the demands of his several "bosses" and their clients, time becomes of increased importance. All this affects both the busy lawyer and the considerate interviewer, who feels the pressure of time and may be embarrassed at taking too much of this valuable commodity.

In spite of these reasons for declining to participate in a sociological investigation, the majority of the subjects I approached did change their minds. Success came after three months of failure.

MODIFIED RESEARCH DEMANDS

WHAT brought about this change in attitude on the part of these men is important to the understanding of both the research approach and the lawyer. The first step called for changes in my own demands. At the beginning of the project I had asked permission to observe the work situation of an office. After receiving a number of refusals because the lawyers felt that such permission would constitute a breach of the canons of ethics (the investigator might after all, be able to see a client's confidential material), I dropped the request. This did not entirely eliminate the legal concern about breach of ethics, but it did make the objection less serious.

Other demands were also modified. I had at first thought it necessary to study all the members of a firm. (And for all practical purposes this was accomplished for one firm.) It was a costly procedure, however, and later it was recognized to be unnecessary for the purposes of the study. I no longer requested records of legal cases. In fact, it was agreed that questions concerning specific clients and some financial matters would not be asked.

On the advice of a law professor the research proposal designed for sociologists was repackaged for distribution among lawyers. The working title was changed from "The Effect of Large-Scale Organization on the Lawyer" to "The Impact of the Large Law Firm on the Legal Profession." Words which seemed threatening—for example, bureaucracy, ethics, and money—were omitted, especially in the initial contact with a firm. The fear of losing anonymity was dissipated by the assurance that other lawyers and law firms would also be studied. The managing partner of a firm was promised that if his organization were described, a member of his firm could see that portion of the manuscript. If the characteristics of the organization had not been camouflaged properly, the material would be reworked further to assure anonymity. This offer did not include the right of censorship, nor the obligation not to use a firm's name if, in connection with a specific item, it had appeared in the public press. And individual lawyers were told their names would not be mentioned in connection with specific interviews. In other words, there would be almost no way of ascertaining, from the published study, who said what.

I adopted a policy of not naming other lawyers or law firms (for any reason) while interviewing respondents, which offered assurance to the attorney being interviewed that his secrets were safe. Later in the course of the study some firms offered permission to refer to them if it were thought an aid in gaining entry into other organizations. Their names were used for this purpose only after a number of firms had been studied, however. Quantity then offered the anonymity that silence once had given.

THE SOCIALIZATION OF THE SOCIOLOGIST

ON a much more subtle level, some changes were required which hardly related to usual problems of research techniques. For example, the relatively informal clothing usually acceptable on university campuses created some uneasiness or mild disapproval, as did my habit of going hatless. I acquired a hat quickly, and took to wearing Ivy League type, conservative suits, button-down Oxford shirts, and striped ties. When some attorneys were asked well along in the course of the interviewing whether the change in dress had made a difference, they said: "Yes, but we don't want you to be too much like ourselves—it takes some of the interest in the meeting away. We can see lawyers any day."

In the process of gaining acceptance I interviewed a great many individual lawyers. (This was arranged with the help of law professors from Columbia University Law School and the secretary of the Association of the Bar of the City of New York.) Many of these men were prominent advocates from large firms. Although they refused permission to study their firms, they did not object to being questioned. These interviews gave me an opportunity to learn something more about law firms and to pretest a questionnaire. The situational questions which had been placed in doubt by the law professors in a previous study were almost totally eliminated in this one, since these respondents reacted in the same manner as had the professors—they kept questioning the questions and asking for additional facts. These preliminary experiences also led to the decision to redesign the questionnaire, which was then changed from a structured to a semistructured schedule. This change allowed me to probe into pertinent areas of my own greatest ignorance. Furthermore, every new contact made it easier to approach the next, so that I developed a sort of expertise.

Thus, the socialization of the sociologist, the change in demands for information and in the questionnaire, the polishing of the package, and the development of the approach to the lawyer all helped me gain final acceptance. The first major breakthrough, however, came when Samuel J. Silverman, now Justice of the Supreme Court in New York State and formerly a partner in a large firm, asked members and associates of his office if they were willing to be interviewed—with each person to decide for himself. All those I then approached directly decided favorably. Although this firm was not typical of most large law offices, useful similarities existed, and studying it gave me further experience.

In the course of this portion of the study, I met a young lawyer from a major large firm who asked why his office was not being studied. His law office through a senior partner, had previously rejected participation in the project because the partner felt it would take too much time to try to obtain the acceptance of the other partners. The young lawyer, although informed of this rejection, took the outline for the study and secured an appointment for me with their managing partner, who allowed himself to be interviewed. He was in reality interviewing the interviewer. He agreed to bring the request to the firm meeting (a meeting of partners), and later reported that after some discussion the members of the firm had agreed to allow the study, although they had refused similar previous requests.

As the Wall Street community learned of this cooperation, resistance to the study began to thaw. Perhaps of even more importance was the help given by the managing partner of this firm, who personally vouched for me to the managing partner of each firm I wanted to approach. His personal recommendation to this legal ingroup eliminated most of the difficulties I had encountered at an earlier stage. Even where a firm remained officially negative, however, some interviews were acquired. I had made an initial error in not attempting to obtain, or in one instance in not accepting, the sponsorship of a major bar association or law school. Perhaps with their recommendation some of the initial reluctance to the study might have been avoided.

Even after various firms accepted the idea of being "researched," individual members and associates showed varying degrees of interest in the project. Some were difficult to interview; many did not like the tenor of the questions. This was especially true of inquiries dealing with conformity, bureaucracy, and finances.

INTERVIEW TECHNIQUES

INTERVIEWING an especially sophisticated and articulate elite who are themselves highly skilled interviewers heightens the normal difficulty of the interview and calls either for special techniques or for the adjustment of old techniques.

Interviewing the Interviewers —

Although some of these lawyers were experts in the interviewing techniques of the courtroom situation, more significant for the present discussion was their experience in interviewing clients. Here, forceful cross-examination gives way to suggestion and the use of persuasive charm. A researcher approaching these men on their "home grounds" must be wary lest he become the respondent and the lawyer the interviewer! As the investigator sits in one of the soft chairs usually offered, it may be he who is beguiled by his respondent's charm and taken in by his interviewing approach; it may be he who finds himself confiding his feelings and revealing his problems. The danger in interviewing interviewers is that they sometimes forget the role they are expected to play. To meet the danger of losing control of the interviewing situation, I learned systematically to refuse the soft chairs, to ask the first question, to avoid the respondent's direct queries, and to try to interest him in the project as early as possible.

The respondents' own skills as interviewers made it necessary that I be particularly cautious in the use of methods and techniques which might be perceived as tricks (for example, employing false statements designed to arouse the interviewee) lest they boomerang. It was dangerous, difficult, and unnecessary to try to fool these respondents. It was much wiser to seek their aid.

In one respect, however, the respondents' knowledge of interviewing and the tendency of some to think in terms of courtroom procedure—which is designed to eliminate the irrelevant—was helpful. If they tried to control the interview, they could be appealed to on the ground that the information they offered did not meet the needs of the problem. In fact, many of them spontaneously suggested, before the interrogation began, that if they should wander from the subject they be stopped and asked questions designed to bring them back to the heart of the matter.

Specialized Functions of Lawyers —

Adaptation was required on my part to meet the sharp differences in respondents connected with lawyers' specialized functions. Senior partners in large law firms are accustomed to dealing with policy questions of their clients. Young lawyers are trained to deal with the details. This occupational differentiation carried over into the interview and called for diverse approaches.

Senior partners who were interested in the study, for example, did not require as many questions to elicit the desired information as did younger partners or associates. Trained to make policy, to deal with general problems, the senior members answered broadly and boldly. Picking them up on minor details and interrupting their train of thought with innumerable questions curtailed the interview, making it difficult for me to get the picture from the respondents' point of view. If these men were properly briefed at the outset and not interrupted, they tended to ask and answer the relevant questions themselves. Toward the close of the interview, if their interest in the project had been maintained or increased, I could then ask for specific details and refer to any broader questions which they had overlooked. Interested senior partners were most fruitfully approached with the initial use of broad stimulating questions, not detailed ones.

With the younger lawyers the process was reversed. The detailed background queries were welcomed. They served as a "warm-up period" and as a means of generating interest. Such an approach fits in with the kind of detail work done at the beginning of their employment with a large law firm.

Modification of interview techniques also had to be made on the basis of a lawyer's area of specialization. For example, a different approach might be needed when talking to a litigator than when questioning a tax specialist. Generally, however, these adjustments were not so sharp as those used to deal with the differences found between a young associate and a senior partner.

I used two methods to reduce the reluctance to being interviewed that I occasionally encountered. First, I asked the taboo questions in an indirect, generalized form; e.g., instead of inquiring, "What do you earn?" I would ask, "What does a senior partner in a large Wall Street law firm earn?" or "What would you say a junior partner earns?" After this information was offered, and it usually was, the respondent was less reticent about answering the question which followed: "Does this apply here, also?" Perhaps in time he might even answer questions dealing with his own income.

The second technique for breaking down reluctance to talk was to display previous knowledge. For example, when I could show that I knew something about how much money lawyers earned, or what partnership agreements were like, or when I displayed a knowledge of the organization of law firms and the respondent's firm in particular, the familiarity partially offset my status as an "outsider." It also made it easier for the lawyer to discuss the taboo topics, for, if my information had been essentially correct, the topic was no longer secret or taboo. A display of previous knowledge was also effective in dealing with the respondent's desire for anonymity and in handling his fear of revealing too much about his firm.

In general an informant's tendency to withhold information lessened if I could show that some information was already in my possession. Furthermore, the discussion was more interesting for the respondent when we could proceed directly to essentials, skipping preliminary explanations. Corroborating this—interviews collected early in the study, when the researcher's previous knowledge was meager, were shorter than later interviews; often, the answers in these earlier interviews resembled those given to law students applying for a position with a law firm.

Sometimes the difficulty of getting respondents to talk was due less to reticence in the face of the topics discussed then to an overwhelming pressure of time in their lives. The key to obtaining information from this busy elite was to make the questions penetrating and interesting. If they were not, I would not get thoughtful answers and would find the interview terminated. In fact, the key to successful interviewing with this elite is to create interest and maintain it. While this is probably true for any interview, the background, training, and the importance of time for these lawyers make it a more difficult task than one ordinarily meets when questioning a random sample of a community.

Through the course of the interview process, which can be perceived as a series of stages, different lawyers entered the various stages of that process at different times. Not all interviewees exhibited all stages, and not all were unidirectional. My approach had to be adapted to the demands of each stage; three were readily observable. These may be labeled the "polite" stage, in which the respondent is motivated mainly by a sense of social obligation to fulfill his promise of an interview; the "interest" stage in which the respondent's curiosity about the subject matter is aroused; and the "challenge" stage in which the interviewer tries to stimulate interest which failed to develop or to continue.

Some respondents started at the "interest" stage and, with minor fluctuations, sustained their interest. With them the danger of premature termination of the interview was not present. Some, who started in the "interest" stage or reached it, later lost interest. Others never did develop real interest but tolerated the interview out of politeness, and many of these continued in a stage of sustained politeness. Since time is money for the lawyer, even for these socially well trained individuals there was often a limit to how polite they could afford to be in face of the demands of the job.

Thus, the task of the researcher, especially in those cases in which the life of the interview was threatened, was to create sufficient interest to keep on with the questioning. One technique I used to arouse interest was to present the respondent with an hypothesis, or a series of hypotheses, from the study and thereby make him a partner in the investigation, or at least an advisor to the interviewer—a familiar role for the lawyer. For example, if through normal questioning it was impossible to get a respondent to talk about conformity among lawyers, a reaction to the subject was usually stimulated by explaining Merton's hypothesis[6] of the bureaucratic personality. Although this technique is time consuming, it nevertheless is quite effective.

The use of questions focused on hypothetical situations also kept the interest of the respondent and often provided passage into untapped areas of information. For example, some associates were asked, "Suppose that, after returning from a vacation, you were to receive a 'memo' from a partner about a matter you had worked on prior to your departure. The 'memo' which is designed to bring you up to date briefly describes what action had been taken in your absence. You think the partner had proceeded incorrectly. What would you do about it?" For the very reluctant informant I provided alternatives to situational questions and asked the respondent to explain why he might take one course of action as against another. Merely varying the type of questions helped keep or develop the curiosity of the respondent.

If interest thus stimulated wore off, and it was still necessary to continue the inquiry, I then presented the respondent with challenges[7] designed to be provocative. I offered contradictions either in the respondent's "testimony" or in evidence I had found elsewhere, and asked the respondents to explain these discrepancies. (This technique is especially good for lawyers, for they are trained in, used to, and seem to enjoy disputation.) For instance, if a man replied, in response to a question about conflict between partners, that there was no conflict, he would be asked (on the basis of previous information), "Didn't the fact that one partner had skipped over other partners on the letterhead (and presumably in terms of power and distribution of profits) cause conflict?" While the respondent's answer might be evasive, e.g.,

"We don't spend all our time looking at letterheads," he had, nonetheless, been challenged, and his interest continued. The next question, which was more general and less challenging, further opened the discussion on conflicts between partners. The respondent was asked if the changing of the "name" partners when one of them died or retired was a cause of conflict in some firms.

Although this approach can be dangerous—it may cause loss of good will[8] and lead to biased answers, since the advocate tends to favor his own position—it does keep the interview alive, opening the way to additional, less provocative questions. In a study of an organization, the danger of using the possibly biased answers is lessened by the opportunity to verify these answers by questioning other individuals in the same organization.

One mechanical device was used to extend the interview. When possible, interviews were scheduled an hour before the respondent usually went to lunch. If he proved interested, and if continuation of the interview seemed indicated, I suggested continuing the interview at lunch. (Often, however, especially when interest was strong, the initiative for the luncheon came from the respondent.) When this suggestion was favorably received (and often it was), the interview could be extended an hour and a half under favorable circumstances with neither the interviewer nor the respondent feeling the pressure of time. This hour was generally not scheduled for partners, as they do a great deal of business during luncheon and are usually booked in advance. Complications may arise if the suggestion is refused, for then it may be too late to ask some of the important questions which should have been raised in the time alloted.

SAMPLING

PROBLEMS concerned with sampling were also encountered. Two main samples were needed—one of large *law firms,* the other of large law firm *lawyers.* The location of these law offices and lawyers was New York City, and the large law office was defined as one composed of fifty or more attorneys. Of the twenty[9] law firms which qualified as large, eighteen were personally studied. Material on the remaining two firms was obtained from the

Martindale-Hubbell Law Directory. Good fortune and the kindness of Spencer Klaw,[10] who had collected material for an article on the Wall Street lawyer and who made his case histories available, gave me additional information on the two firms not in this sample as well as a way to check the data collected for the 18 firms studied. For practical purposes, then, what we are working with is not a sample of large law firms but with the universe, since some information on all the large firms in New York City was available. Within this universe, however, a sample of informants was taken. In the first firm studied, thirty-eight of its fifty lawyers were interviewed. No one refused to be questioned. Interviewing was terminated in this firm when the answers received on major issues became repetitious and the researcher was confident that he knew what he needed to know about that firm. I did, then, what Francis and Stone had done in their study *Service and Procedure in Bureaucracy:*

> When certain patterns became manifest, when certain values were uniformly expressed, when the content of the interviews and observations became similar, a point of diminishing returns was felt. When this point was reached, we would move to another section of the agency until we had interviewed . . . in every section of the agency. Forty people out of a hundred employees were interviewed in this way. This procedure is characteristic of anthropological field work.[11]

Experience with the first firm gave me enough information about the organization of law firms to allow me to know how to choose a stratified sample in the next, so of the hundred lawyers connected with the second organization, only twenty had to be interviewed; this number was gradually reduced in each succeeding firm. Eventually only a few lawyers in each firm were queried. In the few instances, where a respondent's answers were not consistent, additional attorneys were questioned until the discrepancies were resolved.

The advantage of studying people in an organization is that validity can be checked relatively easily, since answers of one respondent can be compared with the replies of colleagues who share some of the same experiences. An additional check was made by interviewing lawyers who had left one of the large law offices. Other steps were taken to assure accuracy; for example, three lawyers have read the entire manuscript and stated their opinions. When they thought an error in fact had been made, the questioned material was reanalyzed.

There were approximately 1700 lawyers in these large Wall Street offices. One-hundred eighty-eight, or 11 per cent of them, were interviewed. These attorneys, however, provided information both about their firms and about the Wall Street lawyers. The same people, then, were interviewed for both samples. As previously indicated, most of these respondents were chosen so as to obtain representation in each firm which would take into account its stratification and specializations.

Some categories are more heavily represented than others. Senior associates just on the verge of partnership or of being "passed over" proved to be among the best informants, since they were at a vantage point just below the partners and above most other associates, and the importance and intensity of this situation made them more conscious of organizational structure and organizational changes. An attempt was made to see managing partners and executive partners who had final power in a firm. Lawyers in these categories were interviewed out of proportion to their numbers.

Still, this sample seems representative of the Wall Street lawyers who practice in the large firms, mainly because of the homogeneity of these lawyers—a fact documented in Chapter IV. It will suffice for the moment to point out that when the background characteristics of all the partners from the twenty large firms were compared with the partners in the sample, little difference was found.

Finally, although most of the information on which this study is based was drawn from the two samples just described, supplementary information was obtained, in a variety of ways, primarily for purposes of checking on the reliability and the meaning of the data. For example, I arranged for repeat interviews with over thirty of the original respondents and for a larger number of informal individual and group meetings with original respondents as well as with lawyers outside of the main sample. I also held informal interviews with law professors, particularly at Indiana University and the University of Chicago, office managers, legal secretaries, "summer boarders" (second-year law students working for the summer in law firms), and court clerks.

Additional Steps —

In addition to these informal means of obtaining information, the following supplementary studies were undertaken:

1. In order to estimate the meaning of size on the organization of large New York law firms, interviews were completed with forty-four lawyers from four large law firms located in three different areas of the United States outside of New York City. This was done so that size could be held constant while new factors, i.e., locality and kind of business, were introduced. To clarify further the meaning of size for organization, twenty smaller Wall Street firms (composed of fewer than fifty lawyers—usually about twenty) which also had corporations among their clients, were selected to serve as a comparison group. Forty-three lawyers from these firms were interviewed.

2. Other checks on findings were obtained from Part II, Biographical section of the 1957 and 1962 editions of the *Martindale-Hubbell Law Directory*. First, background data on all partners (435) and counsel[12] (9) in the twenty large law firms in New York at that time (1957), as well as listings from *Who's Who* and the *Social Register*, were analyzed to extend our knowledge about the partners in these firms and to check the validity of the sample of partners. Second, the material on all 543 partners from the 1962 *Martindale-Hubbell* was analyzed to see if 1957 trends had continued. Then, every fourth firm, excluding those already studied, was selected from the same *Directory*—a total of 84 small firms.[13] These small firms were compared with the original sample of large firms, and the 471 partners and 27 counsel from these smaller offices contrasted both with the universe of partners from large organizations obtained from *Martindale-Hubbell* and with the original sample of partners in order to single out differences, if any, in the type of lawyer recruited to the various sized firms.

3. A three-volume history of the Cravath firm[14] contains case

histories of 402 associates who had left the firm between 1902 and 1948, the 16 associates who remained with the firm, and the 44 lawyers who had been made partners. These records were analyzed for possible information about differences between lawyers who became partners and those who do not. Comparison of these records with the total roster of A Cravath-like firm, and of another large office (which was more "social") for which the records for all lawyers as of 1957 were available, permitted analysis of differences between firms and over time.

4. As a check on the lawyers in the large firms, thirty attorneys who had formerly been with them were interviewed.

5. Fifteen older famous lawyers and judges, including one from the Supreme Court of the United States, were interviewed in an effort to obtain their insight into and views of the large law offices and their lawyers as they see them now from their independent and perhaps more objective positions.

6. House counsel[15] and/or corporation executives from seven large corporations were called on to determine what legal work they kept for their own legal staffs and what work they sent to the large law firms. They were also questioned about the influence of the large law offices on the corporations and about the corporations' influence on the law firms.

7. To determine recruitment, placement, and job hunting procedures, I visited the Harvard Law School Alumni Placement Center and the employment agency run by the Association of the Bar of the City of New York and interviewed five placement officers from leading law schools. The placement records of three of these schools were analyzed.

8. To get the picture from the student's point of view and to determine more about the meaning of law review for the functioning of large law firms, students from three law schools were interviewed, although in an unsystematic, unstructured way. Special attention, however, was given to law review students and members of the *Harvard Law Review* staff.

9. Available records concerning law firms were examined along with a number of books on large law firms.

What was done, then, was to pursue pertinent information from all available sources, in much the same manner as the social anthropologist studies primitive tribes, in order to obtain additional information but mainly in order to check on the validity of the answers I had received from my two main samples—the 188 Wall Street lawyers and the 18 large New York firms. The following chapters describe the firms and lawyers which comprise these samples.

NOTES

1. Erwin O. Smigel, John W. Martin and Donald Horning, "Legal Ethics and Education" (unpublished study, 1958).
2. Roger B. Siddall, *A Survey of Large Law Firms in the United States* (New York: Vantage Press, 1956, privately distributed), p. 142.
3. Martin Mayer, "The Wall Street Lawyers," Parts I and II, *Harper's* 212 (January, February 1956), 31–37, 50–56.
4. Ferdinand Lundberg, "The Law Factories: Brains of the Status Quo," *Harper's*, 179 (July 1939), 180–192.
5. Lawyers use the word *matter* to indicate a legal problem. The word *case* is used only with reference to a legal problem which is to be or is being litigated.
6. Robert K. Merton, "Bureaucratic Structure and Personality," *Social Forces*, 18 (May 1940), 560–568.
7. A similar technique was used by Harold L. Wilensky, *Intellectuals in Labor Unions* (New York: The Free Press, 1956), p. 283.
8. This technique was pushed too hard with a Chicago law firm and some lawyers reacted negatively to it.
9. The following law firms are Wall Street's largest as listed by Spencer Klaw, "The Wall Street Lawyers" *Fortune*, 57 (February 1958), 194. This list was compiled as of December 1957. Except for the total number of lawyers in each firm it is substantially the same in 1963. Klaw listed Cleary, Gottlieb, Friendly & Hamilton (now Cleary, Gottlieb, Steen & Hamilton), with forty-six lawyers, as the twentieth largest firm. I list Paul, Weiss, Rifkind, Wharton & Garrison, with fifty lawyers at that time (although it is not located in the Wall Street district), as the twentieth largest law office. The sample of large law offices used in this study is composed of eighteen of the following twenty law firms:

Shearman & Sterling & Wright (now Shearman & Sterling), 125 lawyers (35 partners, 90 associates).

Cravath, Swaine & Moore, 116 lawyers (28 partners, 88 associates).

White & Case, 109 lawyers (34 partners, 75 associates).

Dewey, Ballantine, Bushby, Palmer & Wood, 105 lawyers (23 partners, 82 associates).

Simpson Thacher & Bartlett, 97 lawyers (23 partners, 74 associates).

Davis Polk Wardwell Sunderland & Kiendl, 97 lawyers (30 partners, 67 associates).

Milbank, Tweed, Hope & Hadley (now Milbank, Tweed, Hadley & McCloy), 94 lawyers (28 partners, 66 associates).

Cahill, Gordon, Reindel & Ohl, 84 lawyers (28 partners, 56 associates).

Sullivan & Cromwell, 84 lawyers (32 partners, 52 associates).

Chadbourne, Parke, Whiteside & Wolff, 70 lawyers (21 partners, 49 associates).

Breed, Abbott & Morgan, 66 lawyers (22 partners, 44 associates).

Winthrop, Stimson, Putnam & Roberts, 63 lawyers (17 partners, 46 associates).

Cadwalader, Wickersham & Taft, 61 lawyers (17 partners, 44 associates).

Wilkie Owen Farr Gallagher & Walton (now Wilkie Farr Gallagher Walton & Fitzgibbon), 60 lawyers (20 partners, 40 associates).

Donovan Leisure Newton & Irvine, 58 lawyers (21 partners, 37 associates).

Lord, Day & Lord, 56 lawyers (16 partners, 40 associates).

Dwight, Royall, Harris, Koegel & Caskey (now Royall, Koegel & Rogers), 55 lawyers (21 partners, 34 associates).

Mudge, Stern, Baldwin & Todd (now Nixon, Mudge, Rose, Guthrie & Alexander), 55 lawyers (20 partners, 35 associates).

Kelley, Drye, Newhall & Maginnes, 50 lawyers (22 partners, 28 associates).

Paul, Weiss, Rifkind, Wharton & Garrison, 50 lawyers [19 partners, 31 associates (approximate)].

10. *Ibid.*, pp. 140–144, 192, 194, 197–198, 202.

11. Roy G. Francis and Robert C. Stone, *Service and Procedure in Bureaucracy* (Minneapolis, Minn.: University of Minnesota Press, 1956), p. 26.

12. "Of Counsel" or "counsel" in a law office is an ambiguous term. It usually refers to an attorney who is neither a member nor an associate of the firm. He is usually a senior person who has client power either because he controls clients and/or because he is exceptionally respected.

13. While these eighty-four law offices were randomly selected, the universe they were chosen from does not contain all the small law firms in New York City, thus limiting our ability to generalize from it. The list of associate lawyers in part II, biographical section of *Martindale-Hubbell Law Directory* is very spotty, so no attempt was made to select a sample of associates.

14. Robert T. Swaine, *The Cravath Firm and its Predecessors*, 3 Vols. (New York: Ad Press, 1946 and 1948, privately printed).

15. The term "house counsel" refers to lawyers who work directly for a corporation rather than for a law firm.

THREE

THE RECRUITMENT OF

WALL STREET LAWYERS

THE functioning and perhaps the survival of any social system depends on its personnel, which in turn is contingent on how well the system is organized to recruit and maintain its supply of competent manpower. The recruitment mechanism is not a separate or distinct department or organ of a social system. Any feature of such a system may enhance or depress its attractiveness to the prospective member and from this point of view be considered an aspect of the recruitment system or mechanism, such as conditions of job security or an organization's reputation for fair dealing. Any part of an organization, then, may be important to the recruitment process.

Alterations in the environment, for instance in the available labor market, in the competitive system, or in the functions of an organization requiring personal qualities and/or skills which are different from those the system currently recruits, may result in changes in a social system. Since so much depends upon the nature of personnel, both the failure of a system to recruit individuals capable of carrying on its activities and the difficulty or insecurity of obtaining such personnel are serious sources of strain. Organizational changes are often made to reduce such strains.

The large law firms, which depend for their success upon the quality of the men they hire rather than on the new clients they enlist, find themselves in an environment where competition for men is increasing and the nature and practice of the law is changing. This chapter describes what the law offices are doing about it. It analyzes (1) some of the personnel requirements for their legal staff, (2) the changes in environment which influence recruitment mechanisms and processes, and (3) the way these factors have resulted in adaptive organizational change. It thus provides information about recruitment techniques and about the kinds of men who come to the giant firms, and offers examples of some aspects of structural alterations in an organization.

PERSONNEL REQUIREMENTS

THE large law offices, especially the huge Wall Street firms, have, as one associate put it ". . . an inflated idea of what they want. They're looking for well-rounded men who are law review."[1] Actually they want more than that. They also want lawyers who are Nordic, have pleasing personalities and "clean-cut" appearances, are graduates of the "right" schools, have the "right" social background and experience in the affairs of the world, and are endowed with tremendous stamina. A former law school dean, in discussing the qualities students need to obtain a job, offers a somewhat more realistic picture: "To get a job they [students] should be long enough on family connections, long enough on ability or long enough on personality, or a combination of these. Something called acceptability is made up of the sum of its parts. If a man has any of these things, he could get a job. If he has two of them, he can have a choice of jobs; if he has three, he could go anywhere . . ."

The big firms prefer the man with all three attributes: lineage, ability, and personality. What they want, what they need, and what they get are related, but are not necessarily the same thing. These organizations recruit manpower in order to do their job, provide continuity to the firms, and keep existing performance up to the clients' expectations and to the lawyers' own high standards. It is not essential for the operation of a firm that all their lawyers have all three attributes. This is so if only because the firms have developed an hierarchical system of practice which allows the best and most experienced counselors to supervise those less able and less experienced. The firms' actual needs, in fact, include lawyers who can and are willing to do routine work. Their recruitment policies, however, are generally geared to what is wanted rather than to what is absolutely needed. The senior men are accustomed to dealing with able and energetic people and would be impatient with others. In addition, seeing themselves as an elite and viewing their work as highly important, they want to perpetuate this image. Thus, there is keen competition for the preferred lawyer.

Academic Achievement —

That academic achievement is important in recruitment is noted in a Harvard Law School report which states that many firms request "as a qualification that a man have 'B' or better grades."[2] The law firms maintain that they want the best men and academic competence is one important element in what they say is meant by best. This policy is not a new one. Walter S. Carter, whom Otto Koegel has labeled "the collector of young masters," is credited with initiating in 1860 the recruiting policy adopted by the larger law firms. It was his practice to pick the best students from the law schools and take them into his office. Koegel finds that in doing this "he [Carter] set an example of great value to firms and students."[3]

That this example continues to be followed is proved by a breakdown of the initial jobs held after graduation by the Yale Law School classes of '55, '56, and '57. It revealed that 53 per cent of the Yale men whom the large New York law firms employed came from the top quarter of their classes, and that 27 per cent were from the first decile. The Harvard Law School placement records, which were analyzed for a selected three-year period to determine the hiring practices of ten Wall Street firms, indicate that an even higher proportion of men in the top 10 per cent of their classes went with the large law firms. These firms hired seventy-one men from Harvard; thirty-two (45 per cent) were in the top 10 per cent of their classes. Only nine of these lawyers had less than a "B" average and these were near-misses. Spencer Klaw[4] points out that the large firms do even better in getting these men from the very top of the class. He takes a Harvard Law School compilation which shows that, of the five top men in the classes of 1950 through 1956 (thirty-five in all), sixteen went to work for large New York firms. One of these big organizations could boast that fifty of its seventy-five associates were law review students—an exceptionally high proportion.

To cite confirming evidence, a note in a *Harvard Law Review* issue of 1958 reports that of the twenty-eight law review editors who had taken jobs, twenty-six would either clerk for judges or work for large law firms: "The figures are revealing. Six men will be clerks, two in the Supreme Court and the others in the lower federal courts. The larger 'Wall Street' firms have claimed twelve editors while large firms in other cities have taken another eight. . . . And this year is not unusual—these figures are representative of the past several years."[5]

Preferred Law Schools —

The large offices also prefer and obtain their men from what they consider to be the best eastern law schools. Seventy-four per cent of the sample of Wall Street lawyers graduated from Harvard, Yale, and Columbia law schools. A survey of the *Martindale-Hubbell Law Directory* 1957 listings of the 468 partners from the 20 large New York firms which had 50 lawyers or more, discloses that 71 per cent were graduates of Harvard, Yale, and Columbia law schools. A resurvey of these same twenty firms in 1962 indicates that while the number of partners had increased to 543, the percentage graduating from Harvard, Yale, and Columbia Law Schools had remained about the same—71.8. These figures take on additional importance since most men who become partners in large law offices begin their careers as associates fresh from law school or after a brief period as a judge's clerk.

Lineage —

Since lineage is also mentioned as important, it is significant that 30 per cent of these 468 partners are listed in the *Social Register*. It should be noted here, however, that although not all large firms are as concerned that a recruit be listed in the *Social Register*, most of them are interested in family background at least to the extent that it reflects on social behavior.

Personality —

Nevertheless, the firms look for more than grades, schools, and family background—they also want the man with personality. Even these very verbal men, however, have difficulty in spelling out just what they want in this department. An interview with a managing partner suggests what they mean:

Q. What do you look for when you hire an associate?

A. We do look for a good college and law school record. As a professor once said, "You can't go against the record. It indicates capacity and information." We look for someone who has that intangible quality of inspiring confidence in people. He should be intuitive, imaginative, with a readiness to take responsibility.

Q. How do you determine these qualities?

A. It is difficult. But we talk to his professors and we quiz him.

The law offices do not obtain all they want and different firms put varying emphasis on the qualities they prefer. In some organizations one finds proportionally more law review men, in others, more people listed in the *Social Register*, in still others, men with special experience.

Men Needed to do Routine Work —

In addition to capable men who can please both clients and partners, these firms need some lawyers who can and are willing to do routine jobs and/or specialized work in fields which are growing or in areas which the firms have previously not developed. Also needed are some lawyers who know their way around the courts. Furthermore, since many firms have rules prohibiting nepotism, an unofficial arrangement exists whereby the various Wall Street law offices employ one another's close relatives or hire someone as a favor for a friend or a client. These "political" requirements make for what little unevenness—in the sense of relaxation of customary criteria—exists in their hiring practices.

Turning first to the men who do the more routine work, the

apt remarks of one respondent points up the necessity for varied employment criteria:

> If a large law firm has a big anti-trust case with a lot of detail factual work, a number of men are required. We have one team of twelve persons working on a case like that and the men are doing mostly factual studies—not law. They are indexing and cataloguing. It is obvious that you can't keep the president of the *Harvard Law Review* on that kind of case and keep him around for long. So you have to hire people who are not that bright.

When, occasionally, lawyers are hired to fill these jobs, they are told that employment is only for the duration of the job. Many offices do not count them, psychologically at least, as part of the firm, and practice this conditional recruitment only when they do not have on their regular staff men already appraised as being unlikely to succeed, who can do these jobs. If the firms cannot afford a temporary crew or do not want outsiders, they rotate their regular lawyers through these jobs.

Other specialized routine jobs must be filled. Some, for example, involve banking, others securities. One job in particular appears to be avoided by most lawyers. They call it "blue sky work." It requires knowing and keeping up with the securities laws for each of the fifty states. It is not considered a creative position. Much of it is tedious, repetitive work of almost a clerical nature. The firms have difficulty in keeping young lawyers at this task.

One solution to this problem calls for placing older men in these positions. Sometimes the firms hire these older lawyers as specialists from the outside, but more often they are the men who have been passed over and will not be given partnerships.

Men not trained by the firm are also hired to fill positions in growing specialties of the law because, until recently at least, the law offices had not properly prepared enough lawyers for specializations such as tax and labor law. Five per cent of the sample said they were hired because of their previous special legal experience.[6] In the tax field this need was especially prominent. Law offices would employ men who had worked in the government tax department. When firms require the immediate services of the specialist, social qualifications are less important than competence and experience.

The large law firms also need men who act as managing clerks. These men are expected to know the courts and their routine. If they are lawyers they usually come from the local schools—often from local night schools such as Brooklyn, Fordham, and St. John's. Many of them come from Jewish and Irish families. Partners feel these men can get along best with the clerks in the New York courts, who generally stem from the same background. In effect, they serve as liaison between the lower level bureaucrats of the courts and the Ivy League lawyers in the firm. Although Harvard and Yale provide broad legal education, they are not the places to learn how to deal with New York law clerks.

RECRUITING PARTNERS

OCCASIONALLY the firms take in partners who have not come up through the ranks. These men are generally well known, mostly from the world of politics, and/or business-getters. Some, however, are taken into a firm because of their special training in an area of the law. This is especially true when a new department is being developed or a specialty is needed which has not been previously covered.

The associates who are specialists, the men to do the routine jobs, the men brought in to work as a liaison with the court's law clerks, and the partners brought in from the outside are the exception rather than the rule. While their entry into the organization calls for the hiring of a variety of people, the firms' main concern in terms of quantity, as well as self-image, is in recruiting their ideal lawyer. We are also primarily interested here in these young counselors.

CHANGES IN THE ENVIRONMENT

WHILE the large firms obtain some of the preferred men they want, each office wants a greater proportion. The increasing competition for these elites initially stems from the increasing amount of practice going to this kind of firm. This expansion of legal work is generally attributed to the continuing growth of big business and to the multiplication of laws affecting commerce.[7] David Riesman also suggests that "it takes more people to do the same amount of work and that ever higher standards of conspicuous production go into the definition of the standard of work —Parkinson's law, in other words."[8] And personal observation does suggest that while Wall Street lawyers work very hard today, they probably do not work as hard (as indicated by historical sources)[9] as did their predecessors—another reason why more lawyers are needed to do the job now.[10]

Competition —

The growing number of large law firms throughout the country is perhaps of more importance as an explanation for the growing competition for the preferred lawyer. One author, by examining the legal directories published up to 1900, found that most firms were very small (by current standards) during the nineteenth century.[11] Today, in addition to the approximately twenty-one offices in New York (some of which are still growing—for example, both Cahill, Gordon, Reindel & Ohl and Simpson Thacher & Bartlett have doubled in size since 1936), there are seventeen large firms operating in other sections of the country. In 1949 only five of the seventeen could have boasted of having fifty or more lawyers. These firms along with most of the other large legal organizations have grown in size.

Available figures for the population of lawyers for fifteen of these large firms located outside of New York indicate that in 1959 about 347 more lawyers were connected with these organizations than in 1949. This increase indicates only a portion of the demand for lawyers, for during the 1949–1959 decade some lawyers left the firms and other law school graduates had to be found to replace them. These organizations look for the same kind of attorneys as do the more numerous large Wall Street firms. Forty-one per cent of the lawyers from one large California law office graduated from Harvard and Yale law schools. Generally, however (and this is particularly true of Texas firms, although not of the largest Massachusetts firm), large offices outside of New

York seem more willing to hire lawyers from schools other than the eastern elite institutions.

The turnover in the New York firms is sizable, often more than ten men a year for the larger offices. This occurs in part because of the weeding out of misfits and malcontents and in part because a number of Wall Street firms have recently adopted an "up-or-out" policy. If a firm decides that an associate is not going to be made a partner, he is informed of the decision so that he may either look for another job or accept one found for him by the firm. This policy, plus the insistent demands made by the firms' corporate clients for lawyers to work in their organizations,[12] creates a constant call for the preferred lawyer. Thus, the usual demand for such attorneys is increased by the departure of additional numbers of associates from the law firms. This gives the large firms another advantage over the smaller offices, for they can predict hiring needs much in advance of other firms, thereby gaining a head start in the search for legal talent. Other sources of increased competition for the preferred lawyers, however, are governmental agencies, the courts, corporations, and universities.

As competition for lawyers has increased, the proportion of men admitted to the Bar has been decreasing in the United States. The rate of admission in 1930 was 81 per million population; in 1958 it was only 57.[13] The problem is further complicated by the large law firms' preference for men from the Ivy League schools and the fact that these institutions have had no significant rise in the number of registrants. Comparison of the combined law school registration of Harvard, Yale, and Columbia for 1948 and 1958 indicates a gain of only 151 students, an increase of 5 per cent. However, the 1960 registrants represent a decrease of 527 students from the year 1947.[14]

Jewish Lawyers —

While most large law firms are now employing Jewish lawyers as associates, they probably limit the number of Jews they will accept. Justice Proskauer, a senior partner in a major "Jewish" firm, in 1949, observed, "It did not take me many days to discover that the doors of most New York law offices in 1899 were closed, with rare exceptions, to a young Jewish lawyer. Fifty years have elapsed since then and I am happy to record that there has been a distinct improvement in the situation; though it still remains true that generally the Jewish student must qualify twice for such employment."[15]

This continuing, though impressively modified, restriction against Jewish lawyers cuts down the number of potential recruits from among the group who meet the high academic requirements. Although it is hard to get direct admission that this restriction exists, the assumption seems supported by deductive evidence: the proportion of Jewish students in Ivy League law schools has increased, according to the estimates of law school officials (estimates buttressed by the B'nai B'rith report of a 54 per cent increase in Jewish enrollments in Ivy League colleges between 1946 and 1955).[16] Furthermore, the number of Jews at the top of their classes is large. At Yale Law School, for example, it was estimated by contributors to the *Law Journal* that 63 per cent of the members of the *Journal* for 1955–56 and 1956–57 were Jewish. By eliminating some of these men from consideration, the firms cut down their potential supply of academically superior Ivy League lawyers.

Catholic Lawyers —

Discrimination against Catholics has not greatly affected recruitment practices. Discrimination against Catholics is based more on their "lower-class" origins, their foreign-born parents, and their lack of "proper" education. Their religion does not seem to be a significant bar to employment, although some firms will not make them partners; consequently some Catholics do not apply for or accept employment in "Protestant Law Firms."

Negro Lawyers —

In the year and a half that was spent interviewing, I heard of only three Negroes who had been hired by large law firms. Two of these were women who did not meet the client. Applying the basic standards of the large offices, this is understandable. Few Negroes go to Ivy League preparatory schools or colleges. Few go to the eastern national law schools. So few Negroes are "eligible" for positions in these firms that the issue of employment is rarely raised.

Women Lawyers —

Women are discrimated against to a greater degree than are Jews, further restricting the law offices' supply of potential recruits. Not until 1869 was the first woman lawyer, one Arabella A. Mansfield of Mount Pleasant, Iowa, admitted to the Bar. Not until 1950 did Harvard Law School begin to accept women students. There were almost no female lawyers in the Wall Street firms until World War II brought about a shortage of male attorneys. Cravath, Swaine & Moore, for example, hired their first female lawyer in 1943. While most large law offices now do have some women in their organization, very few become partners. This researcher came across only one woman partner practicing in the New York City branches of the large firms. An analysis of a directory of women lawyers[17] reveals that, of the 1755 female attorneys in New York in 1956, only 18 list themselves as working in large New York offices (this figure, however, is low).

Barbara Armstrong, referring to a New York University report, writes that: "90 per cent of the lawyers who wish to engage a law clerk refuse even to interview women, and . . . such openings as there are often call for stenography." She herself believes that: "A well-dressed, well-acquainted, well-endowed woman applicant arouses immediate suspicion in the law offices, although all this is just what they pray for in a man."[18]

Interviews revealed that female associates felt they had little chance of becoming partners. Most of them thought that the large firms were "too much like a male club—they don't want women in them." Other less pessimistic judgments were offered, "I have children and hope to have more"; "I can't work as consistently or as hard as male lawyers because of my family obligations— otherwise I think I might make it." Some other female associates said that they hoped to get married and did not expect to stay in the law "and the partners know this."

Professor Soia Mentschikoff of the University of Chicago's Law School, one of the few female law professors in the country who also for a time practiced in the Wall Street district, believes that many women themselves are to blame if they don't become partners. She attributes the delay to their own defeatist attitudes, which start them out on their career assuming that they are second-class citizens who do not and will not have a chance at a partnership.

Other women attorneys insist that discrimination exists in fact. Nancy Young, a graduate of the Harvard Law School class of '54, writes after surveying thirty-four girls who had graduated from the classes of '53, '54, and '55, that "it is still far more difficult for a woman attorney to find a position today, than it is for a young man, even though he may not have as good an academic record. . . . The barriers remain highest in the city firm, which is often bound by tradition, precedent, and a wary eye to the reactions of the clients with substantial retainers."[19]

She finds the two principle arguments against hiring young women were (1) objections from the client, and (2) the expectation that the girls would get married and leave. When they are employed, women are generally expected to work in certain fields —probate, estate planning, and tax. A number of other areas are almost completely closed to them. Few women, as an illustration, can expect a niche in the litigation section of a large firm. One warning which comes from many girls sums it up: "Beware of the firm looking specifically for a woman lawyer. They want you for work they cannot get any man to do."

The partners I interviewed offered reasons similar to those Nancy Young found for limited employment of female attorneys: "They don't stay in the law."[20] "They can't work as hard as men" or "make the same kind of trips." "The clients prefer not to have them." The bias against women is so strong that one firm still elects to employ male stenographers when it can get them.

WHAT LAW SCHOOL GRADUATES WANT

THE factors of bias and of competition are further complicated by the changing initial desires of law students. The students who do not have to go into military service express early preferences about where they want to go, what they want to do, and how they want to practice.

Job location is often mentioned as a consideration, with the west frequently cited as a preference. The evidence, however, (obtained mainly from an examination of Harvard Law School records) indicates that if the fledgling lawyer believes that opportunity lies in New York City and the east instead of San Francisco and the west, he will go east.

Many law school seniors had no particular preferences as to the fields of the law in which they wished to practice. This undecided group constituted the largest number in the 1957 graduating class at Harvard.[21] A more detailed report of the Harvard Law School class of '56 indicated that the law they preferred to practice was distributed in the following order: 121 were undecided; 119 sought a general practice; 125 liked corporation law; 101 preferred taxation; 59 were interested in trial work; 29 wanted labor law; 44 hoped to be international lawyers.[22] These preferences fluctuate somewhat each year with changes in preferred law professors and legal fads and fashions. The stated desired fields of work named by most seniors often differ from their later choices. This was true for members of the sample. Again, the larger opportunity rather than the specific branch of the law seems to be the most important element influencing job choice. As the market becomes more competitive, however, the neophyte can become more selective, and the ability of the firm to offer the location and specialty the potential recruit prefers becomes correspondingly more important.

Perhaps of greater significance to the young lawyer is the setting in which he chooses to practice. A major decision the job seeker from the eastern elite schools must make is whether or not to practice in a large law firm. Many of these students want to practice in the large offices, as evidenced by the many uninvited but welcomed applicants each year. It is understandable that these offices should draw a considerable number of men, for they offer prestige, good starting salaries, and a potentially high future income; they also handle the largest and probably the most interesting corporate matters and are at the center of the business community's power structure. But many other students have clearly decided against the large firm for such reasons as the following: "I don't want to get lost in those law factories." "They make you specialize too soon." "I don't care for that kind of impersonal practice: I want to help people with their problems." "The work is too routine." "You're not your own boss." "You don't get enough responsibility." "The work is too hard." "You have to wait too long to become a partner—you can move up faster in a small firm." "I want to have some time with my family." "You don't see clients or learn how to get them."

The dilemma involved in deciding between the large firm and the small one is detailed by John William Sterling, who eventually became a name partner in Wall Street's largest law firm, Shearman & Sterling:

> To be a partner of David Dudley Field, Dudley Field and Thomas G. Shearman is an offer never made before and one I think which will be sparingly extended to others. So far as honor and reputation are concerned, I suppose, without doubt, that I should be a great deal better off than if I went anywhere else. But then on the other hand I should not be expected to have any business of my own and as the cases which they take hold of are only those involving millions I should never have an opportunity of developing myself in speaking or arguing. And I am not willing so early in life to settle down without having had a trial of my own powers in almost every direction. . . . To try small cases in an inferior court, where I am not so closely watched by those whom I respect or in whose presence I am awe-stricken and dumb, is an advantage which I shall have at Hill's and one which I cannot hope to secure elsewhere.[23]

Many lawyers who do finally enter the large law firms nevertheless share these attitudes, and therefore look for, among the large organizations, one in which they will not feel as lost, will not have to specialize as quickly, and will do more responsible and interesting work. In addition to this desire to modify the negative aspects of work in the large law firm, some men explain their choice of a particular organization by citing available postgraduate education, a chance to get ahead quickly, the opportunity to deal with "big matters," work with interesting people, or several of these reasons.

MYTHS AND LAW OFFICE CHOICE

WHILE opportunity seems to be the most significant factor in job choice, law students often base their choice of jobs, according to placement officers and the evidence obtained from interviews with seniors and individuals in the sample, on personal bias, half truths, myths, fads, and other factors not generally considered important in making such decisions. The recruiter must take these factors into account in a tight job market.

The most frequently heard "reputational myth" involves the notion that one or two firms work much harder and much longer than other large firms. There are legends about the kinds of clients a firm has. Associates in one firm supposedly play bridge all afternoon and then have to work all night. Some offices are known as "friendly" firms where everyone knows everyone else and social life continues outside the firm. Certain offices are known not to hire female or Italian lawyers. These myths can hamper—or help—a firm's recruiting from year to year.

Often a firm is given a "short-term halo" based on the report of a returning alumnus. A dean in charge of placement at one of the Ivy League law schools corroborates this finding:

At one time X firm couldn't get anyone, but now that isn't so. Y firm was going great, but now they can't get anyone. There's usually some student with leadership and he gets the rest to want to go where he goes. To some extent, their choice is based on impressions and sometimes law firms gang up on a firm like Z firm and run them down. Also, students' interests change from year to year—one year it was taxation, the next international law. They try to go to the firm where they can get this kind of work. I think the law student picks his job on the basis of feel—a year later, all of them say their firm is the best in the world. They develop strong loyalties.

The interviews bear out the experience of the dean that some choice is based on how a recruit "feels" about an organization. Thus, one associate reported on a position he refused: "While they offered me a job, I didn't feel they wanted me"; and a student respondent, speaking of a partner who had just interviewed him, said, "He's the nicest fellow I've ever met." To the anxious recruit the hiring partner represents a symbol of things to come.

These findings are not intended to mean that law students are completely naive—they are not. Much of their information is correct, is partially correct, or was correct. There appears to be a correlation between the truth of a statement and how close a student is to law review men. Law review students usually get first chance at the best jobs. Their review colleagues from the previous year are already working at preferred positions and this gives the current review man an edge over his fellow student. It is difficult not to believe a persistent rumor especially when one's information comes from a brother student or alumnus, even though the information is second-hand.

Recruitment Techniques —

The law firms try to cater to the wishes and stereotypes of the law student, and when appropriate they attempt to manipulate or change them. In a competitive market, with its scarcity of preferred men, students can be selective. Under these circumstances, the firms first sell the idea of practicing in the large organizations to the reluctant or ambivalent recruit. The firms then try to sell themselves individually, hoping that these devices will maximize their chances to attract preferred men.

Image-making Machinery —

To change, maintain, or create attractive images, and to assure or reassure the recruit, the firms send notices to the placement offices of the law schools in which they plead innocent to certain detrimental charges and claim desirable attributes. This is part of their "image-making machinery." In order to determine the content of these notices, announcements sent to Harvard Law School were analyzed. Examples from these bulletins illustrate the main theme. Most of them are designed to bolster a desire or defeat a fear.

Some firms belittle students' anxieties about too-early specialization by statements that they are "not as rigidly departmentalized as some very large offices," or by reporting that "insofar as possible, law clerks are given an opportunity to work on problems in those fields in which they are most interested and are not required to select a speciality or confine their work to one field." Another firm emphasizes: "We are departmentalized only to a slight extent and none of our younger men specializes in a particular field unless he requests it."

This anxiety goes hand in hand with concern about not receiving "proper training," and attempts are made to allay both of these fears. Representative notices read:

> While all large firms must inevitably be departmentalized in varying degrees, nevertheless, we try not to put new men into any particular department. We regard the practice of law in the early years in the nature of an internship and feel a responsibility to any young lawyer we hire. We take pains to see that he receives supervision and good training and we give him responsibility as soon as we believe he is ready for it.

> Men coming with the firm directly out of law school are not assigned to a department of the office until they have been with the firm for one or two years. During this period conscious effort is made to see that these men have the opportunity to work with as many different partners in as many different fields of the law as possible. Emphasis is placed on broad general experience. This will include not only research work and preparation of memoranda of law but also drafting legal papers, participation in conferences and with clients, attendance at court hearings, and several weeks' experience in the managing clerks' department.

Some firms announce they do not use the pool system (through which a lawyer can be assigned to do anything for anybody), hoping this statement will help blunt the senior's fear that he will "get lost" in the large organization. To assure him of his independence one firm declares: "It is the purpose of our training to bring a man to the point where he can work independently as quickly as he is able to." To assure recruits of security, firms announce they do not place men from the outside over old associates; or that they receive requests from corporations for lawyers, so that if individuals are not admitted to partnerships their futures are nevertheless assured. For the shy, or the "consciousness of kind" graduates, one firm writes to Harvard that "30 per cent of our staff came from Harvard."

Other techniques designed to capture the fancy of the recruit are also used, although generally not by the large firms. These inducements are in the nature of extra benefits. They include communiques assuring work in an air-conditioned building, group life and disability insurance, and a contribution toward a hospitalization plan.

These promotional notices to the law schools make a difference. In addition to announcing opportunities, they may weaken the resolve of some men against the large law firm and strengthen favorable predisposition of others. Mainly, they make claims for their firms and assist in creating an image. Over a period of time, however, such promotional activities can have only limited effect. For if the claims are not implemented by commitments which correspond to the reality of the organizational experience, a seriously damaged public image spread by disaffected personnel is the result. In the long run, then, the credibility of the firms' claims depends to a great extent on their readiness to back up their statements by corresponding changes in organizational structure and functioning.

The law schools function not only as communicators of law firm images but also as employment middle-men. They bring together persons needing jobs and firms with positions to be filled. This is a very important function, for there are very few employment agencies which deal with the employment of lawyers. Dean Toepher of Harvard found that "36 per cent of the law school seniors received substantial help from the school's placement services." Occasionally an alumnus asks the placement office to find jobs, but they are rarely able to fill this kind of request. Their work is mainly with the graduating senior. The placement offices solicit firms for jobs, sometimes visit them, and occasionally investigate an employer. As an Ivy League employment official put it: "I don't want these boys to start on the wrong foot. They might get mixed up with some negligence lawyers." One placement officer prepared a list of 237 firms for his students after having circularized a larger list of 700 law firms.

Most law schools keep close contact with their alumni and as their alumni find themselves in positions of power they can be of help to the young graduate. The placement office sees to it that the new graduate and the old can get together. Sometimes they publish a list of alumni and their firms because alumni often give preference to applicants from their own school. Some law schools have local placement offices run by alumni. The men who come to these placement centers usually are not, academically at least, the best men. They are somewhat older and many are from the harder-to-place minority groups. These graduates generally are placed with the small law firms and corporations. Some few lawyers in this study, however, did get jobs with the large law firms through these New York Alumni offices.

In addition, the Harvard Law School Association of New York City, Inc., has a placement smoker at the Harvard Club during the Christmas holidays, which is still the main job-hunting season. At one session, for example, former Justice David W. Peck (class of '25) presided and Walter R. Mansfield (class of '35) from Donovan Leisure Newton & Irvine, represented the large firms. He and some other Harvard alumni stated the benefits of different kinds of legal practice and in this way offered job hunters a belated orientation. Also present were a panel of alumni hosts, a number of them from large law firms. At this meeting Harvard, through its alumni, gave its graduates not only an orientation lecture but also job contacts.

At the various placement offices advice is given to both the law firms and the graduates. The firms are told which men the placement officers think best suited for them; the men are told which firms to apply to and how to behave in an interview situation. As we shall see later, this is part of the selecting-out and socialization process. For example, young men have been advised to talk about themselves: "within the realm of strictest modesty, colored to reach the law firm," or to "endeavor to reflect within limits, of course, the personality of the individual you are talking to. If he is conservative, be conservative. If he does all the talking don't interrupt him. If he expects you to talk, talk."

Law School Visits —

The law firms send representatives to visit the law schools. More of these men go to Harvard and Yale than to the other schools. Competition, however, has forced some partnerships not only to advertise in the midwest and western national schools but also, to an increasing degree, to send representatives to the universities of Chicago and Michigan. An examination of the placement records at the University of Chicago reveals that few students are actually employed by the eastern large law offices; nor are the men who are hired necessarily at the top of their class. This may be due to a shortage of the types of lawyers the large firms prefer or to the fact that fewer lawyers from the University of Chicago want to go to these big firms. In a sample of the student body at Indiana University law school, no one stated that he wanted to go to Wall Street.[24] Since few graduates from Midwestern law schools go to the large New York firms, and since face-to-face recruitment in this area is not as persistent as it is in the east, little desire has been developed for these firms. This makes it more difficult for the large firms to obtain the kind of men they want from the Midwest.

Interviewing Procedures —

The representatives of law firms, when they visit the various universities, interview seniors who are interested in practicing with their firm. The interview takes between fifteen and twenty minutes and the weeding-out process continues. Only 6.1 per cent of the sample (interviewed for this study) were hired directly through school interviews. Another 7.1 per cent were invited to visit the law firms and then were employed.

The hiring partner is usually the man who sees applicants; sometimes he brings with him a recent and well-liked alumnus in the hope that school ties and still-warm contacts will influence the prospective employee. While at the law school, the various representatives of the firms may wine and dine the students they want most. There is a correlation between the difficulty of obtaining men and the efforts of a firm to get them. Each organization would like to obtain the best and most popular man. When a firm succeeds in getting this man, the impression left with the school is that this firm just takes the best men. This makes recruiting easier that year and the next. Seniors at the lower end of the first quarter of the class will then feel it an honor to be accepted by the firm which has hired the top man in the class. A former placement officer is unhappy with the hiring techniques used by the law firms. He reports that, except in their concern for grades, the:

> People who hire do not do so as much on logic as on feeling. They have an image of themselves or some other ideal type. It is sort of like a blind date—if they don't like them, they are courteous, but not enthusiastic. If they like them, that's another story. These days they go to all sorts of lengths to get the man they want. They pick one man by first hiring his roommate. It's like fraternity rushing. They work up a lot of early enthusiasm. I don't think this is the right way to go about professional employment. They should proceed to walk handily and slowly. They're not being entirely frank. Their effort not to offend anyone is wrong. They never tell a man, "No, you won't do."—they string people along so as not to offend them. Now they take care of them for the summer—give them a delightful time—because the summer people carry the information back to the school and they may get their man. They also send the most personable junior partner to convince the best law student. I don't like it.

Although some high-pressure recruiting does go on (and reports from the case histories collected confirm this), most of the recruiting is more sedate. Most firms, for example, may interview a special possibility at lunch or dinner, paying his fare to New York and perhaps also the fare of his wife. Nevertheless, the recruitment techniques are not so high-pressure as those often associated with large corporations. Perhaps this will come about. At the moment, however, fancy courting is the exception rather than the rule.

In addition to the employment offices at the universities there are a few lawyer placement services. The two most effective placement offices are in New York and Chicago.

Mrs. Trainer, the former head of the placement office in New York, reports that two-thirds of their jobs were for experienced people and very few requests for men came from the large law firms. (Less than one per cent of the sample was recruited in this manner.)

Almost 29 per cent of our sample of lawyers said their appointments to the law firms were obtained at least in part through influence. This does not mean that they did not have some of the requirements the law offices desire. Because they did and because influence was generally defined by spokesmen for law firms as client pressure, which was relatively rare, the law offices deny this charge and say that influence plays only a very little part in recruitment.

Two per cent of the sample claimed, however, that they received their position because clients had requested it. Another 15.5 per cent reported that other outside contacts had intervened in their behalf. The intensity of the intervention varies from a pressure request for a favor to a more gentle nudge by a social contact. One respondent in answer to a question concerning recruitment describes how he obtained his job:

> I told my father that I wanted to get the best possible training to be a lawyer. He consulted friends and they told him that the best thing to do was to work for several years with a large New York law firm.
>
> The next question which occurred was which law firm to go into. He [father] looked around and mentioned me and my record to some partners in the firm whom he knows. I came down and they looked at me and I looked at them and they were nice enough to offer me a job.

Eleven per cent felt they had obtained their position because they knew someone in the firm.

LIMITS ON RECRUITMENT

COMPETITION for lawyers among the large firms in New York City is limited in two major ways: the firms will not pirate an employee from another law office, and they maintain a gentlemen's agreement to pay the same beginning salary, commonly called the going rate. However, a small number of cases, mostly of editors of law reviews, have been reported in which these agreements were not strictly adhered to. Bargaining, however, was the exception for most members of the sample.

The going rate in 1963 was $7500 for a beginning lawyer, somewhat higher for a man who had been in service or had clerked for a judge or had some other kind of desirable experience. Beginning salaries for each succeeding year are set by a few representatives of the major large firms, usually, one respondent reported, informally at lunch. These people spread the word. Generally this is simple, for members of other firms call the rate-makers just before the hiring season begins and then continue to pass on the information. Eventually it becomes almost common knowledge both to firms and to recruits. The further (in geographical distance) the firm is from the decision as to the going rate, the less necessary it is for it to honor the agreement, unless it is competing for preferred men; then the necessity increases. The large Washington firms also pay the New York going rate; the Boston or Chicago firms pay somewhat less—but they know about the gentlemen's agreement.

The law firms justify standardizing the starting salaries, since they feel that it is best for professional people not to base a most important career decision on initial salaries. This does not mean money is not considered—it is, and in two ways. The competition among the Wall Street lawyers for the same kind of men tends to increase starting salaries. In 1953, for example, it was $4000; in 1963 it was $3500 higher. Ethically, the only real additional monetary inducement the recruiter can offer involves future income. Suggestions of large bonuses or indications that partnerships "are more possible in our firm" are sometimes made. Some of the middle size firms allow associates to bring their own clients into the office, with the right to a share of what is earned from these clients.

Although these basic agreements limit salary competition somewhat, they intensify competition in other respects. The firms compete by raising psychic as well as other kinds of relatively intangible "income." Competition for the preferred lawyer is further pointed up by the willingness of law firms to hire some law school seniors, although they are scheduled to go into the armed forces before they can practice, in order to insure the firm of their services after they are discharged.

ORGANIZATIONAL ADAPTATION TO MEET RECRUITMENT NEEDS

NEVERTHELESS, most of the firms studied are old and conservative, proud of both these attributes, and therefore reluctant to extend the limits of what they will do to attract attorneys. Since, however, it is necessary for the immediate and long-run survival of a firm to recruit "proper" legal talent, some changes in the organization of the law firms have been made to meet the demands of the recruit. This has occurred despite the resistance to such change especially on the part of the older, more conservative partners. These men, who often seem to think of themselves as akin to small-town general practitioners, do not like the notion of a segmented, departmentalized, hierarchical organization, regarding it as something not quite professional. They also resent the time reorganization may take away from the practice of the law, and make changes only when they believe that they must. When changes do take place they do not happen quickly.[25]

The Hiring Partner —

As previously suggested, law firms no longer believe they can afford to wait until the candidate comes to them. More and more, firms are sending lawyers to visit the major schools to look over the crop for the next year. Harvard, for example, which in 1947 did not have a placement office, was visited in 1950–51 by 64 firms, in 1955–56 by representatives of 185 law firms and corporations, and in 1956–57 by 194 prospective employers. This practice, and the tradition of seeing anyone who wants a job, have led to the formalization of the role of "hiring partner," who is generally one of the most attractive and personable of the partners. Creation of this position is an early attempt by a firm to put its best foot forward. The hiring partner is needed not only to attract graduates but also to save the valuable time of other partners. While visiting the various law schools, the hiring partner weeds out the poorer prospects and invites the better ones to visit the firm in New York. The hiring partner is also better able than his colleagues to evaluate the candidates, since he sees a good percentage of all applicants.

In addition to the men invited to visit firms, there is, each year, between the Thanksgiving and Christmas holidays, a mass migration of other young lawyers to Wall Street. Many third-year students making the rounds of the large law firms do not know all the firms; they tend to visit only the offices with the best reputations. Thus, these offices get the greatest number of applicants and presumably have a better chance of obtaining the best men. Thirty-six per cent of that portion of the sample who were asked how they obtained their job reported that they had come to the firm "off the street" during the hiring season and were interviewed and eventually employed. This figure, however, is misleading as an index of what most large law firms do since two firms account for 54 per cent of the "off-the-street recruiting."

One law reviewer tells the story of his visit to the law office that hired him:

> It was quite by accident that I came to this firm. In my senior year of law school, during the Christmas holidays, I had some free time so I went around to the various firms. I had no idea of joining because of rumors of night work and overspecialized specialization which persisted around Columbia. However, it did have a reputation for quality. After I'd been interviewed I was more impressed with the place and when a job was offered, I took it.

A lawyer who no longer works for a large firm sketches his job-hunting experiences. "It was pretty much a pavement-pounding proposition" and he continues to say that his choice was made "largely out of ignorance." He had friends who were scattered around the downtown firms but he found that the ideas he received from them and from the partners who interviewed him in the firms he went to see "turned out to be erroneous." He doesn't think you can really know much about a firm unless you are part of it.

Graduating seniors report that they hear of firms not only through rumors or friends or acquaintances who work for them but also through an organization's famous client, or the reputation of some of its partners. The late Randolph Paul, for example, was a well-known and respected tax specialist and because of this (even though most of his time was spent in the firm's Washington office) he was able to attract some additional men to visit Paul, Weiss, Rifkind, Wharton & Garrison. There are many other examples.

Formalizing Office Interviewing Systems —

Some firms—in self defense but also to maintain good will and a good reputation with the law schools and the legal profession, while at the same time continuing their work and recruitment—have set up elaborate systems to take care of the estimated three hundred to four hundred candidates seen during the year. One large office developed the following system:

Any lawyer who applies for a position is interviewed; no one is turned away. Ten to twelve associates are designated as interviewers. The receptionist tries to spread the work around. Each associate rates the candidate as a "one," "two," or "three." If rated "one," the candidate is sent to a partner who sits on the hiring committee. If rated "two," the applicant may be "all right" but the associate does not think him acceptable; but he is also sent to a partner—though generally he is given less time. A "three" rating means that the applicant is rejected; even rejected candidates, however, are sent to a partner, though not necessarily one who is a member of the hiring committee. The partner spends five minutes with a "three" and then sends him on his way— but he tries to leave the applicant with a favorable impression of the firm. If the partner disagrees with the associate, he refers the candidate to a member of the hiring committee. The man rated "one" is sent to this committee immediately, and at least three people on the committee see this applicant. If the candidate passes this test, then the hiring partners have him see other partners.

Not all firms have such an elaborate procedure. One law office assigns fourteen partners, three different ones each day, to do the screening. This procedure reflects the view that better public relations are maintained if partners rather than associates do the initial interviewing. If one of these partners passes favorably on an applicant, he is sent to two or more partners. Eventually he is interviewed by the hiring partner, who sees all candidates and compares them—a process which requires valuable time but is thought to be necessary and worth while.

Summer Boarders —

Another device of the large law offices to further selective recruitment is to invite second-year law students to clerk with them during the summer. Six per cent of the sample had been "summer boarders" in the firms that finally employed them. Most firms do not really need these summer boarders as workers, but their value is threefold: the boarders get to know the firm; they provide the firm with a preview of their ability; if they are good and are liked, they are offered jobs when they graduate; in any event, they return to the law schools and report what they have seen—hopefully, reporting favorably.

When a firm makes a major revision in its organization because of recruitment, it does so to meet the demands of a number of candidates; generally, however, the change also satisfies other internal requirements.

The Firm as a Postgraduate Law School —

One request most applicants make of law firms is that they provide opportunities for training, a request closely related to the seniors' fear that they will be forced into quick specialization. Candidates are told that diversified work will be available and the firms try to make good on this commitment. But when an associate who has been successful in one kind of work becomes known as "good" or "expert" in that particular area of law, more of his colleagues then send him work in his acquired "specialty," so that soon he becomes an expert in fact. Thus, it is costly for the firm to change his functions, and partners who have been relieved of this particular job are reluctant to take it on again. Consequently, the associate remains in his special area and does not get the broad training he desires. More and more firms, however, finding themselves committed to training their new men (because it is a good recruiting device, to be sure, but also because many partners think that it helps to make better lawyers and therefore benefits the firm), are beginning to further formalize their educational programs. In a sense these firms are becoming postgraduate vocational schools.

One of the largest law partnerships is more formalized than the others in this respect. The hiring partner in this office, who had devised the educational program, found that it was attracting candidates and was becoming known in law schools and throughout the "Street." This formalized program, designed to provide for varied experience, is described by its sponsor as follows:

We have a rotating system. An associate has to spend a portion of three years in three different departments. I keep a chart of where they've been and how long they stay and when they've been in a department long enough I move them. We found that unless you have regular notices that the man is changing departments you don't move the man properly. If you do it without the records and without the formality, you find that a man is never free and the people involved in the problem have forgotten about rotating.

This firm decided that this program had to be installed if they were going to give good training. Despite this, it still meets with individual resistance. A partner will say "I just get a man trained and you take him away from me." Some of the partners said that "we aren't running a school." They feel, however, that eventually they will get good lawyers. The associates like it and that's one reason why I get such good results in hiring. We do a lot of things for our associates. We even send them to special courses, like tax courses.

ADDITIONAL ADJUSTMENTS

AS they debate the merits of large firms, recruits often complain that "you don't get ahead fast enough—it takes forever to make partner." Some few firms assign the title "Junior Partner" to people who would normally be senior associates, perhaps creating the illusion that the associates are moving up faster than they actually are—and this illusion may aid the firm in its recruitment efforts. Many organizations have initiated rules and other changes to reassure ambitious recruits. For example, candidates fear competition from relatives of partners, and members of a firm may fear the possibility that a colleague's unqualified son may be taken into the firm as a partner. Hence the increasing adoptions of rules against nepotism.

Anxiety about being lost in the giant firm is often mentioned by both the applicant and the young associate. The pool system, although it functions formally as a training device, adds to that concern. In addition many associates do not feel that this plan for work assignment is "professional." Because of the disapproval of the assignment of bright young lawyers to more or less mechanical jobs, some offices are doing away with the pool system.

Employment "Agencies" —

The "up-or-out rule" is designed to insure that lawyers who are not going to be made partners leave the firm, permitting a constant flow of new talent into the organization. This rule (not all firms have it) also has the side effect of counteracting the complaint that "you never know how you're doing." It requires that eventually (usually within a ten-year period) associates be informed that they are not going to be partners. (This same rule can be found in most major universities except that the period a professor must wait before he gets tenure is shorter). Some offices therefore function as employment centers, with a threefold aim: to give security to their associates, to demonstrate their own view that it is not "professional" (or at least not "nice") to fire a lawyer, and to provide their corporate clients with good legal and executive talent. Generally, the managing partner solicits jobs and suggests associates from his firm to fill them. Some offices cultivate this function more than others and can provide excellent employment opportunities for their future alumni. While not every man can become a partner, very few leave the firm without a good position—often one paying a higher salary than the partnership they did not get. The firms which best provide employment outlets win the reputation of "taking care of their men."

Increased Employment of Minority Groups —

During World War II many large firms began to accept Jewish lawyers as associates at an accelerated rate. Those respondents I queried, when asked why this change occurred, most frequently said that it was due to the impetus of the Fair Employment Practice Act. That, however, is probably not the main reason, except as passage of such a law reflects changing public opinion. A dean from one of the Ivy League law schools suggests that the Jewish lawyers now coming in greater numbers from Ivy League colleges and the best law schools are in a different position from their predecessors. He points out that discrimination "is becoming less and less of a problem. In almost every case it is not being Jewish that throws a man back but lack of polish that accompanies anyone who is half a generation away from another country."

Jewish lawyers who are employed by these large offices usually come from the top of their classes in the Ivy League colleges and law schools, and the firms, initially at any rate, hired them mainly because competition made it difficult always to secure an attorney with all the preferred background factors. Employment of Jewish lawyers probably may continue to be a problem to both the Jewish law students and to the firms. The law students will want to know if some Jews will be promoted to partnership. And, although many large firms do have Jewish partners, the question will remain as to whether the giant firms plan to restrict this practice by some sort of quota system. As one associate put it: "We will accept some Jews if they don't have a New York background. We have one partner who is Jewish and we have a surprising number of Jewish associates—all are the acceptable kind—and this is going to be the firm's big problem because they can't make so many Jews partners." The reluctance of some Jews to accept employment in gentile firms is documented by an American Jewish Congress survey of lawyers' employment experiences. They found that: "over one-third (35 per cent) of the Jewish respondents [from the 1951 graduating class of Chicago, Columbia, Harvard, and Yale law schools] reported that they refrained from making appli-

cation to certain law firms and business houses because of a belief
that these firms used discriminatory employment practices. . . ."[26]
More recently, a respondent declared, "We don't have more Jews
[in the firm] because too many of them feel that they won't become partners; so they leave. Some won't even take a job with the
firm."

Those Jewish lawyers who have become partners prove to
Jewish candidates that success is possible. By 1963 many of the
law firms which had earlier hired Jews as associates had made
some of these attorneys partners. Still, the fear of discrimination
lingers on in the fact that sometimes these members are regarded
as "the Jewish partner." In the past a few firms have included
Jews as members, usually "German" Jews whose families had been
in this country for generations, many of them with important
business connections. And one large firm, Paul, Weiss, Rifkind,
Wharton & Garrison, has an almost equal number of Jewish and
gentile partners. Respondents believe that most of the big firms
will make some Jews partners. This change in policy not only
represents new unofficial rules but offers the possibility of altering
the social complexion and perhaps the "family" and club-like
atmosphere of some law offices. Even "social"[27] firms are now
recruiting Jewish lawyers, and these organizations too will find,
if they wish to hire the bright Jewish law review editor, that it is
a good recruitment policy to provide models of success.

Still the firms[28] probably feel that they must consider a man's
religion because, as one hiring partner put it: "Prejudice is very
strong among many clients. [To the extent that this is so it makes
finding Jewish associates corporate positions difficult.] There are
clients to whom you can't take a Jewish lawyer; sometimes Catholic lawyers present problems too, but not as often." The firms do
worry about what their clients feel (sometimes a needless concern
as indicated by an experimentally-minded partner who reports:
"Occasionally, just to be obstinate, I take a Jewish fellow up with
me [to the client] but nothing has ever happened"). They also
worry about prejudice among their own partners and about the
change in the social composition of the organization. Since the
firms hire only the best of the Jewish candidates, they worry about
the numbers of these recruits who would normally be seriously

considered for a partnership. It seems safe to assume that, after the initial prejudice breaks down (as it is doing), some informal quota against Jews will probably prevail. For this reason one gentile associate who was given a recruitment assignment was told not to encourage Jewish applicants unless they were extremely outstanding. Over all, however, it is clear that discrimination is waning.

ORGANIZATIONAL SIDE EFFECTS

CHANGES designed to aid recruitment affect the organization beyond the desired goal, and each alteration produces side effects. The formalization of the position of hiring[29] or assignment partner, for example, means that the lawyers occupying this postion assume new managerial duties and are compelled to curtail their practice of the law. The development of these managerial posts also signifies that the younger partners who usually fill them must be given enough authority to carry out their roles. This necessity results in a slight shift in the power relations within the firms.

In some instances, what began as a small alteration has snowballed into something of major importance. Many firms, as noted above, now promise the recruit job security—either within the firm or elsewhere. It was not too difficult to fulfill this promise until some law offices instituted the "up-or-out rule"; then, the increased placement needs required a great deal of effort. It is important that the firms satisfy both their corporate clients and their associates, since their activities in these areas are closely tied in with their ability to recruit and to place more men. The relatively minor task of finding jobs for some of their associates with corporate clients has grown to large proportions; one firm estimates that it has as many as eight hundred alumni.

Similarly, the promise to provide advanced training for their recruits has led some firms to formalize their educational procedures. Among the side effects of this change is the development of additional managerial and tutorial duties and the loss of some measure of freedom by partners, for it is now difficult for them to keep men they have personally trained and whom they like.

There are other unanticipated consequences: for example,

tasks which were meant to be temporary or minor tend to become fixed—for example, running employment bureaus, recruiting at law schools, taking in summer boarders. Almost all such changes call for new rules and further integration on the part of the law firms.

SUMMARY

TO summarize—the recruitment standards of the large law firm are high, and they are hard to meet because competition for preferred men is strong and increasing. Therefore, law school graduates who fulfill the high standards can be more discriminating than formerly in their choice of jobs. The law offices try to satisfy some of the demands of the preferred graduates in a number of different ways, but not all firms have adopted all methods.

The development of "image-making machinery," however, is an adaptation made by all of the large firms. Most offices also have formalized the role of "hiring partner." Other changes include provisions for training, speedier advancement into the rank of junior or limited partner, "up-or-out" rules, regulations against nepotism, and reduction of discrimination against the employment of Jews and women.

These alterations are designed partly to help the firms meet the manpower problems, and the adaptations constitute changes in the recruitment mechanism. This mechanism includes any aspect of the structure or functioning of the system that affects the intake and loss of personnel. Therefore, changes in the mechanism refer not only to the recruitment process in the narrow and commonly understood sense but also to alterations in the firm which affect its attracting and holding power. These alterations can take place in any part of an organization, for in reality the whole system is part of the recruitment mechanism.

Organizational changes to meet the demands of growing competition for preferred lawyers often produce unanticipated consequences, mainly in the direction of increased bureaucratization. This tendency is indicated by the development of formal rules and stratification and the formalization of training duties.[30]

Some changes and side effects of planned change lead to new

strains and dilemmas. Concerning the function of the law firm: "Are we a law firm or a school?" On the employment of women and Jews: "What will our clients think?" What will it do to our little family?" In satisfying short-term needs as against possible long-term benefits: "If we inaugurate an 'up-or-out' policy will we be losing men who know their job and are valuable to the firm?" On the use of corporation techniques of recruitment: "Is it professional?" There are other problems, but the most interesting development has come about because the best students and young associates wish to be treated in what they consider to be a more professional manner—they want more independence and responsibility—and the firms needing these young lawyers set up systems of rules to protect them from the severity of impersonal organization. The young associate receives short-run protection; the firm in the long run becomes more bureaucratic. It is the fear of some that the law firms soon may be facing another and perhaps more important problem growing out of the need for further bureaucratic procedure at the possible cost of a less professional staff.

NOTES

1. Law review or law journal men are law students who run the law journals and who usually academically are at the top of their class.

2. *Harvard Law School Placement Information* (a leaflet published at Harvard), September 1956, p. 3.

3. Otto E. Koegel, *Walter S. Carter, Collector of Young Masters or The Progenitor of Many Law Firms* (New York: Round Table Press, 1953), pp. x, 3, 8.

4. Spencer Klaw, "The Wall Street Lawyers," *Fortune*, 57 (February 1958), 192.

5. "Editors' Employment," *Harvard Law Review*, 71 (March 1958), vii–viii.

6. Percentages cited on the topic, "How the sample of Wall Street lawyers received their position," are calculated on the base of 99 respondents—the total of that portion of the sample asked how they obtained their jobs.

7. See, for example, J. D. Wright, "The Lawyer's Role in Modern Industry," *Western Reserve Law Review*, 9 (September 1958), 425–426.

8. Letter from David Riesman, September 8, 1958.

9. Henry W. Taft, *A Century and a Half at the New York Bar* (New

York: privately printed, 1938), p. 40. Taft quotes Mr. Strong, a member of
a firm which eventually became the large Wall Street firm of Cadwalader,
Wickersham & Taft, who in 1824 wrote: "During the whole winter I have
been confined in the office from about 8 in the morning till about 10 at
night and at work as busily as a man in harvest."

10. See David Riesman, "Law and Sociology: Recruitment, Training
and Colleagueship," *Stanford Law Review*, 9 (July 1957), 666.

11. Edwin C. Austin, "Some Comments on Large Law Firms," *The
Practical Lawyer*, 3 (April 1957), 9.

12. Wright, *op. cit.*, p. 427, finds that private industry employed 15,063
full-time practicing lawyers in 1954, 3789 more than they did in 1950.

13. Ross L. Malone, "Lawyers—Supply and Demand," *Trusts and
Estates*, 98 (March 1959), 186.

14. These figures are based on data compiled by John G. Harvey, "Law
School Registration, 1949," *Journal of Legal Education*, 2 (1949), 218, 220,
221; and "Law School Registration, 1958," *Journal of Legal Education*, 11
(1958), 259, 263, 266.

15. Joseph M. Proskauer, *A Segment of My Times* (New York: Farrar,
Straus and Young, 1950), p. 30.

16. Robert Shosteck, *The Jewish College Student* (Washington, D.C.:
B'nai B'rith Vocational Service), 1957, p. 37.

17. Dorothy Thomas (Ed.), *Women Lawyers in the United States* (New
York: Scarecrow Press, 1957).

18. Barbara L. Armstrong, "Women in the Law," *The Harvard Law
School Record*, Part II (December 1951), 108.

19. Nancy Young, "Alumnae," *Harvard Law School Bulletin*, 8 (December 1956), 13.

20. Edith Fisch's survey of Columbia law school graduates from 1929–
1951 indicates that while there is some merit to the statement, a good portion of it is a myth. She found that 70 per cent of the alumnae are active as
against 77.5 per cent of the over-all alumni. Edith L. Fisch, "Occupational
Discrimination Against Women and the Law," *Fordham Law Review*, 20
(June 1951), 199.

21. *Harvard Law School Placement Information, op. cit.*, p. 2.

22. *Harvard Law School Placement Information*, September 1956.

23. John Garver, *John William Sterling: A Biographical Sketch* (New
Haven: Yale University Press, 1929), pp. 40–41.

24. Erwin O. Smigel, John W. Martin, and Donald Horning, "Legal
Ethics and Education" (unpublished study, 1958).

25. Cf. Emily P. Dodge, "Evolution of a City Law Office, Part 1: Office
Organization," *Wisconsin Law Review*, 2 (March 1955), 182.

26. "A Survey of the Employment Experiences of Law School Graduates of Chicago, Columbia, Harvard and Yale Universities" (New York:
American Jewish Congress, Commission on Law and Social Action, 1954),
p. 2 (mimeographed).

27. Firms composed in large part of lawyers from Ivy League schools who possess Social Register backgrounds.

28. Time after time respondents would point out that "Jewish" firms do not hire gentiles, or at least very few of them. Members of these firms reply that they can't get the best gentile lawyers, but can obtain the best Jewish counselors.

29. Marcson's study of scientists in industry indicates that the recruitment of scientists is similar to the recruitment of lawyers. However, industries' recruiting procedure is more formalized. For example, the personnel office designates a staff member who specialized in Ph.D. recruitment. He himself is a Ph.D. and is often employed especially for recruiting purposes. Simon Marcson, *The Scientist in American Industry: Some Organizational Determinants in Manpower Utilization* (New York: Harper & Row, 1960), p. 52.

30. While these features are not in themselves equivalent to bureaucracy, they are among its defining characteristics.

FOUR

THE SELECTING-OUT PROCESS AND RESULTANT CAREER PATTERNS

THE process of selecting lawyers for positions in large law firms starts long before the new graduates come into an office. It is as we have seen, part of an ascriptive system, beginning, if we care to go back that far, with the accident of birth and continuing long after. The individual who is healthy, bright, and the offspring of educated and well-to-do parents whose families have had long tenure in the United States or come from preferred European countries, has an advantage. This hereditary accident insures that a child from this environment will be able to go to the proper schools[1] and also will know which of them is the most proper. Once he has gone to one of these institutions, he can acquire a quality important to his future should he ever wish a partnership in a distinguished Wall Street law office.[2] As many as 55 per cent of the lawyers in one admittedly atypical firm had gone to prep schools, mainly the very social Groton, St. Paul's, St. Mark's, and Kent. As one eastern-born St. Paul's graduate put it when talking about some fellow lawyers from the less socially acceptable Midwest: "If they had just gone to St. Paul's they would not be so naive about human relations in a law firm." Another lawyer, commenting on the value of an Eastern prep school, said, "I went to Culver, and while it is a good school, it did not help me get into the right clubs when I went to Harvard. If I had gone to a top eastern prep school I would have had no difficulty." Whatever the merits of the various private schools may be, one thing seems certain: they provide a base of common experience and knowledge and a bond which seems to bind people together. The elite prep schools provide contact with power and wealth and help train men to deal with people who have these attributes.

Ivy League Schools —

Social class membership provides knowledge not only about appropriate preparatory schools but also about colleges and universities. An analysis of the background of all partners in large New York City law offices drawn from the 1957 edition of the *Martindale-Hubbell Law Directory* reveals that the 468 lawyers listed attended 79 colleges and universities. (The *U.S. Office of Education Directory* registers nearly 2000 colleges and universities.) Two hundred and ninty-eight (64 per cent) attended 19 colleges which would be judged socially acceptable; 40 per cent of the total went to Harvard, Yale, or Princeton. The persistence of this pattern is indicated by the 1962 figures, derived from the same law directory, which reveals that 41.5 per cent of all partners from these same large firms attended these three elite schools.

The relationship between attending a preparatory school and a socially acceptable college is made evident when the records of the atypical firm mentioned above, which was very conscious of social class, are examined. All the partners (55 per cent of that firm) who have attended prep school are graduates of socially acceptable colleges and all but a few attended Ivy League colleges, whereas less than half of the public school graduates (21 per cent of the total in that firm) attended socially acceptable colleges.

Most lawyers described here who did not go to a preparatory school or to the socially acceptable college did attend the "right" law schools. Harvard, Yale, and Columbia law schools have previously been mentioned as providing the largest number of re-

cruits for the large firms. Only 17 per cent of all partners in the
large firms do not have some combination which includes either
a socially acceptable college or one of the preferred law schools.
And if the law schools at the Universities of Virginia, Michigan,
and Chicago are included in the list of preferred law schools, that
figure is reduced to 12 per cent. For the men who have not gone
to the prep schools or to the socially approved colleges, appropriate
training and indoctrination takes place in the law school and
many lawyers feel that it must continue in the firm if the man
who is initially without the proper social qualifications is to
become a partner.

WHY THEY LEAVE

THE weeding-out process does not stop with recruitment but
continues after a lawyer is initially selected by a firm. The turnover is heavy, and men leave for a variety of reasons long before
they are ready to be considered for a partnership. Although most
associates want to become partners, others know when they enter,
or decide soon after, that they do not want to stay.

An important reason for accepting a position with the large
firms is the desire for the postgraduate education they provide.
If the apprentice comes only to be educated, he leaves when he has
finished his "internship" and learned the basic ingredients of
large office practices and techniques.

Financial Considerations —

Some lawyers use the large law offices as stepping stones to positions with big business. They leave the law firms as opportunities
present themselves and accept positions as "secretaries," house
counsel, or corporation executives. A significant number of
lawyers take these corporate jobs because they pay more. Some,
in fact, leave because they cannot afford to stay with the law firm.
They often have large families and their desired standard of
living is high. When a good position in a corporation comes along
or is sought after and found, and offers a pension plan, methods
of reducing immediate income tax, and a substantial increase in
pay, these lawyers feel they have to accept the offer. Many an

important executive position is filled by the alumni of these firms. As one law review graduate who willingly left a large prestige office for many reasons testifies:

> I came with X law firm because I wanted the experience with them. I thought it would be of value to me when I entered business. I liked it there very much but only stayed two years and left because I was offered a good job. I made the switch with the definite decision that I would give up the law. I had found that the things that I liked were the business aspects; also, the remunerations were greater. I became one of the two or three top people in Y corporation. A job in order to drag one away from X firm has to be good. I have to explain to people [who tended to assume otherwise] that I did not give up the law because of failure—people at X firm leave only because of opportunity elsewhere. I noticed at a recent dinner for alumni of the firm that the guest list read like a register of big business.

One complaint lawyers sometimes make is that they find it difficult to do their jobs well and spend what they consider to be enough time with their family. Some of these men value family over firm and leave the large law office. One associate who is very conscious of this problem reports:

> I like to go home. Sometimes you can't. When you stop coming home you have trouble with your wife over the effect your work has on the children. My wife says, "It is harmful not to have a father around for a reasonable time. It affects the security of the child." For me, going home is a conscious choice. It may affect my becoming a partner. In fact, one member of the firm said that he knew a lot of men who lost their partnership on the New Haven Railroad.

Since hard work and long hours are important for the success of both man and firm, default by men who do not want to meet these requirements is generally welcomed by the large firms. It eliminates a type of lawyer they cannot use.

Dislike for Large Law Firm Practice —

Another category of associates separate themselves from the large firms because they do not like what they are doing. They feel they are not aiding "people" or that they are really not functioning as lawyers in the sense of going to court, solving clients' individual problems, working on a great variety of "human" matters. In contrast, those who stay say that what they are doing is operating at the summit of law practice ("We are working on the very heart of the law—where else can a young associate work on problems involving such vast sums and such important people?"). The associates who want to stay are impressed with the importance of the legal issues, the money, the clients, and the general significance—or power—involved in some of their duties. The men who go are nevertheless impressed with what the large law firm does but feel that other aspects of law are also important. One man who had been an associate in a large firm and who is now a professor of law presents additional reasons for breaking with a large law office:

> At the professional level the job was nearly perfect. The only real shortcoming was that it did not teach all phases of the law. In terms of operation I felt inhibited in not being able to have my own clients and I wanted to find out what the rest of practice was like. In terms of relationships in the office, they were good. My primary objection is that it was too impersonal. I wanted more social primary relationship—in my observation, very few of the thirty partners had much social contact with each other. And there was very little close contact between the associates and the partners. I left in part because I had a more personal attitude toward practice than was traditional there, or than I had been led to believe happens in firms of that size. I left because I did not like a 100-man practice; I wanted my own clients; I did not like the financial limitations. But my main reason is my feeling that the practice of law should be personal and that you should have close contact with your partners.

On the other hand, a number of lawyers who stay with the big firm chose it because it already had its clients—this too is a selective factor. Then there are those who say about the people who go into the large law firms or stay with them that they have no initiative or that they are seeking the security of the "womb." These conjectures will be discussed later. For the moment it is sufficient to surmise that differences in attitude serve their function in the weeding-out process. This self-selecting-out functions so well for the firm that when associates are being considered for a membership, the firm need not be concerned about dissident attitudes; the dissidents will already have left.

"Failures" Who Leave —

In addition to those who do not want to stay, there are also those lawyers who fail. Failure may be evident at the very beginning of a man's career because he does not fit in, is unwilling to work, is incapable—any number of reasons which indicate that he is not good for the firm. On the other hand, excellent lawyers may be considered unsuccessful even after ten years of satisfactory practice if they are not chosen for partnership. There are, then, different levels and reasons for failure. Failure itself is carefully disguised by the firms with the knowing help of their members and associates. Because of the widespread feeling that it is not professional to fire a lawyer, termination of employment often is a long, drawn-out affair. Usually failure is so well disguised that only the expert and educated eye will recognize it. The difficulty in discerning failure is compounded because some potential successes choose to leave and some of those who stay have settled for inferior positions without much hope of advancement. It is difficult also because the men involved—both the judges of success and the candidates—often do not label lack of success as failure. The firm often gives ego-saving reasons to men who have to leave. And, when they first accept positions with giant law firms, associates start preparing themselves for the possibility of not being taken into a partnership. They tell themselves and others that only a very few can make partner, or that it is just a matter of luck—for example, so-and-so who left was a topnotch lawyer but the firm had no opening for him—or that jobs in big business offer greater challenge and opportunity.

Some of this rationalization is true. The difficulty of determining what is failure or who is the failure thereby increases. It is further compounded because failure is redefined by the experienced attorney. There are many types of failure—failure to get the legal job done correctly or the social failure to get along with colleagues or clients. Most men have to be able to handle these functions adequately if they are to become partners. And partnership is the sure indicator of success.

When Do They Leave? —

It is difficult to estimate exactly the timetable on which associates decide to leave the large law firms. It differs by firm, and records generally are hard to obtain. (This information is available in some detail for one large law office. See Chapter V.) The first real movement away from the law offices coincides with the completion of postgraduate training. Though this period is flexible, such internships last no longer than three years. At Simpson Thacher & Bartlett, another firm for which records are available, slightly more than half (22) the associates who entered the firm in 1945 or after and who left by 1959, left in the first three years; all but three left in the second and third years.[3]

At this time the young lawyer can still go home, especially if home is not a metropolis, and open his own office, for his contacts and those of his parents are still available to him. Equally important, he has not yet become so specialized in big business law that his training has incapacitated him for general practice.

One assignment partner, however, claims:

> They won't leave us in the first three years unless they don't work out. In fact, they don't start to leave us until after the fifth year. They know that when they get out they're either going to another law firm [small one] or into the corporate field and they are not going to change that decision unless they did not make the right decision in the first place. These associates are happy because they are getting new work. We've had offers for them paying as much as $15,000 a year, three times as much as their present salary [old rate] and they say "I don't want it." Now when they are here five years and they feel someone is passing them or they get family responsibilities, then they start looking around for corporation jobs

with their special benefits. I know of one man who was with the firm for nine years. He had an offer for $50,000. He couldn't turn it down. We did not offer him a partnership. We would have if we'd wanted him. He was a good lawyer but a marginal case.

The fifth and sixth years are important ones in terms of deciding whether to stay, not only because competition is becoming more clearly defined but also because client and colleague contacts have come to play an increasingly important role in career opportunities. Many associates begin to investigate these job opportunities seriously at this time, particularly because they are better able, after five years, to evaluate accurately their chances with the law firm.

The longer an associate stays, the greater the necessity for him to decide whether he has a real chance of being asked to join the firm. If he feels his chances are poor, he must ask himself when is the best time to leave. It is generally agreed that this period must come before the lawyer loses his attractiveness to another law firm or to a corporate client, and before his colleagues feel he has been passed over. An outside position must, therefore, be found before the tenth year with the firm, depending of course on how long it customarily takes to become a partner in a particular law office. In Simpson Thacher & Bartlett, where it took associates who entered the firm as associates in 1945 or after that date 10.6 years to become partners, all but three of the associates who left did so by the end of their sixth year with that firm.[4] One middle-ranked partner from the sample of lawyers interviewed provides additional reasons for this time unit:

In the pre-war days, there used to be a standard theory that a man should stay for ten years. Then the firm would decide to keep him or place him somewhere. Things have speeded up a great deal now. Our feeling is that finding a permanent place should start after six or seven years. This is partly due to economics. If a man stays here for ten years, his salary is so high that what the corporations can offer him is not so desirable, though it is more than the firm pays. The corporation wants a man earlier, partly because of economics, but partly also because they can train him to fit into their organization.

The lawyers who gamble on the chance of being made a partner and lose, try to leave soon after they know they have been passed over. In firms where there is no "up-or-out" rule, they can spend a longer time looking for a job, but men who were in serious competition for a partnership find it uncomfortable to remain with the firm, and try to leave. They usually go to the client corporations or to smaller law firms as partners. Although they, and their immediate colleagues, feel such men have failed, the larger world may consider them successful. Their salaries are higher and their power appears, on the surface at least, to be greater. Many who did not want to leave, as well as those who had planned to, become successful in the law and in business. This, of course, is true of lawyers in general.[5]

Difficulty of Determining When to Leave —

It is not easy to know when to leave; the decision involves a formidable test of judgment—judgment which depends upon being able accurately to measure one's progress. An associate, when asked how he knew where he stood, replied:

> It's awfully hard to get a commitment. If you ask, and you usually do not, they say "I think you are doing well." This is only a hint, but enough; by a process of osmosis you get to know. I think I have great possibility. I've decided to take the risk and stay on and see. You feel it in the air if you are going places. One way of telling is the responsibility they give you. But anyone is foolish to think it's in the bag.

The earliest, most enduring, and continuous signs come in the form of the work assigned. If a man receives the more difficult or more desirable work, he can usually estimate that he is making more progress than the others in his vintage. If not, he has to decide whether this is due to chance and if it will change. If he decides it will not change, then he must consider leaving unless he is willing to stay on as a perpetual associate. He has, it is true, any number of clues, but these often are not definitive. Probably the most extreme use of work as an indicator of progress or lack of it, occurs when a firm wants to fire someone. A female associate who has been with a law office for eight years reports that she is being eased out. "They feel it is not professional to tell you officially to leave so they punish you by taking away work. It is the classic way of firing someone. I know this is happening because I was told by my immediate partner that the senior partner did not like me. I did a small job for him and he thought I didn't do it well."

It is customary around the Christmas season for the senior partners or the partner in charge of a department to distribute a bonus, if there is one. While it is not proper and not generally considered "good form" to ask how salaries compare, it is considered acceptable to ask how bonuses compare. Usually it is not necessary, for the distributing partner will tell a man as he comes around with the firm's "gift," "You have done as well as anyone." This indicates that the associate is still in the running. If he is told, "You did the best in your group," then he knows he is ahead. The responses become standardized and so this particular indicator is regarded as a good one.

It is true that occasionally an associate is told that he has no future in a firm. One partner reported: "We generally tell people we don't want, or can't keep, 'See if you can't get located by the end of the year; if you can't, see me.'" An associate also often receives hints and suggestions from friendly partners who insist they are not speaking for the firm. Generally signs are not so clear and an associate has to decipher them himself. One of the most difficult clues to interpret develops when the law office offers an associate a position outside the firm.[6] Is he to feel that the firm does not want him, or simply that he is being offered an opportunity to decide his future for himself? There is evidence that both possibilities exist. The lawyer who does not receive the outside job offer through the firm feels he has the edge. One associate reportedly slated for partnership states a little proudly:

I have never had an outside job offered to me by the law firm or a client, but have had some from outside the firm. I know that clients have asked about talking to me—the firm tells them that they can't talk to me, that I am not interested. About two or three months later someone in the office will casually say that T asked about me and was told that I was not interested. It clearly means that my efforts for the firm are satisfactory and that there is a possibility of a partnership.

A managing partner was asked if it were true that if an associate was offered a job it meant that the firm did not want him. He states:

> No. If we want a man but are not sure if he will make it here we have to tell him this does not mean that he has to leave. We tell him that this does not indicate his future. However, if we offer him a great many jobs, this may be taken as an indication that we do not want him.
>
> We are asked to fill many kinds of positions and distribute them in a variety of ways. (1) Some jobs are so good that they must be offered. (2) Some positions are just good and these are offered to men we haven't made up our minds about—mostly young men. (3) Some jobs are just so-so, and we offer these positions to men we want out. We usually tell these men that their position with the firm is indefinite.
>
> We only offer jobs to men who can handle them. We have to be especially careful of our clients. We offer lesser jobs to men who are not too good. For example, we had one man who was not good. He couldn't even pass the bar examination. He got deeper and deeper in worry. I thought he could do a job as assistant secretary —he tried one and it did not work out. We took him back till he could get another one. He found a job as assistant secretary in another concern and is doing fine. But we could not offer him a job he could not do—it's a reflection on us.

One of the clearest indicators that an associate must leave is the announcement that other lawyers who graduated when he did have been made partners. Unless specifically told that this was an exceptional situation and that he is still being considered, an attorney must then recognize that he has been passed over and look for another position. The following case history indicates how difficult it is to make this decision. The lawyer in this example had a number of clues which indicated, to him at least, that his chances of being made a partner were good, yet he was not asked to join the firm.

In 19——, X firm was just starting its reorganization and they needed a corporate lawyer with experience. The head of the government agency I had worked with had been with the firm and he recommended me.

I was a trouble shooter. I was given the tough cases which did not fall into traditional channels. I evaluated the work and decided who should try it—in or out of the office—or whether to settle it. I worked on a great many reorganization cases. I was an associate but was in general charge of many cases, with nominal supervision. I worked with about four partners. I did most of my own work; the amount of partner time was very little. In fact, the SEC evaluated my time as partners' time—they do not evaluate lawyers on the basis of whether they are partners or associates.

I was put in charge of ten men to do another case. When that case ended they announced four new partners. I was not one of them. These men were my equivalent in age, but in other respects, my junior. They explained that they needed partners for different jobs from those I was doing. They wanted to be sure I didn't starve in the street, but it was getting notorious that I wasn't a partner. I had been concerned for some time about not being made one. I had partners working for me. At first I was told I was too young. Then I was told I hadn't worked with enough partners, and they made a determined effort to get me known.

I decided then I should leave. I asked some of the partners who were friends of mine what was the matter. If I had thought it was personality, it would have been easier. I know they regarded me highly. I was the one they turned to for the hardest jobs in the office, except in jobs like taxes.

The associate's dilemma grows as he nears the date when his partnership should be announced. In some offices the time spent with the firm is the best index of when to leave. One associate who had carefully examined this process in the Wall Street community reports: "Sullivan & Cromwell is the guide to use as far as time is concerned. They have a system there. When you are about thirty-five or thirty-six years old, you come up for your first year of eligibility. Somehow you know this is your year—if you miss it that year and someone in your class makes it, and if you miss two years, then you know you haven't made it—then they try to get you a job in two years. At S & C this is a conscious process—not so here. In addition, the age for partnership here is about thirty-eight or forty years. That includes the difference made by going into the service."

The following case indicates some of the factors which must be considered.

This is a crucial year because I have opportunities coming up and because I have favorable indications that my work is very highly regarded—that gives me some assurance as to my future, but which way I step is important.

Q. When the firm offers you outside possibilities does it mean that they want you to go?

A. No, it is a policy of the firm that every opportunity will be passed along. [*This is not what the partners or other associates said.*]

Q. Does the fact that you've been here ten years mean that you've been with this firm too long?

A. No, it now takes longer than ten years to become a partner.

Q. If you had an opportunity to take another job, would you present this alternative to the partners?

A. It would be useless to say I'd rather be a partner. If I had that real choice, they would present it to me. If I leave, it is assumed in the firm that it is my decision. I would know when to leave if for example they had four tax partners [the respondent was in the tax department]. I would know that they would not make a fifth, because it would constitute too large a group. I think in this department, making a partner is a very delicate thing because they have four very competent associates. If two were to make partner, the others would leave—the longer they can maintain the balance by dangling the partnership in front of the four of us, the longer they can keep us, and in the tax department, that is important. If they make one or two of us partners, then the others will leave.

The rules concerning permanent tenure in large law firms are not clear and it is considered in poor taste to ask about them openly. Some also consider it bad strategy. As one associate put it, "I don't ask them because to do so would be a sign of weakness and of lack of confidence." In the final analysis, the employee lawyer is reduced to interpreting a difficult set of clues. This holds true for all except the obvious failures and the obvious successes.

"Failures" Who Stay —

Not all men who stay with a firm become partners. Some who stay remain as permanent associates. Many of these—but not all—are regarded as failures by the younger lawyers. Thirty-one members of our sample were asked to describe the role of these associates. The descriptions, listed in order of the frequency with which the role was performed, were: handles routine matters (blue sky or everyday banking matters); has specialized knowledge (immigration law or labor law); gives assistance and comfort to young lawyers; and completes work which involves limited responsibility. Because most of these jobs involve routine work and because implicit in these roles is the knowledge that these associates have been passed over, colleagues consider them failures. The fact that they stay on reinforces the judgment. They are examples of potential defeat to the young associates. Nevertheless, the average permanent associate is financially secure—some earn as much as twenty-five thousand a year, and in a very few instances, even more, although this is unusual—and most perform useful functions. Generally, they are asked to stay because the firm needs them. Even those offices which have an "up-or-out" rule occasionally find it advantageous to break it. These "failures" are useful because they do not often make mistakes, are usually specialists in narrow areas of the law, and are willing and able to take on jobs the young associates on the make prefer not to do.

ALTERNATIVE CAREER PATTERNS

THE career patterns of those who leave differ according to when they leave and to a degree according to the firms they leave. Some older associates who do not expect to stay on with a law firm remain until they get what they consider to be their big chance—not with the firm but with a client. The managing partner in one law office noted for its ability to obtain jobs for its associates claimed that 50 per cent of the lawyers who left went with the firm's clients. His predecessor ran down the list of the fifteen men who had left the firm in one particular year. From his report it is easy to see the correlation between age and the job obtained. Most went to work for corporations. Three went into the service. He listed the others by graduating year and by the type of job they accepted.

Case 1: entered the law office in 1935, stayed for twenty years, and then accepted a top-notch job with a large steel company.

Case 2: entered the law office in 1942, stayed for thirteen years, and then accepted a top tax job with a large electrical corporation.

Case 3: entered the law office in 1943, stayed for twelve years, and then accepted a position as top counsel for a corporation.

Case 4: entered the law office in 1945, stayed for ten years, and then accepted a junior partnership in a large Florida firm.

Case 5: entered the law office in 1947, stayed for eight years, and then accepted a second echelon job in the legal department of a large automobile manufacturer.

Case 6: entered the law office in 1948, stayed for seven years, and then accepted an important job with the same large steel company as case 1.

Case 7: entered the law office in 1949, stayed for six years, and then accepted a job with the same Florida law firm, which needed another man, as case 4.

Case 8: entered the law office in 1950, stayed for five years, and then accepted an important legal job with a large paper company.

Case 9: entered the law office in 1950, stayed for five years, and then accepted a legal job with a chemical company.

Case 10: entered the law office in 1951, stayed for four years, and then left for a job with a camera company.

Case 11: entered the law office in 1951, stayed for four years, and then went to the Bureau of Internal Revenue to get some tax experience on the other side of the fence.

Case 12: entered the law office in 1953 and stayed for two years; it is not known where he went after that.

Some associates, if they are young enough and have sufficient contacts, go back to their homes to practice. Others join smaller firms as associates or partners, some join the government, and others go to the law schools as professors. Walter R. Mansfield, a partner in the firm of Donovan Leisure Newton & Irvine, at a smoker for Harvard Law School seniors in New York City reported on what happened to the 145 associates and partners who had been connected with his firm up to that time.

Donovan-Leisure alumni—145 former lawyers of the office located as follows: 43 in industrial concerns; 22 in government agencies; 2 in educational institutions; 34 practicing in other cities; 32 in New York firms; 6 for whom whereabouts are unknown; 6 in military service.

Those with industrial concerns include presidents and counsel for many different types of business, including leading motion picture concerns, drug concerns, electric companies, chemical companies, film corporation, and advertising concerns. Graduates are located as far away as Beirut, Lebanon, Hong Kong, and Switzerland.

Those with the government include two judges in New York— one a justice of the Supreme Court, New York County, and one a justice of the Circuit Court of Appeals; most of the others are state or federal prosecutors. We have graduates practicing in such cities as San Jose, California, Manila, P.I., Dallas, Texas, Phoenix, Arizona, Milwaukee, Wisconsin, and Parkersburg, West Virginia. The great majority of graduates in other New York law firms are to be found in small firms, many of which were started by graduates themselves, such as Bethuel M. Webster, of Webster, Sheffield & Chrystie and Horace R. Lamb of Leboef Lamb & Leiby.

Some associates are well thought of, but for a variety of reasons are not asked to join a firm. One type of career adjustment for them involves setting up what might be called, though not always correctly, satellite firms. These organizations, usually composed of alumni of the large law offices, receive excess business from the parent firm. Sometimes the client is referred to them (they bill the client personally), other times they act as part of the large office (the client is billed by the large firm). The large offices find the satellite firms valuable because they have men who are easily available, who know the methods of the parent firm, and on whom they can rely. It also means that the large firms need not add more lawyers to their own staff, especially men they may not be able to sustain. The story of a lawyer who helped set up such a firm offers additional information on the difficulty of knowing when to leave and which position to take.

W is a partner in a small law firm, born in the Midwest. He attended public and parochial schools there. He received his A.B. from an elite eastern college and graduated from a not so elite eastern law school. He is a liberal and "still votes Democratic."

Here is his story as he tells it: "After graduation from law school, where two New Deal professors made an impression on me, I applied for a job with the SEC. Before that I had worked as a law clerk for a law firm in Detroit so I had had a smattering of private law. Then I went to Washington and stayed for some time. They [large law firm] chose me and offered me more than both my jobs paid. I stayed with X firm for eleven years. When I went there I did not know X firm from a hole in the ground.

At X firm, their policy, I learned at the beginning of my stay, is to take a class. You work along and you see that very few become partners—during the war it was abnormal, there was no basis of comparison to see how you were doing. No partners were made for a long time because so many good men were in the service. It became difficult for older people to know whether they should hang around. There was no assurance despite raises that this would mean that you were going to be a partner—lawyers proceeded on the assumption that it was a postgraduate course and if you did well then you would end up in a good spot.

After the war, with the return of many lawyers who were around my class, many of those who were brought in during the war were sloughed off. About this time I had an offer to teach at University of Y law school; I also was senior associate with the Z case. I thought it would be interesting. I had to decide—do I want the hectic pace of New York or the more leisurely pace of a University campus. I decided to stick with the Z case. I worked on the case from 1948 to 1952. I had a major role under two partners as the senior associate. I had eight or nine associates under me, plus about ten temporary lawyers. I became a little executive in my domain. The case was actively litigated, we had two to four deposition rooms going five days a week. Two and a half years of deposition, at least two a day. I had a lot of litigation experience; on the other hand I didn't get individual trial experience on small cases.

When the case was finished I was at loose ends—it was clear that my time had come to move on. I decided I liked active litigation work. I was a little unhappy with a large corporation's machinations, so I didn't want to be a house counsel. There is a certain atmosphere about executive groups and house counsel groups which I didn't like, so I decided to be an independent lawyer.

After any big case there were companies wanting young lawyers with experience; for example, M steel company was interested in me, but I said no.

At about this time two former associates of X firm were trying to organize a law firm. One of them had his own small one; the other had left X because he had a business flair and did not like the hierarchy in the tax department and felt he could do better on his own. A friend of his who also had been with X firm but now was president of a corporation wanted him to do his corporation's work. This client said "While you are my lawyer you have to have a firm to cover all our needs." The tax lawyer got together with the lawyer who had his own small firm. They decided they needed a real estate man and a litigation partner—the two original partners picked us from X, so that we all had the same tradition.

The other three had business, I had none (though X firm sends litigation work to us), but they wanted to say they had full coverage and that they could take care of litigation, and while I did not plan it, I came here.

Partnership—Exceptions to the Rule —

Before investigating the interesting process by which some associates stay on and come up through the ranks to become partners, another avenue toward partnership must be mentioned, for there are three exceptions to the rule of promotion from within. The first involves leading politicians or public figures. Generally, partners selected from the outside are either famous, though often defeated candidates for high office, former cabinet members, or other important government officials. A firm may have a number of reasons for making this kind of choice—usually, because these people can attract important clients. Unlike the young associate, the contacts of prominent men are far-reaching and significant to a law office. Sometimes new leadership is required and a respected lawyer from the outside is chosen to put an end to severe internal squabbling, or simply because members of a law office admire the outsider as a person and a lawyer. Some are chosen for all these possibilities.

Although such appointments constitute only a small percentage of the lawyers who become partners, the examples that come quickly to mind have high visibility. Thomas E. Dewey was asked to join the law firm which is now called Dewey, Ballantine, Bushby, Palmer & Wood. More recently, Adlai E. Stevenson joined Paul, Weiss, Rifkind, Wharton & Garrison, although he gave up this position when he became Ambassador to the United Nations—the "lawyer" for the government. And former Vice President Richard Nixon became a member of a large Los Angeles law firm and then of the Wall Street firm, Mudge, Stern, Baldwin & Todd. Cabinet members are also sought after; Secretary of War Royall, of Harry S Truman's Cabinet, is a senior partner in the firm of Royall, Koegel & Caskey; former Attorney General Brownell of the Eisenhower Cabinet returned to his old firm of Lord, Day & Lord.

The second exception to promotion through the ranks occurs either when a firm needs a specialist in an established field or when a firm decides to expand into another branch of the law. Law firms entering tax law for example, brought in as highly placed associates or partners, men who had been trained by the tax department in Washington.

A third exception occurs when two offices merge or when a large firm takes over the main clients of a smaller one (a large bank provides one example), bringing some of the lawyers from the smaller firm with them. If they are particularly important to the client and his work, such lawyers are then appointed partners.

Up Through the Ranks —

Partnership is a sign of occupational success for the associates. Richard Powell's hero, in his novel *The Philadelphian*, after being warned by the senior partner of the difficulties he is likely to encounter on the road to membership in a large law firm, replies: "The way I look at it . . . in a big firm it's a tough climb to the top, but a mighty nice view if you can get there. I don't want to get to the top in a small firm and find I still can't see over the heads of the crowd. I'll take my chances in a big firm." When associate lawyers who were members of the sample were asked if they wanted to become partners, 62.3 per cent answered affirmatively; 18.8 per cent said no; and 18.8 per cent did not know. When asked if they thought they would be made partners, these same lawyers were not very certain. Only 35.6 per cent said they felt they would, and 14.4 per cent of these had already been told that they would be asked to join the firm.

The attorney who is offered a partnership is an individual who in the judgment of the firm is worthy of sharing assets and liabilities with them and is worthy of signing the firm's name. In many ways becoming a partner is equivalent to an enlisted man becoming an officer. In both instances few do, and in both instances, these few have passed an important work and social barrier.

It is interesting to note that few associates know the exact meaning of partnership. They know it is an important award. They think it will mean more independence, that the work will be of greater interest and excitement, and that they will have more money and respect. In most of these beliefs they are right. On some points however, they are sometimes incorrect. This is especially true of the new associates, but even the senior associate is not always correct in his judgment about what a partnership really means. For example, they do not know how much money they will be making as partners. The subject of percentages and salary is particularly "hush, hush"—the image about money is unclear. It is unusual for people to work long hours for nine or ten years for an occupational position for which they can set no definite monetary value. Brand new partners are usually given a salary until a proper percentage can be worked out for them. One man was eight thousand dollars off his estimate of what he would earn as a partner. He had guessed twenty-two thousand dollars a year—he started with thirty. Some associates are unrealistic about the amount of additional independence they will have when they first become partners. The new associate just beginning the long path to partnership often does not realize that he still will have to work for someone even when he becomes a partner (even at forty, he is considered a young man by senior partners). When he "arrives," he is just putting his foot on a new ladder, and the struggle up to an even more important position in the firm is also a difficult and hazardous one.

How Long Does It Take? —

It is not an easy task to become a partner. Very few do. Those who do generally take between nine and eleven years. This figure differs by firm. At Simpson Thacher & Bartlett, over the course of its seventy-five years as a law firm, it took the forty-seven men who started as associates (five lawyers who entered the firm as partners are not included in these figures) an average of nine years to become partners.[7] In the newer offices where associates are allowed to bring in their own clients it takes less time because these organizations have a more urgent need to hold the associate and his clients. One attorney, for example, became a partner after serving six years as an associate. In some offices, mainly the very social, nepotistic ones, two patterns are seen: (1) some lawyers become partners quickly, in fact, 25 per cent of the partners in one "social" firm reached this position by their eighth year of practice with the firm; and (2) at the other extreme, 34 per cent spent thirteen or more years as associates with one man waiting thirty years before he became a partner. Despite this, the average time it took to become a partner in the law office was 11.7 years, with most partnerships awarded in the twelfth year. This same average was found to hold in a more bureaucratically run firm where rules against nepotism prevailed and for which figures for all partners were also available. The average for the present sample of Wall Street lawyers was however, 8.5 years.

What must an associate do before he is invited to be a partner? What steps does he go through before this happens? What do the firms look for in a partner? To answer these questions it may be profitable to trace the general career patterns of ten imaginary apprentices hired from the class of 1951. The firm usually considers this lawyer with the class that graduated before him and with the one that graduated after. Probably only three men from these three classes will eventually be invited to join the firm. When they first arrive, little overt competition is found. The pay scale is about the same for all beginning lawyers and remains so for the first three years. They start out in a pool or doing research on a variety of subjects and are on general call. They have similar interests and tend early in their careers to form close ingroups. This pattern was intensified when early marriage was not as prevalent as it is today. After approximately the third year, individuals begin to specialize and are distributed among the various departments and work for different partners. As this specialization occurs some colleagues begin to leave the firm for the various reasons previously described, until in the eighth year only two or three of any "vintage" are left. It is from among these attorneys, and those left from the classes immediately before and after, that the firm at that time chooses its partners.

Competition —

Competition among associates at this point is at its height. Competition, however, started earlier and plays a part in the selecting-out process. It is rarely, especially at the beginning of their stay, severe and usually covert. Its existence, however, is recognized. Sixty members of the sample were asked about competition among associates. Fifteen per cent denied its existence, most giving *esprit de corps* as the reason. The others felt that competition did exist, as evidenced by (in order of the frequency with which the specific reasons were given) (1) efforts to do better work than the next man, (2) seeking of additional work and responsibility, (3) the taking on of additional night work and the showing of excessive drive, (4) miscellaneous intangible ways, (5) efforts to work for important partners and (6) the need to take risks. Sixteen per cent who felt that competition existed cited its bad aspects, calling particular attention to "knifing," the harming of reputation, and, finally, to wives' campaigns at social affairs. Ten per cent felt that some competition existed but maintained that it was not extreme; they did not offer illustrations.

The following quotations from interviews provide a less terse view of competition among associates:

It is genteel. Though there is some subtle knifing, it is done in an adroit way—innuendoes, shadings, often at social events.

It doesn't get so marked as in *Executive Suite* [a book and movie about big business]. I know of no instance where there is a deliberate effort to knife someone. Once in awhile you get the feeling that someone is an apple polisher. He knows what to say and how to say it. Obvious attempts of this nature will get nowhere. These people [partners] are too sophisticated. There are two approaches, (1) a very adroit kind of flattery, or (2) the giving of the impression of being able to handle work responsibly. I personally don't have the feeling that people do this consciously. The main thing is not flattery, but whether or not the partner feels that he can rely on an associate.

A lawyer who has been with a large firm and now works for a client of that firm reports:

Partners are made according to the need in a particular field. If a firm has a great need for a specialist in that field then they may take you. I have never seen cut-throat competition. When a partnership opened up there was always a logical choice. There is no real feeling of competition—you want to do the best job you can because you have pride in your work and because you want recognition in the firm, but not just to get ahead of someone else.

A partner in a small law office discussing his experience in a large firm remembered:

> There is competition. It isn't just for money—the need for recognition becomes important. From the very beginning the associate is trying to be a partner. Ten years out of law school the feeling of competition becomes very great—very intense—but there are few ways of showing it except by working late and taking on every job. There really is little opportunity to "tote" up to the partner. You have to keep from being forward. And if he is wrong you have to argue with him. However, at other times I could play it Grey Flannel Suit—if something he [partner] did was good, I might go a little beyond what I would normally say. However, it is difficult to have a real campaign because you don't get sufficient opportunity and it is difficult to sustain.

Other lawyers maintain that competition is seen in efforts "to get the right job so that you can show yourself." Also there is "an attempt to work with partners who have the more important clients." A young attorney observes that "if three associates are in conversation with a partner, each tries to look intelligent." Or "some people work at night so that they can be seen." An ex-associate reports that "there is an attempt to make a good impression on the partners. If a senior partner has a party they will feel that they have to come."

In general, competition between associates shows up in the amount of work they are willing to take on and in the time they are willing to spend on it. It may appear in the quality of production and have some effect on obedience to minor house rules. Many associates claim that competition is impersonal and that the associate really competes against himself, as you can in golf. Those who try the more obvious approaches of flattery are in danger of losing more than they could possibly gain. Competition among associates is based mainly on competence and perseverance. It rarely becomes conflict, partly because even serious contenders for a partnership usually do not work on the same matter. In fact, competition throughout the firm is kept down because people of different ages work on different levels, on different matters, in different departments, and because overt extreme competition is not considered professional. This relative lack of severe competition, as we shall see later, is important because it has implications for professions and professional organizations.

Competition nevertheless exists and its effect as a selective agent depends in part upon the personality of the participants. Some lawyers leave because they cannot stand or do not like the competition. In a way, what those who leave for this reason say is that they feel they do not have the competence or that they are not willing to work hard enough to make the grade; others report that they find the competition so minor that they can say the atmosphere in their law office is relaxing. By the time a man is ready to be considered seriously for a partnership, those who found the competition too severe, or did not like it, have left.

The senior associate who is up for consideration for partnership has survived many tests. He has ignored the call of immediate riches ("I damn near left three times. One job was many times my salary"); judged correctly the managing partner's mention of a position with a corporation ("I was asked once if I wanted to take a job. I remember I was upset because I thought this an invitation to leave"); stuck it out when it did not look as if an opening existed in his field ("When after I had worked for eight years in the tax department, they asked me to change to corporation law, I did not know what to make of it, but I changed. They had an opening in this other department and were trying me out").

In terms of work, the associate who started out as the broad researcher and postgraduate student gradually finds that he is a member of a department and a specialist. As this narrowing process takes place, so does the final weeding out occur. Members of his class have left or were asked to leave and only three or four people from his group remain. These few who have survived face still another test, despite the fact that they have been under observation for at least eight years. They now begin to receive assignments from most of the main partners, instead of just from members in their department. This new work pattern functions in two ways— it tends to broaden the attorney and it gives an opportunity to the senior partners, who may not know the associate's work in detail, to judge him. For two or more years these senior associates will be under tremendous pressure to pass the test of working for the most powerful partners. At the end of this period one of the class of 1951 will probably have been made a partner.

What Qualities are Needed to Become a Partner? —

Associates, partners and lawyers who had worked for the various large firms studied were asked: "What can an associate do to further his ambitions for a partnership?" and "What does the firm look for in a partner?" Table IV-1 lists the attributes mentioned in order of frequency.

Table IV-1—What Can an Associate Do To Help Himself Become a Partner?

Techniques to Partnerships	ASSOCIATES		PARTNERS	
	(N)	(%)	(N)	(%)
Be a good lawyer, work hard	33	18.8	32	24.0
Bring in business	23	13.0	19	14.3
Maintain good relations with client	21	11.9	12	9.0
Have proper social background and contacts	20	11.5	7	5.3
Obtain sponsorship	18	10.2	6	4.5
Have proper personality	14	8.0	14	10.5
Have luck	13	7.4	12	9.0
Fulfill needs of the firm	6	3.3	7	5.3
Become indispensable to firm	5	2.8	4	3.0
Choose right department	3	1.7	0	0.0
Take responsibility	3	1.7	4	3.0
Go to right schools	3	1.7	0	0.0
Engage in outside activities	2	1.1	2	1.5
Don't know	2	1.1	1	.8
Have leadership ability	0	0.0	3	2.3
Other	10	5.7	10	7.5
Total	176*	100.0	133*	100.0

* Totals more than the lawyer sample since multiple answers were given.

It is interesting to note that both partners and associates agree that hard work is one of the keys to partnership. Proportionally, however, partners mention it more often. Associates and partners do not agree on the role of sponsorship, good relations with clients, the importance of social background, proper connections and right school. In all these instances the associates believe these items play a larger role in selection than do partners. Partners believe that the personality of the candidates, needs of the firm, luck, and ability to take responsibility are more important in choosing firm members than do associates.

Most answers contained a combination of techniques which might help the associate to become a partner. Hard work and ability, however, even when not specifically mentioned in answer to the question, were assumed by the great majority. In fact, these two attributes were thought of as minimum requirements. Those who survived eight years of observation could most assuredly claim both ability and hard work among their traits. But these two attributes are not considered enough. A former associate who had been passed over, and who now is a partner in a smaller firm, thought client-getting and client-keeping a surer road to partnership:

> There is no set pattern. One of the best ways is to become so essential to a particular client that the firm feels that they have to make you a partner. I suppose the best way is to get a lot of business, not marginal business. In fact there is no fixed rule even about getting business. We had a man whose father was head of a large insurance company and the firm got business because of that, but they never made him a partner. He brought in a large amount of business but he was a strange person and not liked by the associates—although he was an able lawyer.

An associate in a large office claimed he did not know how to become a partner but knew how not to be one.

> You won't be a partner: (1) if you don't have awareness of interpersonal relationships on the partnership level—and poor relations with the client doesn't help either; for example how you dress is a factor; (2) if you're married to a girl with no money or client contact; (3) if you're a man trusted to do a job by the top people in the office, think you can do a job, and then don't do it well; (4) if you're not one of those fellows who are reaching out and looking for work.
>
> One thing I do know: if there is anything that typifies these downtown firms it is thoroughness. If you're sloppy in the clutch, you're in deep trouble.

Some associates do have formulas for success. One reports:

> We have no rules about becoming a partner. However, there are a number of things that might help. (1) In a small firm you get to be a partner if you bring in a lot of business. In this firm [large office] that doesn't work. We don't pick associates because they can or cannot bring in clients. I'm a poor boy. It is impossible for me to bring in substantive business. (2) Another way of becoming a partner is by being a specialist in some field. Then if a firm has a place to fill and you are there with the special knowledge, you fit the bill. They often pass over men who are good because at a particular time they have to have someone who is skilled. You have to see a hole ahead where you are going to be needed. (3) If, after you become familiar with the client's business and the client sees that you are doing good work, the client says to a partner, "Such and such an associate is doing well, isn't it about time we had a partner working on our account?"—This kind of thing may happen on the golf course. (4) It is best to work for as many different partners as you can. However, it doesn't hurt to do good and effective work for top partners. Actually, though, one partner can't shove anyone down anybody else's throat.

Partner Sponsorship —

While a number of people thought partner sponsorship was important, others felt that it could do an associate some harm. A partner states this position:

> Seeking sponsorship is a mistake I think some associates may make. Partners resist someone who is being sponsored solely by one man. I would advise an associate to work for a number of key men. When you get nineteen lawyers sitting around a table—a great many are independent people and won't be pressured—it gets to a point where the "family" wants to get along. They don't fight —someone gives in or there is bargaining.

There is a great deal of debate among associates about the advantages and disadvantages of sponsorship. Some argue that it is best to have a senior partner's endorsement because he has the power. Others believe that this is not so good, for many older partners do not feel they should pick the men the younger partners will have to live with. Some suggest that the older members of the firm may not be as aggressive as a young partner on the make.

> A great deal depends upon the partner you're working for. Not necessarily the senior partner because he isn't a pushy one. It is better to work for a partner who himself is bucking. He needs younger partners to help him. If a man has arrived he is not always as good as the man who is still on the make.

Whether sponsorship is or is not the best way to attain partnership, such situations do exist. They grow out of the intimate work associations which occur in law firms where the partner is dependent on the associate for certain kinds of information and service and the associate is dependent on the partner for advice and protection. In firms where associates work mainly for a single partner or a few partners, and are highly regarded, this reciprocal relationship is bound to occur. Since it occurs for a number of associates at the same time, however, the question remains which partner's sponsorship means the most. Associates often try to place themselves so that they can be in a position to work for the partner who they think can do them the most good.

Many other bromides are offered. An attorney more sophisticated than most in the ways of the large law firm decided to specialize in trust and estate work: "By going into the Estate and Trust department I thought I'd have easier competition. The bright boys head for the corporate department and work their asses off. Unless they are asked they won't go into Estate and Trust." Choosing a department is important. Perhaps, however, not as important as one law review student thought. He planned to get into a department where there would be a partner who would be retiring ten years later, when the associate estimated he would be ready for partnership. Whether such long-range planning is feasible seems doubtful.

Client Sponsorship —

Others think that client sponsorship is the sure path to success. "The best way to become a partner is to work for clients who contribute substantially to the firm, so that eventually they call directly and begin to depend on you and you become more and more important." Others feel the same way. One associate testifies: "Sometimes you can be made a partner when a corporation says, 'We think a partner should be handling our work.' They are really recommending the associate who is working for them." A partner, when asked how the firm chooses new members, replied that: "We decide what is in the best interest of the firm. A client will sometimes say, 'We think we're entitled to a partner.' This does influence us but does not compel us. Many of the boys are averse to getting a friend in a corporation to sponsor them."

Both associates and partners, when asked specifically about the influence of the client on the law firm, thought that the client could not make a man a partner but that he could help him become one. Clients of those firms who were interviewed agreed. The large law firms, they felt, resent pressure from their clients and in most instances are able to withstand it. The client knows this. One ex-large law firm associate, now a client of his old office, gave the following reply when asked whether his corporation could make a partner in a law firm:

Not my firm, but if a big steel company wanted to, they could. To the extent that a man has a client under his belt, he can use it against the firm. However, that doesn't happen often since men are rotated; furthermore, the big corporations have many lawyers working for them, and the partners do much of the contact work.

Additionally (1) most clients feel that an attempt to insist that a man be made a partner might spoil their relationship with their law firm; (2) clients' contact with the associate, especially on high levels, is limited—the more important executives do not know the associate well enough to go all out for him; (3) the law firms are very proud of their independence and, in periods of prosperity at least, feel that they do not have to make this kind of concession; (4) partnership is very important to the firms—it would take a great deal of pressure before they would be willing to take on a man as a member of their organization whom they do not think should be a partner.

There is no doubt, however, that the client has some influence in the decision to make a man a partner. Influence is not used here in the derogatory sense. It means that the law firms want and seek out the opinion of the clients and weigh it with other factors. All three parties (clients, partners, and associates) know this and take it into account.

Social Background —

Many young lawyers mentioned social background as a help toward partnership. That this is important was shown in the figures on the number of members who are in the *Social Register*, although it is true that some lawyers were listed in the *Social Register* after they became partners. An associate from a large firm believed that proper social background was "a plus if you have it, but it is not a minus if you don't." A partner from the same firm, when asked specifically what part social background and contact plays, stated, "For us it won't produce much because in the long run what pays off is work."

A junior associate has this observation to make:

> I suppose you could go to the right golf club. One associate is joining up right now, but he's not working hard and the rest of us do not think he'll get anywhere. If you look at the young partners, you'll find that they got there by hard, hard work. There is no substitute for being a good lawyer, though other social things might help.

Must Work Hard —

Social background does help and in some firms it is a necessary condition for membership, but even in these law offices ability and "hard, hard work" are musts for the associate if he expects to become a partner. Weymouth Kirkland, head of Kirkland, Ellis, Hodson, Chaffetz & Masters, the largest law firm in Chicago, when asked by a reporter from the *Chicago Daily News* (May 31, 1958) what advice he has for the new men his firm takes on every year, replied: "Just work—all the advice on earth is no good without that." There is a great deal of evidence obtained from the sample indicating the importance of hard work and long hours. All associates in most firms, except those who have been passed over and possibly those who work in the Trust and Estate departments, work some evenings each week. (Now that so many of the married associates are living in the suburbs, taking work home has become the practice.) Some of it is necessary for the client and some of it develops out of law review habits. This is especially so for the bachelor who comes from another city, is accustomed to night work, and knows very few people in New York. One (who seems slightly masochistic) analyzes it this way:

> We have a great deal of night work. A slow guy can produce a hell of a lot of work if he doesn't go home. We also have a breed of lawyers who never go home. Some of them are bachelors and some of them are on the make. Some of these people get breakdowns. I've never gotten to a point where I couldn't go on. Once I worked twenty-four hours straight and then I worked six more hours just to see if I could do it. I've heard of people who've had breakdowns after six months of steady work.

Still another associate from the same firm confirms the need for night work: "I average about two nights a week. It is unusual for me to go a week without night work." Another man from a firm that has the reputation of having a great deal of night work said: "I'm going into the army in two months—so I'm not working as hard now. I still come in two evenings a week, maybe three, though I rarely come in now on Saturday." Another young lawyer reports: "For three weeks I've worked without a night off. I don't think the man who works at night is trying to impress the partner. He's putting in his hours." A former associate who is now with a small firm remembers: "We had some showoffs who didn't have to work at night but did so in order to show off not only to the partners but to other associates."

Not only do some associates show off by working at night, but some of their wives when the opportunity presents itself show off for them by talking about it to impress senior partners. Hard work seems to be part of the tradition of the law and if we look back at the lives of successful lawyers, we see that they took hard work for granted. Harrison Tweed, senior partner in the large law firm

Milbank, Tweed, Hope & Hadley, tells of his encounter with the demands of the law and its practitioners:

> I have a story of my old boss in New York, James Byrne, . . . I remember a time shortly after I came with the office, when on a Friday afternoon, he gave me a memo to write on a question of law which seemed to be very difficult. He said, "I would like to have it at nine o'clock on Monday morning," . . . so I went to work.
>
> On Monday morning Mr. Byrne sent for me and said, "Do you have the memo, Tweed?" I said, "Mr. Byrne, I am sorry, I have not had time to finish it." He looked at me and he said, "Did you work all day Saturday?" I said, "Yes." "Did you work all day Sunday?" I said, "Yes." "What time did you go home Sunday night?" and I said, "I went home at eleven o'clock Sunday night."
>
> "Well," he said, "then don't tell me you did not have time to do that memorandum. Tell me the truth—tell me you wanted to go home early Sunday night."[8]

While it is no longer the custom for people to work as long as they once did,[9] lawyers in large law firms still put in long hours working some nights and weekends. It is true that some of this "overtime" is unnecessary, and that some are trying to impress the partners; that some stay downtown and eat supper on the client; that others have nowhere else to go or are in the habit of working nights; still, most of it is necessary and due to the demands of their practice and of the law. There are very few people in the large law firms who will not agree that hard work is one of the major requirements an associate must fill if he expects to become a partner.

Personality —

Do attorneys take personality into consideration when they choose their new partners? What exactly do they look for? As in the reasons for recruitment choice, partners found it difficult to answer this question succinctly. While they want similar attributes in a partner as they looked for in associates, they have higher standards for their future peers. The attributes they want in the recruit must now have been developed. The difference in choosing a lawyer just out of school and a partner is that the latter has been under observation for at least eight years. Now the firm knows what it is getting.

One law office describes its selection of partners[10] by showing how they keep tabs on their associates:

> Each year we review the progress of the man for the purpose of deciding raises. We have these records through the years. When I was managing partner we spoke to each man. I kept pretty familiar with the men. I judged what they should get [salary] in consultation with their partners.
>
> At one time we used to debate these things for hours. When you discuss these issues it is natural to think of the potential partnership of the man. The managing partner constantly has to think of men because we're always getting outside calls for talent. A great many associates never get to the time of decision because they take these good jobs.
>
> A man's usually here eight to ten years. We have that time to watch him. Still, what we want gets down to intangibles. Some of the best technically equipped lawyers we did not take because of personality difficulties, primarily because we did not think they could inspire confidence in clients. Our big job is to keep the client. Bringing in work is no longer important. A man has to be technically capable, get along with lawyers, and get along with clients. He should have the quality of leadership and be able to inspire people, make people have confidence in him.

When pressed for the qualifications an attorney needed to be a partner, one member of a law firm listed the following: He must (1) be able to see all the angles of a problem, (2) be painstakingly careful, (3) have a legal sense of the law, (4) have ability to get along with people, which includes patience and tolerance, (5) have ability in the field of negotiation in order to try to get the best possible deal for his clients. All this adds up to being an able lawyer. Most partners insist that their future co-participators must have these qualifications. However, some members of a firm have different concepts of what makes an able lawyer. A partner in another firm lists the following qualities as necessary for a potential partner:

> He must be a man of top intellectual ability: he must have no quirks in his thinking.
>
> He must be a man devoted to the practice of law as we practice it.
>
> There are intangibles. We see a man for long hours over the years, see his wife, know his family background, what outside charity activities he participates in. You get to know about these people over a ten year period. You see them in your home or when you're away on a trip with them—the word comes down about them from judges and clients. We encourage extracurricular activities. On a personal level, if we never see a man at functions we wonder if he has the qualities we want—if he measures up.
>
> He must be able to play team ball—if he can't we will not take him, for we are also looking for personal qualities, including his ability to go along with you.

Another partner reports that a man grows into a partnership:

> You don't really pick them—they develop. It becomes quite obvious who will be a partner and who will not. Sometimes there is a wealth of riches for a certain vintage and you don't want too many men of the same age. To be considered, a man must be doing good work, handle people well, show interest in staying with the firm rather than going into business. When he shows other interests he writes himself off. It is a hard decision when you have a number of stars or when business is bad and we don't take on any new partners.

Other lawyers who have been involved in these decisions are even less precise:

> That's an awfully hard question to answer: a man who will grow in a profession. You've got to remember that this individual will do work not very different from the work of an associate. We have to determine the need. But you can't put your finger on a pro-

cedure or method. Perhaps because of a series of events or because a man did exceptionally well, we begin to decide that he will go places. It's a flexible thing.

What these partners and others have said is that they want able lawyers with whom they and their clients can get along. They recognize that this is not enough, however, and that they need more. What this "more" is they can't specifically say. However, they do know what they want and often can pick a man long before he has developed into the kind of lawyer they will choose for a partner:

When you interview these men [seniors in law school] as they come through, you can make a fairly good guess whether they would become partners in a large firm or not. The large law schools have gotten the interest of the highest type of boy, generally with great intellectual ability. These people have social instinct. You look at their records and you see that they were presidents of their high school class, president of the debating society, on the newspaper, took summer jobs, had high scholastic records, have lots of energy. Then you see the force of their personality, you judge them in part by the kind of questions they ask. They are interested in getting ahead in the law.

You can pick out the above type but then there are some that don't have these qualities at the beginning. They are shy and will blossom. You hear about them when people start expressing interest in one person and his reputation grows. Some of the balls of fire may be too much so. They may be the itchy type and lack judgment. These boys who have top grades and who get into the large law firms have to be at the top. They can get jobs easily. I would say, in the course of time, we lose more than we want to of our best men. At least, that is the placement problem in boom time. I don't know how many companies call us for lawyers with a certain age and experience.

The heirs apparent are usually known throughout the firm and they are obvious. Even when interviewing, it was possible to pick out the men who would (on the basis of personality, social background, and ability to answer questions) probably be chosen as the next partners.[11] The chosen people are treated like heirs and the quality of their work is held up as a model. As one partner said, "If we have such a man, we will take him on, opening in the firm or no opening." When there are a great many golden boys or when there are none currently on the horizon and a firm needs a partner, or when a number of partners are needed, the choice is more difficult. Generally, in a situation involving two or three men of equal ability, personality, social background, or the strength of the sponsoring partner would tip the scale in favor of one candidate or the other.

The process of selection is similar for all the firms in this study. However, different law offices stress some different aspects of lawyer's background when they make their choice. While there is some variance in taste, it is only a question of degree, and the Wall Street lawyers comprise a very homogeneous group. An analysis of all the partners in New York City in large law offices, listed in the 1957 and 1962 issues of the *Martindale-Hubbell Law Directory*, indicates little difference in the background of these partners as revealed by their vital statistics. Tables IV-2 and IV-3 attest to their homogeneity, while presenting a brief picture of where they were born and from what schools they graduated. The 1962 figures indicate the consistency of the findings.

Table IV-2—Place of Birth for all Partners in New York City Large Law Firms—1957 and 1962

Area	1957 (N)	1957 (%)	1962 (N)	1962 (%)
New York City	130	27.8	156	28.7
New York State (not including city)	53	11.3	70	12.9
Northeast (not including N.Y.C. or state)	98	20.9	116	21.4
Southeast	22	4.7	25	4.7
South central	28	6.0	32	5.9
Southwest	8	1.7	23	4.2
Midwest	91	19.4	91	16.7
Far west	8	1.7	10	1.8
Foreign	11	2.4	19	3.5
Not given	19	4.1	1	0.2
Total	468	100.0	543	100.0

Source: Basic data were obtained from the 1957 and 1962 listing of all partners in 20 large New York law firms as found in the *Martindale-Hubbell Law Directory*.

Table IV-2 reveals that 59.8 per cent of these partners from the 1957 list and 63 per cent from the 1962 list were born in the northeast. The facts must not be construed to mean that place of birth per se is a prime determiner of who becomes a partner. What it probably means is that people in this section of the country either prefer the east more than people not born in this region, and so prefer working there, or that easterners, knowing more about large law firms, have less hesitancy about working for them, or that they more often have the required social qualities desired by those making the selection. A simpler explanation is that a great number of easterners go to Ivy League colleges and to the preferred law schools. Since these schools are located in the east, they are also located nearer to the large firms. Lawyers from the Midwest, for example (19.4 per cent of the 1957 partners and 16.7 of the 1962 partners were born there) and those who have these same attributes have no real handicap.

One hundred of the 468 partners are listed in *Who's Who* and 133 of them in the *Social Register*. Over half are graduates of Ivy League type colleges, as shown in Table IV-3, and most of them attended colleges outside of New York City. This finding concurs with Carlin's[12] data which places 79 per cent of lawyers in large law firms attending colleges outside of New York City. (His large firms are composed of fifteen or more lawyers.)

Table IV-3—Colleges Attended for all Partners in New York City Large Law Firms—1957* and 1962

College	1957 (N)	1957 (%)	1962 (N)	1962 (%)
Yale	75	16.0	84	15.4
Harvard	67	14.3	79	14.5
Princeton	42	9.1	51	9.4
Columbia	19	4.0	25	4.7
Cornell	18	3.8	21	3.9
Williams	16	3.4	22	4.0
Dartmouth	15	3.2	12	2.2
CCNY	11	2.3	14	2.6
Univ. of Mich.	10	2.1	8	1.5
Others	173	36.9	213	39.2
Not given	23	4.9	14	2.6
Total	469	100.0	543	100.0

Source: Basic data were obtained from the 1957 and 1962 listings of all partners in 20 large New York Law firms as found in the *Martindale-Hubbell Law Directory*.
* Only colleges with ten or more graduates are listed in the 1957 figures.

Homogeneity can also be seen in the law schools attended. The most striking figure derived from Table IV-4 is that 68.9 per cent of all 1957 partners and 71.8 per cent of the 1962 list of members of Wall Street firms graduated from Harvard, Yale, or Columbia law schools. Carlin's figures for attendence at these schools is 60 per cent.[18] The law school attended is probably the most important factor in the selecting-out process.

Table IV-4—Law Schools Attended for all Partners in New York City Large Law Firms—1957 and 1962*

Law School	1957		1962	
	(N)	(%)	(N)	(%)
Harvard	158	33.9	201	37.1
Columbia	102	21.9	115	21.2
Yale	61	13.1	73	13.5
Cornell	16	3.4	18	3.3
NYU	14	3.0	11	2.0
New York Law	10	2.2	10	1.9
Others	105	22.5	114	21.9
Total	466†	100.0	542†	100.0

Source: Basic data were obtained from the 1957 and 1962 listings of all partners in 20 large New York City law firms as found in the Martindale-Hubbell Law Directory.
* Only law schools from which ten or more partners graduated are listed.
† In 1957 listing, two lawyers did not attend law school or law school was not listed; in the 1962 listing, one lawyer did not attend law school or law school was not listed.

The weeding-out process has been described and career patterns of young lawyers who entered the Wall Street law firms have been traced. Most careers led out of the large firms into smaller ones and corporations. The homogeneity of those who remained to be partners is not a product of chance but of the selecting-out process.

In the next chapter we will see detailed evidence from one firm of this weeding-out process and career pattern. The findings about partners' career patterns presented in Chapter V are supported by the data gathered from the sample of lawyers. In essence, what was found was that partners seldom are forced out of firms because of scandal or disagreements and that when they leave they do so voluntarily. Many return after they finish their tour of duty with the government or as a top ranking man in a major corporation—the major reasons other than retirement for leaving a Wall Street law office.

NOTES

1. Charles McArthur, "Personalities of Public and Private School Boys," *Harvard Educational Review,* 24 (1954), 256–262.

2. McArthur and Stevens assert that for prep school boys at Harvard, law might almost be considered one of the ascribed careers. Charles McArthur and Lucia Beth Stevens, "The Validation of Expressed Interests as Compared with Inventoried Interests: A Fourteen Year Follow-Up," *Journal of Applied Psychology,* 39 (1955), 184.

3. *Seventy-Five Years of Simpson Thacher & Bartlett: 1884–1959* (New York: Bowne & Co., 1959), pp. 48–57.

4. *Ibid.,* pp. 45–47.

5. See W. Lloyd Warner and James C. Abegglen, *Occupational Mobility in American Business and Industry* (Minneapolis: University of Minnesota Press, 1955). They found that in 1952, 6 per cent of the business leaders had been lawyers, and this figure would probably be considerably higher if they had just studied top business leaders.

6. As observed by Louis Kriesberg, in a personal communication, in most jobs, presumably being offered another good or better job can be used as a bargaining point in one's present position. This is generally true in academic life. While associates have been known to use this device to try to force the partners into giving them an estimate of where they stand or to see if a major offer can be turned into a partnership in the law firm, this behavior seems to be the exception rather than the rule—partly because paternalistic partners do not like to be pushed; partly because the associates generally want to be partners and do not care to jeopardize their chances of such an appointment. In addition, there is a basic difference between the law firm and the university department in that it is rare that a lawyer can transfer from one large law firm to another, whereas this is common in academic circles. The law firms want to train their own men, in part because the men have to work together, in part because they have strong feelings about their own legal methods. The university department, on the other hand, frowns on inbreeding and often looks for diversity. Therefore, people experienced in one or more universities can be hired by another institution without loss of status for employer or employee. This is not true for the large law firm.

7. *Simpson Thacher & Bartlett, op. cit.,* pp. 45–47.

8. Harrison Tweed, "Extra Curricular Opportunities and Activities of Law Years," *New Jersey State Bar Association Yearbook,* 1947. Condensed from the dialogue on pages 83–84.

9. Harold L. Wilensky, "The Uneven Distribution of Leisure: The Impact of Economic Growth on 'Free Times,'" *Social Problems,* 9 (Summer 1961), 32–56.

10. Roger B. Siddall, in his questionnaire survey of forty-two firms reports on the partnership-making process of these large offices :"My questionnaires elicited the information that no standard practice regarding the

admission of new partners is prevailing. About half of those answering said that they dealt with this matter in firm meetings and the other half arranged the business informally. About half required the new partner to contribute something from his savings to the capital of the firm and the other half did not. Rather more than half of the offices admitted the new partner suddenly as a fully participating partner, while the remainder eased him more gently into the entrepreneur class by placing him first on a partly participating basis. Roger B. Siddall, *A Survey of Large Law Firms in the United States* (New York: Vantage Press, 1956), p. 89 (privately distributed).

11. In an unsystematic manner, my guesses were tested in some firms by asking the managing partner who he thought would be made partner among the upper echelon associates I had interviewed; the guesses generally proved accurate.

12. Jerome E. Carlin, "Current Research in the Sociology of the Legal Profession" (New York: Bureau of Applied Social Research, Columbia University, August 1962, mimeographed).

13. *Ibid.*

FIVE

THE
SELECTING-OUT PROCESS:
PAST AND PRESENT

CRAVATH, SWAINE & MOORE is well-known, influential and large; in all three categories it is among the first firms in the United States. It is old; it is prosperous; it is known for its clients, its system of organization, and its lawyers. It serves as a model for other law offices. Like most of the other large firms, it is housed in a skyscraper in the heart of New York City's financial district. The staff today is composed of partners, associates and non-professional workers. By 1948 the late Robert T. Swaine published a three-volume history of the firm[1] which included biographies of all the lawyers who have ever been connected with it. Because of this valuable source material, which provides us with some longitudinal information and which can be compared with the data drawn from our current sample of law offices, it was thought to be a particularly good firm to serve as a detailed example of the selecting-out process and the resultant career patterns.

HISTORY OF THE FIRM

CRAVATH, Swaine & Moore has gone through many stages; always, however, with some members overlapping. In fact, it has been many firms. Founded in New York City in 1819, under the name of R. M. Blatchford, it eventually merged (October 1854)[2] with an Auburn, New York, law office. Nineteen predecessor firms[3] in New York City (the firm names have contained sixteen surnames) helped create and develop the present-day law office called Cravath, Swaine & Moore.

Over the years, the emphasis of the predecessor firms changed in six major ways, shifting from the practice of law through politics and political connections to the separation of politics and legal practice and an increased devotion to legal proficiency; business-getting to business-keeping; litigation to preventative law; general practice to specialization; a great deal of familial and social nepotism to almost no nepotism; and small-firm practice to large-firm practice and concomitantly from a relatively unorganized office to an organized office.

The Cravath System —

Much of what has come to be called the "Cravath System" grew out of Cravath's experiences with Walter S. Carter.[4] "Cravath," according to his partner, Swaine, "had a definite philosophy about the organization of the law firm, its partners, its practice and its relation to its associates."[5] This philosophy, put into action around 1906, became the Cravath System. The following brief outline of that system is important,[6] for it will help us interpret the data to follow.

The Cravath System is divided into a number of major categories, the first four being of special interest to us in this chapter.

Recruitment—(1) In general attorneys are to be recruited directly from law schools. (2) Preferably lawyers are to be recruited from law schools with the best reputations. (3) The recruit *should* have a good college record but *must* have a good law school record—B or better; Law Review experience is preferred. (4) The recruit should have physical stamina and "warmth" and "force" of personality.

Training—(1) A young lawyer should not become a specialist too quickly. This rule is to be applied not only to a field of law but also the specialization involved in working for one client or one partner for too long a period. (2) A beginning attorney should generally not be given small routine matters to handle by himself, but, rather, he should be given a small section of a large matter which he is to cover thoroughly and with supervision. (3) A man's responsibility should be increased as his ability increases. This increased responsibility should include opportunity to delegate work to younger associates.

Tenure—(1) A life career is possible in the firm but only by attaining partnership—in other words, the office should have an "up-or-out" policy. (2) An attorney is expected to remain with the firm as long as he is "growing in responsibility," however, he should not stay more than ten years unless he has been told that he still has a chance to be made a partner. (3) Lawyers, and this is part of the system, should therefore be constantly recruited, move up in the firm, and then leave or (some few) remain as partners. (4) It is part of the firm's policy to find positions for those who leave.

Partnership—New partners are to be chosen from those trained by the firm, unless special circumstances makes this policy unwise.

Compensation—Each new associate should receive a more or less uniform beginning salary.

Outside interests—(1) The practice of the law should be the primary interest of all lawyers in the firm and that practice should be solely as a member of the "Cravath team." (2) All business in the office must be firm business. (3) To insure objectivity: (a) associates should not get special fees for the business they may bring into the firm; (b) neither partners nor associates should have financial interest in a client's business.

Relationship among partners—(1) Cooperation among partners is expected. (2) Cliques among partners are forbidden. (3) Partners will continue to be judged so that merit may be recognized.

Scope of practice—The major work of the office should be a civil business practice.

Use of influence—Knowledge of the law and the skill of the lawyer is and should be regarded as much more important than "influence."

Management—The firm should have a philosophy of organization, a strong senior partner, a managing clerk and a managing partner.

There have been breaches in adherence to the system: some of them were caused by national emergencies, some by the changes wrought by time, and some can be traced to changes in personnel, although the impression in legal circles is that Cravath's philosophy still serves as a model for the firm. Elements of this system have been adopted by many large firms and have a decided effect on the careers of young lawyers and the organization of large law firms.

ANALYSIS OF BIOGRAPHICAL MATERIALS

AN analysis of the case histories Swaine so providentially provided will, hopefully, yield additional information on the weeding-out process and career patterns of lawyers who have been with large firms. The biographies of all the attorneys connected with the Cravath firm from 1906 to 1948 were studied and IBM processed. Four hundred and sixty-two subjects had been with the firm during these years. For purposes of analysis these lawyers have been separated into those who became partners, those who were associates when they left the firm, and those who remained as permanent associates. Of the 462 subjects, 44 were made partners (though some of these became partners after 1948, the date the last volume was published), 402 were associates who left, and 16 were permanent associates who remained. The available data drawn from the biographies, on these attorneys were compared with the 1956 data gathered on all the lawyers connected with another law firm, similar in organizational structure to Cravath, Swaine & Moore, to help determine generational differences. (Obviously, the Cravath firm does not represent what would be found in all large firms, but it does serve as the prototype for many.) The two sets of findings are then compared with the 1956 findings on all the lawyers of a "social" firm which in turn is the prototype for another set of large law firms. The social firm is so labeled because a majority of its partners are in the *Social Register* and its recruitment, not as open as that of Cravath or the later comparison firm, allows for nepotism, which is reflected in the selecting and weeding-out process. These comparison firms will be referred to as Comparison Firm I and Comparison Firm II, respectively.

Analysis of these data reveals that a selecting-out process does take place in both kinds of firms and that at least in part the process uses social background as one of its criteria. While differences between categories of lawyers studied is generally slight, the trend is in the predicted direction; that is, in the selection of partners, as compared with that of associates, stricter social requirements (among others) seem to be operating. These differences, however, would have been greater if it had been possible to further refine our categories. The statistics concerning the permanent associates, for example, tend to blur because there are men in this classification who stay with a firm for different reasons —some for economic security, others because they are "gentlemen" and want to be able to work "with gentlemen."[7] Nor do all of them perform the same general functions in an office. A much clearer picture of selection occurs when you contrast the Wall Street lawyer with other lawyers.[8]

However, even when we compare the Cravath firm lawyers with those of the two comparison firms, a fairly consistent pattern of differences can be seen, so that, in terms of place of birth, for example, we find differences among the groupings. A look at Table V-1 confirms this statement.

In the Cravath firm, aside from permanent associates, the largest number of practitioners were born in the northeast. When New York City is included in that classification, then the percentage from these localities for all categories adds to over fifty. The same predominance of easterners seen in the 1906–1948 firm is found in the 1956 statistics on the comparison firms, although the percentage of those born in New York City is growing. (This is especially true for associates.)

These are national firms, and their business comes from anywhere in the nation, including corporations whose entity know no state boundary. Members of such firms, for these and other

Table V-1—Place of Birth (in Per Cent)

Firm	Place of Birth	Partner	Associate	Permanent Associate
Cravath 1906–1948	New York City	23	16	50
	Northeast*	41	38	25
	Midwest	23	23	13
	Other areas	13	23	12
	Total	100	100	100
		(N:44)	(N:401)†	(N:16)
Comparison Firm I 1956	New York City	31	39	44
	Northeast*	31	28	22
	Midwest	27	19	22
	Other areas	11	14	12
	Total	100	100	100
		(N:26)	(N:65)	(N:9)
Comparison Firm II 1956	New York City	29	42	59
	Northeast*	42	32	32
	Midwest	21	9	5
	Other areas	8	17	4
	Total	100	100	100
		(N:24)	(N:43)	(N:22)

* Northeast includes New York State except for New York City.
† The total number of associates for Cravath 1906–1948 is 402. The birthplace of one associate is not listed.

reasons, want to hire attorneys who come from all over the country. Despite this expressed desire, now as in the past over half of their recruits were born in the east. This contradiction is easily explained: (1) the preferred law schools are located in the east, and although these academic institutions cater to the nation, much of their student body comes from the east coast. (2) It is easier for the firm to recruit in its own locality and easier also for the easterner to apply for jobs during the hiring season. (3) The desire of the young lawyer to be near home may play a part in the fact that easterners apply for positions with a New York law office in higher proportion than do lawyers from other parts of the country. (4) Interviews with law students at various schools (including two Midwestern law schools) showed that students from the eastern schools were more predisposed to practice in large law firms. (5) To the extent that social requirements are necessary for the job, the easterner may have the advantage, for eastern society provides the model. The data for the social firm indicate that over 70 per cent of its members were born in the northeast. (Those born in New York are included in this percentage.) This figure gives added credence to the relationship between birth in the east and the ability to fulfill social requirements demanded by the firm.

Although it may be significant that more partners come from the northeast than from any other section of the nation, the most startling figure (for the Cravath firm) is seen in the 50 per cent of the permanent associates who come from New York City. This finding also holds approximately true for other large firms, and these figures are relatively easy to explain. The three major reasons for this finding, in terms of the over-all lawyer sample, emerge quite sharply from the interviewing. (1) Some lawyers were hired to do specialized work, i.e., managing clerk and liaison with the clerks in the courts; an unwritten, rarely expressed requirement for that job seems to be that the holder of these positions come from New York City. These permanent associates knew when they came to the firm that they would not be considered for a partnership. (2) Although most of the liaison lawyers were from minority groups, so too were some of the attorneys practicing in the more prestigeful areas of the law. Few, if any, of these were promoted to partnership. Since from the point of view of the law office, they were doing their job well, and it was difficult to place them with the large corporations;[9] and since from their own vantage points they were earning respectable salaries, practicing in a major law firm, and practicing at "home," they stayed on. (3) Other lawyers, born in the city of backgrounds similar to the majority of associates and partners, liked the atmosphere of the firm; despite the fact that they were not and would not be invited to membership, they preferred to practice law in an organization with which they felt compatible. Comparison Firm I showed this continued domination of New Yorkers among the older associates, although to a lesser degree.

(It is important to warn the readers at this point that Comparison Firm I figures have to be interpreted differently from the Cravath statistics. In the Cravath firm, all but sixteen associates were no longer connected with Cravath and therefore had been selected out; in the Comparison Firm I, the associates were still with the firm and some still had the chance of becoming partners. The most significant pruning process in the 1956 data is found in the comparisons between partners and the associates who have been passed over.)

Education —

A firm considers schooling to be one measure of a man's worth— but schooling, in this context, means not only the candidate's marks but also his school. In an effort to measure more accurately what effect attendance at socially proper schools had on selection, three scales were developed. Each scale rated groups of preparatory, college, and law schools from one to five. (Again, it is pertinent to remark that, among those schools commonly regarded as socially elite, no matter whose criteria be used, are a number which are also educationally superior. This fact must be kept in mind in evaluating the influence of social position in the selecting-out process.) The higher the social rating a school received, the lower the number it was given; for example, among preparatory schools, Groton, St. Paul's and St. Mark's were rated one and public schools were rated five.[10] Among the colleges, Harvard, Yale, and Princeton would be placed in the number one group of colleges and St. John's (New York) and Brooklyn College would rate the fifth spot. For law schools, Harvard, Yale, and the University of Virginia were given a social rating of one[11] and night law schools were rated five.

The combined scale indicates that partners have the best social schooling and associates the poorest, whether the mean, the mode or the median is used as the measure.

When the frequency distributions for the social status scores of the 1906–1948 firms are compared by rank, we find that over half (53.5 per cent) of all partners had scores in the top (most social) five positions (out of a possible thirteen) contrasted to 37.4 per cent for associates and 43.7 per cent for permanent associates. The finding that an education at a socially approved school is important is reinforced by the observation that only 11.6 per cent of the partners fell in the lowest five spots and no partners were in the last two cells, as compared to 21.4 per cent for the associates and 12.4 per cent for permanent associates. This

Table V-2—Frequency Distribution for First Five Cells
Compared With Last Five Cells* for the Total
Social Status Scores (in Per Cent)

Firm	Social Status Rating Cells	Partner	Associate	Permanent Associate
Cravath 1906–1948	First five cells	53.5	37.4	43.7
	Last five cells	11.6	21.4	12.4
	N‡	(43)	(398)	(16)
Comparison Firm I 1956†	First five cells	50.0	32.8	33.3
	Last five cells	11.6	29.0	22.2
	N‡	(26)	(64)	(9)
Comparison Firm II 1956	First five cells	62.6	69.0	22.6
	Last five cells	4.2	16.7	18.2
	N‡	(24)	(42)	(22)

* Middle three cells not reported. First five cells equal highest social rating; last five the lowest.

† Data for prep schools are not complete for associates and permanent associates. All that was available was information on whether an associate attended public or private school. Those who attended private schools were scaled arbitrarily, the proportion of partners attending 1-, 2-, 3-, and 4-rated private schools was used for associates. Still, evidence of difference between partners is conclusive.

‡ The N's for these three firms may vary by table because information was not always consistently available for each lawyer.

distribution may mean that while it is not an absolute necessity to have graduated from social schools to be a partner, graduation from a combination of least socially desirable schools practically eliminated the chance of becoming a member of the firm during the 1906–1948 period.

Comparison of the data for the (Cravath-type firm) Comparison Firm I with the Cravath firm reveals a de-emphasis on the importance of the attendance at socially approved schools. This relaxation of social requirements started some time ago, and slight changes in this direction were found even among lawyers born in the decade 1890–1900 compared with those born during the years 1910–1920. Table V-2 indicates that despite a relaxation of the social requirements as measured by the kinds of schools attended, the social factor still seems to play a role in the selection process. This factor, however, is much more important for the social firm, which still hires a preponderance of graduates from the socially proper schools; these candidates have the best chance of becoming partners. The difference in the importance of the social factor is seen when the scores of partners and permanent associates for Comparison Firm I and Comparison Firm II are contrasted. Forty per cent more partners attended the best social schools in Comparison Firm II as compared to a 17 per cent difference between these two categories in Comparison Firm I.

When social status scores are examined separately, that is, by social ranking of schools at educational level, it is discovered that each category in the Cravath firm received socially higher scores as they climbed the educational ladder—and partners did the best of them all. This finding also holds true for both comparison groups in 1956. In the social firm, however, as expected, almost all social status scores were higher, although proportionately fewer partners than associates were graduates of the most social law schools.

Preparatory School —

An attempt was made to evaluate the part preferred schooling played in the pruning process. Again the statistics for the 1906–1948 firms are blurred and again the blurring exists because it was impossible to further refine the classificatory system. Despite this, the figures for the 1906–1948 firms show a 9 per cent difference between partners and associates, with more partners having attended private school. The trend for the Comparison Firm I-type legal staff is also in the expected direction, although fewer lawyers in all ranks attended private school. In fact, 14 per cent fewer partners went to private schools in Comparison Firm I. This reduction can be explained if we assume, as the evidence indicates, that Comparison Firm I has a system of organization similar to the Cravath System. Rules involving nepotism and initial selection on the basis of high scholastic grades and tenure were observed with special stringency. It accounts also for the change in schooling over the years of the two groups of permanent associates (from 56 per cent attending prep school in the Cravath firm to 25 per cent in Comparison Firm I). Since this comparison firm permits only a small number of lawyers to stay with it if they are not going to become partners and insists that those who stay must fill special needs, these needs are usually satisfied by people who are not members of a social elite.

Table V-3—Type of Secondary School (in Per Cent)

Firm*	School	Partner	Associate	Permanent Associate
Cravath 1906–1948	Private	52	43	56
	Public	48	57	44
	Total	100	100	100
		(N:42)	(N:362)	(N:16)
Comparison Firm I 1956	Private	38	33	25
	Public	62	67	75
	Total	100	100	100
		(N:26)	(N:65)	(N:9)
Comparison Firm II 1956	Private	62	62	45
	Public	38	38	55
	Total	100	100	100
		(N:24)	(N:43)	(N:22)

* The N's for these three firms may vary by table because information was not always consistently available for each lawyer.

Despite the lower percentage of those in Comparison Firm I who attended private school, graduation from these schools seems to play at least a small part in initial and final selection. This tendency is much more noticeable in Comparison Firm II where nepotism, both familial and social, is accepted, and where membership in the *Social Register* is still considered important.

College —

Graduation from a socially proper college or university seems to be of greater significance to the law firms than prep school education. For example, for the Cravath office, it was found that 33 per cent of the partners and 31 per cent of the associates and permanent associates went to Harvard, Yale, or Columbia Universities. Comparison Firm II places more stress on graduation from these three schools; it drew 75 per cent of its partners and 76 per cent of its associates from these schools. As might have been predicted, however, fewer (only 38 per cent) of the permanent associates attended these elite schools.

When the social scale for universities and colleges is examined, we observe that partners had the best scores. A further breakdown of these scores, which does not appear in Table V-4, reveals that over 50 per cent of all partners are graduates from socially elite colleges. Again, for all firms, associates did not do as well as partners; so that when the first cell is examined by itself it was found that 20 per cent fewer permanent associates in Comparison Firm I attended the "proper" social schools; just as significant, no partner graduated from the least socially correct college (last cell), although some of the permanent associates did. Still, since in all categories at least 50 per cent attended the better rated schools, it probably can be said that graduation from choice schools was and remains important for selection both as an associate and partner.

Table V-4—Frequency Distribution for First Two Cells Compared With the Last Three* for College Social Scores (in Per Cent)

Firm†	College Social Rating Cells	Partner	Associate	Permanent Associate
Cravath 1906–1948	First two cells	63	54	60
	Last three cells	37	46	40
	Total	100	100	100
		(N:43)	(N:373)	(N:15)
Comparison Firm I 1956	First two cells	73	56	50
	Last three cells	27	44	50
	Total	100	100	100
		(N:26)	(N:62)	(N:8)
Comparison Firm II 1956	First two cells	92	81	61
	Last three cells	8	19	39
	Total	100	100	100
		(N:24)	(N:43)	(N:18)

* The first two cells equal the highest social rating, the last three the lowest. This scale divides into five segments.

† The N's for these three firms may vary by table because information was not always consistently available for each lawyer.

Law School —

Law school is perhaps the most important item determining selection into a firm either as an associate or partner, and the data show that proportionately more partners than associates attended the prestige law schools. Further refinement of the data reveals even greater selectivity of the law firms. A higher proportion of partners, for example, went to Harvard than to any of the other two most preferred law schools—Yale and Columbia. On the other hand, Harvard graduates three times as many students as Yale. Selectivity is further indicated when it is recognized that the percentage of partners in all the firms who studied at Harvard Law School was higher than that for the associates. When the figures for the three preferred schools were combined, it is clear that men who have attended these academic institutions have a better chance of becoming partners than those who did not. Strengthening the hypothesis that academic excellence is a major factor, today, in the selecting-out process, is the datum that only 20 per cent of the members of both 1956 firms did not attend one of these three law schools.

Since many of the law schools thought to be the most socially elite are usually also considered to be academically among the best, it was difficult to know whether the scales measured desire for the best education or for the highest social status. Because of this, two scales were constructed, one a social scale, the other an educational scale. The results showed little difference between them, although the scores on the educational scale were slightly (for partners it was only a matter of 2 per cent) higher for all categories. This occurred mainly because Columbia Law School was rated "one" academically but "two" socially, and the University of Virginia Law School was rated "one" socially, but not rated that high academically. Since many of these attorneys are Columbia graduates, educational scores were higher than the social ones.

Regarding selection it is probably safe to say, then, that it is more important to have been graduated from a law school with the best academic rating than from one which is only socially approved. Table V-5 indicates just how important this is when it is observed that all the partners in both the Cravath firm and in Comparison Firm I graduated from the schools rated educationally best. The fact that the figures for Comparison Firm I record a 33 per cent difference between partners and permanent associates indicates the partners' superior education and strengthens the selecting-out process hypothesis.

Table V-5—Frequency Distributions for First Two Cells Compared With the Last Three* for Law School Education Scores (in Per Cent)

Firm†	Law School Rating Cells	Partner	Associate	Permanent Associate
Cravath 1906–1948	First two cells	100	77	81
	Last three cells	0	23	19
	Total	100	100	100
		(N:43)	(N:398)	(N:16)
Comparison Firm I 1956	First two cells	100	88	67
	Last three cells	0	22	33
	Total	100	100	100
		(N:26)	(N:65)	(N:9)
Comparison Firm II 1956	First two cells	83	91	64
	Last three cells	17	9	36
	Total	100	100	100
		(N:24)	(N:43)	(N:22)

* This scale divides into five segments.

† The N's for these three firms may vary by table because information was not always consistently available for each lawyer.

COLLEGE ACTIVITIES AS A SELECTOR

OTHER items, such as college and law school honors and activities, point up the differences between the three categories of lawyers being compared. Partners were more active in college sports and debates than associates. Permanent associates were more active in student government and on the student newspaper than were the other lawyers. Membership in Phi Beta Kappa provides another index of the possibility of success in the large law firm. The Cravath statistics indicate that 62 per cent of the partners, 40 per cent of the associates and 30 per cent of the permanent associates received this award—a 32 per cent difference between the partners and the associates who have been passed over.

Law Review Membership —

In law school the most important item separating those who became partners from those who did not was membership on the law review. The eligibles for the law journal had been awarded a high honor. Proportionately more partners (73 per cent) than associates (42 per cent) received this honor. Permanent associates in the Cravath firm, however, have done better than would have been predicted, and 69 per cent of them were on the law reviews. It seems that those who had earned the privilege of being on a law review or who had the special experience it offers had a better chance of staying with the firm either as a partner or as a permanent associate. The figures, however, also point out that it takes more than law review to become a partner. Not enough is known about these permanent associates who were successful in law school to explain why they were not invited to become partners.

In Comparison Firm I the figure for permanent associates who had been on a law journal had dropped to 22 per cent, a reduction which reflects this firm's support of an "up-or-out" policy. Lawyers who are among the most capable but who for one reason or another cannot be made partners leave; a few lawyers who are doing capable routine but necessary work stay on as permanent associates. There is no need to place the law review men in these jobs.

Table V-6—Percentage on Law Reviews

Firm*	Partner	Associate	Permanent Associate
Cravath 1906–1948	73 (N:44)	42 (N:402)	69 (N:16)
Comparison Firm I 1956	65 (N:26)	71 (N:65)	22 (N:9)
Comparison Firm II 1956	21 (N:24)	22 (N:41)	10 (N:20)

* The N's for these three firms may vary by table because information was not always consistently available for each lawyer.

The 43 per cent difference in this firm between the partners and permanent associates who had been on the law journal indicates that law review membership, its training, and its function as an initial weeding device does affect selection of partners.

CAREER PATTERNS

THE weeding-out process makes for a variety of different career patterns. The general possibilities were outlined in the last chapter. Briefly, they consist in: (1) staying with the firm and becoming a partner, (2) staying with the firm and remaining a permanent associate, or (3) leaving the firm and going to various kinds of other positions. These possibilities will be detailed for all associates who were employed in the 1906–1948 Cravath firm. First, however, we should analyze the jobs these lawyers held before they came with that office, for their previous positions are also part of their career pattern, and the data indicate that these jobs may play some role in the pruning process. Partners, for example, had a somewhat different career prior to entering the firm than did most associates.

Prior Job Experience —

Comparison Firm I seems to prefer attorneys who have had no prior job experience. Exceptions are made for those who clerked for a judge (Supreme Court Justice having the highest status), or for those who took an academic post, but stayed in academic life for no more than a year or two. Exceptions are also made for lawyers who hold honorific government positions; such as posts in the Federal District Attorney's office. (Possibly the law firms are more interested in the honor attached to a prior position than to its apprenticeship aspects, although, alternatively, they may simply seek competent men wherever they are apt to find them.) Usually, the large firms today prefer to train their lawyers in their own system and in their own way. Permanent associates, however, have been hired who have had prior job experience which was felt could be of value to the law office.

In the 1906–1948 firm on the other hand, over 50 per cent of lawyers in all categories held at least one prior job. On the average, for all prior positions taken, however, partners held slightly more jobs than did associates—partners 1.3 jobs, associates 1.0, and permanent associates 1.1. An analysis of prior employment by generation indicated that the trend was to hire fewer and fewer associates with previous job experience. Sixty-five per cent of the associates born in the decade 1870–1879 held at least one prior job, but only 48 per cent of those born between 1890–1899. And the number of previous positions held continues to decline, so that only 38 per cent of the associates born between 1900 and 1909 held previous positions; this number declined to 36 per cent for those born in the 1910–1919 decade.

Table V-7—Number of Prior Jobs Held by Rank

Firm	Number of Prior Jobs	PARTNER* %	PARTNER* N	ASSOCIATE* %	ASSOCIATE* N	PERMANENT ASSOCIATE* %	PERMANENT ASSOCIATE* N
Cravath 1906–1948	1	55	24	52	209	50	8
	2	32	14	27	108	31	5
	3	21	9	13	54	13	2
	4	11	5	7	27	13	2
	5	7	3	4	14	6	1
Number of lawyers studied		(44)		(402)		(16)	
Comparison Firm I 1956	1	35	9	55	36	44	4
	2	8	2	28	18	22	2
	3	8	2	5	3	11	1
	4	4	1	2	1	11	1
	5	0	0	0	0	11	1
Number of lawyers studied		(26)		(65)		(9)	
Comparison Firm II 1956	1	63	15	40	17	73	16
	2	38	9	23	10	59	13
	3	25	6	9	4	41	9
	4	4	1	5	2	36	8
	5	0	0	2	1	14	3
Number of lawyers studied		(24)		(43)		(22)	

* Percentages are based on number of lawyers studied.

N's are cumulative from 5 to 1 "prior jobs," therefore their aggregates exceed the number of lawyers studied in all cases but one. Likewise, percentage aggregates exceed 100 in all cases but one.

Further inquiry into the nature of prior employment reveals that the more recently a person was born, the fewer jobs he accepted after the second position and the greater is his choice of prior jobs. Associates born between 1870–1879 tended to hold their first jobs with a small law firm, their second jobs mainly with small firms and with positions peripheral to the law, their third jobs with the government. For those born between 1910–1919 the job market continued to expand. In other words, associates are likely to come from more sources with a decrease in proportion coming from any one source.

While the numbers involved for partners and permanent associates are small, analysis of the first prior job, as seen in Table V-8[12] indicates that partners held more jobs which were peripheral to the actual practice of the law, i.e., judge, law professor, than did associates. Partners also had more experience with other large law firms. Perhaps more interesting is that the data reveal that few lawyers had prior experience with other large law firms. Only 34 of the 462 lawyers who practiced in the 1906–1948 firm had previous practice with other large law offices. This is in keeping with Cravath's ideas about recruitment. His ideas, however, were not so scrupulously applied to lawyers who had worked for small firms. Over 25 per cent of all categories have had experience with small firms although both categories of associates had more of this type of work than did the partners. When all types of prior jobs ever held are totaled, a pattern similar to that found for first prior employment persists.

Table V-8—Types of First Prior Jobs Held by Rank for the Cravath Firm, 1906–1948*

Type of First Prior Job	PARTNER		ASSOCIATE		PERMANENT ASSOCIATE	
	%	N	%	N	%	N
Large law firm	17	4	6	12	0	0
Jobs with business	8	2	17	36	25	2
Small law firm	25	6	37	78	38	3
Government	8	2	11	22	13	1
Solo practice	4	1	4	9	13	1
Clerk	4	1	4	8	0	0
Peripheral to the law	33	8	21	44	13	1
Total	99†	24	100	209	102†	8

* Figures for the 1956 Comparison Firms, are too small to be relevant.
† Totals of 99 and 102 per cent due to rounding.

Jobs After Leaving The 1906–1948 Firm —

The associates who left Cravath were of varying caliber. Some were true rejects; others could probably have become partners had they stayed. They left for a variety of reasons, to go to a variety of jobs. Most of these positions have been categorized and follow the patterns presented in the last chapter. Fifty-nine former associates, however, took jobs which did not fit these patterns; some left the law to become actors, writers, farmers, one worked as a curator, another became a professor of music, and others to go into still other pursuits not directly related to advocacy.

Some alumni disappeared, others became famous. Those who became well-known arrived at this position mainly through government service, academic pursuits and important business positions. John Lodge is one of these men; his biography in Swaine's book reads:

b. Washington, D.C., Oct. 20, 1903. Ecole Gory, Paris 1913–14; St. Albans, Washington, D.C. 1914–15; Middlesex Sch. Concord,

Mass. 1915–18 and 1920–21; Evans Sch., Mesa, Ariz. 1918–19; A.B., Harvard 1925; Hasty Pudding Club; Pres. Cercle Francais; Ecole de Droit (U. of Paris) 1925–26; LL.B., Harvard 1929. Adm. N.Y. [bar] 1932. With R. A. Knight 1931–1932 [With Cravath Oct. 1, 1929–Aug. 31, 1931]; indiv. prac. 1932; actor with Paramount Pictures 1932–33; featured film player with RKO, Paramount and Fox, stage actor with the Pasadena Community Playhouse and in Max Reinhardt production 1933–35; starred in 14 films in England, France and Italy 1935–40; played leading roles in summer stock circuits 1940; on New York stage 1941–42. Member 80th Congress (1947–49) . . . World War II: Commd. Lt. . . . Lt. Commdr., USNR, Oct. 1944 (overseas); . . . demobilized Jan. 1946[13]

Since 1949 he has been Governor of Connecticut and Ambassador to Spain. William O. Douglas[14] is another notable alumnus. He was with Cravath from September 14, 1925, to September 3, 1926, and then left to become a law professor, first at Columbia and then at Yale. While at Yale, he served as a consultant to the government on various matters. He has been an author and, since 1939, Associate Justice of the United States Supreme Court. Thomas Knite Finletter[15] is another alumnus who became well-known through government service. He spent five and a half years with the firm, practiced with the Coudert Brothers from 1926–1941, then became Special Assistant to the Secretary of State. Under Truman he was Secretary of the Air Force, and, in the Kennedy administration, Ambassador to the North Atlantic Treaty Organization.

Others became known through their academic roles, although many of these men also held government positions or were active in politics. Leading among them are Dean Eugene V. Rostow,[16] of Yale Law School, who spent a year with the Cravath firm, and Paul R. Hays,[17] who after two brief stints with the firm left to become an Assistant Professor of Law at Columbia University. Early in 1961, he was Professor of Law at that school and Chairman of the Liberal Party, and by the end of the year he had been appointed to the Federal bench.

Most ex-Cravath associates, however, went into positions which

can be more regularly traced. It is of interest for an understanding
of the total picture of the Wall Street lawyer to follow the career
patterns of the majority, for the alumni of the large law offices
are important to these firms, and their subsequent careers affect
recruitment by pointing out what the recruits face. These
regularized patterns were discovered by analyzing the third volume
of Swaine's history, which lists up to five jobs held by an alumnus
after leaving the firm. The number of those who held four or five
jobs is small. Table V-9 lists the totals for all positions held for
the main employment categories. The largest numbers of alumni
took jobs with smaller firms (32 per cent) and with business (27
per cent). Most of those who went to work for business (13 per
cent) accepted positions which combined both legal and executive
tasks.

Table V-9—Types of Jobs Held After Leaving Cravath by Former Associates of the Cravath Firm, 1906–1948

Type of Job	Per Cent	N
Large law firm	5	42
Executive legal*	13	104
Business legal*	3	26
Business nonlegal*	5	39
Miscellaneous business*	6	49
Small law firm	32	249
Government	15	116
Solo practice	11	88
Peripheral to the law	9	71
Total	99	784

* When figures for business are combined, the N is 218, per cent is 27.

Table V-10 presents just the final jobs (as listed in 1948) held
by the alumni and reveals that the last positions of more lawyers
is in some capacity in business (31 per cent) while a slightly
lesser percentage (28 per cent) stay with the smaller law firms.
No matter which way you look at it, these two patterns remain
the most important and account for 65 per cent of the final jobs
taken by these alumni.

When these figures are examined by generation, we see
changes in the rates and types of final jobs taken. The youngest
associates seem to experiment with a variety of positions when

Table V-10—Final Jobs Held by Former Associates of the Cravath Firm, 1906–1948

Type of Job	Per Cent	N
Large law firm	6	22
Business	31	108
Small law firm	28	96
Government	12	42
Solo practice	11	37
Peripheral to the law	11	38
Total	99	343

they first leave the firm, although, like the older associates, most younger ones also accept final jobs with business or smaller law firms. Generational differences have already been noted for the rate of entry into business. These rates have seesawed. Of lawyers born in 1870–1879 period, 38 per cent had final jobs in business; of those born between 1910–1919 only 18 per cent. (Analyzing the data on Comparison Firm I, I found evidence that there is a renaissance of this preference today.) At the same time, the choice of smaller law firms as the final working place has increased steadily from 25 per cent for those born in the 1870's to 40 per cent for those born between 1910–1919. In line with the general trend in the legal profession there was a drop in percentage of those going into individual practice. Government service, one outlet for the displaced attorney, proved itself not to have an equal appeal in all generations. More lawyers took jobs with the government in times of emergency or in periods of experimentation.

Length of Service —

In order to further delineate the correlation between how long a man stayed with Cravath and his career after leaving it, years of service were divided into units of two, and positions taken in these periods were compared. Eighty-one per cent of that firm's associates left within a six-year period, with 41 per cent separating in the first two years. Only 10 per cent stayed over ten years and one per cent over twenty. As expected, the longer a lawyer remains with one firm, the fewer positions he holds after leaving it. Consequently, of those who stayed as long as twelve years, only 9 per cent took fourth or fifth positions, while of those who remained three to four years, 32 per cent took fourth and fifth jobs.

Table V-11 indicates the relationship between the number of years an associate stayed with the firm and the type of position he held after he left. As has been noted, the two jobs most often filled were with small law firms and with business. The longer a person stayed with Cravath, however, the greater the possibility that he would go into business (except for a slight decline for those who left after their fifth or sixth year). This holds true until we reach those who remained with the firm for eleven or twelve years and then the percentage going into business declines. No one who served eleven or twelve years, for example, accepted employment with business after the second job, and no one who spent nine to ten years with that office worked in a business after their third position.

At the point where the percentage going into business declines, the percentage deciding upon practice with a small law firm increases. This is probably a result not only of desire on the part of lawyers, but of reluctance to hire on the part of business and a renewal of interest in the "older" lawyer by small law firms. Smaller law firms often find themselves in need of specialists whose skills are not available among their staff; if the need is immediate and great enough they often look for the man with the experience to fill their gap and are willing to pay him with a partnership. Business, on the other hand, prefers not to hire men who are nearing their forties; they are considered harder to retrain, they can add an extra expense to pension funds, and the possible number of years of service with the corporation is shorter. A similar situation is seen with regard to entrance into another large law firm. No associate, for example, went into a large law office who had spent more than six years with Cravath. If a lawyer intended to stay with the large firm, he left Cravath early and quickly went with another large firm. In fact, 76 per cent of those who did go to another giant law office did so in their first two jobs. This finding corroborates the statements gathered through interviews in which members of large law firms main-

Table V-11—Occupational Positions by Years of Service for Former Associates of the Cravath Firm, 1906–1948

Type of Job	Years of Service											
	0–2		3–4		5–6		7–8		9–10		11–12	
	%	N of Jobs	%	N of Jobs	%	N of Jobs	%	N of Jobs	%	N of Jobs	%	N of Jobs
Large law firm	6	(25)	6	(9)	6	(7)	0	(0)	0	(0)	0	(0)
Business	23	(91)	30	(49)	26	(30)	46	(26)	56	(14)	31	(5)
Small law firm	34	(132)	28	(45)	35	(41)	25	(14)	24	(6)	38	(6)
Government	16	(61)	17	(28)	11	(13)	13	(7)	8	(2)	6	(1)
Solo practice	11	(45)	12	(20)	7	(8)	9	(5)	12	(3)	19	(3)
Peripheral to the law	10	(39)	7	(10)	15	(17)	7	(4)	0	(0)	6	(1)
Total N of jobs		(393)		(161)		(116)		(56)		(25)		(16)
N for lawyers in each year group*		(176)		(83)		(64)		(37)		(17)		(11)

* Total number of lawyers, 388.

tained that they wanted to be able to train the men they hired and so preferred to reach them early in their careers.

Table V-11 also tells us that those who enter government service, not including judgeships or other major federal posts, follow a similar career pattern; that is, they do not stay with Cravath long and go into government employ early in their careers. The figures show that 16 per cent of those who spent zero to two years with that law firm went into government service (not including military) as against 6 per cent of those who spent eleven to twelve years with the firm. Those lawyers who did stay for longer periods of time and then went into government service tended to do so in their initial post-Cravath job.

Lawyers who became solo practitioners, on the other hand, tended to go into individual practice both after spending only a few years with the firm and after spending many years. The percentage choosing solo practice diminishes considerably for the attorneys who spent between five and eight years with the 1906–1948 firm. Twelve per cent of those who stayed up to four years tried solo work while only 8 per cent of the attorneys in the five to eight year category went into individual practice. An upturn is witnessed for those who left the firm between their ninth and twelfth years; so that 16 per cent of these lawyers became individual practitioners. This seeming discrepancy in career patterns may be accounted for by two hypotheses: The youngest attorneys still had contacts at home with people who could be clients and could better afford to take the chance on this precarious means of earning a living. Older attorneys had become specialists, and while their contacts at home had declined, their contacts with fellow lawyers had increased. The combination of being a skilled specialist and having colleague contacts meant that some older alumni could afford to go into individual practice. The older men, however, were specialists who worked for other lawyers, giving advice or writing briefs; the younger attorneys were mainly in general practice.

Career Patterns of Partners —

The men who stay with the 1906–1948 firm and who "succeeded" were chosen (if the data from Swaine's volumes may be interpreted) by their colleagues to be partners. This goal was achieved in various ways and at various rates. Six of the forty-four who were partners came as partners; two were made members of the firm after a brief period as associates. The rest came up through the ranks. The largest number, 34 per cent, made partner between the ninth and twelfth year of their stay. The mean number of years as associates for partners who worked their way up through the firm was 6.8 years. In the 1956 Comparison Firm I the mean number of years was 9.1. This fact does not necessarily indicate a general trend in large law firms—it may merely reflect the reluctance of many law offices to make new partners during World War II, on the grounds that war-time promotions would not have been fair to the associates who were in the armed forces.

While the majority (73 per cent of the partners in the 1906–1948 firm had served over ten years (36 per cent over twenty years), most held other positions during these years. Generally, they involved shuttling between government and the law firm or between business and the firm.

John J. McCloy,[18] went to Peddi School and Amherst; received his LL.D. from Harvard in 1921; practiced with Cadwalader, Wickersham & Taft (a large law firm), left that firm (contrary to the norm) to join Cravath, Swaine & Moore as an associate on December 1, 1924. He became a Cravath partner on July 1, 1929. On December 7, 1940, he was appointed a Special Assistant to the Secretary of War; April 1941, he was named Assistant Secretary of War, resigning on November 24, 1945. On January 1, 1946, he joined still another large law firm as a name partner—the firm is now known as Milbank, Tweed, Hadley & McCloy. McCloy left them on February 28, 1947, to become President of the International Bank for Reconstruction Development. During the years 1949–1952, he became United States Military Governor and High Commissioner for Germany. He left to become Chairman of the Board of the Chase Manhattan Bank (the Chase Bank merged during his administration), leaving again for government service. He returned to Milbank-Tweed for a short time, then President Kennedy asked him to become his dis-

armament adviser. More recently he again returned to the practice
of the law.

McCloy's career is unusual not only because of his tremendous
success and fame but also because as an associate he left one
large law office to go to another and as a partner he left one
large law firm for another. He not only shuttled between the
practice of law and government service, but between the two of
them and business. The late Alexander Iselin Henderson is illus-
trative of the normal successful career pattern for Wall Street
law partners. His obituary, in the July 24, 1961, *New York
Times*, outlines his life and highlights this pattern:

> Alexander Iselin Henderson, a partner in the law firm of Cravath,
> Swaine & Moore, died here yesterday at his summer home. His age
> was 69.
>
> Twice during his law career, Mr. Henderson withdrew from
> practice to go into government service. In 1940, he worked with
> W. Averell Harriman in the National Defense Advisory Commis-
> sion and later with the Office of Production Management and the
> War Production Board as director of materials. He also served as
> deputy director of industrial operations.
>
> Again in 1948, he left his practice to take the post of general
> counsel of the Economic Cooperation Administration, a position he
> held for a year and a half. He then returned to law and remained
> in private practice until his death.
>
> He was born in New York, graduated from Harvard College in
> 1913, attended Trinity College of Cambridge University, returned
> to Harvard Law School, became editor of the Harvard Law Review
> and graduated in 1916.
>
> Mr. Henderson saw service in both World Wars. He drove an
> ambulance for the American Field Service in France in 1915, and
> later enlisted in Squadron A of the New York National Guard and
> served with it on the Mexican border. He then re-enlisted with the
> American Field Service until the United States entered the war.
>
> He joined the French Army at that time and was later trans-
> ferred to the United States First Division in which he served as a
> First Lieutenant and later a Captain. In 1919 he was assigned to
> the Peace Commission.

During World War II, he was commissioned a lieutenant colonel in the Army Transportation Corps and served in North Africa. He later became the deputy port commander in Naples and Marseilles. For his duty he received the Legion of Merit, the Croix de Guerre and the French Legion of Honor in the degree of Chevalier.

He was a member of J. & W. Seligman & Co., stock brokers, from 1928 to 1932. At various times he served as director of the Visiting Nurses Service of New York, the American Field Service and the New York United Service Organizations Fund, Inc. He was also a trustee of Smith College and the Educational Testing Service.

Mr. Henderson was a member of the Association of the Bar of the City of New York, the New York County Lawyers Association and the New York State and American Bar Associations.

His clubs included the Broad Street, the Century Association, the Down Town Association, the Harvard and University of New York, the Piping Rock of Locust Valley, L.I., and the Metropolitan of Washington.

NOTES

1. Robert T. Swaine, *The Cravath Firm and Its Predecessors*, 3 Vols. (New York: Ad Press, 1946 and 1948, privately printed). The books are valuable for their presentation not only of the history of the firm but also of the times. There are other firm histories but they are less complete and, therefore, for our purposes less adequate. Among these histories are: Henry Waters Taft, *A Century and a Half at the N.Y. Bar* (New York: privately printed, 1938); Arthur H. Dean, *William Nelson Cromwell, 1854–1948, An American Pioneer in Corporation, Comparative and International Law* (New York: Ad Press, 1957, privately printed); *Seventy-Five Years of Simpson Thacher & Bartlett, 1884–1959* (New York: Bowne & Co., 1959); Albert Boyden, *Ropes Grey, 1865–1940* (Boston: Lincoln and Smith Press, 1942, privately printed).

2. Swaine, *op. cit.*, Vol. I, p. 44.

3. The names and dates of all the New York City firms follow: R. M. Blatchford, 1819–1822; Blatchford & Clizbe, 1822–1826; R. M. Blatchford, 1826–1832; R. M. & E. H. Blatchford, 1832–1842; R. M., E. H. & S. Blatchford, 1842–1845; R. M. & E. H. Blatchford, 1845–1853; Blatchford & Crosby, 1849–1854; Blatchford, Seward & Griswold, 1854–1869; Blatchford, Seward, Griswold & De Costa, 1869–1884; Seward, De Costa & Guthrie, 1885–1890; Seward, Guthrie & Morawetz, 1890–1893; Seward, Guthrie, Morawetz & Steele, 1893–1896; Seward, Guthrie & Steele, 1896–

1900; Guthrie, Cravath & Henderson, 1901–1906; Cravath, Henderson & de Gersdorff, 1906–1913; Cravath & Henderson, 1913–1920; Cravath, Henderson, Leffinwell & de Gersdorff, 1920–1923; Cravath, Henderson & de Gersdorff, 1923–1928; Cravath, de Gersdorff, Swaine & Wood, 1928–1944; Cravath, Swaine & Moore, 1944. Swaine, *ibid.*, p. vii.

4. In 1886 Cravath was a clerk in the office of Carter, Hornblower & Byrne. Three years later he was a member of the firm. Otto F. Koegel, *Walter S. Carter: Collector of Young Masters or the Progenitor of Many Law Firms* (New York: Round Table Press, 1953), pp. 380–381. Also see Swaine, *op. cit.*, Vol. I, p. 3.

5. Swaine, *op. cit.*, Vol. II, p. 1.

6. For details of the "Cravath System" see Swaine, *op. cit.*, Vol. II, especially pp. 1–12.

7. In a few firms the position of the permanent associate is even more complicated because some are regarded as successes. In one law office this was true of a labor lawyer, in another it was the Jewish or Irish litigator whom that firm refused to make a partner but gave a percentage of the profits as well as important cases.

8. For example, Jerome E. Carlin, *Lawyers on their Own* (New Brunswick, N.J.: Rutgers University Press, 1962).

9. A *New York Times* item, April 28, 1961, p. 10, quotes an American Jewish Committee report which documents this lack of job opportunities in the banking industry.

10. The preparatory school scale was devised with the help of E. Digby Baltzell.

11. An educational rating scale was also designed. This scale placed Columbia Law School in the number one group and lowered the law school at the University of Virginia. On the social scale, Columbia Law School was rated as part of the number two group.

12. While the figures for the comparison firms are too small to report, they do indicate the differences between the firms. More partners, for example, in Comparison Firm II had prior job experience.

13. Swaine, *op. cit.*, Vol. III, p. 131.

14. *Ibid.*, p. 120.

15. *Ibid.*, p. 108.

16. *Ibid.*, p. 148.

17. *Ibid.*, p. 138.

18. *Ibid.*, pp. 467–469, 654–657.

SIX

WORK OF THE WALL
STREET LAWYER

FEW people know exactly what lawyers do,[1] despite the fact that law is among the professions about which the public has most knowledge.[2] Carlin,[3] studying individual practitioners in Chicago, provides some detailed information about their activities. These, he observed, consisted of the following, roughly in the order of the amounts of time devoted to them: (1) conferring with clients, (2) doing office paper work, (3) doing court work, (4) negotiating, (5) conferring with lawyers, (6) reading legal matter, and (7) doing legal research.[4]

On the surface, at least, the lawyer in the large firm is involved in similar tasks, but despite this the solo practitioner's activities are radically different from that of the lawyers in the law firms. This must be so if only because, in the case of the large law office, the nature of clients and their problems requires (because of their complexity, volume, and stakes) a system of specialization and teamwork. Perhaps the only accurate way to determine the work of the lawyer is through the use of "time and motion" studies. No such method was employed in this investigation. Instead, most lawyers were asked to list what they had done the day before they were interviewed. In answer to this question, which was designed, incidentally, to help us understand the organization of the firm and not primarily to obtain detailed information about the types of work performed, most lawyers reported their duties as they had listed them in the diaries they are required to keep. Additional information was collected through further questions, by observation, and by analysis of several histories of large law firms. While these techniques give us an over-all picture of the kinds of work involved in a large law office and which of the various types of lawyers within them perform these tasks, they do not provide a great deal of specific detail. For example, what does a man mean when he says, "I worked on a security issue?" Actually a great deal of activity is hidden behind such a seemingly simple statement.

Even physically obtaining a deceased person's will offers complications. Where, for example, does the lawyer get the will—from a vault, from the client, from a bank safe deposit box? If it is in a safe deposit box, the attorney may have to prepare a petition to have the box opened. He has to secure appointments with the safe deposit company and representatives of the tax department. He may have to prepare an estimate of the contents of the box to be checked against the actual contents. He has to obtain a certified copy of the order for the safe deposit company's file. All these steps are, however, relatively minor when compared with the procedure involved in applying for probate of the will. In the latter instance, the lawyer may have to attend to many of the following details: petition for probate of the will, executor's oath and designation, trustee's oath and designation, citations, supplemental citations, waivers of citation, personal service of citations before first publication, proofs of service of citation, adjournment of calendar, depositions of subscribing witnesses, application to dispense the testimony of absent witnesses, giving notice of probate, filings in court, affidavits as to person in military service, decree, obtaining letters testamentary, obtaining short form certificates as to the issuance of such letters, obtaining certified copies of the will.

There is more to the procedure, often with a great many other duties listed under each of the main tasks involved. The will, for example, may have to be recorded in other jurisdictions. Estate assets have to be collected which may call for applications for waivers by taxing authorities on bank accounts, stocks, bonds, etc.

There are special proceedings to discover property withheld. A petition for discovery may be needed and this petition also calls for numerous legal steps. Counsel has to take care of claims against the estate. The serious business of income tax returns, local and federal, as well as the estate tax has to be attended to. Again each of these pursuits may entail a variety of additional procedures and a variety of additional legal techniques.

It is not important for our immediate purpose to know the meaning of the legal terms used above. All that is intended here is to point out the difficulty of arriving at an exact picture of the attorney's job. Broad outlines of the kind of law a man practices in the large law firm as he progresses from legal fledgling to senior partner are available, however, from the respondents' own comments.

TRANSITION FROM LAW SCHOOL TO LAW OFFICE

THE neophyte coming to the large law firms quickly learns that what he knows is not the "living law," but an academic version of it. His first job is to find out what the law "really" is and how to practice it. He discovers that he must not only do research, write memoranda and briefs, give advice, learn the "ins and outs" of the courts, but also confer with partners, learn to dictate, gain familiarity with the filing system, and compete with older women stenographers for small power symbols.[5]

The Beginning Associate —

The newcomer does have areas of skill—he can do legal research and does know something about writing briefs. This is especially true of the law review man. The managing partners know this and invariably assign that kind of task to the incoming lawyer.

Walter R. Mansfield, a member of Donavan Leisure Newton & Irvine, when addressing a group of Harvard Law School seniors who were in New York looking for positions, described what they could expect if they worked for his firm:

We have a managing partner whose job it is to keep track of the work load of the entire staff. All requests go to him, frequently in hysterical tones from those with deadlines to meet. The new young lawyer is assigned by him to work with the lawyer requesting help, who is supposed to give a rough estimate of the time the job will take. Perhaps it's a very short job like researching a statute, drafting a subpoena, or the like. Or it may be much longer, such as getting thoroughly familiar with the pleadings and evidence in the case being prepared for trial. This may involve reviewing documents, preparing questionnaires to be used on depositions, researching evidence questions expected to be raised at trial, assisting in writing memoranda of law, and doing the many other jobs needed before trial. In this case the young lawyer will work steadily with the partner in charge, attending hearings and helping out wherever possible. If the case becomes temporarily dormant, he will handle other jobs, usually with other partners, in the meantime. It is the rare instance where one case will absorb all his time for months on end. Most associates have several matters on their lists.

The beginning associates' work involves a wide variety of experience, both in the law and in terms of new human contacts. While they do not often meet the principal clients alone (though they may deal with the client's subordinates on an equal basis), they are occasionally taken by partners to conferences with the clients. Their new social interaction calls on them to develop the ability to get along with the partners, with fellow associates, and with the stenographic staff; later on they may develop techniques for securing and retaining clients.

One associate analyzed his first year and a quarter in a large firm. His experience offers a more comprehensive picture of what the young lawyer does at the beginning of his legal career:

I have been with this office 15¼ months. I have been assigned to work under ten partners and about seven associates. My main activities have been as follows:

　1. United States v. ———— (46½ working days)

This was a Sherman Act antitrust case. My work consisted of reading and preparing summaries of documents from our client's files, preparing an extensive memorandum of law relating to defenses under the Sherman Act, and preparing a draft of a consent decree.

2. _____ (40 working days)

This was a Clayton Act, Section 7 case. My work consisted chiefly of researching and preparing a brief in opposition to defendant's action to enjoin plaintiff's purchase of defendant's stock, preparing a memorandum dealing with the right of a board of directors to dismiss its officers, and researching and preparing a brief in opposition to defendant's motion to hold plaintiff in contempt for alleged violation of a court order.

I also researched various problems in connection with plaintiff's application to the Interstate Commerce Commission for approval of a merger between plaintiff and defendant.

3. _____ (35½ working days)

We are general counsel for these two associations. My work has consisted of reading current correspondence and documents of the association, and preparing a memorandum of manufacturers' products liability and product liability insurance which was printed in booklet form and distributed among the members to assist them in connection with prospective sales of their products to private atomic power plants.

4. _____ (22 working days)

My work consisted of preparing a memorandum on the Government's right to enforce or modify a 1921 Sherman Act consent decree.

5. _____ (18 working days)

We represented plaintiff in an action to recover a commission for the sale of real estate. My work consisted of preparing the evidence for the case and assisting the partner trying the case in court.

6. ABA Moot Court case (17 working days)

My work consisted of researching the law of corporate opportunity and assisting in preparing a brief in connection with a moot court case argued by a partner at the ABA meeting.

7. Merger (13 working days)

My work consisted of preparing a memorandum on Virginia law on appraisal of stock and research on various other matters related to the merger of Virginia corporations.

8. _____ (9 working days)

My work consisted of preparing one memorandum, interpreting a sales contract and analyzing the New Jersey law of fixtures, and another memorandum dealing with the definition of a public utility under New Jersey law.

9. _____ (9 working days)

We were counsel to plaintiff in a trade mark infringement action. I did research in the law of trade marks and assisted in the preparation of plaintiff's brief.

10. _____ (10 working days)

Researched and prepared an opinion letter on the enforceability of a management contract entered into by this Connecticut corporation.

11. _____ v. United States (10 working days)

Prepared various memorandums of law in connection with plaintiff's action against the United States for breach of contract.

12. Diamond Distributors (7 working days)

Research on the law of bankruptcy in connection with our client's claim against an insolvent company.

13. _____ (7 working days)

Researched and wrote opinion letters on validity of our client's fair trade agreements.

14. _____ (6½ working days)

Prepared a memorandum on the applicability of Foreign Agents' Registration Act to our client and this office in connection with our efforts to restore assets seized by the Alien Property Custodian.

15. _____ (6 working days)

Prepared one memorandum on the cost defense under the Robinson Patman Act and another memorandum advising our client on types of contract clauses limiting liability.

16. _____ (5 working days)

Researched our client's files in connection with a Sherman Act antitrust charge made against them in a patent infringement action.

In addition to these projects, I have prepared short memoranda of law on various points of law including the law of evidence, the

Interstate Commerce Commission's power to regulate passenger railway traffic, contract law, New York divorce law, etc.

I have also spent a total of 4 or 5 days answering calendar calls, making brief motions in court, delivering documents for registration with the SEC, etc.

What Young Associates Say They Do —

Answers to the questions concerning the legal duties of young associates were subjected to a rough content analysis. The results indicate that most of their work consists in researching various fields of the law, writing preliminary briefs, and conferring with partners about what they have discovered. In this process they learn both the law and how to get along. The firms, by design, see to it that they have contact with many aspects of the law (this formal training was detailed in Chapter III) and with a great many partners.[6]

Analyzing the information gathered in this study, I was able to prepare a rough list of the jobs done by associates who have been with their respective firms for as long as four years. This record is not complete and no attempt has been made to put it in order of importance or of time spent on each type of work. Despite these shortcomings, the list does add to the picture of the daily legal occupations of the young attorney. The record reveals that they do research, write and revise briefs, confer with partners, fellow associates, and clients, give advice, draft letters, revise corporate charters and bylaws, prepare trial memos, take depositions, work on new issues of securities, engage in general corporation work, banking matters, employee pension plans; they also work up exhibits and continually use the telephone.

JOB SEGMENTATION

THE large law firms often find it necessary to divide an enormous matter into smaller parts in order to achieve greater efficiency. This job segmentation saves time and money. It employs the same principles of division of labor found to be so effective in the production of manufactured items before the advent of recent automated devices.[7]

The efforts of the larger law offices sometimes require the application of a production line system. This most intimately affects younger lawyers, especially those who have been with the firm for under two years, although instances where others were required to work on segments of a legal matter are easy to find. In any event, it is considered a resented necessity by many partners and associates. As in a factory, it means that it is more difficult for the persons involved to see the entire situation. The disadvantages of this are clearly recognized; for the lawyer, it limits his value because he cannot give constructive advice on the larger issues, it interferes with a portion of his training, and it tends to reduce his interest in a matter. Some lawyers feel it somehow is not professional. A partner in a large firm located outside of New York offers his view of the situation:

> It is not the practice of this firm, in spite of its size, to divide work up in the manner you describe. In the larger New York firms which are so systematized and regulated, many offices don't take their men into full consideration. They don't tell them the full problem and the man who does the brief might not know its full import. That practice is directly opposite to our policy. We tell them the objectives—then, when a young man does his work he can be brought in on the consultation with the client. We make them feel as though they are partners as far as the work is concerned. We gain greatly in efficiency and build up morale. That is not possible in New York.

Members of New York firms say they too try to limit the amount of work they must divide into small pieces and that when it is necessary to portion out parts of a matter they try to give the associates the broader view of the problem and to keep them informed on the progress made. Even when that is not done, one associate claims it is possible to see the larger picture: "The longer I stay here, the more I find out about a case. A lot of it I have to find out for myself, but nobody tries to prevent me from doing so." Still, it is difficult for an attorney to visualize the entire problem when he is working on only a small part of it.

The most and probably the best use of a system of minute division of legal labor, is to be found in the handling of the "big case." Most large law firms are involved in at least one "big case." The "big case" usually is a large anti-trust or patent infringement suit.[8] Breck McAllister writes that "a BIG CASE is typically a documentary case. . . . Thus Alcoa's records bulged with 15,000 pages of documentary evidence while the National Lead record contained 1,400 exhibits."[9] The cases[10] often take many years and many people work on them. The work is customarily divided into small fragments and assigned to young associates. These units often require research on specific areas of the law, the taking of depositions, and the compilation of information about the client's business. When the associate finishes his task he feeds the completed assigned segments back to a partner or to a senior associate whose task it is to put the parts together.

The "big case" is an extreme example of the use of segmentation in the practice of the law. Illustrations of the division of legal labor requiring lesser amounts of fragmentation were also recorded. These examples, however, are not looked upon by most lawyers in as bad a light as those described above. One associate, asked if he had an over-all picture of the matters he worked on, replied:

> Yes, but there are some things the partner knows that I do not know about—he talks with the executives about things which are in the future. I won't know about these plans till they reach an advanced stage. If I'm swamped on things I'm working on, he may bring in another associate and then I may not know what's going on. On a particular matter we do see all of it—if the matter concerns the corporation as a whole, then we do not see all of it.

Specialization —

Another form of segmentation is specialization. This, however, does not involve the breaking up of the job into its most minor components. Lawyers specialize in many different ways—in the client, for example, or in a broad field of law or both, in the beginning of the case (young associates) or in the end of the case (senior partners). Many attorneys object to specialization just as they objected to other forms of work segmentation. They appeared pleased to be able to say that "I don't specialize," or that "I suppose I do specialize, but I'm in corporate law which is a pretty broad field." Or as one partner put it: "I don't specialize; I do corporate financial work." When a Wall Street lawyer, however, reports that he is in general practice, he really means that he is specializing in business law. The emphasis on specialization was borne out when 118 members of the sample of lawyers were asked specifically if they had a specialty—101 said yes, 13 reported no, and 4 were uncertain.

The large law firms limit their practice by refusing to take most divorce and criminal cases (except some white collar crimes) and negligence work. They further restrict themselves when they discourage, either overtly or through their public image, the work of the individual (unless he is wealthy or connected with a corporate client) and that of small business. At the same time, they encourage the business of the large corporation. These events immediately color the kind of practices most large law offices have and the type of law to which their members and associates must give special attention. All large law offices, therefore, have experts in real estate, estate and trust, tax, litigation, and corporate law.

Despite the recognition of the need for specialization, the law firms fight it. Harrison Tweed's writing exemplifies this schism. While he advocates specialization, he is afraid of the overspecialized specialist. He would like to see "the judgment of the generalist and the expertness of the specialist . . . combined. . . ."[11] The large law firms try through their training programs to give the associate the broadest experience in the law that their practices allow, at the same time the needs of the firm, both temporary and long-run, demand planning to promote specialization. One partner describes the situation in the following manner:

> We think by necessity you have specialization—you can't be a jack of all trades. Actually even the solo lawyer has a relatively narrow range of practice—he takes care of the demands of his particular community. Here it is the demands of the corporate clients and those demands dictate a certain amount of specialization —a man can't stay current in all fields. There is specialization, but if you have only registration men you can't be trained to be a good

lawyer. A lawyer, however, can't be too general and he can't be too specialized. I think that too much specialization is undesirable. If a man wants to be a tax lawyer it is impossible for him to be a good one without knowing the other parts of the law—you can't practice in a vacuum. A man has to be broader than one narrow field.

There are a number of reasons for specialization. The most important ones appear to be the complexity of the client's operation; his desire for positive answers; the impossibility of keeping up with all aspects of the law; the preference of the practitioner.

When and Why Lawyers Specialize —

In general, the associate has moved toward a particular course of work by the end of his third year with a firm. This time period is very flexible and depends in part on the demands of the firm and how formally it is organized. An associate describes the process of becoming a specialist:

> After you've been here a year to eighteen months you tend to go into some sort of specialization. The firm decides where you're to go and you start to do more and more of a particular kind of work but you do not lose all the other work because law suits keep dragging on. I'm still on three or four pieces of litigation, and then there are always emergencies and crises which come up and you may find yourself in one of these.

Another young lawyer who had worked on a "big case" for two and a half years was told by a senior partner, "It's time you decided what you want to do." The associate, who had been working in both litigation and financing reported: "I'm now in the financial side. It is terribly difficult to do two fields. It is an extremely uncomfortable position to have a foot in both areas."

Partners view this process toward specialization in the following manner: A senior partner:

> We give the first-, second-, and third-year man work which will not tie him up. We are interested in trying to move him around.

Eventually, if he's going to practice in a downtown office, he will have to specialize. Nowadays, you can't keep up with all phases of the law.

A managing partner:

Whether or not you specialize, sooner or later depends on you. Early specialization is really the line of least resistance. What happens is this: X comes from Columbia, and he waits for an assignment. I find an assignment for him. If he does well, I may give him the same kind of thing again and again because he can turn out a piece of work faster. He gets proud of this work and reaches for it. This goes on for a year or so. He becomes specialized. If you ask him to do another type of matter, he may say, "It's out of my line."

In addition to the pressures on the firm to specialize, there are pressures from the firm on the practitioner to specialize. There are various reasons besides the institutional ones presented above for an individual to concentrate on one area of the law. In some instances the young lawyer has decided upon a field before he enters the law firm. The evidence presented earlier concerning Harvard Law School graduates, however, indicates that most beginners are willing to change their area of specialization. A number of factors play a part in determining what a man will become expert in: accident, volume of work, vacancy, and just drifting are among these. Sixty-six specialists, members of the sample, were asked how they chose their area of specialization. Thirty-two per cent had been asked by partners if they wanted a particular field of concentration, 23 per cent had been assigned a specialty, 18 per cent had had previous experience in a definite area of the law and were used in that area, 11 per cent felt they had drifted into it, 10 per cent thought that the choice was accidental and 5 per cent offered a variety of other reasons. While 55 per cent had to some degree been assigned a specialty, this did not come about quickly for the firm or for the man. Most descriptions concerning the development of a concentration involve a gradual process. Mansfield sketched this process at a Harvard Law School smoker for job hunters:

As time goes on the young lawyer becomes more acquainted with certain clients and cases and more proficient in certain fields. With us his proficiency usually results from interest and enthusiasm for a particular field to which he has been exposed. There comes a time when others having certain problems, as well as certain clients, will look to him. In this way some men develop into specialists. We have no departments as such except for tax work, we do not assign a man to a special field on a permanent basis. If an associate grows into a specialist, it is a Topsy-like process with us.

A young associate reports on how he became a specialist: "I think you do tend to do one job or become familiar with a certain procedure. When you get known as an 'expert,' either partners or clients will call you on a particular item." A partner from another firm confirms the associate's impressions:

What happens is that when you do a job no one else has done you get special knowledge and it gets to be known around the firm. You then get all the jobs of this sort and become known as a specialist in this area. If some area is missing then it is a designed policy to have a partner specialize in it. So that if someone died or retired, we would have a specialist in that area. The managing partner keeps an eye on that and so does the senior partner.

A number of associates report that they became experts by accident:

I went into the litigation department without any training. I did not want to—I was fully unqualified and had even ignored some of the courses in litigation when in law school. In the last ten years 80 per cent of my time has been spent in litigation. Any progress I've made in the firm has been made while in that job [he is now a partner]. You can't overestimate the element of accident.

All specialization does not come about in this haphazard fashion and one partner reports:

After a couple of years the associate drifts into a field. He or the firm may ask him to shift to another area of the law to fill a need of the firm. There is one important exception to that policy and that is in tax work. It is very exacting and a man who goes into it is very apt to stay in it.

Some lawyers also have a number of subspecialties. Whether the choice of a subspecialty is accomplished by drift or design depends on how well a firm is organized. It is important that someone in an organization know about legal subjects in which there is little general interest, for example, immigration and emigration laws. This principle is often applied in tax departments where a lawyer is expected to have both a broad knowledge of tax law and an expertise in a smaller segment of it, e.g., merger taxation. One associate who feels strongly about the importance of having some minor areas of expertise reports that while 95 per cent of his time is spent in estate work, "the other 5 is all over the shop." A portion of this time is devoted to a subspecialization. "I have elected myself expert on one area of foreign law. You know a man can maneuver to some areas of the law."

There are obviously many degrees of specialization. The practice of business law is broad while blue sky work is narrow. Many lawyers say that they have become so specialized that they cannot easily draw a will; or, as one associate reported: "We had a corporation man who went to Europe for a client and had to call back to the United States on a relatively simple tax question." How narrow a lawyer becomes depends on the man and the firm.[12] In some instances both agree that the narrow speciality is best for a particular person.

MIDDLE RANGE ASSOCIATES

THE middle range associates, those who have been with the firm four to eight years and who follow the average career pattern, take on more and more responsibility and become more and more specialized. One of these associates discusses this development:

I find myself getting more responsibility; I negotiated a contract for sale of residential property, did some drafting on a long-term lease for a block of land in New York, and answered telephone calls on rent law. When I first came into the department I was only allowed to do assignments of mortgages and simple forms of sales situations.

It is difficult to present a true picture of what middle associates do. For while there is overlapping of the kinds of work in which each category of associate is engaged, there is more overlapping for middle associates. This group of men are sometimes treated like novices and at other times treated like experts. Much of this seemingly schizophrenic behavior depends upon the needs of the office. Occasionally it is based on the actual expertise and superior competence of an individual associate.

SENIOR ASSOCIATES

FOR most lawyers length of service means greater client contact and with it more independence and responsibility, in addition to some responsibility for supervision of younger associates who now are doing the leg work. By the time a man has been with a law firm for approximately eight years he is engaged in almost the same kind of work as a younger partner, especially if the firm regards him as partnership material. The big difference in what they are allowed to do, besides that of degree, is that the senior associate is not allowed to sign opinion letters and does not attend firm meetings and therefore has less influence than junior partners upon firm policy. Of equal importance is his inability, usually, to command the same status response from his colleagues or from the firm's clients. One senior associate reports his activities in the following fashion:

My day consists and has been progressively consisting more and more of client contact, conferences with clients, assigning research to younger members, reviewing and evaluating their work, corresponding with clients, and advising partners other than tax partners on tax matters. People in the rest of the firm call me or the tax partners, who then call me.

Senior associates listed, as representative of the kind of work in which they were engaged, corporation acquisition, conferring and advising clients, litigation, drafting and briefs and conferring with partners and younger associates.

PERMANENT ASSOCIATES

THE job of the permanent associates has previously been described. Here I only list the type of work in which they say they are engaged. Their work histories indicate that they interview witnesses, draft briefs, draft mortgages, do blue sky work, dictate leases, prepare for closings, work on general banking matters and take care of a great number of odds and ends.

Just before a man is made a partner or is eliminated from the firm, his work noticeably broadens. He now has more contact with clients and their demands call for increased general knowledge. At the same time senior partners, checking for the last time the credentials for partnership of these associates, start assigning them a variety of legal tasks. Suddenly the associate finds himself working again for a number of partners, although on matters of a different and higher level than when he was the new recruit in the legal pool.

JUNIOR PARTNERS[13]

THE young partner goes to the firm meetings and begins to see something more of the over-all picture. He may be given an associate or two to help him with his work. He sees much more of the clients and receives more responsibility from the older partners. The junior partner, however, still remains fairly specialized. A young partner from one large law firm describes one of his days:

I came in and got rid of my correspondence and prepared for a meeting about a hearing. I met with an outside lawyer. We came back to my office and met with another lawyer and spent an hour and a half with him. We then reported to our respective clients and then drafted an answer between us. I'm sitting as a referee and did some preparation for that. I had a hearing which lasted two hours—I had been chosen from a panel. I came back and worked on a letter for the Federal Trade Commission and discussed it with the client who came to the office. Then I went out to supper and worked for three hours last night preparing a deposition.

The diary of a second junior partner from another firm indicates that he was involved in a greater variety of work. This is partially explained by the nature of the business of the firm he is connected with, which has smaller accounts and more clients than the typical Wall Street firm. His diary lists the following items:

1. Phone call—advised client.
2. Called another executive in the same company as (1) about figures which are relevant in the case.
3. A number of calls with another client about a different matter.
4. Reviewed a long memorandum on a tax matter before discussing it with the client.
5. Had a conference on the figures needed in items (1) and (2). It was held in our offices.
6. Analyzed a very complicated plan on reorganization and assigned my two associates to different matters relating to this reorganization.
7. Had a long conference with tax people.
8. A number of phone calls. One about a client tenant who was going bankrupt.
9. Wrote a letter of recommendation.

Young partners are involved more directly with clients and have greater responsibility than associates. Their diaries revealed a larger spread of activities: advising both clients and colleagues, supervising associates, general counsel work, letters and telephone calls, preparation for a trial, analysis of an estate problem, meetings with outside lawyers, preparation for a meeting, contact with the Federal Trade Commission, preparation of a deposition, meeting with an accountant, preparation of questions for arbitration, writing an article.

MIDDLE PARTNERS

IT is difficult to ascribe a separate set of duties to middle partners. Their work, if they are successful, continues to involve greater client contact, including giving a great deal more business advice and increased supervising and responsibility. The following answers offered by two middle partners to the question "What did you do yesterday?" help fill in the picture:

I spent a good deal of time on a memo regarding estate tax apportionment between a large trust and the beneficiaries under a very wealthy lady's will. The tax amounted to eight or ten million dollars and we are trying to find out how the tax can be reduced.

I spent a long time on the phone with a guy who wants his deceased brother's estate. His father has it now and the father thinks the brother really wanted his brother to have it. I then spent considerable time in preparation for an examination before a trial. A husband, when he died, turned over the management of his business to his second wife. Her step children don't like the way she is managing the business.

I still have a couple of corporate clients that I continue to take care of. I had them before I switched to the tax department. I was also involved in some correspondence concerned with getting Italian securities accepted for trading in this country.

I worked 9 and ¾ hours yesterday. I worked through lunch but that wasn't so bad because we had a business lunch going on at the same time. Only had nine items, which is a fairly small number. I often have as many as fifteen to twenty matters.

I wrote a letter to a client on a new case, on something we had given him an opinion on and on which the Supreme Court had ruled in what to a layman would appear to be similar case and told him his was different. I was trying to allay any fears he might have. Had an extensive telephone conference on the proposed sale of a book to one of our clients.

Received a call from a partner in another law firm. His tax partner was out of town. We have a great deal of stuff which is just a matter of professional courtesy. On another matter I dictated a memo to the files. On still another matter I put the final touches on a petition in a case we lost.

SENIOR PARTNER

WHEN a man becomes a senior partner he is no longer the narrow specialist, the researcher, the brief writer, but is usually the broad advisor and administrator. As one upward-looking junior partner remarked: "The older partners are the general practitioners and so they need younger people to do the research. Now it is true that we have certain people who do trial work. Some who do tax work. The other areas of business law are done by the other partners." Except then, for the partners who were in the tax department or estates and trusts or other service divisions of a firm, the senior partners become general practitioners of business law. This does not mean that the partners who retain their specialization do not broaden also. They do, but in a different way. They, too, depend more and more on the younger specialist but tend to answer the larger questions in their field themselves. The other senior partners become the managers and coordinate the work of various specialists in their firms—"He must," in Proskauer's words, "direct a legal orchestra."[14] Their job is to put the different segments of a matter together, in a meaningful order, so that they can advise the client. The client expects the senior partners to have the answers. As one partner said, "You can't always say you don't know." He advises the client not only on legal matters but also on business matters. For example, the late Boykin C. Wright, who was then the senior partner in the firm of Shearman & Sterling & Wright, was also a director and counsel for a number of corporations including Corning Glass Works, Georgia-Pacific Plywood, Investors Management, First Railroad and Banking Firm of Georgia, and the Home Insurance Company.

The senior partner's advice-giving role increases as he gets older. Not only does he counsel clients but he advises younger attorneys. He does this because it is expected and is part of the traditional role of the older lawyer. In his position as senior partner he must make recommendations to the younger members of his staff, for in some ways he has final responsibility for the work the firm turns out. In addition to the counseling tasks mentioned above, the senior partner is often called upon by the government, the bar association, and various private philanthropic associations for recommendations. Managing and advice-giving, then, are the main roles of the senior partners.

What we have seen is that legal practice in large law offices means different things for people at different stages of development and for lawyers in various departments. The practice of the law changes for the attorney as he rises in the firm. In terms of scope of work, at least, it can be likened to an hourglass. The practice of the beginning lawyer is broad because he works on a great many matters in a wide variety of fields. If he stays with the firm he becomes more and more specialized, although he now has increasing opportunity to see more of the large picture. If he is made a partner, he begins to broaden again. This time the broadening does not involve research on a number of problems, but advising about these problems. Both advising and responsibility increase as the lawyer grows into a senior partnership. When he arrives at that position he becomes the final interpreter of the law for the firm, its over-all manager, and advisor to colleagues, clients and government, as well as to civic organizations.

WHAT THE LAW FIRMS DO

THE work the lawyers do adds up to what the firms do. Still, a different picture is obtained when one looks at the problems which come to the large law firms and the product they turn out. It is clear that, in the main, these law offices represent big blocks of power and money. The following partial list[15] of corporations and countries which have been clients of the Cravath firm during the 1928–1946 period[16] validate that claim: The Chemical Bank and Trust Co., The Bank of America, Kuhn, Loeb and Co., Westinghouse, Bethlehem Steel Co., Columbia Gas and Electric Co., Squibb and Sons, Dupont, Time, Inc., Armour and Co., Paramount and RKO, Studebaker and Ford Motor Companies. The list could go on, for the Cravath firm had (and probably still has) regular clients who ran chain stores, hotels, investment banks, oil industries, railroads, motion picture companies, real estate firms, utilities, automobile companies, steel and glass factories, ships, magazines and newspapers or were in aviation or credit companies. In addition to corporations, Cravath had as clients a number of foreign countries, among them Russia, Germany, Roumania, Peru, Colombia, Mexico, Great Britain, Finland, and Japan.

Generally, the power the large law firms represent is controlled by their clients. When the client is a corporation, the law offices in effect help operate these businesses in an arena which is terribly complex. It is this very complexity which demands that corporate heads give up some of their authority to their legal experts (although Arthur Dean would disagree with this interpretation).[17] The complexity involved, even in what would seem to be the easiest thing in the world to do—give away money—is demonstrated in a further passage from Arthur Dean.

That legal partnerships have attained a large size in the United States is in part a reflection of the scale of American enterprise, but is also in considerable measure attributable to the enormous complexity of nationwide and foreign commerce under our federal system, the powers reserved to the several states and the perplexing congeries of laws under which we move and have our being. Consider, for example, the recent secondary offering of Ford Motor Company common stock by The Ford Foundation in which Sullivan & Cromwell represented the several underwriters. Six lawyers in the firm worked seven days a week for several weeks on the investigation of relevant questions of law and of fact, on the preparation of registration statement under the Securities Act of 1933 relating to the stock with a care commensurate with the problems implicit in a $657,900,000 offering, on the qualification of the stock under state Blue Sky laws in many instances before the effectiveness of the federal registration statement (so as to permit under the various state laws the early solicitation of offers to purchase to the full extent permitted by the 1954 amendments to the Securities Act of 1933 to which most state laws had not yet adjusted), on obtaining approval for the use of advertising matter in the several states, in the Canadian provinces and certain foreign countries, on the preparation of material pursuant to Rule 134 under the Securities Act of 1933 through which selected Ford dealers and employees could offer to purchase before the effective date of the registration statement portions of the $100,000,000 of stock initially reserved for offering to them so that the remainder could be released to the public on the effective date, on the preparation of a prospectus for use in Canada, on the preparation of the underwriting agreement, the agreement among underwriters and the selling dealer agreements to be used in the United States, Canada and foreign countries, and in an analytical review of questions of Delaware law relating to the reclassification of the stock and the unique arrangement of voting rights in the several classes of Ford Motor Company stock, on the possible effect of the exercise of stock options previously granted by the Company to Ford executives and on a host of other related matters all involving investigation, conferring, and drafting.

In addition, other lawyers in the firm worked from time to time on other matters such as the stock pledge and bank loan agreement by which the underwriters raised funds to meet the purchase price, questions of federal and state taxation relating to the offer and a review of certain legal questions arising from the listing of stock on stock exchanges and the registration of the stock under the Securities Exchange Act of 1934.

All of this work was, of course, in addition to the intensive work done by the special counsel for The Ford Foundation, by counsel for the Ford Motor Company and by counsel for the Ford family. As the offering of the Ford stock may suggest, a considerable amount of close cooperation between specialists in a number of fields, and therefore of practice in partnership, is simply unavoidable if today's commerce is to receive the competent advice required to permit its nationwide and frequently worldwide scope of operations to continue on the unrelenting and exacting time tables now customary in financial matters.[18]

That much of the business of the large law firms is complex and important is recognized by their legal staff and is documented in the histories of law offices. Members of the sample kept referring to the fact that they were working in the grey areas of the law—those portions of it which no one really knows and where what is done may help define the law. They talked also about the large sums involved in the cases they handled. A not untypical remark offered by young lawyers reads: "The first week I arrived here I was working on a matter that involved many millions of dollars."

Young attorneys were often also impressed with the importance of the clients and the power they represented. All in all, beginning lawyers felt they were helping to shape the destiny of the nation. The fact is that they are.

In addition to representing the wealthy and the powerful, the firms occasionally change their menu when they become the lawyers for the poor and the weak. The daily diaries sometimes record work performed for the servant of one of their wealthy clients. One entry mentions the rape of a client's maid and goes on to report how the firm was providing legal help. Occasionally they also take glamourous though unpopular civil liberties cases. William Remington, for example, was represented by Winthrop, Stimpson, Putnam & Roberts. This more or less gratis legal aid extends also to institutions and so a number of charities are among the large firms' clients.[19]

The firms, however, prefer the large commercial clients. They do not generally want the legal problems of the "average" man. In answer to a question on that subject, many of the lawyers in my sample said they would suggest the man consult a "local" lawyer he has confidence in. One partner sees the picture this way: "If a small man comes in completely cold with an accident case, we probably would not take it. If he were the secretary to the president of one of the corporations we handle, we would do it for him as a favor. Incidentally, that just happened."

Not all matters coming to the large law firms are exciting, nor are all of them concerned with the grey areas of the law. Much is routine and unexciting. Boyden, of Ropes-Gray, writes:

> The simple fact is that the great bulk of office-practice is not of sufficiently romantic nature to be of general interest. . . . A corporation reorganization where first and second mortgages bond-holders, general creditors, holders of two or three classes of pre-ferred stock, common stock holders, etc., are, figuratively speaking, locked into a room together, and told they must fight it out to a just and equitable division of the assets, is no mean test of in-tellectual agility, financial acuteness and personal character—but its details have no dramatic interest. . . .[20]

Not all work is intellectually stimulating,[21] and even partners must do some of the dull chores. One lawyer reports that in his firm thirty of one hundred lawyers worked full-time on bank matters. "Most of these are second-class citizens [permanent associates] who just stay on to handle the routine of looking over line-of-credit agreements and corporate mortgages, of bringing suit on promissory notes, and of checking stock transfers."

The work of the large law firms is not static; it varies with the times and with the events which affect the business community. So, as would be expected, there is a strong relationship between income tax law and tax work; between antitrust law and antitrust work. ". . . as the depression gathered momentum, the business of marketing securities dried up. For the Cravath firm and many of its colleagues, the lost issue practice was replaced by litigation, receiverships and reorganizations largely arising out of the boom-time securities."[22]

To help clarify a complex picture, the work of the large law firms has been divided into three main categories. The first concerns the internal operation and day-to-day interests of their corporate clients. The content analysis of Swaine's book reveals a number of examples of this type of practice. Consolidations fall into this category, as do recapitalizations. The Cravath firm also helped with the organization of subsidiaries, acquisitions, pension plans, conversions, reclassifications of stocks, liquidations, registration and listing of stocks, and special distribution. These are all internal problems of the clients with which the large law firms concerned themselves.

The second category includes their work as representatives for the client with large elements of the outside world, i.e., other big businesses, the consumer, the general public, labor unions, and the government. Problems with the government are so numerous that they may be divided into those with government agencies—Department of Justice, Federal Power Commission, Federal Trade Commission, The Treasury Department. These are just some of the agencies with which the Cravath firm had to deal. Though it is difficult to separate agencies from the laws they supervise, it is the law firm's concern with problems which grew out of government acts which comprises the other major segment of the firm's dealing with the government. Swaine mentions a number of problems which fit into this subcategory involving the Assignments of Claims Act, Bituminous Coal Act of 1937, Federal Banking Act of 1933, Federal Fair Labor Standards Act, Federal Food and Drug Act, and the Robinson Patman Act. Dealings with other business and national labor unions also were important, and some of the controversies reflecting these relationships had to do with problems over land, inventions, licensing agreements, and contracts.

The third main type of work may be called personal law. When dealing in personal law, the large firm usually represents wealthy individuals in personal matters—often on questions involving trusts and estates. But other personal matters also come up. Among the cases processed by the Cravath firm were adoption proceedings, guardianships, divorces, problems arising from personal "indiscretions."

There are numerous other ways of classifying the duties of the law firm or of its department. Emily P. Dodge divides the work of a Milwaukee law firm in two main ways—in terms of per cent of total business and of the legal skills[23] needed. For example, she found by examining the November 1950 letter files that contracts composed 23 per cent of the work, torts only 2.1, real property, 9.9, and business organization and operation, 41.6, personal property, 12.2, while government relations were 3.5 per cent, procedural problems, 3.5, and miscellaneous substantive law problems, 4.2 per cent[24] of the work load. The types of skills involved for the same year according to Dodge, were litigation, 8.1 per cent, counseling, 59.7 per cent (this category was divided into three subgroups, advice, 47.1 per cent, drafting, 11.1 per cent, appraising advice or papers of others, 1.5 per cent), negotiation, 31.6 per cent and involvement in client's organization, .6 per cent.[25] While these figures would not be exactly the same for large New York firms, they provide another look from a different vantage point at the work done by any "large" law firm.

Other researchers[26] have divided the work lawyers do into client-getting and client-keeping. There appear to be two types of these lawyers, the "public partners" and the "trappers." The "public partners" bring in business partially because of their public reputations—for example, Thomas E. Dewey. The "trappers" bring in clients because of their social background and wide social contacts. They spend a portion of their time refining this asset. Many of them work in estate and trust departments. There are also "private" partners who are known around Wall Street, and many of these are regarded as "scholars"—they put all their effort into the practice of the law. The Wall Street lawyers have also been classified, by Martin Mayer, as the "keepers of the business conscience"[27] and by the late Justice Harlan Fiske Stone as the "servants of business."[28]

While each classification system provides a slightly different picture, and is important from that point of view, what is most needed for this volume is an understanding of how the work is divided by the firm. Two associates who were members of the sample offer us a brief preview. The first merely categorizes the kind of law practiced in the litigation department with which he is connected:

1. Antitrust—these are big cases. They take a lot of time, they make money and require manpower. One partner concentrates on that kind of work.

2. Personal injury work—mostly for a railroad. This work is handled almost exclusively by a permanent associate. He has a younger man who helps him.

3. General commercial work—breaches of contract, breaches of warranty of equipment.

4. Junk—anything from a small criminal case (usually someone who works for an important client) to postponement of jury service.

Breaking an entire firm into its component parts is more difficult and the second associate divides the work of his office in the following fashion:

Four of the sixty-one lawyers are the name partners. They do general advisory work. Two partners and two associates do tax and estate work, though there is some overlapping with corporate work. One older associate does immigration work. He's an expert at it. Two partners do corporate work. They and two associates, an older one and a bright young junior, spend most of their time as general counsel to one corporation. Two name partners and six other partners are primarily antitrust—one of these half-time. Twenty associates also work in this area, eight of them on any one big case. One partner and one senior associate do securities work. One partner is a general all-round think man (We have three former college professors). The senior partner is a summit by himself. He is *the* senior partner. One associate does nothing but handle the work that he does for a foreign country. Five partners and one name partner are in the general practice of law and litigation. In estates we have an older associate and one of the all-round partners. The rest of the people are in general practice, which is mostly litigation. There are no strict work boundaries in this firm.

The business of the large law firms then is complex; it involves people working together to turn out a product. As the last quotation indicates, some amount of organization is needed for efficiency. Thus the various jobs the lawyers do in the large law offices have to be coordinated and this is generally done on the basis of broad specialized areas, or on the basis of the client, or both. It is this organization to which we now turn our attention.

NOTES

1. Harrison Tweed, a well-known Wall Street lawyer and a name partner in the firm of Milbank, Tweed, Hope & McCloy, writes: "Surprisingly little has been written about lawyers which has literary merit and is reasonably accurate. Both biographers and autobiographers have had little success in their efforts to give a true picture of what a lawyer is and what he does." *The Changing Picture of Law* (New York: Association of the Bar of the City of New York, 1955), p. 9.

2. Robert K. Merton and Paul Hatt, "Election Polling Forecasts and Public Images of Social Science," *The Public Opinion Quarterly*, 13 (Summer 1949), 185.

3. Jerome E. Carlin, *Lawyers on Their Own* (New Brunswick, N.J.: Rutgers University Press, 1962), p. 41.

4. A study of 101 counties (Cook County was excluded) revealed the "main fields of practice" of local lawyers in Illinois. Different categories

were presented and different answers received. The following, in order of their highest frequency, are the seven top fields of practice: estates and wills, land titles and sales, mortgages, personal injuries, collections, commercial practice, and criminal law. *Opportunities for Young Lawyers of Illinois* (Rochester, N.Y.: Lawyers Cooperative Publishing Co., 1940). Also see Jerome E. Carlin, *Current Research in the Sociology of the Legal Profession* (New York: Bureau of Applied Social Research, Columbia University, August 1962, mimeographed), Table 5. Carlin lists the percentages of lawyers by their main area of practice. His figures are based on a sample of 801 lawyers. The list follows: business law, 44 per cent; personal injury, 17 per cent; probate, 14 per cent; real estate, 13 per cent; matrimonial, 2 per cent; criminal, 2 per cent; workman's compensation, 2 per cent; individual income tax, one per cent; other, one per cent; no answer, 4 per cent. His sample is drawn from New York City.

5. Albert J. Harno writes that "the greatest weakness of a young law-school graduate is that he is inept in dealing with facts." *Legal Education in the United States* (San Francisco: Bancroft-Whitney, 1953), p. 152. The statement finds support in a study conducted by a Committee of the Harvard Law School, which sent out a questionnaire to a random sample of Harvard Law School graduates. In one question six skills were listed: "negotiation, draftsmanship, advocacy, legal planning, 'knowing the law' in a practical sense (the ability to predict how cases will be decided), and ability to secure an understanding of facts and motives." Those answering the questionnaire were asked to rank these skills in the order of their importance for the type of work they were performing. The results follow:

"The number of lawyers giving first rank to skill in dealing with facts was more than twice as great as that of those giving first position to any of the other skills. Averaging the numerical indices of the positions assigned these skills (so that the smaller the number reported, the higher the ranking), the relative ranking of the six skills was as follows: dealing with facts, 2.3; predicting how controversies will be decided, 3.4; legal planning, 3.4; negotiation, 3.5; draftsmanship, 3.8; advocacy, 4.1. The margin between 'dealing with facts' and the next skill in order is 1.1, while the margin between the top and the bottom in the other five skills is only 0.7. A 'sense of fact' is therefore given the highest position by a wide margin over any of the other skills." Preliminary statement of the Committee on Legal Education of the Harvard Law School, 26 (1947). In Harno, *op. cit.*, p. 153.

6. While associates appreciate the opportunity of becoming skilled in the law, at the same time they complain about the type of work they are given and at the lack of meaningful client contact. One young associate put it this way: "I do the research and write an outline for the brief. The partners decide most of the cases themselves on the basis of past knowledge; the difficult points they give me to look up, and then they make a decision. Then they see the client—I have no relationship with the client, unhappily—but this will not always be so."

7. The latest automative devices tend to take the small segmented jobs performed by the man on the production line and integrate them into the process of automation, thereby relieving many men of small jobs but in the process, creating larger and more professional positions.

8. "Reference of the Big Case under Federal Rule 53 (b): A New Meaning for the 'Exceptional Condition' Standard," *Yale Law Journal* 65 (June 1956), p. 1057.

9. Breck P. McAllister, "The Big Case: Procedural Problems in Antitrust Litigations," *Harvard Law Review*, 64 (1950–1951), p. 32.

10. A more detailed organizational description of the "big case" will be presented in the next chapter.

11. Tweed, *op. cit.*, p. 17.

12. A countertendency is beginning to appear, i.e., for all lawyers to learn something about some "specialties," e.g., taxes.

13. "Junior" in this chapter simply refers to new or young partners.

14. Joseph M. Proskauer, *A Segment of My Times* (New York: Farrar, Straus and Young, 1950), p. 121.

15. The large New York firms do not list their clients in The *Martindale-Hubbell Law Directory*, as do firms in most other parts of the country. The names of present clients mentioned during the interviews held with various members of law firms are not used since this information is regarded by some firms and clients as confidential. However, the major clients of these law offices are generally known in the Wall Street area.

16. Robert T. Swaine, *The Cravath Firm and Its Predecessors* (New York: Ad Press, 1946–1948), Vol. II, interspersed between pp. 481–718.

17. Arthur H. Dean, *William Nelson Cromwell, 1854–1948: An American Pioneer in Corporation, Comparative and International Law* (New York: Ad Press, 1957), pp. 83–85. The two paragraphs preceding those in the text indicate that Arthur Dean would not agree that executives in corporations have delegated any of their authority to make decisions to their lawyers. In addition he does not see law partnerships as limiting the individual responsibility of the attorney (a factor which this present study of Wall Street lawyers is examining). On pp. 82 and 83 Dean states:

"The development of large partnerships in law is, however, not the cause of specialization but merely one of the effects of a highly complicated society in which trained people increasingly wish to think out their own individual opinions and make their own decisions, and can only be assisted by experts. The influence of lawyers in their area of competence is not necessarily lessened because professional people or persons with specialized training other than themselves are intelligent, have ideas and are equally capable of rationalization, but the lawyer of today cannot expect professional assurance, unnecessary legalisms and the aura and ritual of a quasi-priestly caste to be accepted by his intelligent contemporaries as a substitute for expert knowledge, sound reasoning, thorough research, incisive and accurate analysis and constructive and timely solutions.

"The emergence of large partnerships reflects the attempt of lawyers to offer clients in a more complicated society the competence, the breadth of view, and the ability to cope with the present, complex network of laws and regulations in as efficient a manner as the solo practitioner could offer in a simpler one. As always, individual clients repose their confidence in individual lawyers in such partnerships. Though these lawyers may in a greater or lesser degree rely on the reasoned opinions of their partners, individual responsibility is not lessened.

18. *Ibid.*, pp. 83–85.

19. See Albert Boyden, *Ropes-Gray 1865–1940* (Boston: Lincoln and Smith, 1942), p. 128.

20. *Ibid.*, p. 123.

21. Martin Mayer, "The Wall Street Lawyers: Part I: The Elite Corps of American Business," *Harper's*, 212 (January 1956), 34. The author provides additional evidence of tedious business and cites the preparation of documents for new security issues as an example.

22. Swaine, *op. cit.*, Vol. II, p. 486.

23. It is difficult to break down the practice of law into minute areas of skill; for example, one respondent, when talking about securities issues, said, "Anybody can read regulations, but nine tenths of the real work is reading between the lines. And it's the Wall Street boys, with all their experience, who know how to read between the lines."

24. Emily P. Dodge, "Evolution of a City Law Office, Part II. Office Flow of Business," *Wisconsin Law Review* (1956), 41.

25. *Ibid.*, p. 48.

26. Harold D. Lasswell and Richard C. Donnelly, "The Continuing Debate Over Responsibility: An Introduction to Isolating the Condemnation Sanction," *Yale Law Journal*, 68 (April 1959), 869. Lasswell and Mc-Dougal also list various professional activities and the skills needed for these activities. Harold D. Lasswell and Myres S. McDougal, "Legal Education and Public Policy: Professional Training in the Public Interest," *Yale Law Journal*, 52 (March 1943), 203–295.

27. Martin Mayer, "Keepers of the Business Conscience—The Wall Street Lawyers, Part II," *Harper's* 212 (February 1956), 50–56.

28. Harlan Fiske Stone, "The Public Influence of the Bar," *Harvard Law Review*, 48 (1934). Reprinted in Elliott E. Cheatham, *Cases and Materials on the Legal Profession* (Brooklyn, N.Y.: The Foundation Press, 1955), p. 56.

SEVEN

DIFFERENCES IN THE

PRACTICE OF LAW:

A Glance at Various Types
of Large and Small Firms

VAST differences exist in the practice of the law as well as in how that practice is organized. This chapter attempts to describe some of these differences, mainly those among large firms in New York, between these giant New York firms and large out-of-town offices, and between large and small law firms. No attempt will be made to account for all the variations possible in the bar or even in the metropolitan bar.[1] The distinctions easily discernible, however, could be put on a continuum which ranges from the very loose agreements between the general practicing, solo lawyers, to the individual practitioners who may share an office, a secretary, and a telephone, and a variety of specialists who fill them in on problems requiring particularized knowledge, to the comparatively intricate and relatively tight organization of the large law firms.

Between these two poles can be found a great variety of types and degrees of organization.

SOLO LAWYERS

COMPARING the "average" solo lawyer with his "average" large firm colleague is our easiest task. Carlin's study[2] of the individual practitioner in Chicago and the material presented in this volume detail the differences. These can be found in who they are and in the kind of work they do. The solo lawyer, Carlin's investigation points out, is usually a graduate of a night or local law school. Unlike the large law firm lawyers described here, few attended Ivy League law schools. Their background is different (mostly they are members of minority ethnic and religious groups versus majority protestant Anglo-Saxon large-firm lawyers); their clients are different (individuals versus corporations); their practice is different (often fairly routine, clerical-bookkeeping and manipulation of minor local government officials[3] versus complicated business law involving vast sums of money and dealing with federal agencies); and their average net income is different ($5759 for the member of a one-man firm to $27,246 for members of law offices of nine or more[4]). They even tend to join different bar associations. The solo and small firm lawyers join the New York County Lawyers Association and the attorneys from the large firms tend to join the Association of the Bar of the City of New York.[5] Solo lawyers are more likely to be general practitioners; they work directly with individuals on kinds of matters most large firms will not handle. They are, according to Carlin, at the margin of their profession "enjoying little freedom in choice of clients, type of work, or conditions of practice."[6] The solo lawyer has little or no library, and to get to one takes precious time. Usually he needs a great many clients to survive, since most small clients do not require continuous legal service. This means, as one large firm associate put it, "The solo practitioner practices largely by ear," and an individual practitioner concurred, "We can't spend a great deal of time looking up the law—it is pretty nearly hit or miss."

The separation between the individual and large law firm

lawyer is cavernous; it is almost caste-like. These lawyers rarely have contact with each other because of the differences in background and type of work they do. The division between them was deepened by discrimination on the part of many large law firms against graduates of night or local law schools and against members of minority groups. This separation leads to a series of mutually derogatory images.[7]

The solo practitioner sees himself ideally as the defender of the poor and the needy, an independent man with real responsibility. He is the spokesman for the people, not the mouthpiece for big business. Lawyers from large law firms who would talk about the solo lawyer did so with more tact and less emotion. They could not see how the law could be adequately practiced by the single lawyer. One partner from a large firm states, "I don't think there are any good solo lawyers; there is too much to know and he has so little time to learn it." Some large firm lawyers felt that there were more unethical people among solo lawyers, although they hastened to add: "Perhaps they are forced into it." Others felt it was nonsense to speak of the solo lawyer having more responsibility, or of being more professional. The Wall Street lawyer claims these attributes for himself; after all, doesn't he deal with larger matters on a more important and difficult level? These mutually negative images tend to perpetuate the social distance between the two groups.

DIFFERENCES AMONG THE LARGE FIRMS

Jewish and Gentile Firms —

It is not uncommon to find law firms staffed with personnel from the same ethnic or religious groups; consequently "Irish," "Jewish," or "Anglo-Saxon" firms are easily discernible. Most of the minority group firms are not large. However, a number of Jewish offices[8] are approaching the arbitrary mark of fifty lawyers—(three have already passed the necessary number to be considered large). Three of these offices were visited in an effort to determine something about the difference between the major Jewish and the major Anglo-Saxon law firms. Questions were asked about the types of lawyers recruited, the kinds of clients they had, and the structure of their organization. The last two questions jigsaw together, since the type of business processed affects the structure of the organization. What variance was found seemed due to the smaller size of the Jewish firms and the differences in clients. Although the large Jewish firms have important corporations as clients, these companies are not as large, as old, as conservative, or as important as the major clients of the large Wall Street firms. For example, if a Jewish firm has a bank as a client, it is usually a small bank. When you extend this finding to other clients, it means that the Jewish firm, if it is to remain large and survive, needs many more clients than other large firms. While the partners in Jewish firms are usually all Jewish, all of their clients are not. In fact, one major Jewish firm reported that half of its clients were not. A partner in that firm states:

> There are two types of Jewish law firms. One only has Jewish clients (generally the smaller ones), the other is the "Texas" kind, where the client says, "Get a Jewish lawyer, he'll get you off." It's a back-handed compliment. While I personally do not have a major Jewish client, the firm's greatest dollar volume comes from firms that are Jewish. Over half our clients, however, are not Jewish.

A partner from another large Jewish firm observes:

> Our clients are predominantly Jewish, despite the fact that many of the large Jewish businesses like to be represented by large gentile firms. This may be especially so for Jewish clients who have "Washington" problems. I don't think, however, that this pattern is deeply set.

Jewish law firms do not necessarily get the largest Jewish concerns as clients, and generally when they receive gentile business, it is not from the largest organizations. Again this points up differences in size of the client. For the moment, it is sufficient to say that this means that there is less need for teamwork in the Jewish firms (though teamwork is still the major feature of their organization), and this in turn means there is less super-vision, that the associate can be more independent and has more individual responsibility, although on smaller matters.

Perhaps the greatest difference between the large Jewish firms and the gentile firms lies in their recruitment patterns. Although they enlist in much the same fashion and from the same elite eastern law schools, the Jewish firms can hire very few gentiles but are able to obtain the top Jewish law review students. Proskauer's firm, which, like other large New York offices, does not list as-sociates in the *Martindale-Hubbell Law Directory*, reveals in that publication that eight of the eighteen partners were law review editors. The Anglo-Saxon firms, as indicated elsewhere, are hiring Jewish lawyers. However, because many Jewish law students still fear they cannot become partners in the large gentile firms, they will not accept appointments with them. This fear makes it easier for the Jewish organizations to obtain top Jewish law review graduates even though it is claimed that until recently, they paid their associates less.

When members of Jewish firms were asked why they did not employ gentile lawyers, they generally said that they did when they could. As one lawyer put it:

It is difficult to attract top-notch Christian associates and partners, and there is a tendency to have firms stand much as they were when they started. We do have some gentile associates but no non-Jewish partners. The reason for that is that we compete for top law review people, which means the top gentile lawyers go to the gentile firms. We get Jewish law review people here because they feel they can become partners here.

Uptown and Downtown Firms —

Another distinction, although one which is passing into history, is found between uptown (midtown Manhattan) and downtown (Wall Street district) firms. To be called an uptown firm was to be looked down upon. It implied poorer lawyers from smaller law firms. The distinction was based partially on size of firm and partially on size of clients, the downtown firms being larger and having the largest and most important clients. Some psychic income is obtained by being labeled a downtown firm. It reflects itself in the difficulty uptown firms have in recruiting the best lawyers. As business moves away from Wall Street, however, law firms are beginning to follow. Paul, Weiss, Rifkind, Wharton & Garrison, for example, moved uptown. Other large firms are now developing uptown branch offices and some medium size firms with excellent reputations have moved away from Wall Street. Others will follow and, as one lawyer stated when asked the difference between uptown and downtown firms and why his firm had moved uptown:

> There was a period of years when there was a difference between uptown and downtown firms in terms of size and respectability. However, some sections of downtown also have this stigma—Broadway, for example, is known as Shyster Hall.
>
> We moved from downtown and it was difficult for two of our partners to make the move, but the advantages of moving became overwhelming. Most New York business had moved to the Grand Central area and there's a general comfort in uptown living and our airconditioned buildings. We moved uptown with many other large firms [he considered his firm large]—Coudert, Rifkind, and Proskauer. The trend was to move uptown; now there are enough good firms uptown to take the stigma away. When we moved, we were afraid we were not getting enough stock issues, but we did. There still is a difference, however, there is a tendency of firms who represent big banks to stay downtown, and the downtown firms are more conservative. Downtown is also a lower-economic rent district. On our side, when the Bar Building moved uptown, it increased the respectability of uptown.

Social Firms —

Among the large firms studied, those offices where many of the associates and partners are listed in the *Social Register* or are "social register types" (upper-class), are called social firms. Davis-Polk, for example, in 1961, with thirty-eight partners, has twenty-six who are in the *Social Register*, although half of these were listed in the *Social Register* after they became partners. On the other hand, one large firm, Donovan-Leisure, with twenty-five partners, has only six who are in the *Social Register,* and Paul-Weiss, with twenty-five New York partners, has three listed.

The importance of this distinction is reflected in a slight difference in the organization of the various kinds of firms, the type of business they attract, and in their recruits. For example, many social firms will employ relatives. They do not have rules against nepotism, in fact, probably prefer relatives to inherit their practice. They try to maintain an upper-class image. This is one way they attract and keep a relatively greater proportion of the trusts and estate business and perhaps banks and security issues than do other large firms. Much of the work dealing with trusts and estates is done on an individual basis (although tax lawyers are being consulted more and more frequently). Even a young lawyer with a wealthy contact can bring this kind of business into the firm and, except when he foresees or runs into difficulty, can work by himself. The clients tend to be considered the individual's clients rather than the firm's. The obvious then occurs—the less the need for teamwork, the less the need for complex organization. It must be remembered, however, that while some large practices have proportionately larger assignments of trust and estate work which can be handled on an individual basis, all firms have a variety of legal departments; thus, real differences of organization are relatively slight.

Social status differences between the firms provide one distinction which affects their organization. Prestige differences based on their rating as lawyers make for another division, although some of the law offices overlap in that they fit into more than one category. The thirty attorneys from the sample of Wall Street lawyers who were asked to rate the ten best large New York law firms in terms of their proficiency in the practice of the law consistently agreed on eight of them. And four of the eight always headed the list. These prestige firms often acted as models for the other large offices and were instrumental in deciding beginning salaries for the Wall Street legal community. Their *esprit de corps* was high; their organization was desired by both clients and lawyers. These facts made management of these firms somewhat easier than in the other large partnerships. Indeed, some claim that the prestigeful firms' reputation for proficiency helps them win in court, in that the judges know that their briefs have been thoroughly prepared (Riesman feels they are overprepared),[9] and their accuracy can be counted on.

Of greater importance for this volume than the difference between large firms in New York City are the distinctions between small New York offices which aspire to large law firm practices and the larger firms themselves, and the distinction between these giant New York firms and their out-of-town "equivalents." These comparisons are important not only because they shed additional light on the organization of the large Wall Street firms but also because information is garnered about the relationship between size and organization and between location and organization.

Large Law Firms Outside of New York —

There are relatively few large firms outside of Manhattan. Most of these have only recently become large. Because of this it was difficult to find out through routine channels how many there were and where they were located. During the fall of 1959, letters were sent to bar associations in cities with a population of 500,000 or more. The associations were asked to list all law offices with fifty or more lawyers and, if none of that size existed, to name the largest firm in their city. The replies from the above query indicated that there were seventeen[10] firms composed of fifty or more lawyers in cities outside of New York. None of these organizations had more than one hundred lawyers. Geographically, they are distributed as follows: one large law firm in Boston, Pittsburgh, and Washington, D.C., respectively; two such firms in practice in Cleveland, Los Angeles, Pittsburgh, and San Francisco; Chicago and Houston each list three large law firms.

A number of questions are immediately raised by this breakdown. Why, for example, does Houston have three large offices and Detroit none? One possible answer involves the size of the city; its distance from New York, and the amount of big new business it has developed. Law firms in Houston probably expanded with the opening of the new oil fields and with the development of new local wealth and new big business in that area, much of which had only loose ties with Wall Street. Generally, the old giant national corporations send their intricate legal work to Wall Street. Most large firms outside of New York have to have a special major function to survive; for example, Covington & Burling, in Washington, D.C., nationally known and highly respected, does a great deal of work for corporations from all over the country. Generally, their work involves dealing with government agencies and the federal courts. Charles Horsky, author of *The Washington Lawyer*, and a member of Covington & Burling, writes:

> Washington lawyers are peculiarly ubiquitous. Representing as they do clients everywhere in the United States who have Federal problems, Washington lawyers must be able to pack their brief cases and speed anywhere to do battle with the Department of Justice, or the tax collector, or the Office of Price Stabilization.[11]

It is probable that in each region some special circumstance exists. Large firms, therefore, in the various sections of the nation may have somewhat different kinds of clients and problems. I suspect that while there are distinctions between the seventeen large firms located outside of Manhattan, especially between Covington & Burling and the others, all those large firms nevertheless have much in common which sets them apart from the New York offices.

In an effort to determine some of the differences between the large firms located away from New York with those in the city, four large law firms situated in various areas of the nation were studied. In addition, information about all seventeen large out-of-New York firms was obtained from the *Martindale-Hubbell Law Directory*. While the four offices visited were not the same in terms of organization or "personality," they all were somewhat different from the majority of the large New York firms. It is to these differences and the differences discovered by an analysis of the *Directory* that the next few pages are devoted.

LARGE LAW FIRMS OUTSIDE NEW YORK CITY

A COMPARISON of the *Martindale-Hubbell Law Directory* for 1962 with earlier records reveals that, at their inceptions, large law offices outside of Manhattan chose mainly local men for their legal staff—probably potential business getters. Between 1941 and

1961 there was an increase of 6.3 per cent in the number of partners who were not born in the state in which they practiced. However, even the 1962 records indicate that 54 per cent of the partners in these firms had been born in the same state in which their law firms were housed.[12] For the New York law firms the comparable figure was 39 per cent. Table VII-1 shows a tendency for New York firms to hire men who were graduates of eastern elite colleges rather than those who went to local schools. Except for the Boston firm, (in which, to pinpoint it, 64.5 per cent of the partners had graduated from Harvard College) law offices outside of New York did not go out of their way to employ eastern elite school graduates; despite geographical distances, however, the indications are that this tendency is being modified.

Table VII-1—College Background of Law Partners in Large Law Firms in the United States for 1962

| | College or University | | | | |
| | LOCAL | | EASTERN ELITE | | |
State	(%)*	(N)	(%)*	(N)	(Total N)
California	47.1	57	14.1	17	121
Illinois	22.5	23	20.6	21	102
Massachusetts†	0.0	0	79.4	27	34
New York† ‡	6.0	28	61.5	288	468
Ohio	22.2	18	34.6	28	81
Pennsylvania†	3.6	4	55.8	67	120
Texas	54.2	52	4.2	4	96
Washington, D.C.	2.9	1	48.6	17	35
Totals	17.3	183	44.4	469	1,057

* The percentages for other colleges are not given; therefore the percentages do not add to 100.

† These states had colleges in them which were considered as Eastern elite and figures for these local institutions are included under Eastern elite.

‡ The New York figures are for 1957.

As the offices outside of New York City grow in size (from 1941 to 1961 they added 255 partners, a growth of 84 per cent), age, and reputation, they look for men who have the same qualities as those which the Manhattan firms seek—i.e., men with high scholastic averages and broader legal training; they then begin to flirt with recruits from the eastern elite schools. They now turn for their recruits, as Table VII-3 points out, first to the best local law school, then to Harvard, then to Yale. Thirty-nine per cent of the partners in the California law firms had graduated from Harvard and Yale law schools; in one office, 54 per cent of its members were alumni of these schools. The proportion of Harvard law school graduates was much higher, as would be expected in the Boston firm (94 per cent) since Harvard is both an eastern elite school and a local one. (Seventy per cent of the partners in the large New York firms graduated from the eastern elite schools but the majority did not come from Columbia, which to New York is almost what Harvard is to Boston.) The movement to recruit from the eastern elite law schools seems to have affected the Texas firms least; only 13.5 per cent of their members graduated from elite eastern law schools.

Table VII-2—Law School Background of Law Partners in Large Law Firms in the United States for 1962

	Law School				
	LOCAL		EASTERN ELITE		
State	(%)*	(N)	(%)*	(N)	(Total N)
California	38.8	47	38.8	47	121
Illinois	37.3	38	22.5	23	102
Massachusetts†	3.0	1	94.0	32	34
New York† ‡	13.3	62	69.2	324	468
Ohio	19.8	16	50.6	41	81
Pennsylvania§	47.5	57	27.5	33	120
Texas	71.9	69	13.5	13	96
Washington, D.C.	11.4	4	54.3	19	35
Totals	27.8	294	50.3	532	1,057

* The percentages for other colleges are not given; therefore percentages do not add to 100.

† These states had law schools in them which were considered as Eastern elite. Figures for these locally housed institutions are included under Eastern elite.

‡ The New York figures are for 1957.

§ Forty-five per cent of the large Pittsburgh firm graduated from the University of Pittsburgh.

While New York firms rarely hire attorneys who have not been trained by the firm, it is not uncommon for law offices located elsewhere to do so. Many of these partnerships are still growing quickly and they cannot wait for men to learn a specialty, so they often recruit attorneys who have gained the needed experience in other places, in other firms, or with the government. One interviewee, who had worked for the OPA, explained why he thought a large firm had employed him: "A key man in this firm left to go to work for a corporate client. This left a gap in an area in which my government work made me especially competent, and his departure also created a shortage of lawyers of my vintage." As these large firms mature, they will be better able to predict the needs of their clients and to train their own experts, except in cases where a specialty becomes very important quickly.

The practice of filling gaps in an organization with outside men tends to create personnel problems. Men who have been with an organization for many years do not like seeing outsiders placed over them. This procedure affects the socialization process and can make a firm less homogeneous. It also means that orientation practices in these firms must be developed more fully than is necessary in the New York offices.

Some non-New York legal offices send associates or partners to the eastern schools to recruit, but this is not done in the same systematic fashion in which large New York firms pursue their task. Most large partnerships have a recruiting agent or a committee in charge of obtaining new lawyers for the firms, but again the position is not as important or as formalized as in the New York firms. This is in part due to the relatively smaller turnover in these offices. For example, one of the largest out-of-New York firms had only three men leave them in a seven-year period. In the same period, however, they hired twenty-six lawyers. Little evidence is seen of up-or-out rules which force a flow of lawyers through an organization; earlier partnership possibilities encourage the associate to stay at his job longer than in New York. These reasons, plus the fact that in many out-of-New York offices the associate can bring in his own business and receive a percentage of it, hold associates to their firm.

Recruitment procedures and rules are not as formal as they are in the large New York firms. Men need not come from Harvard, Yale, and Columbia—nor is it necessary that they start their legal careers in these firms. This makes for greater heterogeneity and fits in with the less formal tradition of the Midwest and the smaller city.

ORGANIZATION

THE organization of these firms resembles those in New York. Size and the requirements of the law make this so. The mere fact of largeness, for example, means that there are similarities in housekeeping problems. Firms in or out of New York must ask some of the same questions. Who gets which office, which rug, which desk? Who goes on vacation, when, and for how long? How can one system for filing, for signing papers be instituted? What is the best way to use secretaries and other personnel? The mere fact that much of the business of the large law offices deals with the legal needs of large corporations means that their organizations will resemble each other. Nevertheless, there are differences. For example, they are not as formal as the Manhattan offices. (Incidentally, this is also true for how they dress.) The proportion of associates to partners is much higher in the New York firms no matter how partner is defined.[13] The stratification of the professional side of the organization differs in that the out-of-town firms make more use of a classification other than full partner and associate. This category is the junior or "limited" partner—nonpercentage partners who are not responsible for the firm's debts.

Partnership —

Partially because of the junior and "limited" category, partnership is generally easier to attain, and lawyers are younger when they reach this goal. One respondent who received his LL.B. in 1947 and became a nonpercentage partner in 1952, tells of this progress:

In 1952 I became a limited partner; in 1954 I became a percentage partner—I've been going up fast. Our letterhead does not indicate who are the limited partners and who are the percentage partners and they do not jump you on the letterhead. There are partners ahead of me who are limited partners. Our letterhead is based on when you made partner, irrespective of the kind of partner you are made. There are some senior partners who are now salary partners—and modest salaries at that. We feel that when a man gets to a certain age, he should retire whether or not he wants to.

Q. When does a limited partner become a percentage partner?

A. When it becomes advantageous to the firm not to guarantee the man a definite salary because that salary is too high. They say, "Why not let him take some of the risks?"

Making a man a nonpercentage partner quickly is one way the firm keeps its men, this also satisfies smaller clients who want the prestige of having a partner working on their matter.

Despite the fact that the letterhead in a particular firm does not indicate status among partners, a status differential does exist, and there is a cleavage between junior, or nonpercentaged, and full partner. In one firm the correlation between junior or nonpercentaged was not absolute because some very old and formerly powerful senior partners, as they neared retirement, became limited partners. One of these men offered the following information:

> We have two kinds of partnership: percentage and nonpercentage. Those who are nonpercentage get bonuses, as do the associates. The people who make policy come from among the percentage partners and about four, five, or six of these do the deciding.
>
> *Q.* How does a nonpercentage partner become a percentage partner?
>
> *A.* He becomes one when he is ready to. Let us say he inherits a large account. If we let him have it, we don't want him to leave with it, so we have to make him a percentage partner.

While it is impossible to generalize on the basis of the organization of four out-of-New York firms, these organizations have fewer rules and these, as in all firms, are not always enforced. Few out-of-New York law firms have regulations against nepotism or rules preventing an attorney from staying with the office, even though he will not be made a partner. Since training a new recruit is not so important to these firms, rules and organization concerning training are practically nonexistent. While conflict of interest situations must be avoided, it is done in a more informal manner, through office conversation and the judgment of the main partner in the matter—in fact, some of these offices did not have a new matter list, a precaution against conflicting interests which most New York firms insist on. In one firm it was the responsibility of the managing partner and the office manager to see that a conflict of interests did not occur.

Unlike most New York offices, most out-of-town organizations do not have as many office meetings. A partner reports: "We do not have a firm meeting. We do have a luncheon every Friday, but here we discuss the law." Many law offices do have a table at a club where members of the firm eat when they do not have other luncheon appointments, and it is here that a great deal of the business of the office is transacted.

Just as they are not so formal in terms of regularized training or in the way they have their firm meetings, so, too, are they less formal in terms of departmentalization, except for service departments—like tax—which are much the same as in the large New York firms. Lawyers out of New York seem to depend less on other lawyers and more on themselves. Probably, as is true for the New York Jewish firms, this is because they work on more individual and smaller clients. One large out-of-New York office estimated that they had 850 separate clients. There is more of a tendency to consider clients as belonging to individual lawyers rather than to the firms. However, as these firms become larger and older they too are tending to become institutionalized, and clients, libraries and equipment are passed on to the younger lawyers. As in the New York firms, then, continuity is assured.

Differences in Kind of Work —

Of great importance to both the organization and the men involved is the kind of work a firm obtains. While out-of-New York large firms do a great deal of corporate work, much of it is for smaller clients, and when large clients are involved, there are fewer of them. A partner from a large eastern firm refines the last statement: "X area is not expanding. We do have a substantial amount of big business, but not a substantial amount that comes in a steady flow as do the New York firms—so we cannot depend on it to keep us steadily busy. This means we do a great amount of individual practice."

Banks are the New York firm's most basic client, and while large out-of-Manhattan firms generally service banks (one of the four out-of-New York offices studied did not), these banks are smaller and require more of their routine law work be done for them. This again tends to individualize the work of the lawyer, as does insurance work. Most New York firms do not handle the small matters of insurance companies. In fact, in New York both banks and insurance companies customarily employ their own lawyers to take care of most routine matters. In addition, a greater proportion of the practice of out-of-New York firms deals with trust and estate matters. They also have more trial work, and some law firms will take on patent matters. They have less blue-sky work and prepare few or no prospectuses or security issues. The antitrust cases they handle generally concern small matters (not so for the Washington firm) or the locally based portions of a larger matter. In any event, they handle less of it. What this type of practice means is that the individual lawyer has a greater opportunity to practice the law by himself. He is less specialized, less supervised. He appears to have more independence. In some firms the associates are allowed to sign opinion letters—a tabooed practice in most New York firms. He needs fewer rules to guide him because his work does not call for as much synchronization as is needed in the more team-oriented New York firms. The out-of-town large firm lawyer is much closer in his working relationships to the small firm lawyer than are the members of the giant Manhattan firms. He sees more of the client.

One young partner explains how he was able to work on his own:

> They put me on collection work, justice of the peace cases. I took any small case they had. I was convinced that the same principles involved in a small case are involved in large cases. I took all the crap I could get and I had no trouble getting it, and as I learned, they gave me some more important trial work.
>
> At this firm we want men to try cases and, since large clients have lots of small business, we use these cases as a way of training new men. I'm all for it. If he learns nothing else, he learns how to make a decision.

In turn, the fact that more of the work is individualized means that the young associate has more responsibility (although not on matters as measured by the money involved) and can show more initiative. Associates would commonly report: "I have a lot of responsibility. I take it because I want to be a partner. We have a lot of independence—no one is riding on your back. You work at your own pace and you have a diversified practice."

The men interviewed in the four firms under discussion generally feel that there are differences between their firms in terms of both types of practice and the milieu in which they do their legal work. Said one lawyer:

> I think we're different from the New York firms because we do not live with our clients. When you do, you tend to think like your client. They talk about Standard Oil as "We." The great men in New York are not that way though. We have different friends and different lives. We are not dependent on any client. No client gives us 10 per cent of our work. [New York firms make a similar claim.] I think that, therefore, we are independent. And one reason that we have succeeded is because we are independent. You'll find a pattern more like our firm in Houston, Philadelphia, and Chicago. The other big factor is that we emphasize litigation practice.

A partner in an out-of-New York firm who had worked for one of the large New York firms commented:

> They were roughly comparable in size to us but they do more day-to-day corporation work than we do. We do more trouble cases. They do bank work and corporate minutes. We do more day-to-day business advice. They represent big banks. Our firm is somewhat peculiar. In New York you have almost homogeneous groups. When I worked in N.Y., I worked on a big corporation merger. We are organized more haphazardly, but their hierarchy is grossly exaggerated. A lot of our young people are doing a lot of responsible work. They are much more satisfied. Here, anyone who is good has a chance of doing important work—you write your own letters, and you don't work in the abstract. You do things with the minimum of supervision.

An associate feels:

> I don't think I would like —— "R" (New York large firm), for example. Individuality is not stressed. You are not allowed to

develop on your own. You don't get credit and you do all the
work. Here, if you work on a brief, your name gets on it. [This
is sometimes true for New York firms as well.]

This firm is different because the kind of work is different. This
firm is not in competition with anyone. And there is a very unusual group of senior partners. You have a whole group of top
people and a likeable group. Maybe it's because this is a lawyer's
town.

A man who had worked in close cooperation with New York firms
was asked to compare his firm with the large Wall Street offices:

I was impressed by their formality and regimentation. This firm
is much more informal but this firm is becoming more formal. In
1948 it was in a period of rapid growth. It grew quickly. It had
a number of personnel problems which are old stories to the New
York firms. When I first came here things were informal. People
just got to know each other. Informal parties would spring up. At
X firm, for example, the boys told me that to be a partner you had
to be in the *Social Register*.

A partner from a Midwest firm describes some differences:

This firm is organized around fields of law, rather than by departments. The trouble with the large law firms in New York is
the tight hold they take. I don't think it makes for efficiency and
for personal contact. It does not produce proficient professional
men. Here everyone is treated like a professional man.

In New York they pay attention to the business a partner brings
in, allocate fees to individuals, and are inclined to prepare individuals to go to work for corporations. We don't think it right
that some should do the work and the rest of us get the gravy.
The percentage partners take the responsibility of guaranteeing
the salaries of the rest of the employees. No one grabs everything.
In terms of percentage, we're pretty evenly distributed.

Q. Does this mean that every partner gets the same percentage?

A. No, it means that no one here gets over 20 per cent, as they
do in some New York firms.

A senior partner was asked to compare his firm with the large New York firms, as far as the associates were concerned:

> We are different from them. We don't have the turnover. We are not as formal in terms of rules and we don't have too much supervision. We let the young man do his work. They all seem contented here. More of them make partner here. Some of this is changing. We just have become big; we started taking in young men in quantity after the war. Now we choose the best from Harvard, Chicago, and Michigan law schools. At one time, I knew all the men by their first names—now I don't know a lot of them. But we are much less formal than Q firm, for example.

A partner in a large firm in Ohio who had worked as an associate in a comparable firm in New York remarked about his leaving the New York office: "I felt a little as if I were leaving the big time. I was quite impressed by the aura of superefficiency, the high-priced talent and the big-name corporations. Of course, this all contributes to the Wall Street lawyer's own sense of importance."

Summary of Organizational Differences —

Although the comparison of large New York firms with large firms elsewhere does not keep size perfectly constant, size was nevertheless in most instances close enough to reveal that while it is important in determining organization format, by itself it does not account for a particular type of social structure. Similarities can be ascribed to the function of the organization as well. The primary function of all law firms is the practice of the law. Differences in practice, however, lead to variations in organization, so that while similarities in size call for similar housekeeping regulations, the lessened need for teamwork on the part of lawyers located outside of New York, limits the need for rules designed to help the team function.

Organizational differences between the compared firms occur because of other factors, although some of these are related to both size and function:

1. The location of a law office often determines some variation

in the kind of work obtained and that difference in need will reflect itself in organizational differences. Boston firms for example, have proportionately more trust and estate work than New York firms; Washington offices more litigation.

2. Age of a firm—and particularly the length of time it has been a large firm—affects its organization. Most offices out of New York have grown only recently and they are still growing. They are still experimenting and still trying to keep their old small firm ways. With age comes tradition, and tradition makes change difficult. In general, the large New York firms are older than the others (Ropes-Gray in Boston being a notable exception), and they have to contend with history to a greater degree. The longer a firm has been big, the more likely will it resemble the large New York firms' organizational styles—modified, of course, by the other circumstances mentioned.

3. The type of early leadership is important, for the powerful senior partner can set the tone of an office for years to come. This has been especially so for the "dictator" who leaves his stamp not only directly through his own leadership but also by choosing his successor.

4. The image a firm has of itself is also important. Those with a high self-image tend to try to live up to this image. And this is reflected in the kinds of briefs it turns out and in the kinds of men it hires. New York firms have high self-regard. Some of the others do not.

LARGE VS. SMALL LAW FIRMS

IN AN effort to determine the differences between large and small law offices that worked on similar kinds of matters, twenty small Wall Street type firms were studied. In all these small offices, at least one partner had had large law firm experience. In addition, every fourth office containing less than fifty lawyers, listed in the Manhattan section of the 1957 issue of the *Martindale-Hubbell Law Directory*, was analyzed.[14] This sample of 84 smaller New York firms produced 471 partners, 27 counsel, and 211 associates.[15] A comparison of the background of the lawyers in these small firms with those in the large offices reveals both similarities and differences. More lawyers in the small firms were born in New York City (40 per cent) or in the entire state (49 per cent), as compared to 28 and 39 per cent of the partners from large firms who were born in New York City or anywhere in New York State, respectively. This finding is logical, given the national characteristic of the large firms, their recruiting policies, and the local contacts necessary to start and sustain most smaller firms.

The *Directory* sample revealed that 55 per cent of the partners of small law organizations were graduates of Harvard, Yale, and Columbia law schools, compared to 71 per cent of the partners from the large firms. While this difference is important, equally important is the finding that 48 per cent[16] of the small firm partners went to local and night schools. Further investigation reveals that these lawyers did not go to the elite colleges in the same proportion, nor were they equally represented in the *Social Register*. Differences in the background of personnel were found for this sample. When the attorneys for the twenty Wall Street type small firms were studied in detail, the distinction between them and the large organizations' lawyers were not as great.

Origins of Small Law Firms —

This study was not designed to determine the origins of small firms. Yet, how they began is critical if their organizations are to be understood. The twenty firms studied, it is to be remembered, were not picked in a random fashion; they cannot be said to represent small firms in general but rather tend to represent small offices similar in practice to the large Wall Street firms. Even among this limited sample, however, we do find differences in how they began.

Friendships and consciousness of kind play their part in who belongs to a firm. It was not uncommon to find people who were friends joining together to start a practice. But more than friendship is necessary if a firm is to succeed. Business is of course one of the prime considerations. For members of these twenty firms, it came, initially, either from personal client contact or from work the large firms did not want or could not handle at a particular period. A senior partner for one of these small firms who had been an associate in a large firm explains how he started:

> As a result of having worked on—(magazine) matters—they were minor publications then—I was offered a job working for X newspaper. At twenty-nine, I was asked to represent the newspaper in a law firm. Another man, two years older than myself, started this firm with a couple of stenographers, an office boy and an investigator. Our main client was the newspaper. Now we have eight partners and six associates.

Some offices survive and prosper because of the business-getting ability of one partner. He decides to start a firm and picks his partners on the basis of the specializations he feels the work he brings in needs. Specialization, then, is another focal point for organization. One respondent pictures this situation:

> V was a tax lawyer with a great deal of business. Y left a large firm because he had always traveled around in society circles and did not want to work twelve to fifteen hours a day to get ahead. Besides, he was interested in people. He married the daughter of a wealthy man and he wanted a normal practice and a little more freedom. They decided they needed a real estate man and a litigator. R thought of me.

Most small firms try to have specialists in the major areas of the law. One partner reported: "We figured we needed corporation, litigation, tax and estate partners. Eventually, we added a transportation partner and took in another partner with no specialty." Some small firms, to obtain the men they need for their staff, merge with another small firm.

Satellite Firms —

Some small firms bud off from the large ones. Debevoise, Plimpton, Lyons & Gates is one of the most successful of these (and now [1964] is composed of seventy-six lawyers). It was started by two associates from the giant firm Davis Polk Wardell Sunderland &

Kiendl. In many instances the large firm supplies these smaller offices with clients and regards them as satellites:

> When we started we had no clients, but all of us came from the same large firm and we all had good reputations with that office. The large firm saw to it that we received business. One senior partner was fond of saying that it was the function of the big firm to spawn little firms.

This small firm now grosses roughly a million dollars a year. Overhead runs to about 50 per cent, so that the six partners netted $500,000.

One former associate with a large firm points out the connection between his present outfit, where he is a partner, and the giant office from which he came:

> I did a lot of anti-trust work for R firm [large office], and even now they send me work as if I were still there and a part of their shop. They say, when they get too busy, "Why not get Y [the respondent's firm] to take over a section of this." I know what they want done in that area [anti-trust]. In reality, when it comes to this area of the law, we are an adjunct to the old office.

Many of these spin-offs modeled their organization on that of the large firms. This was modified somewhat if a small firm had had a strong head who controlled the business. In these cases, his idiosyncratic notions could affect the organization. Small firms also varied somewhat from the large firm as a result of trial and error based on the need to get and keep clients, a much more difficult job for the small firm than for the large one.

While the satellite organizations provide the best example of small firms with large firm organizations, other microfirms also copy the large law office structure, although not as minutely. This is understandable for this particular sample of small firms, because at least one person in each of these organizations had had large firm experience.

A partner from an office which merged with another firm reports on their organization:

Since our original group had all come from the large law firms, we had adopted their ways and we were all specialists broken down into little departments. The people we merged with were used to doing everything for all their clients. What we did was to take on the best of both systems. While we still specialize, now most of us have spread out a little.

The work an organization must do in a similar culture probably determines its structure. The small Wall Street firms claim they do the same kind of work as the large offices, that only their clients are smaller. True, they admit they have proportionately more individual clients who come to them with a wider range of matters.[17] This fact alone produces changes in their organization which make them somewhat different than the larger firms. For example, they claim to be broader lawyers and not as tied to office divisions and specializations.

The following quotations from lawyers in small offices indicate these points:

The giant firms have the big banks and big industrial clients; we have mostly personal clients and small firms. We do not have one main area of specialization, but I would say we are primarily engaged in estates—that's my field. In estate work you get a variety of matters—business property, etc. You might have to see or administer it. We combine our real estate with our estate work. We also have a litigation group but we do practically no personal injury work; we do some negligence work if a client gets involved, but we don't take new clients on that basis. We also have a corporation and tax department. [Respondent was a member of a firm which had nine partners and seven associates.]

We have a broader practice than the large firms, but we do have embryo departments and do have some specialization. One partner does just estate and trust work, some others do a little of that kind of work also. The rest do a variety of things, mostly corporation work. One other partner does real estate work and one is a tax specialist. We have several fellows who can do litigation work and we do litigation for our regular clients but don't get any recommended. There is some subspecialization. For example, one partner does a lot of pension plan work. The others, mostly, are not specialized. [Respondent was a member of a firm which had ten partners and eight associates.]

We have the same kind of clients as the large law firm, but they are not as big. We feel we're big enough to take anything and still maintain a close relationship with the client. However, to do a big anti-trust case would be difficult because of the manpower needed. [Respondent was a member of a firm which had eight partners and eight associates.]

We specialize to this extent. One partner spends 80 per cent of his time on tax work. We have specialists in anti-trust. In fact, two of us work in this area. We have more personal clients than the large law firms. Our firm doesn't get SEC work—it is part of the large firm's regular business and it is not too profitable. It requires a department. It is an assembly line job and it is not worth while unless you have the volume. That kind of business goes to the firms set up to handle it. [Respondent was a member of a firm which had nine partners and seven associates.]

What we have is a general civil practice with miscellaneous litigation, corporate, tax and estate work. We also do some admiralty and international law practice. These first two fields will grow tremendously, as have other parts of our practice. I personally have a dozen life insurance companies who look to me, and three or four anti-trust cases. I do litigation all over the country. It isn't dull—my cases never involve just money. [Respondent was a member of a firm which had six partners and thirteen associates.]

There are some differences, then, in the kind of work these small Wall Street firms engage in, and there are differences in whom and how they recruit.

Departmentalization —

To the extent that small firms have specialties they are departmentalized. Lawyers in these firms, however, work in many areas of the law. When this happens, departments have little functional meaning. The exceptions, of course, occur when all the members of a small firm specialize in the same general area, say patent law, or where firms are large enough to keep a specialist busy.

Small offices are not as departmentalized as large ones. A partner from one of these firms makes this point:

> We departmentalize but not to the degree of the big firm. Here I may be the real estate office—in the big firm you may have five people on it. In addition, I find my clients expect me to know other areas of the law, and so I find myself practicing in areas outside of my specialty.

A partner in a small firm now and a former associate of a large one, makes this comparison:

> We aren't consciously compartmented. In the large law firms they are compartmentalized. They also tend to concentrate on an area within their department so that some one or two people will do mostly SEC work. Here there is some tendency to use the same man on similar problems, but so much depends upon whether or not he is busy at the time.
>
> Our young men get a more rounded practice of the law. They might not be as specialized in one field of the law, but with a little extra time they can do the same job as the specialist down-town.
>
> I think in the large law firm you get a good education in thoroughness and meticulousness and we try to observe that here.
>
> One of the small firm's good points—and one of its problems— is to have a congenial group. We make an effort to get a congenial staff on all levels.

The Pioneers —

The founders of these small firms are generally either local individuals who drift into partnership with other lawyers or ex-associates of large firms. Most of those interviewed came from the large offices. They left the giant offices because they couldn't stay or were discontented or wanted to form their own "shop." These pioneers have a great deal of courage because the competition in New York City is great. It is very difficult to take clients away from the large firms, and so business must come from personal contacts or through large firm sponsorship. The risk is great; one small firm partner tells of his experience:

> When you start a firm like this, you take a chance; it is a tremendous risk and responsibility. When you start a firm you have no wills to probate. There is money in the old firms because they have a backlog of this kind of business. The firm I left had a will box so big that two men had to lift it. You can't charge much to draw a will because you want to administer the estate after the person dies.

A partner from a small firm who was in his late fifties commented:

> People who leave the large offices to start their own law firms seem to have greater courage. I think, as much as anything, it takes courage. It may spring from ego—a man at the large firm finds his talents are not being fully utilized and leaves. That is not why I left. I left because I had a good opportunity. The men who stay downtown and become partners are still regarded as boys and not to be entrusted with the full range of responsibility. When I was there, the older partners used to bawl them out. I'm sure this isn't done much anymore. A different approach to people is made now.

Recruitment —

Men who come into a small firm after it is founded are of three sorts: (1) specialists, who come from the large law firms or the government; (2) lawyers from the outside who come as partners because they can bring significant business with them; (3) young associates just out of law school. A good deal of recruitment is on a personal level. An associate from one of these small firms who had graduated from Harvard and from the University of Virginia Law School, where he had been on the law review, reveals that his firm used many recruitment approaches:

I met Mr. X [head of the firm he joined] when I was on my honeymoon. He was in the process of setting up this firm. While I went to see other firms and one of the large ones did offer me a job, I did not seriously consider any other job. However, we do not hire all our associates directly from law school. Recently, we hired a litigation and a tax associate. One had worked for a judge, another with a corporation. Recently our new people have come to us with experience. The reason for that is that we as a small firm have to hire people when we need them. The partners who come from large law firms would like to have people right out of law school.

Those offices which do get most of their associates from law schools report they have difficulty in obtaining the best graduates. One senior partner observes:

We get our associates from law schools in competition with other firms, unless we need a man to fill a vacancy where experience is needed. We pay the going rate [this is not true of all such firms] but still find it difficult to get law review men.

A partner from a satellite firm complains: "We try to get associates from Harvard, Yale, and Columbia. We have trouble getting them, because many of the best want to go to the large firms. However, some prefer small firms and we do get a few."

The older and more successful a small Wall Street type firm becomes, the more it is inclined to attract Wall Street type associates. Still in many ways they are not as homogeneous as those in large offices. They are recruited from a wider variety of law schools. All of them do not go through the firm's socialization process from the beginning, since many start at advanced positions. Their dress is not as formal as those of their large firm colleagues and they do not seem as socially conforming.

Partnership Agreements —

As we shall see in some detail in the next chapter, written partnership agreements are becoming more and more the norm for law firms. They constitute one part of the formal organization of these offices and generally cover arrangements dealing with percentages for partners, distribution of property (if that becomes necessary), determination of final authority, and disposition of the firm name if a split in the firm occurs. In comparing large and small firms, it is important to note whether small firms tend as often as large ones to have partnership agreements and in what detail, for this may be considered an indication of the rigidity of an organization. The satellite firms tend not to have written partnership agreements; when they do, the agreements are brief, following the pattern set by the larger offices. A partner in one of the smaller firms quotes a member of the larger one he had worked for in an effort to explain his own firm's lack of a formal agreement: "We do not have a partnership agreement. Mr. De Gersdorff of Cravath used to say, 'We don't want people for partners with whom we need written agreements.'"

Other small firms draw their agreements in more detail than do the large law offices. This is especially so for offices which do not take the large firms for their model. Members of small offices which grew not out of friendships but from the "accident" of sharing office space may lack knowledge of their partners and their partners' wives and feel additional protection is needed.

Rules —

A sociological guess would have it that small firms have fewer rules than large firms. This is not necessarily so. The satellites have regulations similar to those of the larger offices. An associate from one of these smaller organizations makes this point:

> This firm was designed to be a small Cravath. We use the same forms, the same kind of paper and routing techniques, even though it is costly. Each of us keeps a daily record of our time. Office hours are from 9:30 to 5:30. Associates are here between 9 and 10 and leave anywhere from 6 to 10 P.M.

While these firms have rules, they don't, as far as can be judged from the flimsy evidence available, obey them religiously. Here the informal aspects seem to function. An associate gets to know a partner better; permission to break rules is more easily granted.

The small partnerships which do not have primary models seem to have fewer rules, except for the formal regulations of the partnership agreements. Evidence that associates can on occasion sign opinion letters—a sin for the associate in the large firm—has been cited. Fewer rules are needed to protect against conflict of interest, since the clients are not so large and intricate and it is easier for everyone to spot possible trouble. The fact that a firm is small means it cannot and may not have to train men in the same way as the large offices must. This relieves the small firm of the necessity of making rules which deal with training.

And since the lawyers know one another and know what is going on, it is easier for them to improvise. The large firm can't afford this luxury to the same extent.

Power —

These smaller firms, like the large ones, are divided into partners and associates. Power resides with the people who control or bring in the business. Many small firms depend, at least initially, on one man to attract clients. Although this was also true of some of the larger firms, this dependency tends to be modified as inherited stable business is distributed among the partners. In the small office, the client is more nearly the "property" of the individual lawyer than of the firm. These facts lead to proportionately more one-man control in the small offices.

Another device tending to keep power constant is that many small firms, like the large out-of-town offices, have a policy of making some attorneys nonpercentage partners. There do not seem to be as many firm meetings as in the large organizations. This is understandable. When firms are small, ideas can be exchanged easily. In terms of power, one man can know what is going on in a small firm; if he has the clients, he can control the firm.

Other Differences Between Large and Small Firms —

Lawyers in smaller firms feel they are given more responsibility than those in the large offices. One reason for their saying this is that they have to rely on their own knowledge more than large firm lawyers who can always call on a specialist. As one partner in a small firm, who had been an associate in a large one, puts it:

One of the attractions of a small firm is that an associate sees more live clients. We do not run everything into the ground to the extent they do—we don't spend as much time writing, researching, or reading. We take small chances. The large firms have specialists we can't afford. We cover it by experience—our staff doesn't change as much as theirs. Our people get responsibility early. Their people spend a lot of time in the library.

Another partner from still another small firm points out the individual nature of this responsibility: "I went to a closing where the other firm was [a large firm]. They took five people along; I took myself—I didn't need anyone else. I had done the entire job."

An additional reason offered by these lawyers for their claim of being given greater responsibility than the Wall Street lawyers is based on the fact that in most small firms (though this is not true of all the satellite firms or of the very prosperous offices) associates are allowed to bring in clients. There is a tendency for the lawyer working on his own clients to receive less supervision and to take the initiative on the matter. How well he handles the situation is reflected in his ability to keep the client and this is further reflected in his salary or a bonus. If he brings in enough business which he can control, he has found a way of increasing his independence. Perhaps the difference in the kinds of clients small and large law firms attract is indicated by the fact, as Lortie[18] points out, that lawyers in small firms are active in political life (a technique which may attract clients, but usually small ones), whereas lawyers from larger firms frown on this activity but are active in professional associations (a possible technique to obtain colleague-preferred clients and to increase a lawyer's attractiveness to the sophisticated taste of large clients).

Optimum Size —

Many lawyers have theories about a law firm's optimum size. Attorneys in smaller firms generally feel their organization should be slightly larger; those in the largest firms think theirs should be somewhat smaller. A former associate of one of these giant organizations, who is now a partner in a ten-man firm, throws some light on the difference between large law firms and small ones, while giving his views on the optimum size of a firm:

> The best size for law firms is somewhere in the neighborhood of twenty lawyers. The considerations are these: The lawyers are a workable group. They know each other socially and are happy together. I don't like the impersonality that creeps into many organizations. Below that number you can't have the proper number of specialists. A firm of twenty enables you to give the client the same kind of service offered by the large law firm.

The importance of size is brought out by a partner in a large firm:

> When you get down to fifty lawyers, you bring in the element of bringing in business. And when you get down to a firm of thirty, you have to be able to bring it in and to hold it. The really large firms make their members from people who are not social, who don't bring in business. They are work horses—they have gone ahead on sheer ability.

Now let us look more closely at the organization of the large New York law firms.

NOTES

1. Jerome E. Carlin and members of the Columbia Law School are currently working on a detailed study of the New York City Bar. Some preliminary material from that study has been mimeographed. Jerome E. Carlin, *Current Research in the Sociology of the Legal Profession* (New York: Bureau of Applied Social Research, Columbia University, 1962).

2. Jerome E. Carlin, *Lawyers on Their Own* (New Brunswick, N.J.: Rutgers University Press, 1962).

3. *Ibid.*, pp. 206–210.

4. Albert P. Blaustein, Charles O. Porter, with Charles T. Duncan, *The American Lawyer, A Summary of the Survey of the Legal Profession* (Chicago: University of Chicago Press, 1954), p. 11.

5. Carlin, *Current Research*, pp. 20–21.

6. Carlin, *Lawyers on Their Own*, p. 201.

7. Among those expressing views similar to those held by the solo lawyers are: Adolph A. Berle, Jr., *Encyclopaedia of the Social Sciences* (New

York: Macmillan, 1948), Vol. 9, p. 341; and C. Wright Mills, *White Collar* (New York: Oxford University Press, 1951), pp. 121–129.

8. The firm of Paul, Weiss, Rifkind, Wharton & Garrison, currently composed of eighty attorneys, is consciously made up of approximately a like number of Jewish and gentile lawyers.

9. David Riesman, "Toward an Anthropological Science of Law and the Legal Profession," *American Journal of Sociology*, 57 (September 1951), 133. The author lucidly states: "On the face of it, these lawyers were worldly men, or at least worldly-wise; behind their backs, in their unconscious, operated motives of an unworldly sort they would have done their best to deny. Perhaps something of what Veblen called 'the instinct of workmanship' was also at work here, some desire to do a good job apart from any immediate audience. These non-utilitarian elaborations go on in the law—our office was not unique, though it may have been extreme—not in the search of justice but in search of something which transcends even justice, some kind of quest of the absolute, some kind of art for art's sake. Indeed, I am fairly sure that something of the same sort happens in all occupations, but the lawyer is perhaps less able than others to conceal his intellectual orgies."

10. The seventeen firms are: in California—*Gibson, Dunn & Crutcher* and *O'Melveny & Meyers* (Los Angeles); *Pillsbury, Madison & Sutro* and *McCutchen, Doyle, Brown & Enersen* (San Francisco); in Washington, D.C.—*Covington & Burling*; in Illinois—*Kirkland, Ellis, Hodson, Chaffetz & Masters*, and *Mayer, Friedlich, Spiess, Tierney, Brown & Platt* and *Winston, Strawn, Smith & Patterson* (Chicago); in Massachusetts—*Ropes & Gray* (Boston); in Ohio—*Jones, Day, Cockly & Reavis* and *Squire, Sanders & Dempsey* (Cleveland); in Pennsylvania—*Morgan, Lewis & Bockius* and *Peper, Hamilton & Scheetz* (Philadelphia) *Reed, Smith, Shaw & McClay* (Pittsburgh); in Texas—*Vinson, Elkins, Weems & Searls* and *Baker, Botts, Shephard & Coates* and *Fulbright, Crooker, Freeman, Bates & Jaworski* (Houston). (Now, 1964, there are 23 firms.)

11. Charles Horsky, *The Washington Lawyer* (Boston: Little, Brown, 1952), p. 30.

12. The Boston firm and a Philadelphia office did not list place of birth in the *Martindale-Hubbell Law Directory* and could not be counted in the percentage of those born in the states involved. The Washington, D.C., firm was not counted since it is not located in a state. Associates were not tabulated since most firms do not list them or do not list them accurately.

13. The ratio of associates to partners based on figures from 19 large New York firms is a little more than 2 to 1. Accurate data for one large out-of-town firm indicate that, if the term partner includes both full partners and nonpercentage partners, the ratio is fewer than 1 associate to 1 partner. If nonpercentage partners are excluded, the ratio is 1½ associates to 1 partner.

14. While every fourth firm listed in the *Martindale-Hubbell Law Di-*

rectory ([Rahway, N.J.: Quinn and Boden, 1957], Vol. II), cannot be said to represent all New York small firms or Wall Street type small firms because all firms do not list themselves in the *Directory,* this fact skews the sample in the direction of the Wall Street type firm. It does this because there is a greater predisposition for offices which have or want a "business" practice to list themselves in the *Directory.*

15. The material on associates is not accurate, for not all law offices list them. There is also a question of what is meant by the word "associate," a question which never arose when dealing with large firms. As one partner of a small organization (seven partners and five associates) put it: "First let's define our terms. What do you mean by an associate? We don't call our people that—we employ them. There are a number of meanings to the word. An associate can be the man who shares office expenses; he can be an employee; he can be an expert you call on occasionally. It depends on the set-up." Because of these difficulties, comparisons based on these data between large and small firm lawyers will refer to partners only.

16. This figure includes both Columbia and New York University law schools.

17. The sample of small firms taken from the *Martindale-Hubbell Law Directory* reveals that they list a wider variety of matters than do the large firms. Seventy-seven of the eighty-four small firms studied say they are engaged in general practice. All but thirty-nine, however, list other areas of practice as well. The most popular areas are trademarks, patents, unfair competition, copyrights, litigation, corporation law, estates and trusts, tax law and real estate.

18. Dan C. Lortie, "The Striving Young Lawyer: A Study of Early Career Differentiation in the Chicago Bar" (Ph.D. dissertation, The University of Chicago, August 1958, microfilmed).

EIGHT

ORGANIZATION OF THE

LARGE LAW FIRM

MORE than twenty law firms in New York City now have fifty or more lawyers either as partners or associates on their staffs. Variations in their organizational structure exist, of course. Each has some organizational distinction, its own "personality," and its minor unique physical characteristics. One firm, for example, has decked itself out with modern furniture, a radical departure from the usual decor. Another had a special "secret" elevator which connected it with one of its major clients. Some offices are air-conditioned, some are not; one prefers to employ male stenographers, the others do not. These are minor matters. The firms have more similarities than differences. They all seem to have combined the atmospheres of a university, offices for a group of physicians or a "Mayo type clinic," a country law firm, and a big business.

The fact that this combination of atmospheres prevails is not too surprising, in light of the history of the growth of the large law firms and the attitudes of its various practitioners. The researchers poring over their books in the large library, which usually dominates the office, compare the firm to the university. Even to the outsider the scholastic climate is readily observable.

The client is in many ways like the patient in that both seek advice and both fear the unknown. Both come to a place where "treatment" is readily available, as are specialists if the general practitioner does not have the answer. The litigators go a little further with this analogy and compare themselves to surgeons. They claim that when they are in the courtroom, medicine (or in their case preventive law) has failed and the drastic step of surgery is necessary. The courtroom then becomes the operating room for the lawyer. The law firm is where the litigator prepares and scrubs up for his "surgery."

Many of the oldtimers and some of the new men like to think of themselves as part of small firms in small towns where clients can come in and talk at leisure; these people create a little of the atmosphere of the country law firm. They keep their doors open. They sometimes serve tea. They ask you to "drop around any time." They decorate their offices with pictures of Lincoln and some old-fashioned furniture. They "pretend" they are in general practice. Few like to admit they resemble big business. However, they do and they recognize it. This recognition is seen in the way they organize their nonprofessional staff. The businesslike atmosphere is emphasized by the constant ring of the autocall paging missing lawyers, or by a view of the rows of offices running down the long corridors, or by the meticulous way in which the files are kept.

Location —

The firms usually house their 50 to 125 [in 1964, 158] lawyers and 100 to 230 nonprofessional workers on three or four consecutive floors in the Wall Street district,[1] preferably on Broad or Wall Street (some have recently moved to 1 Chase Manhattan Plaza— a large new building located in the heart of the Wall Street district) and near their main banking client. Occasionally, a firm will be forced to take space in another building or on a floor away from the main offices. If and when they can, however, they quickly remedy this because it affects the organization of their firm. Since law firms come close to making a fetish about keeping papers, more file space is required than is available in the Wall Street area and additional storage space is usually leased in a cheaper rent district. At one time firms had European offices (currently there seems to be more interest on the part of large firms for European branches). Swaine talks, for example, of the Cravath Paris office of 1927–1934, of which he says: "Unlike most of the others [Cravath's Paris office] . . . did not seek business from local or visiting Americans, but operated almost entirely as a facility of the home office in connection with security issues."[2] According to the 1962 *Martindale-Hubbell Law Directory*, only three firms— Cahill, Gordon, Reindel & Ohl; Mudge, Stern, Baldwin, & Todd; White & Case—maintain foreign offices—many firms also had Washington offices, though this is no longer as true. However, most of them now have what they call Washington Correspondents. These are independent or semi-independent small law firms which do some of the Washington work for large New York firms and also provide a desk and some services to the New York lawyer when he comes to the Capitol. Not all partnerships do this, and a few still maintain their Washington branch office. Breed, Abbott & Morgan; Chadbourne, Parke, Whiteside & Wolff; Simpson Thacher & Bartlett; and Paul, Weiss, Rifkind, Wharton & Garrison have Washington offices, and the latter firm also maintained one in Chicago[3] until 1961.

Law Firm Names —

Large law firms usually use as their identification the names of two, three, four, or five of their partners—dead or alive; never one or six names and usually three, four or five. When one phones for an appointment, the operator acknowledges the call by using an abbreviated version of the firm's name; for example, Davis-Polk for Davis Polk Wardwell Sunderland & Kiendl. It is a rare honor to be a name partner, and one which can cause conflict among the partners, although the question rarely comes up because the turn-over among these members is not great. There is also a tendency to keep the names of deceased partners. The firm, for example, which was headed by John Foster Dulles and now by Arthur Dean is still called Sullivan & Cromwell. The names of the firms are essentially trade names and they have monetary and prestige value. Usually the name partners appear horizontally on the office door, with the remaining partners listed vertically. Associates are not listed; the tenure of many is too limited. Furthermore, associates do not own a share of the firm nor are they liable for its mistakes.

Description of a Law Office —

An open entrance door would generally disclose a large wall-to-wall carpeted reception room complete with an attractive, capable, female receptionist. Her main job is to direct clients to the proper lawyer and to keep track of these attorneys. She sits next to a machine which lists the name of each attorney and registers where he is. The receptionist has four mechanical possibilities—she can record the lawyer as (1) not in yet, (2) in, (3) will return, and (4) out to lunch. The machine is connected with the message center and lights up a board so that the telephone operators know where the lawyer may be reached. Firms which have not as yet adopted this automatic device do the same task by hand.

The waiting room, when it is separate from the reception room, is smaller. The walls may be decorated with Vanity Fair caricatures of members of the legal profession, lithographs of famous English barristers and American attorneys, judges, and other important figures in the law. Some firms hang photographs of deceased partners on the walls. The room is always freshly supplied with copies of *Time*, *Life*, perhaps a boating magazine, and the *New York Times* and *Herald Tribune*.

Stairways connect the maze of offices and the library. Some firms have a large stairway connecting at least two of the floors of the firm. Usually an office has two libraries, a large general one and one dealing specifically with tax law. Most of these macro-firms claimed to have the largest private law library in the world— and they all were large. However, a compilation of law libraries reveals that Davis Polk Wardwell Sunderland & Kiendl has the largest private library, with a total in 1960 of 30,776 volumes.[4] Cravath, Swaine & Moore was next with 26,000[5] books.

Individual offices of the partners show individual tastes. Some are unornamented, tidy, and plain. Others have a museum-like quality, complete with original furnishings dating back to the 1800's, a wall full of pictures, many books, a George Washington desk, a sofa and chairs. The desks run from antique to modern Miller. Although decorators are usually employed to design the offices, individual tastes come through. Most offices have pictures which are personal to the occupant. Photographs of wife and children are usually on the desk. The autographed photo of the supreme or other important judge for whom a lawyer has clerked appeared on the bookcase. All the offices had the soft comfortable chair which seems to be almost as essential to the lawyer as the couch is to the psychiatrist.

Office Space Allocated on the Basis of Status —

Large law firms are generally not organized physically on a production line basis, except for some members of the nonprofessional staff. For example, it is rare to find all the men in one department housed near each other, although occasional department heads have insisted on this arrangement. Even if space were not assigned by department, it would seem appropriate for a partner and his associates to be close to each other. This is not the case. Time is sometimes wasted walking from one floor to another in search of the next man on the "team." Distribution of office space is not made haphazardly, however. It is allocated on the basis of custom and status. The size, location, and decor of a room become to a law firm what generals' stars and sergeants' stripes are to the army. They are symbols of status; they tell the newcomer how to behave; they make relationships easier because they provide clues to status. They also are rewards for service and success.

Custom and power have ordained that the senior partners generally have the largest rooms (and an adjoining room for a secretary) with the best view of New York's harbor. Courtesy and the recognition that inevitably everyone grows old guarantees that a very old partner, no longer in power, retains his large office, even though he is not currently "earning" it. Younger members, as expected, have smaller offices. A senior associate has his own room and a secretary who may work just outside his office or come to him from a central secretarial pool.

Generally, a relationship can be found between age, power, and the value of a man to a law firm (although there is a point where this diminishes). This relationship reveals itself in the housing of the younger lawyers. As expected, the younger the attorney, the fewer accouterments he receives—the poorest view, the least secretarial help, and the smallest room. A beginning lawyer is usually placed in a pool or "bull pen" with five or six other attorneys. He may stay there as long as a year. When he graduates from the pool he is assigned to share an office with another colleague. By tradition, the one who has been with the firm longer sits next to the window. In some firms he is called, and not inappropriately, the "window man." The younger lawyer is placed nearest the door and is labeled the "door man." The window man has the responsibility of teaching the door man the ropes and helping him with the law when possible. At one time, firms would merely place older and younger lawyers in the same room regardless of the kind of work they were doing. Now, with the increased importance of specialization, some firms who use this system are beginning to place together older and younger associates who are working on the same matter, or who are in the same department.

Attempts to place as a physical unit a number of lawyers, both partners and associates who are functioning in the same area of the law, is the exception rather than the rule. In one firm, the separation between partners and associates was so great that each of these categories had its own men's room. To be fair, neither the partners nor the associates said they thought of this as a deliberate attempt to keep the firm status conscious. However, when associates were asked if they would use the partners' bathroom (no one had told them not to), they felt it would not be proper. "We have our own on our floor."

FORMAL ORGANIZATION

NOT all is left to tradition, habit, and laissez-faire power struggles. Large law firms do have formal organizations. Partnership agreements constitute their most formal aspect. These agreements have become increasingly necessary for tax reasons, and because the law forbids professional people (to protect the client and implement libel laws) who are working together in the practice of their profession to incorporate. Capital, according to the Internal Revenue Code of 1954, is not a major producing factor in a law firm, and members cannot decide to be taxed as a corporation. It would be thought by many to be unethical. At one time even partnerships in the law were considered unethical, and the hiring of other lawyers was frowned upon.

Nevertheless, the number of partnerships continues to increase. There are innumerable forms of partnership and partnership agreements. Still, there are some sections of these agreements which seem common to most of them. It is primarily these provisions which will be discussed here.

Reluctance to Draft Agreements —

It may seem strange that lawyers who are trained to draft protective instruments for their clients should be reluctant to do the same for themselves. Some even seem ashamed to admit that they have a written understanding. A spokesman for one firm boasted: "We leave out of it [partnership agreement] more than we put in because we feel that this is a group of gentlemen, and a partnership is based on mutual trust." A partner in another organization was proud of the fact that the agreement in his office was "just a page long." One extremely well-known law office does not even have a formal written agreement, although it does have a series of principles which are presented in the form of memoranda.[6] When asked if a more formal accord would not serve their purpose better, the respondent replied: "No, everybody trusts everybody here. Besides, we have experience and precedent to guide us." This firm and many other large old offices regard themselves as special institutions. It is not unusual for them to liken themselves to the British government. They claim that an equivalent to common law grows up in the organization and is passed along and accepted by the new members. It is sort of a continuing gentlemen's agreement. When a partner was asked what happens to a member's share in the firm when he retires or dies (one of the more serious problems of professional partnership), this reply gave further credence to the idea that the law firm was a little like a government in that it had continuity, and that property belongs to the membership:

No one has property in good will or physical rights in the firm. What is being liquidated is the debts that we owe him and his share of what he had been working on. We don't pay to get into the firm and property does not exist for us.

There are other reasons why some firms feel that they do not need written agreements. Perhaps the major one is based on a careful selection process. The rigor of this selection cuts down the number of undesirables and makes formal partnership agreements less necessary. Because of this selectivity and because it usually is economically not preferable, there are few split-ups among modern large firms. Professional tradition probably also influences this reluctance, since it tends to strengthen feelings of fraternity and ingroupness.

Partnership Agreements —

Most firms do have formal partnership agreements. Tax experts say that more of them will have to formalize their agreements if they expect to take advantage of tax benefits. Those that do have formal understandings are most reluctant to talk about them. "I don't think anyone will let you see it," was a common remark which I heard during my research. Some partners were willing to talk about their agreements but not to show them: "I can't, of course, tell you specifically about ours, but I can tell you, in a general way, what it covers." Despite this understandable reluctance, some information was obtained from respondents, and, in addition, numerous articles have been written about what a partnership agreement should contain. A picture of these agreements does emerge.

Agreements differ somewhat in each firm. Some offices include the exact percentage of the profits each partner is to receive in the agreement; others do not. Because percentages change, they are set forth in a separate arrangement. Other differences occur because many were written after some problem occurred; to the extent then, that problems differ by firms, so do the agreements. Two examples offer some idea of why firms have decided to write their agreements and why they differ somewhat:

> We don't have one [partnership agreement] yet; what we have is in draft, but we decided we needed one. After the senior partner died—his wife thought that it was his firm since he was the main partner in it—it caused some needless irritation.

Until a few years ago, we never had a written agreement. The truth of the matter is, we did not know what we were entitled to. We were getting so big, we did not know when some widow would take it into her head to sue us, and then there were tax considerations. We decided to make it [partnership agreement] formal.

Most professional partnership agreements try to take care of three principle problem areas by defining the rights and duties of the partners during the existence of the partnership; the rights of the parties at the time the partnership terminates for one of them by death or retirement, or if more than one of the members want to split-up or in other ways dissolve the firm; what firm income is and how it is to be distributed. The third area is delineated in response to the problem of defining rights and also to implement the relationship with the Internal Revenue Bureau. Subsumed under these three broad areas may be many clauses designed to ease some of the situations which might cause conflict.

Among the questions the partnership agreement tries to answer, generally at the beginning of the document, is the question of what constitutes the practice of law—a very important query and, as we have seen, not easy to answer. It is a question of moment because it involves what is to be considered firm income. The distribution of income is one of the major sources of potential conflict in law firms. One sample partnership agreement lists the types of income which go into the firm. In one sense the agreement is therefore defining what the partners consider subsumed in the practice of the law. The contract reads:

The types of incomes which shall be considered income from the practice of law: directors' fees, executors, administrators, guardians, conservators' fees, salaries as officer of a corporation, fees and compensation of any public or semi-public office, royalties from the sale of books, magazines, articles and pamphlets, salaries, fees and honoraria for speeches and teaching engagements and expense allowances in connection with any of the foregoing, less the amount of expenses actually incurred.

It is easy enough to see how conflict might occur between the lawyer who teaches at a law school at night on what he might consider his own time, and his partners who think that any income from the law must go into the partnership. Other questions in this same area come to mind. Can a partner engage in any practice which is not connected with the firm? How much work shall each partner do? How long a vacation can he take? If he doesn't take a vacation one year, is the time applicable to the following year? What should a partner's income be if he becomes sick or disabled or is called into the army or other government service? What happens if he wants to do less work?

Questions involving bookkeeping and how profits are to be determined and distributed must also be answered. Since there seems to be an almost infinite number of ways of dividing income in a law office, this question is exceedingly meaningful. Generally, large law firms divide profits on a percentage basis. This raises a number of related questions, among them: Who decides how the pie is to be divided? When are percentages to be brought up for reconsideration?

Additionally, the members of a firm must decide how they expect to pay a retired partner. If they pay him one way, it can be considered a capital transaction. If he is paid a second way, it can be thought of as an income transaction. The way an estate or retired partner is paid then has income tax implications. These are sometimes taken care of in partnership agreements. Arthur B. Willis, writing about income tax problems of the professional partnership, states:

> In the tax planning for a professional partnership the matters of principal concern are the problems relating to unrealized receivable of the partnership and the proper drafting of provisions to cover the death or retirement of a partner. There is considerable overlap between the two since the handling of unrealized receivables is one of the primary considerations in connection with payments to a retiring or deceased partner.[7]

Often other areas of potential conflict are dealt with in the partnership agreement. For example, when does a firm take in new partners? Who decides whom the new partners are to be? What kinds of partners—limited or participating? Who shall determine the merits of a conflict? Shall it be a senior partner, an executive committee, an outside person, or the majority of the firm? If there is to be an executive committee, who decides the membership? Who is to manage the firm? How are the books of the partnership to be kept? In the event of a "split," who keeps the name of the firm and its good will? What is a proper business expense? Who shall be allowed to sign checks? In what amount? What clients can a departing partner take with him? What files does he have a right to have? What property is divisible?[8]

Sample partnership agreements usually cover the following areas:

Recitals: including the understanding that "the parties hereto agree to continue their partnership under the laws of the State of New York and under the following terms and conditions":

1. Name and place of business.
2. Purpose of the partnership.
3. Capital contributions, accounts and withdrawals.
4. Profits and losses.
5. Management; salaries.
6. Disability and military service of a partner.
7. Dissolution because of retirement, death or permanent disability of a partner.
8. Voluntary dissolution.
9. Partners' powers and limitations.
10. Miscellaneous.[9]

Most of the above items are suggested by the Uniform Partnership Act which is in force in New York, and by the Internal Revenue Code. Not all items are always covered; sometimes additional items are included in keeping with the history of an individual firm.

Other Formal Rules —

The rules of the partnership agreement are not the only formal regulations enacted by the law firms. In most large legal organizations a new lawyer is given a "Memorandum on Office Practice." This manual usually explains the office organization and management, special rules of concern to lawyers, and the functions of the various service departments. Each lawyer is given this book of instruction and each lawyer promptly forgets most of the rules and often loses the manual, partly because they dislike formal rules (they feel they are restrictive and somehow not professional) and partly because so many guides to correct behavior are found in custom and the informal rules of the firm.

Recognizing this dislike for formal regulations, it is common to minimize and sugarcoat them in order to make rules more palatable—a procedure so successful that lawyers, when asked to list the firm's rules, were hard pressed to think of many. This forgetfulness was probably bolstered by their desire to forget and because the repetitious following of them blurred regulations until they were not considered rules at all. One associate, when asked what rules his firm had, replied, "There are no rules at all. Well there are rules about when to take a vacation, what kinds of paper to use in the office—but these are all logical." Another lawyer who had at first been unable to think of any organizational prescriptions, retreated from this view: "Did I say there were no written rules? Come to think of it there is a memo on how to write a memo. I don't think anyone has paid any attention to it. These memos pretty nearly fall into a form anyway." Another young attorney noticed, "When they make rules the system always breaks down. If they suggest forms, they are forms you would normally follow anyway."

Lawyers took pride in not following or recognizing formal rules. Associates who adhered strictly to the regulations are derogatorily known as "the 9:30 to 5:30 boys." One formal rule ignorer reports: "Our office opens at 9:30 and closes at 5:30, but I've never had the sense of having to be there; I would, however, get in between 9:30 and 10:30. Almost from the beginning you are the master of your schedule. But we do have demands to keep our date-line and if we have to, we work Saturdays and Sundays."

Clerical Regulations —

Despite the attitude of many associates and some partners, some formal rules exist. Not all firms have all the rules discussed below. Certainly not all the regulations were mentioned, and those discussed differ in the degree to which they are obeyed. Some lawyers find most rules especially easy to follow because they rationalize, "They are really for the clerical help." One example deals with clerical rules. These are numerous and some are esoteric. A senior associate cites the following:

> If you write a letter to someone other than someone you have a telephone conversation with, you begin it "Dear Sir" and end "Very truly yours" and the firm name. If you say "Dear Mr. Jones," you end the letter "Sincerely yours," and your name.

A typical "Memorandum on Office Practice" lists many other rules; the following are common:

1. A heading should be dictated to the stenographer for each letter in order to expedite the filing of the routine carbon copies (pink copy for the File Room; green copy for the Mail Room). If the heading is to be omitted from the original, so instruct the stenographer who will make an appropriate notation on the pink and green copies to that effect. If more than one subject heading appears, a pink copy should be made for each subject.

2. For travel money and for expenses on occasions where the amount and possibly the account to be charged is unknown at the time, cash is advanced on a "temporary voucher," which is replaced later with a definitive voucher.

3. When each matter is finished the senior member of the legal staff working on the job must see to it that the files are gone over either by himself or someone else working on the job to be sure that the office file is complete. . . . It is of first importance that the office file shall contain copies of all final documents in connection with the job, and that copies of final documents are correctly conformed to show the exact manner of execution.

4. No papers in any litigated matter should be served or used or sent to the files before they have been referred to the Managing Clerk.

It is impossible here even to begin to present all the details involved in clerical work, or the rules that go with them. Some files in older firms go back more than a hundred years. Many different colored papers are needed and letter forms used. While most of this work remains the duty of the clerical staff, final responsibility rests with the lawyer.

Rules for Personnel —

While our primary interest is in the lawyer, rules promulgated to regulate the behavior of nonprofessional personnel affect the professional as well. As stated by one attorney: "We would still be regularly working Saturdays if the nonlegal staff worked Saturdays. Stenographers just won't come in on Saturday without extra pay." The firm has a number of specific rules for its nonprofessional personnel. Not so convenient for the lawyer as the above example are the following regulations: "Files should be requested before 5:00 P.M.," slightly before the time the nonprofessional leaves his work in one firm. Or another rule which, on paper at least, reverses the hierarchy:

> All letters and papers sent to the File Department must be properly marked by the lawyers for filing. *The File Department will reject and return to the lawyer in charge of the matter all letters and documents not properly marked.*

Numerous other examples of rules designed for nonprofessional personnel which affect the professional staff might be cited. What is important is that these same rules affect the lawyer's behavior. Some of the process of bureaucratization starts from below and changes the organization by affecting the behavior of those above. Norms meant primarily for the stenographer become restrictions for the counselors.

There are, of course, regulations designed specifically for the lawyer—usually for the associate, although they are not always so designated. Some are similar to those listed for the nonprofessional people. This is understandable since co-ordination between the various staffs is important. One firm states in its rule book:

> Office hours for lawyers are traditionally elastic and according to reputation the hours of lawyers in our office are particularly so. Our office hours commence at 9:30 and the entire organization is

geared accordingly. To run the office effectively there must be co-ordination between the lawyers and the service staff, and the service staff is set up to handle a normal day commencing at 9:30. Moreover, most of our clients start their business day at 9 o'clock and it is frequently embarrassing when lawyers are not on hand to handle calls when they start coming in.

Some firms are more definite about office hours. One specifically states: "Members of the legal staff are expected to reach the office by 9:30 A.M. and to stay until 5:30 P.M. . . ." All of them expect the lawyers to report their arrival and departure to the receptionist. For the associates, this regulation comes under the category of "keeping clients happy." Clients like to be able to contact their lawyers when they feel they need them. To please the client and to keep track of associates, law firms require their attorneys to tell the receptionist where they are. Since this rule is not always obeyed, the firms make it convenient for attorneys to report in and out by having the receptionist take note of their movements. One lawyer, in fact, had reversed the situation in his mind so that his coming and going became the responsibility of the receptionist. An office rule book noted:

> It is of utmost importance that everybody leaving the office advise the receptionist of: (1) his destination, (2) length of time he expects to be away from the office, and (3) whether he can be reached. If a lawyer, for some reason, is unable to advise the receptionist of his absence, it is the responsibility of his secretary to notify her. Each secretary is also responsible for telephoning the receptionist daily at 9:20 A.M. if the lawyer for whom she works is absent for any reason.

In the same vein, whenever a lawyer is to be away from the office for any length of time, he must leave a memorandum telling where he will be, when he will return, and how he can be reached.

Vacations are also subject to the same procedure, and the rules often state that the legal staff is entitled to a four-week vacation if conditions permit. But vacations are not cumulative. And the lawyer on leave will have left his vacation address and the needed information about the matters he was handling.

Rules about assignments and rotation of personnel for training reasons are common to most firms. They will be or have been discussed in other contexts. Another regulation found on the books of many large law firms deals with the right of the individual lawyer to practice outside of the law firm. One memorandum allowed for an exception—lawyers could represent themselves and their immediate families if their personal representation did not interfere with office work or involve a conflict of interest. In any event, such representation had to be approved by the managing partner.

Many of the rules previously mentioned have to do with the protection of the communication system. There are, of course, additional regulations. One handbook on office practice and procedures enjoins the associates to "report to the senior associate or partner in charge regularly and promptly any and all communications between you and the client and any actions or decisions taken by you directly with the client."

Keeping of diaries and time records is important. It is important for billing and it has some importance in deciding on promotions and in tracing the work of attorneys, especially since time is one of the commodities lawyers sell. Some firms believe an associate should put in 1800 chargeable hours a year and a partner 1500, with the hours decreasing as the partner gets older.[10] Probably the main purpose of the diary is its use for billing purposes:

Service memoranda are prepared daily for each lawyer showing the time in hours and quarter hours spent by him on the respective cases and the details of the work done. These service memoranda or diary entries are essential in the functioning of our service charge system, and are of particular importance in the preparation of bills. Each diary entry, therefore, should not only correctly state the client but also the particular matter to which the time is charged, and the description of the work done each day on the particular matter should be in sufficient detail to enable one not fully familiar with the matter to understand exactly what was done during the time charged and to prepare bills which will intelligently describe the work.

Though completing a diary is important, many lawyers neglect this duty and the management of the firms must keep after them. The associate who is not directly concerned with management and possible profits or losses to a firm is especially negligent about filling out his diary. A check on the memoranda in one law firm revealed numerous items calling for the prompt completion of the diary sheet. One organization felt strongly enough about this rule to create the position of Diary Clerk:

> Diaries will be expected at the Diary Clerk's desk by noon of the second day after work was done. If the diary is not received by that time, the Diary Clerk has been instructed to check with the lawyer. If the diary is not forthcoming, the Diary Clerk has been instructed to bring the matter to the attention of the Managing Partner.

So great was the problem of getting diaries into the proper hands that the same firm whose regulation is quoted above felt it necessary to issue another memorandum, this one with teeth in it.

> The delay on the part of certain associates in sending their diary entries to the Accounting Department has occasioned a great deal of inconvenience and in certain cases, serious errors in billing.
>
> The purposes of the diary are:
>
> 1. To provide a contemporaneous record for use in case it becomes material to establish, in litigation or otherwise, what was done on a particular day.
>
> 2. To provide up-to-date information for billing purposes. Orderly recording of work is an integral part of law practice. Delay in reporting diary entries deprives the diary of its value, defeats the foregoing purposes, and wastes the time of others in following up the delinquents. It is therefore imperative that each man transmit his daily diary to the Accounting Department as promptly as possible. In the future, whenever an associate's diary is more than one week late the Accounting Department will report that fact to the management committee sending copies of the report to the associate involved. In the absence of special circumstances,

delays in transmitting diaries will be taken into account in the annual evaluation of the worth of each associate to the firm.

The filing system is part of the communication system, as is the use of differently colored duplicate copies. Regulations concerning incoming papers are also developed, and they usually go through the Managing Clerk's office. He is also in charge of keeping the calendar or "tickler" system up to date, in that it is his duty to inform the various lawyers ahead of time when a certain item is due or when they must appear in court.

Some rules are designed primarily to protect the firm's name and pocketbook. The most important of these deal with who may sign opinion letters. These are documents which say essentially that in the opinion of the firm, "such and such" is the law. The opinion is usually backed with appropriate citations. The client is advised that he may or may not legally act in a certain way. Law firms often stake their reputations on these more formal opinions, and it is possible to hold partners collectively liable for them. Most offices are emphatic that only partners can sign the firm's name on such letters. They alone are finally responsible and they must see that the client and the firm are protected. One memorandum on office practice states:

> Every communication written under the firm letterhead, whether signed in the firm's name or in an individual name, must be either signed by or *specifically* approved by a member of the firm if it (a) expresses an opinion on a question of law or a matter of policy, (b) commits the firm or a client to any financial obligation (other than routine disbursements), (c) waives any rights of the firm or client, or (d) could form the basis of an estoppel or an assertion of a claim against the firm or the client. Regardless of the seniority of the lawyer concerned, or his relationship to the particular matter or client, such communications must not be signed by him except with specific approval and authorization of a member of the firm. Opinion letters *must* be signed by a member of the firm.

There are a number of regulations designed to strengthen the canons of ethics or to go beyond them so as to give further protection to the organization and its clients. For example, rules to minimize conflicts of interest are found in all the major firms. It is common for law offices to issue a monthly "New Clients List" so that all partners will know whether they are representing clients who are in conflict. Some matters are weeded out before they can appear on this list; usually, before a client is accepted by the firm, the senior partner or an executive committee or the entire firm decide whether the client is appropriate or not, and one element considered is the potentiality of conflict between new and old clients. Since some corporations are so large and their properties and work so diversified, it is often impossible to predict areas where conflict may occur. Firms have been known to find themselves representing two opposing clients. When this occurs they take one of three paths—give up both clients for that particular matter (this rarely happens), keep their oldest client whether or not he is the most lucrative, or inform their clients of the situation and ask if they are willing to allow two lawyers from the firm to work in opposition to each other (this occurs only when relatively small issues are involved).

There are other regulations which deal with professional behavior. One rule cautions lawyers about statements to the press. Another prevented or sought to prevent firm attorneys from investing in their clients' equities. The firm felt such investments might warp the lawyer's judgment. It also tries to protect him from accusations that he is seeking to serve his own interests rather than that of the client's. Some firms even prohibit their lawyers from serving as members of the board of directors of their clients' corporations. The instigators of this rule reason that lawyers are not businessmen and in any event must be dispassionate and objective —an ideal which some law firms feel is difficult to reach if one is involved directly in the operation of a business.

No attempt was made to cover all the formal regulations of large law firms. In fact, some categories of rules have not been mentioned at all, particularly those dealing with finances. Many of the rules listed under the headings of clerical, personnel, communication, ethics, and protection of the firm overlap among themselves, as well as with other potential categories. At the same time, the point has been made that despite lawyers' protestations, rules do exist in large law firms. Later, however, we will see that they often exist to be broken. In any event, no real attempt was made to map the degree to which a rule was or was not followed. It is my belief that while lawyers do have formal rules, they do not have as many as do workers in nonprofessional organizations of the same size. Many of the regulations for lawyers are designed for their non-professional staff and only later is it seen that these rules also affect the professional personnel. Most regulations are either rationalized away by the legal staff, not obeyed, or thought of as so necessary that they are not regarded as restrictions at all. This minimization of organizational regulations is probably true for professional people working in other occupations who like to feel that they have control of their own destiny.

FORMAL STRUCTURE

MANY respondents have described their law offices as composed of a number of small firms. Some associates even say: "As far as I'm concerned, it's just me and the partner I work for." Most lawyers prefer not to see their offices as giant organizations. They wish to maintain the myth that they are still individual or small firm practitioners. For some this has an element of truth. The facts, however, are that most large law offices are organized around the use of a system of specialists, and members of these firms have become accustomed to this fact. In addition, these offices are connected by their common names, their partnership agreements, histories and traditions, by their rules and their clerical staff. They are joined by the kinds of clients they share, by the reputation and prestige their members receive. The myth is just a myth and these lawyers know it, although where they can, they try to turn the myth into reality.

A large law firm looks like two pyramids, one standing on top of the other with the point of the bottom one protruding into the top structure. This occurs because a few individuals from the lower pyramid, which is composed of nonprofessional staff, have higher status within the office than most of the very beginning professional staff. The arrangement of both pyramids is hierarchical. The professional pyramid is composed entirely of lawyers who divide into various strata, with the senior partner or an executive committee at the top and an increasing number of lawyers in each lower status category. At the very bottom are the greatest number of legal troops. Most of the detailed work is done at that level—the battalion level.

The top pyramid is divided vertically into departments based on various important legal specialties, or by clients and departments, and finally around the "Big Case."

Departments —

Despite the protestation of lawyers that "we are all general practitioners," all the large law firms visited had departmental structures. True, some stood out more distinctly than others. In fact, the more departmentalized a firm became, the greater was the possibility that it delegated a senior partner with the responsibility of overseeing the functioning of a departmental unit. Each department finds itself dependent upon other departments. And even in firms which vehemently deny that they have separate departments, their members always admit to a tax section. In point of fact, all the large offices also have a corporate department; it is generally the backbone of the Wall Street firm and it usually is the largest. Most partnerships also have real estate, and trust and estates departments. Some have a special banking division or one which deals with air law, labor law, or theatrical law and litigation. If the firm's work in an area of the law expands, a department eventually springs up; this holds particularly for the new firms.

Even though departments do exist, lawyers in one section will do some of the work which is the specialty of another division. This is especially so when the task is not complex or, as we have seen, if the lawyer is a very senior or a very junior practitioner. In any event, all lawyers know that appropriate experts are available to them if needed. And both formal and informal systems of consultation have developed which will be discussed at a later point in this chapter.

Client-Team System —

Some organizations, while retaining a departmental system, also divide their lawyers into teams formed around each of their major corporate clients. What this amounts to is an attempt at integrating two systems of specialization; the first based on subdisciplines of the law and organized around departments; the second based on specialization for the client. The latter system works this way: a senior partner (how senior a partner is usually depends on the client and the importance of the matter) is in charge of a team; he works with a younger partner or two, plus some associates. The numbers at the bottom increase with the demands of the client. The team is made up of members of the various specialty divisions who try to handle the entire matter themselves. They feel this is the best way to control the client's work—a problem central to the organization of the firm. If they need help, in terms either of manpower or of consultation with specialists who may not be represented on the team or for confirmation of their own judgment, they call on the various departments to supply them with the needed talent. For example, if they need a litigator or tax expert, they consult men in the appropriate division.

In many firms these departments are essentially service departments; their primary purpose is to provide intrafirm advice. Even when this is done, teams like to call on experts who also have had experience with the particular client. Depending on demand, a member of a team may be and usually is assigned to many teams. However, these teams will not generally be composed of the same lawyers.

Even in offices where the team system is not explicit, there is some tendency for it to occur—especially on matters where knowledge of the business of the client is important. It grows up because certain top partners are put in charge of the client and they tend to call on the same people to aid them. In addition, the client becomes accustomed to working with certain lawyers and begins to regard them as their lawyers.

The philosophy behind the client-team system was explained by a senior partner in a firm where this system has been formalized: "We believe lawyers should work with people, that they should learn the client's business and should only go to the experts after they have tried to do it themselves. We try to have each client-team act as if it were a country law firm."

The law offices which have formalized the client-team system have tried to prevent their attorneys from becoming modified house counsels, i.e., lawyers who work entirely for one corporation and are considered by the client, at least, to work for them rather than for the law firm. The Wall Street lawyers feel that this kind of dependency relationship makes for a poor lawyer—one who can't practice his profession properly. They call the attorneys who work and are paid directly by a corporation "kept lawyers." By placing a man on many teams, this danger has been modified. In one version of the client-team system, however, it has not been prevented. All the large New York law firms probably have banks as clients. Most of them are engaged in only the special legal work the bank sends them. The bank's house counsels do the more routine work. Law firms which do all the work for a bank tend to set up special banking departments. The lawyers practicing in these departments have little protection from the client, for they are essentially house lawyers, with the one difference that they are paid through the law firm rather than directly by the client. Their colleagues often regard them as second-class citizens.

The Big Case —

The "Big Case" is another instance of a client-team form of organization. It generally deals with emergency matters which require a great deal of manpower. No one expects the case to go on forever (although cases have been known to go on for years)[11] so that there is an air of the temporary about it.

A simple line organization is used in the "Big Case." One firm involved in the "Brokers' Case" employed twenty men, although not all of them full time. A senior partner was in charge of the matter. All material collected below was finally digested and submitted to him by a middle partner and a junior partner. These two partners were the "working" members. They translated the senior partners' decisions into more specific terms. The working partners had under them a senior associate; he functioned as the foreman and saw to it that the men under him brought back the information needed at the top. The rank and file lawyers collected vast amounts of data, learned the business of their client, took depositions, went carefully through the files of their corporate clients, and combed them for every minute detail which had some bearing on the case.

When a specialist was needed, then the firm, as in other forms of the client-team system, provided the necessary talent. If a special body of knowledge had to be constantly called on, then the specialist would be made part of the regular team.

Sometimes the case, because of its magnitude, requires that a firm hire outside lawyers. They then do so with the understanding that these men are to be employed only for the duration of the case. Many of the Wall Street law firms were involved in the Brokers' Case,[12] and a separate office was set up so that the individual firms could co-ordinate their common fight against the government. These possibilities pose additional problems for the smooth functioning of the law firm.

STATUS SYSTEM

THE descriptions of the distribution of office space revealed the importance of a status system. In the large law firm there is a high correlation between the informal status system and the formal. The two systems are closely knit. This might be expected if only because age (through the vintage system) plays such an important part in the selection of partners and because both the professional and nonprofessional staffs recognize the differences between themselves and the importance of the work they are doing.

The status system of the large law firm can most broadly be divided into castelike entities. The castes in turn stratify by class, then by age, and to some degree by the area of law practiced. One caste is composed of professional people, the other, the nonprofessional help. Except for their office contacts, the lives of the members in the various castes seldom cross. It is, for instance, not considered nice to socialize with a secretary. One associate was seen lunching with a male secretary and was told that professional people do not eat with their secretaries. When lawyers were asked about this taboo, they would point out (probably in an effort to appear democratic) a member of the firm who had married his secretary. Still, most would admit it was not considered smart to go out with one.

Partner Hierarchy —

Members of the executive committee constitute the first stratum of the professional caste. In the old, powerful firms these men earn from the practice of law between $100,000 and $200,000 a year and a few exceed this figure. Most of them are in their late fifties or sixties, with an occasional old-timer still at the helm. Some old-timers give up their partnership and become "of counsel." Essentially this position is an advisory and an honorary one which provides the semi-retired exceptional lawyer with a place to practice as much law as he wants to. Cleary-Gottlieb (a firm which now has over fifty lawyers and a "break-away" from the firm currently known as Dewey-Ballantine, but previously called Root-Ballantine) has two well-known, distinguished, and highly regarded "of counsels"—Elihu Root, Jr., and Grenville Clark.

Not all older partners are on the executive committee. In terms of status hierarchy they come directly below members of the committee, with the middle partners directly below them. These middle partners are approximately ten years younger than the members of the executive committee and the other senior partners —probably between forty-five and fifty-five years old. Their salaries range from $50,000 to $75,000 a year.

Underneath the middle partners are the junior partners. The ages of these men range from thirty-four to forty-four years, although recently some attorneys have been made partners at a younger age. In most large New York firms, these men are junior only because of age and not because of contract. In some firms partners who are nonpercentage partners are thought of as junior partners. Their position is spelled out in the partnership agreement. They are not liable for the firm's indiscretions, they are usually on a salary, they cannot vote at the firm meetings, and while their names are listed with the participating partners, they are (as in the military) more like warrant officers than enlisted men or regular officers. In general they are younger than full partners, and their salary starts at about $20,000. All of them do not become participating partners. These younger members are not officially called junior partners and are listed on the letterhead (usually in order of their status in the firm), as are all partners. They attend firm meetings and are entitled to a vote. Their influence, in part because of their limited tenure, is not so great as that of some of the other partners, but they are entitled to know what is going on. Their salaries range from $20,000 to $40,000 annually. They differ from the middle partners by age, influence, type of work they do, and income. The three strata outlined here do not exist as separate entities (except for the executive committee), but blend into each other so that some partners are more junior than others and some more senior.

Status Differences Among Lawyers —

Among the lawyers, the first important demarcation is between the associates and the partners. In the hierarchy of the firm, they constitute a separate class. Associates are employees who are paid a salary. They can be fired. They do not participate in the management of the firm[13] nor share directly in its profits and losses. They are not liable for the firm's laxities. They do not attend firm meetings. Because of their age, their lack of tenure, and the kind of work they do in the organization, they are below partners on the status ladder. This is true even though by ascription they may have been born into the same (for some, a higher) social status as the men who employ them. One associate describes the sociometrics of the situation: "We don't eat lunch with the partners because they have their own club. However, if you are down at night with them, then you do. If there is a social line, it is seen in factors outside the office. For one thing, we can't keep up with them."

Another young lawyer, from one of the most respected firms, replied, when asked about the status difference between partners and associates: "Associates are wage slaves; at the same time in some areas they are treated as equals. On the one hand, you're a lackey—on the other, you still have a lot of status." The ambivalence in the self-image of associates, as registered in this statement, highlights both the personal problems of professional people who are employees and the organizational problem of institutions which must integrate these people into their structure.

While there are numerous reasons for partners treating associates as separate and inferior to themselves, there are other reasons for behaving toward them as if they were identical. The hard facts are that some associates are the social equals of the partners who know the families of some of these men. A few will become partners, and treating associates as if they were "common employees" might later prove embarrassing. The values of the profession make it necessary for lawyers to treat other lawyers as equals. In addition, since division of labor exists, each part needs the other, and this mutual dependency tends to help modify somewhat the lower status of associates. An attempt is made to treat them at least as potential equals, if not as equals, whereas nonprofessional help is not treated as equal, and little effort is expended in that direction.[14]

Associate Hierarchy —

Associates also divide into strata. Briefly, since portions of this hierarchy have previously been described, they can be broken down (though this is not done formally) into permanent, senior, middle and junior associates. The permanent associates are divided into two categories—those with relatively high status in the firm and those who are regarded as failures. The first classification is composed of men who because of their specialty (labor law), or their origin are not asked to be partners. These men often are doing important, imaginative jobs. The recognition of this lies in their secure tenure and in their salaries. These men earn between $18,000 and $30,000 a year. One reported a much higher salary. In the second segment of this category, where the majority of this group are found, are the "failures"; models not to follow. They do the routine work. Their salaries however are only slightly lower than those of the other permanent associates. Perhaps what distinguishes these subcategories as much as anything else is that those who are engaged in creative work and are not made partners are supported by group rationalization. Those who are engaged in routine work and are considered failures have to depend upon their own rationalizations.

The senior associates have been with their firm from eight to ten years, sometimes longer. They are, in most offices, on the verge of becoming partners or of leaving the firm. They are looked up to and at constantly; they are under observation both by partners who must decide their futures and by the associates below who are in search of successful career models. They have their own secretaries, or share them, and they often supervise younger associates who help them. Their salaries range from $11,000 to $22,000 a year.

The middle associates have been with their organization from three to eight years. They earn between $9,000 and $12,000 a year. They share secretaries, have less responsibility than the seniors, and less status in the firm. The younger associates are still in training and they earn from $7500 to $9500 a year. They do the spade work. They share secretaries, have less responsibility than the senior and less status in the firm. Their lower status is indicated by their forced use of dictaphones, the number who share an office, and the type of work they are asked to do. In some ways their status is also lower than that of permanent associates. The difference is that these young men have their future in front of them. Not all of these junior associates are committed to stay with a firm. In this respect, they differ from the other lawyers who have not been passed over in that most of the latter have decided to be tested for partnership.[15]

Status and Age —

A high correlation can be found between age and the status system just described. The law firms are very age conscious as indicated by their hiring and promotion policy. Jobs are often assigned by the ripeness of the attorney and lawyers of the same age are seldom assigned to the same matter unless they have different specialties. One partner notes:

> I think there should be a definite echelon every ten years. Now mind you, that is not a definite figure, so that we won't get into a position where there isn't a man coming up. We try to see that this happens but we do it intuitively and it isn't uniform—there is nothing inflexible about it—we can't be inflexible.

An examination of the 543 members of the twenty large New York law firms illustrates the age distribution and shows something of the age hierarchy of the firm on the partnership level. The table also indicates the diamond shape of the age hierarchy. Only a few more lawyers will be made partner from those born in the 1910–1919 decade. Firms are now filling in their mem-

Table VIII-1—Date of Birth of All Partners in Twenty Large
Law Firms in New York City as Listed in the 1962
Martindale-Hubbell Law Directory

Date of Birth	N	%
1870–79	5	0.9
1880–89	32	5.9
1890–99	89	16.4
1900–09	166	30.5
1910–19	152	27.9
1920–29	96	17.8
1930–39	2	0.4
Not given	1	0.2
Total	543	100.0

bership ranks from the 1920–1929 group and just beginning with
the exceptional attorney from the 1930–1939 classification. Those
born in the 1880–1889 category probably have the greatest power
in the firm. Older members are declining in number and power,
but not necessarily in prestige.

Status and Specialty —

No exact—certainly no formal—status hierarchy was erected on
the basis of the kind of legal work performed. There is no doubt,
however, that such a hierarchy exists. It has already been indicated in terms of responsibility involved. It can also be seen in the
type of specialty engaged in. Generally, those in the corporate and
in the litigating departments have the highest status, and those in
real estate, estate and trust, or the large banking departments the
lowest. A relationship can be found between these departments and
the number of permanent associates a department has. This correlation is spoiled, however, because the litigation section, which
has high status, is based on a "star" system which requires
permanent associates and does not need many partners, since the
client usually prefers the top man. One client in trouble indicates
his feelings about the subject: "They took my case [tax]. They
looked over the matter first and they decided they would take it.
I didn't know whether they would or not. They put some subordinates looking up research and then they went on a vacation

and here I am sweating blood." Still, even the status of the permanent associates in this area is better than that of some of the associates in the real estate department.

POWER

THE status hierarchy implies differentiation of power.[16] It is obtained in a law firm from three major sources: within the organization, outside the organization, and through preferred individuality. These three roads to power are not necessarily mutually exclusive.

Within the Organization —

Power in a law firm depends to a great extent upon control of business. In new offices which are still building, or old ones which are rebuilding, power among partners is contingent on business getting ability. Lawyers in these organizations frankly mention this skill as one way up the ladder toward increased power in a firm. Some talk about the men who bring in new clients as having "sex appeal." In older offices which have maintained their roster of clients, power rests less on new business than on the control of old business. While these old, successful law firms do not frown upon new business, associates are discouraged from attempting to bring it in. In any event, it is difficult to bring in new business without disturbing the organization of the firm. These venerable organizations already control the business of the giants of industry, and conflict of interest restrictions often prohibit an office from taking on another corporate client in the same field as an old client. Witness the difficulty which would have ensued if a law firm had been counsel for both the Radio Corporation of America and Zenith Radio when Zenith sued RCA for the use of some patents. New clients also may mean an extension of staff, and many lawyers resist the possibility of any further increase in their numbers. In addition, existing partners have more than they can personally keep up with in taking care of their old clients. Nevertheless, new business is still required. In terms of power, however, it is the man who inherits the old business, usually because he had worked on these clients' matters and had been supervised by those who brought in or controlled the business originally, who controls the old institutional law firms.

Some lawyers gain power by appointment; they are given institutional right to employ power; they have authority. The head of the firm may have his rights listed in the partnership agreement; the managing, hiring, and assignment partners are appointed by the head of the firm or by means of a vote of the firm. The same situation applies when a law office is run by a committee system. The executive committee's power is recorded in the partnership agreement and they appoint, in consultation with the rest of the firm, members to other committees (these positions will be described later in the chapter) such as the management committee, committee on finances, on assignments, and on hiring. Eventually, this authority, which Bierstedt defines as institutionalized power, breeds real power which he defines as latent force, i.e., "the ability to employ force, not its actual employment."[17] The heads of the firm initially have both power and authority. Those appointed work mainly on institutional authority. As the appointees take on their duties, however, they begin to take on pure power, i.e., if the hiring partner employs the kind of men he wants, these men may develop a loyalty to him which provides him with additional control over them; or the assignment partner can build his own little organization through his distribution of jobs. Even when this is not being developed deliberately, the position itself generates elements of pure power.

External Sources of Power —

Some lawyers develop reputations outside the Wall Street community. They do this usually through government service, work with the bar associations, or through their various hobbies and charities. Some of these men build strong outside reputations, and their external prestige may turn into internal power by reflecting on their business getting and keeping ability, the prime source of power in the law firm. Their external prestige may manifest itself simply in the respect that other members of the firm offer them. This in turn may result in the ability to control. Outside reputations do not necessarily, however, indicate inside respect or control.

Power through Preferred Individuality —

Some attorneys find themselves with power because of their superior knowledge. These men have become so expert in an area of the law that the firms would not like to do without them. Others are so bright or so personable or so socially acceptable that they are looked up to and have an influential voice in the organization. It is these elements of preferred individuality which often lead to positions of authority. Sometimes these attorneys are able to take over some important administrative function other lawyers have abrogated. In this way, they are able to increase their power within the organization. Possibilities become open to them to influence decisions about which associates should become partners. This further aids their rise in the firm. When an attorney is a business holder, a business getter, or has superior knowledge and/or elements of the charismatic leader, it is possible for him to dictate to the firm. In fact, it is easy for members to accept such a "dictator" —especially if he is benevolent. The late John W. Davis seems to have held such a position in the firm of Davis Polk Wardwell Sunderland & Kiendl. Many lawyers do not want to be bothered with the details of running the law firm. They are relieved when a well-qualified man is willing to take on these responsibilities.

WHO RUNS THE LAW FIRM?

SOME attorneys believe a law firm with a benevolent dictator at its head is most effective.[18] There even seems to be some inclination to seek out this kind of administration. However, this clearly superior individual is difficult to find, and even if found, there is a tendency for the benevolent senior partners of today to try not to take all the power. A managing partner, who has been watching the process for years, discusses his firm's powerful senior partner:

> All decisions are arrived at by general discussion. Some partners' views are stronger than others. That happens by gradual development over the years. X has a strong voice, but he does not decide on percentages or organization by himself. He is not anxious to run the firm single-handed.

Many lawyers believe the day of the strong man is almost over. A man like Cravath single-handedly dominated his firm. This happened in part because he controlled a good share of the business, and in part because the strong head of an organization was the fashion. Furthermore, Cravath was interested in the organization of his firm and was considered good at running it.[19]

In the absence of a strong leader or the desire for one, an executive committee is set up to take his place. This group is composed of the most powerful senior partners, usually only three, four, or five men. Membership in this group is often decided at a firm meeting and designated in the partnership agreement along with their rights and duties. Some lawyers maintain that a partner is not picked for the executive committee; rather, he takes that position on the basis of the power he controls. In some firms where power between senior partners is equal, the executive board resembles the cabinet of a coalition government. Among the members of the committee are representatives of various specialties and occasionally a lawyer with outside reputation or personal charisma who initially had little inside power.

The executive committee acts as overseer for the firm. It is the deciding group; it settles policy matters and disputes. The main, specific task of the committee is to decide on percentages distributed to partners. Members of the group discuss questions about setting up pension plans or moving their offices. Those at the summit make the initial determination about whether new partners are needed. They decide, if the problem becomes overt, about the optimum size of the firm.[20] The executive committee concerns itself with problems of office morale;[21] of client satisfaction. The committee acts as referee and serves to ease conflict within the firm. For example, the committee may be asked to decide which partner will take what case, or, if a client is unhappy with a lawyer, how to change the assignment tactfully. Still another major problem for the executive committee is to plan for succession. As a member of this top committee for one group expressed it: "If a lawyer retires, the client has the right to expect continuity. We try to organize our departments so there is an assistant. Much of this is by natural selection, but if it does not grow by itself, we plan it and discuss it."

Just as the dictator senior partner is disappearing, so is the desire on the part of many members of ruling committees to dictate. One member of an executive committee reports: "We are much more democratic today; the strong man is not suitable to our times. We run by consultation among the partners, with the members of the executive committee having a greater say." The executive committee seeks advice and many questions are brought to the firm meeting for further discussion and vote. The firm meetings are important, for it is here where major problems concerning management and the law are discussed. The firm meetings are like Town Hall meetings. Every partner has a chance to speak and vote. However, if the executive committee wants something badly enough, the members of the firm will vote with them—after all, they have both the power and the respect of their fellow partners.

The Managing Partner —

Except for settling major disputes and making policy decisions, the executive committee deals with most problems in a general way. The committee passes its thoughts and decisions on to the managing partner or to the members of special committees to deal with in a more specific way. The managing partner's job is to take care of the everyday housekeeping problems. The men who are assigned this task are usually "young" partners in their early forties. At one time this position was filled by one of the major partners. But the situation is analogous to that of university chairmanships. When these once high-status positions began to carry less prestige, they were available to younger men. In both instances, as the administrative functions of the job became more important, the position lost its power to attract important personalities, because the amount of time needed for administrative duties had to be taken from what professional people regarded as their main duties, i.e., the practice of law for the attorney and teaching, research and/or writing for the faculty member. In both the university and the law firm, the men who take these jobs are put into positions of some power, however, and this in part makes up for the loss of professional prestige. The managing partner gets to know intimately the firm and the men. This knowledge makes him additionally valuable. But many managing partners want to return to the full-time practice of the law, and in most firms the position is rotated to allow for this. Many firm members object to this system because they feel the job of managing partner should be full time.

In some offices, the tasks of the managing partner are divided into an assignment partner and/or a hiring partner. Generally, however, these functions belong to the managing partner.

ASSIGNMENT

THE job of assigning work is difficult. Many systems for obtaining work are operating at the same time. For example, a young man may work for many partners and on many matters simultaneously, making it difficult to keep track of him. Emergencies arise which call for shifting of assignments; attorneys are professional people and want to be treated as such, and this calls for special managerial techniques. Powerful partners vie for the services of the best associates.

These difficulties make it necessary for a firm to place responsibility for assignment and to formalize the assignment system. Most firms have done this, at least for new lawyers. Usually a partner or a senior associate who needs a young lawyer makes his request to the managing partner, who sees that the request is fulfilled. Numerous ways of keeping track of lawyers have been devised. One system aims not only at scheduling the work of the novice attorney but at doing it in such a way that he receives a systematic training. In fact, however, in most law offices the better apprentices are recruited and attached to the various departments and specialties long before they have had complete training. To stop this, more and more firms have formalized their educational program. The sponsor of the most formalized plan to keep track of training and assignment discusses his plan:

We have a rotating system. An associate has to spend a portion of three years in three different departments. I keep a chart of where they've been and how long they stay, and when they've been in the department long enough I move them. Sometimes you have to wait

a week or two before we can get them off a case but we do move
them. We found that unless you have regular notices that the man
is changing departments you don't move the man properly. If you
do it without the records and without formality, you find that a
man is never free and the people involved in the problem have
forgotten about rotating.

This firm decided that this program had to be installed if they
were going to give good training. Despite this, it still meets with
individual resistance. A partner will say, "I just get a man trained
and you take him away from me." Some of the partners said that
we aren't running a school. They feel, however, that eventually
they will get good lawyers. The associates like it and that's one
reason why I get such good results in hiring. Other firms have
gone haywire salarywise. We do a lot of things for our associates.
We even send them to special courses, like tax courses.

Other systems to keep track of assignments have been devised. In
one office it was the responsibility of the young associate to list
the client, the matter, the nature of the assignment, the data of
assignment, the estimated completion date, and the immediate
supervisor. It is important to know who the supervisor is, for in
terms of organization, he is the immediate boss and the appropriate rewards or punishment fall on the person with responsibility.
When the associate completes an assignment, he crosses it off the
list. In this way any lawyer looking at the list can make an estimate
of the availability of the listed attorneys.

In another firm, the assignment partner would mimeograph an
availability list. The associate reported to him on a Monday morning, stating his availability. Partners who needed help could consult the list and then make their request through the assignment
partner.

These systems which involve the individual reporting his own
availability do not always work. Associates want to be sought after
and so firms who ask their men if they have enough work often
get a false report, for fear that a "need work report" would indicate some failing on their part. In one office where this reporting
system is used, only one man in a week's period reported himself

partially available. An inquiry revealed that this was a man no one wanted.

Most attempts at formalizing the assignment system meet with some degree of failure. This can almost be expected, given a partnership system where, theoretically at any rate, all the partners are bosses and actually a number are equally powerful. In some firms, despite the formalization of assignment systems, it is still the custom for a partner who needs assistance to go down the hall asking various young associates if they can do a job for him. From the point of view of an associate, here is how the process works:

> They call you and ask are you busy. If you say you're busy, they call someone else. There is theoretically an administrative partner who is supposed to know whether you're busy, but most assignment is done on an informal basis. The associates like this because they don't want to work for one man. By working for more than one, they feel they learn more and it gives them the privilege of saying no.

Another associate from another firm reports:

> Technically, you're on call for any partner or any older associate. You get your work through your schedule which is listed in the library. Or a partner comes in and asks you if you're free. You say, if you're busy, "I can work for you if it is a small job." It's worked out on an individual basis. It has its limitations. I think it's a holdover from the lawyers' desire to be independent.

In some instances, the associate wanting to keep his independence, to get training, and to work on the most interesting matters tries to influence his assignment. In fact, he often initiates the assignment. One partner reports on this method:

> Sometimes I just go to the man. You get to know who is good around here and so sometimes you do it informally. Occasionally the associate comes to you and asks for work. A good many never get on the available list because they pick what they want to do before they can get called.

The partner trying to relieve himself of some work tends to hold on to the associate who has done a good job for him. If he is powerful enough, he may succeed. There are obviously a number of opposing forces pulling in such a way as to minimize the formal organization and to make the assignment partner's job more difficult.

Eventually, generally after a lawyer has served his apprenticeship, associates are assigned to departments or to specific men in a department. This helps minimize conflict between partners over associates and it takes some assignment burden away from the managing partner. Lawyers attached to service departments such as tax, receive their assignment in various ways, despite the fact that in most offices requests are supposed to go through the head of the department. As often as not an associate will be approached directly through informal channels by an associate or partner from another department. In fact, anyone in the firm can call anyone in the service departments and ask for advice. In addition, these departments may have clients who come to them directly for help. Some check on what a man has been doing is provided by the diary he keeps and through the billing procedure.

In firms organized on a client-team system, assignments come from the head of the team and eventually directly from the client. This latter point is true for all lawyers as they grow in experience and in client contact. When this happens the associate must report client-assigned work to his superior. Generally, however, it is the partner who receives the work from the client; he then distributes it to men below him. However, the system is more complex because of the need to consult with specialists from other departments. This is how a middle partner describes the assignment process:

A house counsel calls me and asks, "Will you handle a statement of proxy, a resolution, and a clearance with the stock exchange?" SEC is involved so this meeting then is not a routine matter. Dick Jones works with me on U corporation matters and he knows all the people there. I ask him to draft a proxy statement for me. Since he is not a specialist, he consults a man in the tax department who generally works on the same corporation's problems.

When he consults that man, he doesn't go through me. In this case a pension is involved so I called the tax partner. He found a man in his department who is an expert on pensions. This man and Dick worked together. Both report to me. There is no fixed procedure for this—the men call me on the phone. I encourage them to deal with other associates directly—I give them as much responsibility as they can take. All partners don't do this; some have a master and servant relationship. I regard this kind of work as group practice, and you can't stand on ceremony.

In many of the assignment procedures the managing partner or the assignment partner is eliminated; this is true for some assignments given to senior associates who are being considered for partnership positions. In this special instance, senior partners from various departments in the firm give the men assignments in an effort to determine finally who shall be made a member of the firm.

Of course, assignment procedures change in crisis situations. When an emergency occurs which takes a great deal of manpower, the managing partner is again called in to fill the demand. Men may be pulled out of their respective departments and put to work on the emergency matter. Law firms, unlike factories, cannot predict accurately the amount of work they will be called upon to do at any particular time. The tightness of manpower is aggravated because it is difficult to know exactly how many new men to take on, and is further irritated because most of the hiring is done for September and an exodus from the firms begins after that. By March or April the firms begin to feel a manpower shortage. An emergency can then severely affect the assignment procedure. The "Big Case" is another special circumstance which requires special attention to assignment. As we have seen, the work is distributed in line fashion, from the top of the team down. These cases generally spread over long periods of time and the managing partner must allow for ennui and loss of personnel.

Assignment of Partners —

The managing partner does not handle assignments for members of the firm. Partners get their work in three ways. If it a big new matter, a firm meeting or the executive committee may decide that a certain partner should be in charge of it. He is asked if he can take on this work. If he agrees, he deals directly with the client. In fact, as a lawyer progresses up the partnership ladder, more and more of his work comes directly from the client. Before his ascension, however, he receives his work from older partners in much the same manner as he did when he was a senior associate—through his departmental connections or from his colleagues who know of his specialty and legal talent.

OTHER COMMITTEES OR MANAGERS OF THE FIRM

IN addition to an executive or management committee, partnerships have used the committee system to decide who should be hired, where and when to move the office, and how to make assignments. Generally, the job of running these committees falls to one man, usually the one most interested. Not all of those who manage the office are partners or lawyers. The managing clerk's office, for example, need not necessarily have a lawyer at its head. The job of the managing clerk is to see that practicing lawyers, mainly in the litigation department, know when deadlines have to be met. He is a human "tickler" system. He keeps the calendar. The managing clerk has a staff who help him keep these records and serve summonses. The exact duties of this position vary by firm, and what a given managing clerk does depends in part upon himself. In one office where the clerk is a lawyer, he reads over all the briefs to check on errors. In most firms, besides taking care of the calendar, the managing clerk acts as a liaison between the Ivy League lawyer and the Civil Service tested minority group clerks.

OFFICE MANAGER

ALL large firms also have an office manager. He is not a lawyer and his main job is to see that the nonprofessional section of the office runs smoothly—a large enough job in itself, but one which is not the subject of this book. However, he does have some power over lawyers, especially over young lawyers. Occasionally, he doubles as the managing clerk. In one firm, he even gave young associates their assignments. Office managers were asked what would happen if a lawyer did not follow procedure for filing. One office manager reports: "If he doesn't the head file clerk will speak to him. If the lawyer still doesn't, the file clerk comes to me. I speak to the lawyer, and if he doesn't conform, I'll take it up with the senior partner and then he's really in trouble." This doesn't happen often. The office manager's authority is given him by the executive committee and by the fact that lawyers do not want to bother with everyday housekeeping duties. His power is increased because his tenure is usually longer than most associates' and because he has control over items such as additional secretarial help and new office equipment, which can make the lawyer's life easier. Still, he often finds himself in conflict with young associates. Here the different status systems which exist in a law firm can cause conflict. On the one hand, the office manager is usually older than the young associates and so, according to some norms, must be respected. On the other hand, he is not a lawyer. The associates resent his intrusion into their professional world. Office managers often modify the possibility of such conflict by reporting their problems with lawyers back to the managing partner or to a committee of lawyers set up for the purpose. Actually any major problem is finally reported back to the partners who, for example, decide on salary for the various categories of clerical jobs.

The multiplicity of chains of command, of assignment functions, of disobedience to many formal rules described in this chapter, seems to give credence to the lawyers' claims that their organizations are loose. It is the purpose of the next chapter to examine that claim and to explain why these law firms function successfully.

NOTES

1. Another, Simpson Thacher & Bartlett, according to a report in the January 10, 1962, *New York Times*, has leased a floor in the Manufacturers-Hanover Trust Building, which is also in midtown Manhattan. They will move part of their staff uptown, most probably to take care of the uptown moves of their clients—Manufacturers-Hanover is one of their clients.

2. Robert T. Swaine, *The Cravath Firm and its Predecessors* (New York: Ad Press, 1946 and 1948), Vol. II, p. 440.

3. The firm was called Stevenson, Paul, Rifkind, Wharton & Garrison in Washington, D.C., and Stevenson, Rifkind & Wirtz in Chicago.

4. *Law Libraries in the United States and Canada 1960-1961* (Published for the American Association of Law Libraries by Commerce Clearing House, 1960), p. 30.

5. *Ibid.*, p. 29.

6. Roger B. Siddall, *A Survey of Large Law Firms in the United States* (New York: Vantage Press, 1956, privately printed), p. 35. The author found in his study (his large firms included law offices composed of nine lawyers and over), "The articles of partnership under which we operate are written and complete in themselves (27 checks [responses]); mostly written but with some things left to oral understanding and custom (2 checks); only a brief memorandum, with most things being left to oral understanding and custom (8 checks); entirely unwritten (5 checks)."

7. Arthur B. Willis, "Income Tax Problems of the Professional Partnership," *The Practical Lawyer*, 2 (November 1956), 67.

8. Capital is not as important to a law firm as it is to a business and perhaps this is a reason why many professional partnership agreements do not take all aspects of property into consideration. For the large law office capital assets such as the library and the furniture are by tradition transferred on to the succeeding generations of partners.

9. H. Bradly Jones, "The Law Partnership Agreement," *The Practical Lawyer*, 2 (May 1956), 50-67. In his article, Jones presents a full description of each of the terms and conditions.

10. Some lawyers feel that they cannot expect to charge for more than 1200 to 1500 hours per year. The figures may be higher for the large law firms because work is generally available to them and associates' time can be supervised and scheduled. See Eugene C. Gerhart, "The Art of Billing Clients," *Law Office Economics and Management*, 1 (May 1960), 34.

11. *Life Magazine* (October 23, 1953), 60, 63-64, 66: Regarding the "Brokers' Case" (antitrust suit in which the government attempted to prevent seventeen investment bankers from banding together to buy large portions of securities for resale): "The trial lasted 30 months and 57,531 pages were offered as evidence." The judge's opinion took 424 pages. "The trial cost the government and the investment brokers nearly $10 million."

12. The following large law firms were involved in that case: *Breed, Abbott & Morgan* and *Cahill, Gordon, Zachary & Reindel* and *Covington & Burling* (Washington, D.C.) and *Cravath, Swaine & Moore* and *Davis Polk Wardwell Sunderland & Kiendl* and *Donovan Leisure Newton & Irvine* and *Shearman & Sterling & Wright.* "United States v. Morgan *et al.*," 118 *Federal Supplement* 621 (United States District Court, S.D. New York, October 14, 1953).

13. In one atypical large firm, associates formed committees which advised management and sought to function as a pressure which would help modify management policies in the direction they desired.

14. In the same firm referred to in footnote 13, an exception is seen. The nonprofessional segment of the office demanded the right to join the professionals in their "Thank God it's Friday" evening office cocktail. They won this privilege and spoiled not only the ritual but its function.

15. The nonprofessional help also stratify, with the office manager at the top of the hierarchy and the head of the secretarial staff under him. Next come the secretaries who are divided further, partially on the basis of the status of the partner they work for, i.e., if a woman is working for a major partner, she receives somewhat higher status than another secretary who works for a junior partner. Under the secretaries are the typists, then the file clerks, and then the fifty-year-old, tan-jacketed messenger boys, or their much younger equivalents.

16. Power is used here, except if otherwise indicated, in its simplest, standard dictionary form, i.e., "ability to do or act; strength; control." See Robert Bierstedt, "An Analysis of Social Power," *American Sociological Review*, 15 (December 1950), 730–738, for an excellent discussion of the distinctions between various items with which power has been identified, such as prestige, influence, eminence, competence, knowledge, dominance, rights, force and authority, and social power.

17. Bierstedt, *op. cit.*, p. 733.

18. Siddall, *op. cit.*, pp. 45–46, has classified large law firms into three types: (1) Solar-type organization "has a recognized head partner who pulls on all the other partners and on whom all the partners pull. . . ." (2) Planetary-type organization; in which there is no boss, clients are inherited, custom and tradition run the firm. (3) Pari-mutual organization; in which lawyers sell their time, and their net earning value to the firm is computed. Each year a percentage is worked out.

19. Otto E. Koegel, *Walter S. Carter: Collector of Young Masters or the Progenitor of Many Law Firms* (New York: Round Table Press, 1953), p. 382.

20. Usually the size of a law office is decided by the needs of current clients. Decisions have to be made about taking on large new clients. In general, law offices will not take on the "one-shot" client if his needs are demanding and they entail hiring a temporary staff—although there are some examples of this kind of expansion.

21. Siddall, *op. cit.*, p. 99, gives a composite chart of the answers on handling personnel matters:

"*Personnel Matters*, that is, the employment, discharge, fixing of salaries and of vacations, assignments and so on are handled with respect to:

"*Lawyers*, by a committee of the partners (27 checks); by any partner (1 check); by one designated partner (9 checks); by one or more employers who are not partners (3 checks).

"*Stenographers*, including secretaries, by a committee of the partners (10 checks); by any partner (0 checks); by one designated partner (14 checks); by one or more employers who are not partners (17 checks).

"*Other employees,* by a committee of partners (10 checks) ; by any partner (0 checks) ; by one designated partner (14 checks) ; by one or more employers who are not partners (17 checks).

"With respect to stenographers we use the secretary system (16 checks) ; the pool system (0 checks) ; a mixture of them (21 checks)."

NINE

THE SUCCESS OF THE

ORGANIZATION: RATIONALE

EXAMINATION of the social structure of large law firms allows us to see why a relatively loose organization, one which because of its size[1] would usually be expected to be much more rigid and rule-ridden, can function successfully. At the same time, it offers an equally important opportunity to add to our understanding of bureaucracy. Much has been written about the importance of formal internal controls for the smooth functioning of an organization. Max Weber[2] thought that bureaucracy, which has such controls, was the most rational and effective way to run large organizations.

There are, as the literature on this subject has previously documented, other facts which are important for the success of a social system. Some of these probably can be found in any large institution; others have more meaning for large organizations which employ professional people. For the giant law firms, the following factors are the most important: (1) homogeneity of the persons employed, (2) the special training of many attorneys (law review), (3) the development of *esprit de corps*, (4) control of competition, (5) the stability and easy recognition of some informal rules, (6) the use of judgment, which in some instances involves a knowledge of regulations which are not considered rules at all, (7) the special role of the client, (8) informal external professional rules, and (9) formal external professional controls. Many of these factors can be found in other large-scale organizations, though probably not to the same degree. No attempt is made here to evaluate the relative importance of the above list except to estimate that the external professional controls, both formal and informal, are probably the most important. It is especially salient for this discussion because it points up one major difference in the arsenal of control techniques available to professional large-scale organizations which is not available, certainly to the same degree, to nonprofessional institutions.

The looseness of the organization of their law firms was voluntarily mentioned by 27 per cent of the sample. Only a very few thought this circumstance unfortunate; most felt it offered some advantage. It was more professional, they said, and allowed for greater independence; it also promoted creativity and provided organizational flexibility.

Actually, although large law firms are not quite so loose as the lawyers in them would like to believe, they are not as formal as most corporations or for that matter as the nonprofessional portion of their own firms. Despite this relative looseness, the large law firms are effective, if by effective we mean that they satisfy the main purpose for their existence—to serve the client well and keep him contented.[3] In addition, and perhaps as a prerequisite for effectiveness, they also keep their own lawyers happy.[4]

REASONS FOR ORGANIZATIONAL SUCCESS

ONE hundred one members of the sample were asked to explain why their organization worked even though it seemed to be loosely organized. Their answers, which totaled 158 responses, can be subsumed under two major headings: professional responsibility and quality of personnel; and organizational considerations. Professional responsibility led the list; it was mentioned by forty-eight members of the sample, with intelligence of personnel ranking second—mentioned by seventeen respondents. Other considerations, listed in descending order of frequency, were: *esprit de corps* (mentioned by sixteen respondents); similarity of background (mentioned by fifteen); requirements of the work (fourteen); a more ambiguous response—"type of individual in the large law firm"—which actually refers to a combination of intelligence and proper background, was mentioned by thirteen respondents; mutual confidence as a factor was mentioned by eight; twenty-seven responses which might be lumped together as "other considerations" concerned such factors as the influence of high pay, associates' desires to be a partner, the lack of professional jealousy. These answers provide clues to why law firms are effective. Other reasons or combination of these reasons are based on my own observations and analysis.

Homogeneity of Lawyers —

The meaning of homogeneity for the organization of the law firm needs elaboration. One aspect of this homogeneity is the lawyers' agreement about the right to disagree. The law, which is often complex and ill-defined, is subject to debate. In addition, most of these lawyers are trained in a way which demands a disputatious attitude. This fact at once makes it more difficult to maintain some aspects of formal organization, and provides the law offices with an accepted technique for getting to the heart of the client's matter. Since disputation is not only acceptable but necessary, the organization must be able to allow disagreement between people of different ages and status. Any disputation, however, must be carried on within rules which are accepted as socially proper. The large law firms guarantee this condition by choosing men with similar social and legal backgrounds who recognize these social regulations, thus modifying the chances of conflict and avoiding the necessity for additional formal controls to do this job.

This homogeneity of backgrounds also permits communication short-cuts. In a factory or in a hospital[5] where workers are from different social classes and have a variety of skills and training, additional rules are necessary. Here a single professional category is involved and the needs of co-ordination are not as great as would be the case if several professions were cooperating. A supervising lawyer does not have to describe in detail as many aspects of a job to his subordinate. The ability to short-cut is helped immeasurably by the brightness of the associates, or, as Kriesberg hypothesizes: "The greater the homogeneity of the social origins of the organization's members, the greater organizational consensus is likely to be."[6]

Law Review —

Men on the law reviews of the major law schools are reputed to be especially bright; they are at the top of their class. Many members of the samples had been on a law journal. One firm which I studied, for example, employed seventy-four associates; fifty of them had been members of a law review. The law firms come to depend upon the special training these men receive. Law review training is important for the organization of large firms in that it helps prepare individuals to write, to criticize, and to practice in groups. The law review, especially at the schools from which the large law firms do most of their recruitment, teaches a man how to work with others and how to work long hours. It also teaches responsibility and the need for perfection. David Riesman,[7] an ex-law reviewer himself, writes:

> Let me turn for an illustration of this last point [effect of legal education] to a few remarks about that most remarkable institution of the law school world, the law review. So far as I know, there is nothing in any other professional group which remotely resembles this guild of students who, working even harder than their fellows, manage to cooperate sufficiently to meet the chronic emergency of a periodical. Indeed, this cooperation often develops an island of teamwork in a sea of ruthless rivalry.[8]

A number of present and past review men were asked in detailed interviews to tell how they thought law review affected them or would affect them in the large law firms. One president of the *Harvard Law Review*, describing the work on that journal, amplifies our understanding:

> A man on law review quickly becomes aware of his responsibility. We try to train younger men to the notion that they do a good job by hard work and organized editing. These boys spend eight

hours a day here and work six and a half days a week. Everything is rewritten—comma per comma. We have a tradition of perfection, and a man of wider experience gets a number of cracks at the thing—usually, of course, he is an officer. In all, there are about seven readings of a paper. Law review does offer a special training.

A former law review man who had been with a large law firm and who at the time of the interview was a professor at one of the "national" law schools pointed out some aspects of the law reviewer's job:

It involves intense research and writing and a joint application to a piece of work which can improve it. The fact that law review students spend so little time in class indicates how important law review is. Exams don't test things in a substantive way; the law review does. Law reviews have their own tradition, and the big law reviews, like the big firms, are conservative. Law review men work so hard that they have to apply to get a weekend off. All this training, of course, helps them when they first get to the large law firms.

An editor of the *Harvard Law Review* stated:

We're divided into departments and we're set up like a law firm. I, for example, decide what is to be written. Some other officers have no jurisdiction over substantive work.

Q: Does the law review give you special training?

A: Yes. Here is what we do. We come up here three weeks before the rest of the law school. The first work you do is to read the advance sheets, picking out cases that are important. You learn a lot of law, but it is pretty tedious work and you then appraise each case. In the second step, you give the case to the case editor. Then we have what we call "prelims."

I'm given the name of a case, and then I'm to summarize the issue involved. It is the same process as one goes through in a large law firm when you research a point of law. We do it constantly throughout the year. It is an exercise in quick legal writing. We are encouraged to take on things we know nothing about.

Writing up these cases is one of the most valuable things we learn. After we brief a case, then we write up a case note—the first draft is due in eight days. You are supposed to know everything there is to know about a particular small part of the law.

After your first draft, you are assigned to a third year man, and you go over the notes sentence by sentence—this takes three to seven days. This type of experience is important for the editor because he is getting partnership type experience. There is an intense exchange of ideas also. Then we go through the final editing and polish up the language. Then there is an officers' meeting and they criticize, and it may go back to us.

We write notes about any area of the law. It takes three weeks for the job and the process is the same as the case notes, except that it is more creative and it brings things together.

All third-year law school men have to write a paper. We have to do that, plus the notes we produce. Consequently, we do better on papers than anyone else. This experience should help us in writing briefs.

One other experience that work on the law review provides is that you learn to work hard and also at night. If I only worked from 9 to 5, I wouldn't know what to do with the rest of my time. Most of us work at night. Law review work is the kind of work you do for a partner, only you don't learn strategy.

The choice of law review men by many law firms is not an accident. They want them because being on a law review is a sign not only of recognition and achievement but also of intelligence and special training. Most young lawyers when they first enter law firms are required to do basic research. Law review men have had to do more such work than other law graduates, and they have subjected their work and themselves to the critical scrutiny of their peers and superiors. They learn to work as a team. This gives them an initial head start in the firm, because partners can assume that these graduates will be able to do their research job without detailed instructions. When law review graduates who were actually working in large law firms were asked the value of their law review experience, a typical answer involved ease of adjustment:

My adjustment would have been much harder here if I had not been on the law review. It is very broadening; it also gives you confidence. You can do your work a lot faster when you are not fearful of doing it incorrectly.

Law review work does more than build confidence; it offers training in perfection—a commodity in which large law firms pride themselves. Law review develops devotion to the law—a necessity if an associate expects to survive in one of these firms. Working together on the law review instructs the individual not only in work habits but also in the nuances of organizational life. For example, it helps the recruit adjust to superiors. As one review officer pointed out: "Second-year people know less than third-year people and depend upon them." Editors also see something of the hierarchy which is found in the large firm when they allocate funds or when, acting as heads of departments, they assign work. Their experiences on the law reviews help these men adjust quickly to the needs of the law office and saves the law firms time and money.

Image of Self —

If it were possible to construct a model of an average associate's concept of self, it would probably read something like this:

I feel that I am capable, responsible, and intelligent; that I have received superior training and that success in some form is inevitable; that I am destined to deal with important people and matters.

This concept of self is important for the large law firm. These lawyers feel they must try to live up to their image. The lawyer himself, therefore, provides an important work motivator. Most of the men under discussion have been brought up believing they would be successful. They do what they can to make this belief come true. In a more practical way, however, the associate knows his professional future is at stake if he doesn't perform up to the expectations of the law firm. His chances for a partnership will disappear. His reputation as a lawyer, at least among his Wall Street colleagues, will be demeaned. His chances of being recommended for the choice jobs with his firm's corporate clients will decrease. Thus the lawyer *must* try to live up to this self-concept. Lawyers feel this way not only about themselves, but about most of their colleagues. This mutual respect makes it even more important for lawyers to live up to the expectations both they and the other lawyers share.

Esprit de Corps —

This common enthusiasm for each other and for the law office plays an important part in enabling firms to function without extreme formalization of their organization. Both the existence of *esprit de corps* and its importance to the social structure of the large law firm can be documented. Thirty associates, when asked to rate the ten most important large law firms in New York City, always placed their own at, or fairly near, the top.[9] In every firm visited, lawyers would claim for their office "the top tax man" or the best litigator. In general, they were proud of each other and they were pleased with the fact that they were connected with their present firm. This does not, of course, mean there is no discontent nor any competition, but the discontent and competition are usually impersonal, and if there is criticism, it goes no further than the firm.

Sixteen per cent of those quizzed claim that *esprit de corps* is helpful to the organization because it signifies a willingness on the part of the members to adjust to each other. An extreme statement of this is seen in a young associate's remark: "I have never heard a lawyer talk about another lawyer. It's hero worship. If my partner said, 'Jump from the twenty-eighth floor,' I would consider it; if he said it, there must be a good reason." Another young lawyer reports: "If my officemate is busy and he sees that I am busier, he'll say, 'Can I help?' We really have a school spirit." This spirit is helpful because it allows the firm to be informal. Members are willing to accommodate and to help each other. It minimizes conflict, aids in adjustment, and thereby takes the burden off the formal organization which might otherwise find it necessary to supply formal techniques to keep harmony.

Controlled Competition[10] —

The structure of the law firm is such that it tends to control detrimental competition within its organization without the need to develop the many formal rules to achieve this end which are found in other large social systems. It does this in part through its hiring practice, which in most instances calls for the employment in each hiring year of recruits who graduated at the same time and are of the same vintage. There appears to be a high correlation between age and increased respect lawyers have for each other. This respect may be based on the fact that these attorneys tend not to become obsolescent (although there finally is a point of diminishing returns). Experience and wisdom are assets and the hierarchy tends to reflect actual competence. Marvin Bressler suggests[11] that law be contrasted with other disciplines which are changing much more rapidly, such as sociology or physics or the occupations affected by automation, in which a man trained ten years earlier may not actually be as competent as his juniors. Since firms also restrict the employment of older, more experienced lawyers from the outside, lawyers of the same age rise through the ranks in orderly fashion and generally are assigned to different departments. This assures that men of different ages and status will work together on the same matter, except where specialists are needed, thus limiting some competition. (In fact differential specialization in itself limits competition since the participants are involved in different tasks and work out of different departments.)[12] This is true also for partners, where competition is modified by the age gradation, which starts with vintage recruitment. In addition, partners receive help from their partnership agreement.

The outsiders' restricted access to the firm limits the competition of both associates and partners to the inside group; this offers some career security. Perhaps as important for all lawyers in the firm is the need for teamwork, which limits the nature of competition. That some lawyers recognize this social structural force is seen in the statement of the 14 per cent of those asked about the effectiveness of their law firm who replied by saying that the "work requires it." We have already seen how professional norms buttressed the demands of the firm for teamwork by stimulating both formal and informal "helping out," and thus modifying competition.

Lawyers in these firms share and depend upon the same clients for their livelihood. Partners, at least, are committed to their firm; this in itself may aid *esprit de corp* and control competition. One indication that competition between partners is indeed controlled is seen in the fact that relatively few firms have broken up. Some have, to be sure, and it is these modern exceptions which caused comment. Anyone who has lived for a while in the world of the Wall Street lawyer has heard about the Cleary-Gottlieb rupture with the Dewey-Ballantine firm, the break-up of the Chadbourne office, or the split between the Hughes, Hubbard & Blair offices and the development of what is now called Royall, Koegel & Rogers. In most instances, however, partners do not leave their law firms unless they go on temporary duty with the government or retire. It would be difficult for an attorney, even if he wanted to capture a large corporate client and set up his own office, to do so. The client and the law firm become so entwined that it is hard, both psychologically and in terms of obtaining the best legal advice, for a client to leave a law firm to which he has grown accustomed. This picture is dramatically presented by Louis Auchincloss, himself a former associate in a large firm, who vividly describes the difficulty in his novel, *A Law for the Lion*.

In addition, the partnership name is worth money. Dissolution of a law office means the end of a good thing. Most partners are earning too much to want to rock the boat; therefore, if for no other reason, they are willing to work together and make the firm work well. The glory of the firm is their glory; they could not over any long period harm colleagues without harming themselves. In short, the need for staying together puts a limit on competition and accentuates cooperation.

Rewards —

Throughout this discussion the effectiveness of a reward system has been implied. Merton[13] writes persuasively of the power of reward as an agent for conformity. In this context, it can be considered an agent of cooperation. Both partners and associates are subject to its lure. It is one reason why lawyers stay with the firm and why it operates successfully. Reward is found as a motive for behavior in every large organization. Its pull for associates, however, is not so great as it probably is for most other employed workers. Among these lawyers are some of the best graduates of the elite law schools, and they are eagerly sought after by other employers. The reward system of the firm, therefore, is somewhat weakened by the easy availability of other reward systems. Nevertheless, the associates are surrounded by its potential. The most important acknowledgment is to be asked to stay as a partner. This possibility with its implied benefits is the strongest reward, although there are others (and they do not constitute all possible rewards at the disposal of the large firm): for example, the prestige of being with an important firm; training; relative security; almost annual raises; important, "independent," and interesting work as well as the opportunity to deal directly with the client; seniority, with its psychic income in the form of a larger office and/or a secretary; the possibility of directing other younger associates.

The reward system is more effective for partners; they have more at stake. It would be difficult for them, if they were to start again on their own, to have as much prestige, profits or working conditions which allow for such propitious use of time.

INFORMAL RULES

EVERY organization has, in addition to its formal rules, numerous informal regulations which can be categorized as social (mainly external) and office (mainly internal). Those social rules which are the result of class training are a continuation of practices prevalent outside the law firms. Although rules of this nature seem to be minor, disobedience of a great number of them can be a nuisance to an organization, because recognition of "proper" social behavior helps ease relationships.

Informal internal office rules are in many instances so completely accepted and stable that they might almost be considered formal; for example, the seating arrangement of "door man" and "window man" described in Chapter 8.

As in other organizations, formal rules are often modified and informal ones take their place. Lawyers feel these informal rules give them a bit more independence, although they can work the other way as well.

Some rules are a combination of external social rules and informal office norms. For example, an associate usually does not openly discuss the possibility of his becoming a member of the firm with a partner. To discuss salary with a partner or to ask what the next man is getting is not considered proper, and as far as this investigator could tell, not done very often. One senior associate states about other informal rules:

> You don't get drunk at firm parties. You don't practice on the outside, except work for your close family or friends, and then only with permission. Obeying these rules in itself will not get you a partnership, but if you disobey them and it is a pretty close decision, it might hurt.

Judgment —

Informal rules range from the firmly established informal regulations which are easily determined to the very informal rules which are difficult to codify. They cover behavior which includes dealing with clients and colleagues as well as regulations about standards of work and of progress. Many lawyers used the words "good judgment" when trying to explain why their firm was effective. "Our men have good judgment." An analysis of their statements reveals that to be considered as having good judgment, an associate must either have the ability to determine the idosyncratic behavior of the partner he is working for or the ability correctly to interpret and codify the difficult rules.[14] Partners prefer associates who can do both. Our interest here is with the latter formularization. The firms expected every lawyer to be able to recognize and deal correctly with the formal and the more stable informal rules. They were pleased when an associate could also correctly interpret the not so easily recognizable informal rules. Associates, for example, have to be able to decide when to call upon a partner for help. As one young lawyer put it: "Personal success, or lack of it, depends upon your *judgment* in keeping a partner up to date on things he is interested in—and to get off his back." Another associate when asked, "Under what circumstances do you call on the partners for help?" replied: "It is a matter of judgment to decide what you know and what you don't know. If I'm sure, I'll bring it up with someone at my own level first, and then decide whether this is something for a partner or not." The informal rules involved in this situation seem to be: never bother a partner unless it is absolutely necessary, and never take a chance which might lead to an error. These two rules can conflict. Good judgment implies following the best choice and the best choice in turn involves interpreting the informal rules in the same manner as the partners. An associate gets a good reputation when he consistently demonstrates "good judgment."

There are many other examples which point up the importance of good judgment. Client contact provides one of these. An associate often has to decide whether and/or when he should speak to the client himself, or whether he should ask the partner to do it. This decision is more complicated than it appears because the associate would prefer to see the client personally. It gives him a much desired contact and relieves the partner of some of his duties. The associate has to make sure, however, that the client wants to see him and not the partner, that he is right about the law, that he can sell the client on a course of behavior, and that the partner will not object to his taking this initiative. Since becoming a partner depends a great deal on whether the firm thinks an associate has good judgment, the special dilemma of the employee lawyer is heightened. If he takes his opportunities and is successful fairly consistently over the years, he will be thought of as having good judgment. If he fails, he will be considered to have poor judgment.

It is easy for a lawyer to follow defined precedent. Many of the informal rules of behavior pose no problem. But to know when to write an opinion letter and send it out without a partner's seeing it, is much more difficult. In one case described to me, an associate showing poor judgment was subsequently "let go":

> He [the associate] rushed in at the last moment with a fifty-page brief. The partner needed this brief to bring to a client. He didn't get to read it until he was on his plane. Then he found it was inadequate and that it had not been proofread adequately. On his return, he asked me [also a young associate] what I had thought of the man. I told him. "Why didn't you tell me before?" "Not my place and you didn't ask." "Why," said the partner, "doesn't he have better judgment?" He didn't proofread [rule] and he doesn't organize his work [rule], and he worked on the weekend when it cost more [rule].

Partners, of course, must also show good judgment, because

success for both the law firm and the client depends upon this quality in the partner. It is important, for example, that partners pick the right man to join them, that they know whom to assign to various legal tasks, that they be able to determine whether or not associates are using good judgment.

The Special Role of the Client —

The client directly affects the organization of the law firm in two major ways. First, he requires from it an explanation of its fees. This is normally handled by the firm through the formal organization which sets up elaborate procedures for keeping diaries, for filing, and for converting time spent on a client's matters into dollars and cents. Second, since the large corporate client is sophisticated in the ways of the law and its law firm, the client can delegate some work directly to the appropriate specialist in the firm, rather than channeling everything through the senior partner in charge of their general legal work. This is often made more feasible because many lawyers who have practiced with the large firms join the corporate clients after they leave. A process of parallel escalation then takes place. While the alumni are climbing the corporate ladder, lawyers of the same vintage who remain with the firm are rising in power and status with the law firm. These men tend to keep in contact and to consult each other, and the law firms sponsor this procedure by having dinner parties for the alumni. It is true that a method has to be set up so that eventually the client's senior legal consultant knows what is going on. Nevertheless, client assignment relieves the firm of some of its assignment duties and adds to the client's confidence, for he can better appreciate the depth of specialization in the firm. In addition, the system of parallel escalation helps develop a communication system between the client and the law firm which can bypass the formal communication channels—providing still another short-cut for the law office.

SOCIAL CONTROL

SOCIAL control, which is an essential part of organization, is, as we have seen, affected by both the formal and informal rules of an organization. This control is reinforced by external rules,[15] again both formal and informal, both governmental and professional. The latter regulations, to be discussed presently, were not specifically formulated to be of help to the organization of large law firms. Rather, they were to serve as models of behavior and as aids for insuring conformity,[16] as conceived by the leaders of the bar, for the "free," self-employed professional. However, these external professional controls are especially salient for this discussion for they point up one weapon in the arsenal of control techniques available to professional large-scale organizations which is not available, or certainly not to the same degree, to nonprofessional institutions.

There are a number of pressures which converge on the Wall Street lawyer to prevent him from violating these professional norms. The pressures within the organization come from the heads of the hierarchy, from the colleague work unit, and from the lawyer himself (conscience). Some external pressures to conform come from the lay community, whose general notions of right and wrong are often accepted by the lawyer. If the community's specific demands are held strongly enough, they tend to be reflected in professional canons of ethics and in rules legislated by the state. Nevertheless, it is the profession which formulates these demands for their members and for the state. These rules are policed by the government and by the bar associations and monitored by the general public and the client.

In the case of the attorney in the large law firm, the pressures to conform to ethical rules are particularly strong, for his large corporate client is, Wall Street lawyers admit, knowledgeable about the law. In fact, many top corporate officials are lawyers. Those who are not, often have the readily available services of their house counsel. In addition, the giant corporations are especially concerned with the image their law firms mirror, for it reflects on their business. In addition to public and client control, instances of colleague and state control are numerous and tremendously important. How well all these sources of control are obeyed probably depends on a number of factors. Merton and Goode list the following important variables as influential:

a. How strongly the belief is actually held by the members of the profession.

b. The frequency of occurrence of given kinds of temptations.

c. The attraction of the temptation itself.

d. The likelihood that punishment will actually occur.

e. The seriousness of the punishment.[17]

EXTERNAL PROFESSIONAL RULES

THERE appears to be a consensus among sociologists that recognition of informal values and norms is extremely important if formal codes are to be obeyed. This is especially true for external formal and professional controls, since professional codes are not thoroughly policed, nor are those who break the rules always uniformly punished. They would probably not be successful if professional people did not also have informal professional codes and a professional milieu.

It is this professional milieu that Goode writes about when he considers professions as being a community within a community; the characteristics which make up these professional communities (in reality there are many of them) are important for us at this point. Much of the professional behavior of lawyers in their law firm is due not to their own organizational controls but to those of the community of which they are a part. Goode's criteria for a professional community helps illuminate why this entity, external to the law firm, functions as it does. He lists the following characteristics:

(1) Its members are bound by a sense of identity. (2) Once in it, few leave, so that it is a terminal or continuing status for the most part. (3) Its members share values in common. (4) Its role definitions *vis-à-vis* both members and non-members are agreed upon and are the same for all members. (5) Within the areas of communal action there is a common language, which is understood only partially by outsiders. (6) The Community has power over its members. (7) Its limits are reasonably clear, though they are not physical and geographical, but social. (8) Though it does not produce the next generation biologically, it does so socially

through its control over the selection of professional trainees, and through its training processes it sends these recruits through an adult socialization process.[18]

Wall Street lawyers are a special lot and have their own subcommunity. The fact that it is smaller; that many of its members know each other; that for most part they work in relatively small geographical areas (they also live near each other); that many of them are part of a legal elite and many more expect to be, makes the force of this subcommunity serve as an even stronger instrument of social control than the larger professional unit.

Informal External Professional Rules —

All professions have informal codes. Some of these informal norms are peculiar to a particular profession and others are common to all established ones. Kornhauser lists four criteria of professionalism:

> a. specialized competence that has a considerable intellectual content;
> b. extensive autonomy in exercising the special competence;
> c. strong commitment to a career based on the special competence; and
> d. influence and responsibility in the use of special competence.[19]

These criteria are backed by appropriate professional values. All professions disapprove of emotional involvement with the client; all feel that professional decision-making must not be based on the self-interest of the professional; all say that professional service must be based on the need of the client and not on the ability to pay; all have values to protect standards of excellence; all demand the highest possible standards.[20] There are, of course, many other professional norms, but these suffice to indicate the presence of a value system which underlies formal professional rules.

These values are generally learned in the schools and reinforced or reinterpreted by colleague contacts in practice. Lawyers almost imperceptibly take on these professional norms.[21] In a study of law students at Indiana University, where no course in legal ethics was offered, third-year law students took on the highly ethical attitudes (as measured by situational questions derived from the canons of ethics) of their professors.[22] For the Wall Street lawyer, these professional attitudes are further strengthened by contact with the most respected men in the law firms. Most lawyers in the sample considered it improper to criticize the work of other lawyers in or out of their firm, or gossip about them. It was difficult even to get these attorneys to rate the various law firms, for they thought giving such information unprofessional. There are, of course, many other examples of professional rules.

The informal rules which are external to the firms often serve the function of making both internal and external formal rules unnecessary, and in terms of a general atmosphere of professional behavior, buttress the formal regulations of the profession. That this connection is overtly recognized by members of the sample is seen in the statements of 47.5 per cent of the respondents who thought that professional responsibility (which certainly is part of the general professional climate) was what made the loosely organized law firms work.

It is difficult to separate the impact of formal and informal rules on the functioning of the law firm, for each affects the other; the process is circular. It is possible, however, to separate the formal professional rules from the informal for the purposes of this discussion.

Formal External Professional Rules —

The lawyers in the sample offered, as one reason why the loose organization of the large law firm is effective, that it is directed in part by the formal external rules of the profession. The canons of ethics and the rules of the courts provide the main regulations, and the legislated code another. These are reinforced by the various professional associations and the courts. It is maintained here that these extra-organizational rules provide part of the guidance lawyers need and that the courts and the professional associations provide the sanctions. Therefore, the practicing organization (the large law firm) does not have to create its own rules to the extent that they are provided for by outside agencies who police them to some degree. It is true, however, that large firms do have their own additional rules of ethics which they enforce and which go beyond the official canons; some lawyers feel that the large law firms, not the outside agencies, do most of the controlling.

The main outside organizations which control the lawyers' professional behavior are the bar associations, the government, and more specifically, the courts. One primary source is the Canons of Professional Ethics.[23] Although even the canons state in their preamble that:

> No code or set of rules can be framed, which will particularize all the duties of the lawyer in the varying phases of litigation or in all the relations of professional life. The following canons of ethics are adopted by the American Bar Association as a general guide, yet the enumeration of particular duties should not be construed as a denial of the existence of others equally imperative, though not specifically mentioned.

Lawyers did not always have these written prescriptions. It was George Sharswood who, through his *Essay on Professional Ethics,* was considered responsible for formalizing these ideals of lawyers. Sharswood felt the function of the canons was to define the high moral principles he thought every lawyer needs:

> There is certainly, without any exception, no profession in which so many temptations beset the path to swerve from the line of strict integrity; in which so many delicate and difficult questions of duty are continually arising. There are pitfalls and mantraps at every step, and the mere youth, at the very outset of his career, needs often the prudence and self-denial, as well as the moral courage, which belong commonly to riper years. High moral principle is his only safe guide; the only torch to light his way amidst darkness and obstruction.[24]

It was not until 1908, however, that the Canons of Professional Ethics were adopted by the American Bar Association. The principle additions were passed in 1928. Essentially, the forty-seven canons furnish, as do most professional codes, the clues to proper behavior in three main areas of social relationship; i.e., between the professional and the client, professional and fellow professional, and between the professional and society.

A report of the Special Committee of the Bar Foundation on a plan for the study of the Canons of Professional and Judicial Ethics notes that the canons "contain a mixture of statements of fundamental principles, illustrations of the application of rules to specific types of conduct, statements of the etiquette of the profession, and rules given operative force by courts in disciplinary proceedings."[25] Trumbull, who placed the canons in categories, defined sharply what the canons generally cover.

Responsibility

Canon   1. The Duty of the Lawyer to the Courts
Canon   2. The Selection of Judges
Canon 29. Upholding the Honor of the Profession
Canon 32. The Lawyer's Duty in Its Last Analysis
Canon 26. Professional Advocacy Other Than Before Courts

The Right to Practice Law

Canon 35. Intermediaries
Canon 40. Newspapers
Canon 47. Aiding the Unauthorized Practice of Law

Fiduciary Relationship to Client

Canon   6. Adverse Influences and Conflicting Interests
Canon 36. Retirement from Judicial Position or Public Employment
Canon 37. Confidences of a Client
Canon   8. Advising Upon the Merits of a Client's Cause
Canon 10. Acquiring Interest in Litigation
Canon 42. Expenses
Canon 11. Dealing with Trust Property
Canon 38. Compensation, Commissions and Rebates

Limitations on Duty to Client

Canon 15. How Far a Lawyer May Go in Supporting a
　　　　　 Client's Cause
Canon 16. Restraining Clients from Improprieties
Canon 41. Discovery of Imposition and Deception
Canon 22. Candor and Fairness
Canon 3. Attempts to Exert Personal Influence on the Court
Canon 23. Attitude Toward Jury
Canon 18. Treatment of Witnesses and Litigants
Canon 9. Negotiations with Opposite Party
Canon 39. Witnesses
Canon 19. Appearance of Lawyer as Witness for His Client
Canon 20. Newspaper Discussion of Pending Litigation

Freedom To Serve or Not To Serve

Canon 31. Responsibility for Litigation
Canon 30. Justifiable and Unjustifiable Litigations
Canon 4. When Counsel for an Indigent Prisoner
Canon 5. The Defense or Prosecution of Those Accused
　　　　　 of Crime
Canon 7. Professional Colleagues and Conflicts of Opinion
Canon 44. Withdrawal from Employment as Attorney or Counsel

Professional Fees

Canon 12. Fixing the Amount of the Fee
Canon 13. Contingent Fees
Canon 14. Suing a Client for a Fee
Canon 34. Division of Fees

Solicitation and Advertising

Canon 27. Advertising, Direct or Indirect
Canon 28. Stirring Up Litigation, Directly or Through Agents
Canon 43. Approved Law Lists
Canon 45. Specialists
Canon 46. Notice to Local Lawyers
Canon 33. Partnerships—Names

Relations with Other Lawyers, Clients, and the Public

Canon 17. Ill-Feeling and Personalities Between Advocates
Canon 21. Punctuality and Expedition
Canon 24. Right of Lawyer to Control the Incidents of the Trial
Canon 25. Taking Technical Advantage of Opposite Counsel;
        Agreements with Him.[26]

What the canons say has been added to by what the courts and the
bar associations have determined when trying to enforce these
norms. Henry Drinker, who is considered the foremost authority
on the canons of ethics, has written a book[27] discussing some of
the cases and decisions, thereby furnishing the Bar with additional instructions; he is, in other words, helping to build a
special type of "common law."

It is true, as F. B. MacKinnon[28] says, that the canons are not
up to date, and this is especially so for lawyers in large law firms.
The canons provide few guide lines on the rights and duties of the
employee lawyer, or how a partnership should deal with a corporate client, or what the corporate lawyer's responsibility is for
giving both business and legal advice, or to whom in the corporation he owes his loyalty. Questions of professional ethics arise
when an attorney is on the board of directors of a large corporate
organization and thus becomes both client and lawyer.

Despite the fact that all canons do not affect all lawyers equally
and that additional canons are needed and some old ones require
modernizing, the canons of professional ethics do have an important effect on the organization of large law firms. Some of this
is reflected in the firm's formal rules, but usually these cover only
the most important mandates, as in the care most firms exercise
to avoid conflict-of-interest situations.

The firm takes a hand in seeing that the canons of ethics are
enforced. This is not too difficult a job. The caliber of men hired
and retained (especially law review men who probably become
conscious of professional responsibility before others) by the large
law firms makes it less likely that many would be willing to risk
their reputation by being unethical.[29] In addition, these firms can
afford to be ethical. As one partner said, "It just doesn't pay for
us to be unethical. There is no incentive." A lawyer in a small
firm, talking about the giants, reminisced: "It's a case of *noblesse*

oblige—I remember being asked by a big firm to fix up a phony divorce. I refused; they didn't want to soil their hands." And as a large law firm partner suggested:

> It is difficult also to tell what ethics are. You've heard the story about the man in the grocery store who was given two ten dollar bills which had stuck together, instead of the one that he deserved. His son seeing him keep it asked if that was ethical. He replied the only ethics involved were whether he should tell his partner.

Large law firms work in areas of the law which the canons of ethics may not cover, as well as in the more traditional types of law practice. Large law firms usually will not handle divorce cases or defend professional criminals or accept negligence work. Their clients "are the kind that everybody is looking at and you would have to be careful—there are just too many people out to get you." Higher standards are required by the public of big business as against small business. Glen McDaniel[30] suggests that the changing nature of big business (which implies a change in ownership from the single or family owner to the stockholders) and the development of the corporation manager who is proud of his reputation have made ethical problems of counsel for big business less substantial than if the lawyer were handling small business. In addition, since much of the work in large law firms depends upon team play, it is more difficult for an individual lawyer in the firm to be unethical. As one associate put it: "If they caught you, they would fire you."

The bar associations and the courts all attempt to enforce the canons. It is usually the Supreme Court or the Appellate Court of a state which decides whether a lawyer is to be disciplined for a breach of the canons; it is the bar associations, often after a former client has protested, which initiate the complaint. These cases, according to Henry Drinker, involve two distinct characteristics: those involving conduct demonstrating that the lawyer cannot properly be trusted to advise and represent clients and those involving conduct which would cast a serious reflection on the dignity of the court and the reputation of the profession.[31] The Committee on Inquiry of the Association checks into the merits of the complaints and then determines what must be done. In New York City, for the period 1960–1961, the Association of the Bar of the City of New York reports that 1843 matters were referred to the Committee on Grievances. This was 141 more than for the preceding year and 219 more than were received for the 1950–1951 period. The 1960–61 committee heard the cases on only 44 lawyers, "and the court, upon petitions filed by this Association, took affirmative action against twenty-three members of the bar."[32] The Appellate Court disbarred 14, suspended 5, censured 4, and dropped proceedings against 3 lawyers.[33] Although not many lawyers were punished, the threat exists, and the stigma for a lawyer of even having his name listed is great. It can be presumed, then, that the canons act as deterrents against antisocial behavior (even if the specific canons are not remembered) and as models for proper behavior, and that the bar associations do constitute (even though few are disbarred) disciplinary forces for large law offices. This makes the law firms' policing task easier.

The bar associations, like other professional associations, have at their disposal further techniques for social control—for example, they provide additional ways of gaining client and colleague recognition and many Wall Street lawyers have been president of the Association of the Bar of the City of New York.

Furthermore, the bar association journals,[34] besides serving as outlets for new ideas, as a corollary provide a reward and recognition system for the contributors. Kornhauser, writing about the same phenomena, finds that "professional associations provide *stimulation* of the individual's work, *recognition* of his contributions, and *support* of his identification with the professional community."[35]

Lawyers seeking to fulfill these kinds of social needs may find it necessary to play the game as the bar association wants it played; they must live up to the professional norms prescribed by the association. Since almost all of the Wall Street lawyers are members of the American Bar Association,[36] and many are members of the Association of the Bar of the City of New York (in some instances the firms pay the dues), this membership, plus the potential of important rewards, provides another pressure for this elite to obey the professional norms.

Control by the Courts —

The courts play a part in the organization of law firms in two major ways: (1) they prescribe acceptable modes of behaving in court and set schedules which help determine the working calendar for the firm's lawyers; (2) they can and do discipline lawyers who do not obey their dictates. Eliott E. Cheatham succinctly reviews the sanctions and supports the court offers professional standards. He writes:

> The proceedings in which they [the processes of the courts] are invoked may be classified as: (a) criminal prosecutions, (b) contempt proceedings, (c) injunctive proceedings, (d) actions for damages or proceedings for the denial of fees or liens, (e) the declaration of a mistrial or the grant of a new trial because of misconduct by the lawyer for one of the parties, (f) summary proceedings, (g) disciplinary proceedings for censure, suspension, or disbarment.[37]

The courts have power over the bar and police it. Cheatham writes that this power is maintained through contempt and disciplinary proceedings, through inquiring into the general standards of conduct of the bar, and through deciding who can become or remain a lawyer.[38] The judiciary can help decide the general organization of the bar. Its exclusive field of activity, of major importance to us here, is the power of the "courts to determine their own rules of procedure and practice."[39] Because the lawyers in the large firms must follow these rules which offer guides to proper behavior, the managerial task of the law firm is eased. Most courts have specific rules covering wide assortments of behavior including such items as when to serve a summons, when to answer a pleading, notes on proper pretrial procedure, and manner of taking appeals to the application for rehearing.

Rules of the Court —

The Supreme Court of the United States lists fifty-one Supreme Court rules which affect the lawyer. Some state in detail just how an attorney must proceed to file a notice of appeal, as illustrated in U.S. Supreme Court Rule 10:

1. An appeal permitted by law to this court shall be taken by filing a notice of appeal, in the form and at the place prescribed by this rule.

2. The notice of appeal shall be in three parts: (a) It shall specify the party or parties taking the appeal; shall designate the judgment or part thereof appealed from, giving its date and the time of its entry; shall specify the statute under which the appeal to this court is taken; and, if in a criminal case, shall include a general statement of the offense, the sentence imposed, and the place of confinement if the defendant below is in custody. (b) It shall include a designation of the portions of the record to be certified by the clerk of the lower court to this court. (c) It shall set forth the questions presented by the appeal, expressed in the terms and circumstances of the case but without unnecessary detail. The statement of the questions should be short and concise, should not be repetitious, and should not resemble in form or particularity the former assignments of error which are abolished by paragraph 4 of this rule. The statement of a question presented will be deemed to include every subsidiary question fairly comprised therein. Only the questions set forth in the notice of appeal or fairly comprised therein will be considered by the court. The notice of appeal shall include proof of service on all adverse parties as prescribed by Rule 33. A failure to comply with these requirements will be a sufficient reason for dismissing the appeal. For forms of notices of appeal, see the Appendix to these rules.

3. If the appeal is taken from a federal court, the notice of appeal shall be filed with the clerk of such court. If the appeal is taken from a state court, the notice of appeal shall be filed with the clerk of the court possessed of the record.

4. The petition for allowance of appeal, the order allowing appeal, the assignment of errors, the citation, and the bond for costs of appeal in cases governed by these rules are abolished.[40]

These prescriptions of behavior would have less meaning if in many instances the courts did not have behind them the right and the ability to enforce. U.S. Supreme Court Rule 8, for example, discusses disbarment. In *People ex rel Karlin v. Culkin* 162 N.E. 487 (1928), Justice Cardozo, writing the decision, ruled that the court had the right to discipline a member of the bar. The following partial summary of his argument taken from that case states what is now an accepted point of view:

> Membership in the bar is a privilege burdened with conditions, and one admitted thereto becomes an officer of the court, and an instrument or agency to advance the ends of justice by co-operating with court whenever justice would otherwise be imperiled.
>
> The Appellate Division may direct a general inquiry into conduct of members of bar, and compel one of them to testify as to his professional acts, subject to this claim of privilege, if answer will expose him to punishment . . .
>
> Power of court to inquire into professional conduct of attorneys as its officers imports power to inquire by appropriate and adequate methods, including compulsory process, if necessary.
>
> Refusal of attorney to answer questions as to his professional acts in general inquisition by Appellate Division into conduct of attorneys on petition of bar associations *held* a contempt, under Civil Practice Act, ¶ 406.

To the extent that large law firms are still involved in litigation these procedures make it unnecessary for the firms to create their own regulations to cover required behavior. Nor is it necessary for the law office to do any extensive policing, for the courts have the power to enforce their own standards. This can be generalized for the function of other external rules because what all of them do is provide guides for behavior and make it less necessary for the firm to formulate its own regulations. The minimization of internal rules and the fact that external prescriptions do not usually have to be formally monitored by the firm gives the associate a feeling of independence and responsibility (a necessary part of the informal professional milieu) and makes the task of managing easier and more pleasant.

PROFESSIONAL BUREAUCRACY

THESE observations have importance for social theory for they bring to the sociologist's attention another type, or at least another dimension,[41] of bureaucracy. Gouldner developed Weber's concept of bureaucracy in observing that there were three types (instead of the two Weber implied) which Gouldner labeled *mock, punishment-centered,* and *representative.*[42] Basically, they can be described as follows: in mock bureaucracy, little obedience to the rules can be found because the rules are imposed from the outside and neither management nor labor agrees with the regulations; punishment-centered bureaucracy involves rules formulated by either labor or management and enforced by one upon the other; representative bureaucracy involves formal norms which all groups in an organization accept and follow.

Recently a number of studies have been published which deal with the relationship between professional employees and the bureaucratic organizations for which they work. Researchers in this area observed the strains between the professional and the organization. Independently, all discovered some organizational patterns having to do with the control of the professional worker by the organization or the control or attempt at control of the organization by the professional employee. They have given these patterns various names, and while all overlap, all are somewhat different. In addition, they also differ to a degree from Gouldner's bureaucratic patterns and the pattern discovered through the present investigation.

Wilensky,[43] in his study of intellectuals in labor unions, talks about one type of professional or semiprofessional (intellectual) who was oriented to a colleague group outside the union (this was not true of the other intellectual staff members). Gouldner, in a study of a small liberal arts college,[44] also found a segment of his population of academics committed to larger professional norms and oriented to outside reference groups. In both instances internal social controls are weakened by what Gouldner calls the "cosmopolitan" value systems of the professional employee. Norms of the larger external colleague group affect these professional workers' organizational behavior. (In the large law firm the permanent associates equal Gouldner's locals and associates "on the make" his cosmopolitans and the various types of rules affect them accordingly.)

Kornhauser, writing about chemists and chemical engineers,[45] discusses colleague control but finds that the professional associations of the people he studied were not strong enough to greatly affect their employment relationship. Logan Wilson finds that academic men work in what he calls a semibureaucracy.[46] His pattern is very much like Gouldner's representative bureaucracy. However, it is made up of a combination of professional self-control and hierarchical authority. Kornhauser, discussing the internal organization of a plant, discovered the same phenomena but found colleague control not to be as strong for the people he studied as it appears to be for academic men, or, as we have seen, for the Wall Street lawyer. Simon Marcson agrees, for he found, for the scientist in industry, both "executive authority" and "colleague authority."[47] In the latter instance authority is vested in the group rather than the individual. Marcson sees it as coming "within the framework of Representative Bureaucracy."

It is Mary E. W. Goss who discovers a type of bureaucracy not delineated by Gouldner, although she finds it is similar to Gouldner's representative bureaucracy. In fact, the claim is that they may supplement each other. She calls hers "advisory bureaucracy." Goss writes:

> This type [of bureaucracy] does not involve, as do the three outlined by Gouldner, organization "rules" that are "enforced" or "unenforced" by those in charge, or that are "obeyed" or "evaded" by those in subordinate positions. Rather than rules, specific technical knowledge and guiding principles for the application of this knowledge represent the content focus of advisory bureaucracy. Further, in advisory bureaucracy, the counterpart of enforcement of rules is the formal obligation to give advice based on technical knowledge; while the counterpart of obedience is the obligation to take such advice under critical review when making relevant decisions.[48]

The large law firms exhibited not only the three bureaucratic patterns Gouldner discovered in his study of a gypsum company but a fourth pattern which I have labeled *professional bureaucracy*. This pattern can be put on a continuum, as can the other bureaucratic patterns, and will depict some institutions as having few necessary elements and others many. The law firms, at least those parts which deal directly with its professional staff, seem not to have as many rules which could be labeled mock, representative or punishment-centered, but more rules which could be called professional.

While law firms have Gouldner's three patterns of bureaucracy, professional bureaucracy itself has elements of these three patterns. However, an examination of professional bureaucracy reveals the differences.

Following Gouldner and discussing only rules as the key factor in bureaucracy, since as Gouldner points out "bureaucratic rules are central to Max Weber's theory of bureaucracy,"[49] I find that professional bureaucracy is composed of external formal rules devised by (in the case of the lawyer) professional associations and the government, and supported by a professional milieu and public opinion which is generally favorable to the enforcement of these regulations. As has been pointed out, these rules affect the functioning of the large law institutions; in fact, become part of the organization.

These professional regulations are external to the organization but they are not usually mock, for lawyers (especially the elite) generally agree with the restrictions, or at least do not often question them. While they are representative, they are not representative in the way described by Gouldner, i.e., in terms of some common agreement between workers and management. Most of the canons, for example, are representative because of historical reasons (though large-firm lawyers would still agree with most of them) and are accepted because lawyers have been conditioned to accept them. This is especially true today inasmuch as the present-day lawyers have had little to do with deciding the formal rules and "learn" them in what probably amounts to a subliminal fashion. Only to the extent that external formal rules are currently being fashioned and represent the present sentiment of lawyers can these professional standards be considered to be similar to Gouldner's representative rules. Even then differences remain. Gouldner was writing about agreement between workers and management within the plant. We are talking about agreements between a community of colleagues outside of the office. For some attorneys, of course, some rules are punishment-centered in that the law firm, the bar associations, the courts, and/or the elites see to it that others follow them. All the rules involved apply to all lawyers equally, so that within the firm questions of hierarchy are not involved; in addition, professional bureaucracy is reinforced by strong informal professional norms and values. It is probably true that elements of professional bureaucracy even exist among Gouldner's nonprofessional gypsum workers. Certainly every occupation has its informal occupational rules, though perhaps they are not so strongly entrenched as are informal rules for a profession. Becker, for example, in his work on the dance hall musician,[50] points out the power of their informal external occupational norms. Delineating professional bureaucracy as a separate type does not mean that the three types of bureaucracy Gouldner discusses cannot also be found in the law firm; they can, as the summarizing chart indicates, and probably this will hold true for most bureaucratic organizations.

Professional bureaucracy differs from advisory bureaucracy and colleague authority in that it does directly involve formal rules —rules which are formulated outside the organization. It is similar in that advisory bureaucracy and colleague authority imply outside norms, if not a plethora of formal norms. Professional bureaucracy is similar also in that it promotes efficiency among professional people. The way large law firms are organized makes advising easy, and, because of the specialization in these firms, a necessity. Even if it were not, professional norms require advice-giving when a colleague requests it.

Professional bureaucracy differs in other ways. While most professional rules are internalized and generally accepted or tolerated, especially if these regulations are relatively stable, they are monitored by colleagues. These colleagues break down into three groups. There is an outside hierarchy of power as reflected in the structure of the bar association and the courts. There is an inside hierarchy composed of colleagues within the firm (someone is always in charge of a matter) who have both executive and colleague authority. In addition, all lawyers in the organization, as a

CHART IX-I

Summary of Factors Associated with Gouldner's[a] Three Patterns of Bureaucracy as Exemplified by Gypsum Workers and a Fourth Bureaucratic Pattern (Professional Bureaucracy as Exemplified by Wall Street Lawyers)

	GYPSUM PLANT		
MOCK	REPRESENTATIVE	PUNISHMENT CENTERED	PROFESSIONAL[b]

1. *Who Usually Initiates the Rules?*

MOCK	REPRESENTATIVE	PUNISHMENT CENTERED	PROFESSIONAL
The rule or rules are imposed on the group by some "outside" agency . . . neither superiors nor subordinates identify themselves with or participate in the establishment of the rules or view them as their own.	*Both* groups initiate the rules and view them as their own.	The rule arises in response to the pressure of *either* workers or management, but is *not jointly* initiated by them.	

2. *Whose Values Legitimate the Rules?*

MOCK	REPRESENTATIVE	PUNISHMENT CENTERED	PROFESSIONAL
Neither superiors nor subordinates can, ordinarily, legitimate the rule in terms of their own values.	Usually *both* workers and management can legitimate the rules in terms of their own key values.	*Either* superiors or subordinates alone consider the rule legitimate; the other may concede on grounds of expediency, but does not define the rule as legitimate.	

3. Whose Values Are Violated by Enforcement of the Rules?

Enforcement of the rule violates the values of *both* groups.	Under most conditions, enforcement of the rules entails violations of *neither* group's values.	Enforcement of the rules violates the values of only one group, *either* superiors or subordinates.

4. What Are the Standard Explanations of Deviations from the Rules?

The deviant pattern is viewed as an expression of "uncontrollable" needs or of "human nature."	Deviance is attributed to ignorance or *well-intentioned carelessness*—i.e., it is an unanticipated by-product of behavior oriented to some other end, and thus an "accident."	This we call a "voluntaristic" conception of deviance. . . . It was believed to be *willful*.

5. What Effects Do the Rules Have upon the Status of the Participants?

Ordinarily, deviation from the rule is status-enhancing for workers and management *both*. Conformance to the rule would be status-impairing for both.	Usually, deviation from the rules impairs the status of superiors *and* subordinates, while conformance ordinarily permits both a measure of status improvement.	Conformance to or deviation from the rules leads to status gains *either* for workers or supervisors, but not for both, and to status losses for the other.

6. Summary of Defining Characteristics or Symptoms

(a) Rules are neither enforced by management nor obeyed by workers.	(a) Rules are both enforced by management and obeyed by workers.	(a) Rules either enforced by workers or management, and evaded by the other.

CHART IX-I (Continued)

MOCK	REPRESENTATIVE	PUNISHMENT CENTERED	PROFESSIONAL[b]
(b) Usually entails little conflict between the two groups. (c) Joint violation and evasion of rules is buttressed by informal sentiments of the participants.	(b) Generates a few tensions but little overt conflict. (c) Joint support for rules buttressed by informal sentiments, mutual participation, initiation, and education of workers and management.	(b) Entails relatively great tension and conflict. (c) Enforced by punishment and supported by the informal sentiments of *either* workers or management.	

LAW FIRM[c]

1. *Who Usually Initiates the Rules?*

MOCK	REPRESENTATIVE	PUNISHMENT CENTERED	PROFESSIONAL[d]
Same as gypsum plant, e.g., a sign in one law office reads: "Keep file doors closed. Fire Regulation." This rule was initiated because of insurance company. Obeyed by neither partners, associates, nor nonprofessional personnel.	Same as gypsum plant, *but* partners do most of the initiating of these internal rules. However, associates agree with the rule. E.g., keeping a diary, leaving a place you can be reached with the receptionist.	Same as gypsum plant, *but* in a paternalistic law firm, rules are *rarely* made by associates, i.e., formal punishment goes only from the top down. E.g., the official opinion letter which cannot be signed by an associate is viewed by some of them as repressive and unprofessional especially	The rules are imposed on the group by some "outside" agency, e.g., bar associations. These rules are historical facts and are agreed to because of a socialization process. Lawyers have been conditioned to accept most of the canons. They have little to do with formulating the

	when they did the work. But it was something to which associates were forced to adhere. Many rules refer to housekeeping.		rules. Most rules deal with the practice of the law. E.g., prescription against advertising.

2. Whose Values Legitimate the Rules?

Same as gypsum plant.	Same as gypsum plant, e.g., emergencies are recognized by both partners and associates and so the need to be kept track of.	The values are those of the partners in control of the firm. Others concede (as above) on ground of expediency.	The values of the profession buttress the formal rules. This is the point where the informal norms become of tremendous importance.

3. Whose Values Are Violated by Enforcement of the Rules?

Same as gypsum plant.	Same as gypsum plant.	The values of the lawyers who do not control the firm.	Under most conditions enforcement of the rules entails violations of neither group's values.

CHART IX-I (Continued)

	MOCK	REPRESENTATIVE	PUNISHMENT CENTERED	PROFESSIONAL[d]

4. What Are the Standard Explanations of Deviations from the Rules?

MOCK	REPRESENTATIVE	PUNISHMENT CENTERED	PROFESSIONAL[d]
No explanation needed.	Same as gypsum plant.	Same as gypsum plant.	Deviance is attributed to ignorance or well-intentioned carelessness, i.e., it is an unanticipated by-product of behavior oriented to some other end. E.g., law firm censured for an article in *Life* which the appellate Division of the State Supreme Court (N.Y.) said "touted" their firm. The main partners testified that "they did not know that the article would concentrate on their firm alone, and that *Life* had refused to show them an advance copy." *N.Y.T.*, May 16, 1963.

5. What Effects Do the Rules Have upon the Status of the Participants?

MOCK	REPRESENTATIVE	PUNISHMENT CENTERED	PROFESSIONAL[d]
No obvious effect, however, if lawyers had been carefully observed the effect would probably have been similar to the participants in the gypsum plant.	Similar to gypsum plant.	Deviation from the rules on the part of associates leads to status gains, especially if the deviance is based on professional norms.	Usually, deviation from the rules impairs the status of both associates and partners, while conformance ordinarily permits both a measure of status improvement.

6. Summary of Defining Characteristics or Symptoms

Same as gypsum plant.

Almost the same as in the gypsum plant. Major difference is that only "management" initiates the formal rules.

Almost the same as in the gypsum plant except that the rules are enforced only by "management" and its system of sentiments.

These external rules are occasionally directly enforced by outside agencies but punishment is more informal than formal. Rules serve as guidelines for appropriate professional behavior. Generates a few tensions but little overt conflict. Joint support for rules buttressed by informal professional sentiments which are generally accepted by the community of lawyers and to a greater degree by the subcommunity of Wall Street lawyers.

[a] Alvin W. Gouldner, *Patterns of Industrial Bureaucracy* (New York: The Free Press of Glencoe, 1954), pp. 216–217. Portions of Gouldner's table appear above.

[b] Professional bureaucracy does not appear in Gouldner's table and so that cell is empty when we deal with gypsum workers.

[c] An attempt was made in this section of the chart to use as much of Gouldner's language as possible.

[d] Comparison of groups within the firm only includes lawyers. Nonprofessional workers are not discussed.

body of equals and as a group, have colleague authority. The over-lapping occurs because in the case of the large law firm the executives are practicing lawyers themselves. The employees we are studying are also lawyers who in the main want to stay with their firms and become partners. In addition, and research with other types of legal organizations may indicate its importance, most lawyers in large law offices are part of both a legal and social elite. Elites who may have received better training probably have a clearer view of their profession and its norms. They probably identify more closely with the association imposing or "enforc-ing" the rules. They are jealous of their reputations, which they do not hold alone but share with their firms and their families. In addition, because they can afford to live up to the canons of the professions, this type of rule-following is easier for this group of lawyers.

Isolating, as a phenomenon, what I call professional bureauc-racy has a number of other implications. It is valuable to identify this not only because a label can make a phenomenon easier to see and to investigate but because it brings up a number of im-portant questions. For example, it would be interesting to know whether there is general truth to the implied statement that the greater the external control, the less the need for internal control. Is there then an inverse relationship between the extent to which a given occupation, such as a profession, establishes a set of rules and the necessity for an organization to create its own formal internal rules? We may eventually find that external occupational rules exist for all occupations, but not in the same quantities. This is probably one of the factors that differentiate an occupation from a profession. In a profession, the values involved are more firmly institutionalized. This is probably true of all professions and of some nonprofessional occupations. However, even with external controls, professions are probably less regulated than other oc-cupations. Possibly this inverse relationship can be found in a descending order from the highest prestige occupations to the lowest. This type of examination tends to place a given institution within a larger societal context (where it properly belongs) instead of trying to understand it in isolation.

NOTES

1. For a discussion of this point see Theodore R. Anderson and Seymour Warkov, "Organizational Size and Functional Complexity: A Study of Administration in Hospitals," *American Sociological Review*, 26 (February 1961), 23–24; and Theodore Caplow, "Organizational Size," *Administrative Science Quarterly*, 1 (March 1957), 484–505; and Robert Presthus, *The Organizational Society: An Analysis and a Theory* (New York: Knopf, 1962).

2. From Max Weber: *Essays in Sociology*, H. H. Gerth and C. Wright Mills (Trans. and Eds.) (New York: Oxford University Press, 1946).

3. This statement must not be construed to mean that the organization of law firms cannot be improved—they can.

4. Only in one large firm was this not generally true.

5. The social structure of the hospital differs from that of the law firm in many respects. Pertinent here is that generally the physician does not spend most of his time in the organization and is usually a member of a health team which he heads, but which is made up of a number of different kinds of professional and nonprofessional people. The law firm can be broken down into caste-like categories made up of lawyers working primarily in their office in one division, and of nonprofessional people in the other. It has been shown that nonprofessionals tend to bureaucratize the firm. However, unlike many other work organizations the technology of production in the large firm is such that nonprofessional support personnel do not overwhelm the professionals.

6. Louis Kriesberg, "A Propositional Approach to the Study of Organizations" (mimeographed, no date), University of Chicago, National Opinion Research Center.

7. David Riesman, while a law student at Harvard, led a revolt against the law journal, for he felt that gifted non-law-review students were capable of doing a job as well as the law reviewer. See David Riesman, "Law and Sociology: Recruitment, Training and Colleagueship," in William M. Evan (Ed.), *Law and Sociology* (New York: The Free Press, 1962), p. 12.

8. David Riesman, "Law and Psychology," *Chicago Law Review*, 19 (1951), 39.

9. Caplow and McGee found that 51 per cent of the university department chairmen from important universities thought their department among the five best. Theodore Caplow and Reece J. McGee, *The Academic Marketplace* (New York: Basic Books, 1958), p. 45.

10. Competition is used here in its ordinary dictionary sense rather than as sociologically defined.

11. Marvin Bressler, personal communication, 1963.

12. According to Thompson this appears not to hold for industrial organizations where organizational conflict seems to arise from the inconsistencies between hierarchical and specialist roles. Victor A. Thompson,

"Hierarchy, Specialization, and Organizational Conflict," *Administrative Science Quarterly*, 5 (March 1961), 485–521.

13. Robert K. Merton, "Bureaucratic Structure and Personality," *Social Forces*, 18 (May 1940), 560–568.

14. Karl W. Deutsch and William A. Madow, "A Note on the Appearance of Wisdom in Large Bureaucratic Organizations," *Behavioral Sciences*, 6 (January 1961), 72–78. These researchers statistically try to measure another factor which is involved in correct decision-making and which is a relatively permanent personal quality of the decision-maker. They call it "wisdom."

15. Many external rules affect other organizations as, for example, when certain days are designated by government as holidays. The law firms honor these rules then, if only by allowing the nonprofessional worker the day off. To continue this theme, any rule, whether it comes from the government, the union, or is the informal regulations of the nonprofessional workers themselves which affect them, also affects the lawyers. The current general practice of paying time and a half for overtime to secretarial help has made it increasingly expensive for lawyers to work, or at least work in the same manner, at night or during the weekend. The local rules of the New York Stock Exchange also set the behavior of the law firms. When the Exchange decided to start trading at 10:00 A.M. instead of 9:30, law firms tended to begin their serious business at this new time. While these nonprofessional external rules add little to the picture of why law firms function effectively, they do affect the lawyer and his firm. It is appropriate that they be mentioned here, for these or other regulations not investigated might actually, though inadvertently, affect the efficient functioning of the large law organization. See Robert Tannenbaum, "Managerial Decision-Making," *The Journal of Business*, 23 (January 1950), 33–37, for a discussion of how influences outside an organization affects the management of an organization.

16. Senator Paul H. Douglas, chairman of a subcommittee concerned with the uses of professional ethics, wrote: "the testimony [before committee] brought out a number of arguments for codes, . . . They would: (1) clarify new or complex situations where the application of basic moral principles is far from obvious; (2) . . . anticipate issues so that difficulties could be foreseen and basic policy decided when rational consideration is possible . . . ; (3) [tend toward] the enhancement of the influence of the more progressive elements of the group who will tend to bring the whole group up to higher standards; (4) . . . be a basis for discipline if the group had enough leadership and pride to act; (5) . . . furnish a basis for instructing new members of the group as to their professional obligations . . . ; and (6) . . . instruct the public as to what it should expect of the principal elements in the realm of public affairs." These points probably are applicable to any code of ethics. "Ethical Standards in Government," Report of a Subcommittee (Mr. Paul H. Douglas, Chairman) of the Committee on Labor and Public Welfare, United States Senate, 82nd Congress,

1st Session (1951), p. 35. As quoted in Elliot E. Cheatham, *Cases and Materials on the Legal Profession* (Brooklyn, N.Y.: The Foundation Press, 1955), p. 108.

17. Robert K. Merton and William J. Goode, *Professions*, Chapter XVII, "Professional Codes of Ethics: (mimeographed, 1953), p. 45.

18. William J. Goode, "Community Within a Community: The Professions," *American Sociological Review*, 22 (April 1957), 194.

19. William Kornhauser, with the assistance of Warren O. Hagstrom, *Scientists in Industry: Conflict and Accommodation* (Berkeley and Los Angeles: University of California Press, 1962), p. 11.

20. For a succinct discussion of the professional in a bureaucratic situation, see Peter M. Blau and W. Richard Scott, *Formal Organizations: A Comparative Approach* (San Francisco: Chandler Publishing Company, 1962), pp. 60–74.

21. Erwin O. Smigel, John W. Martin, and Donald Horning, "Legal Ethics and Education" (unpublished study, 1958). This does not mean that the lawyer increasingly becomes more ethical. It was found that practicing attorneys scaled lower on ethicality than did law professors or senior law students.

22. There are a number of studies now in preparation which seem to indicate that students are not socialized in the law schools. One tentatively finds that socialization takes place after graduation, that a Harvard Law School graduate who goes into solo practice takes on the ethics of his fellow practitioner, and that those who go into the large law firms assume the higher ethical standards of their fellow lawyers. However, most recent studies indicate that socialization does take place in professional schools. See, for example, David Gottlieb, "Processes of Socialization in American Graduate Schools," *Social Forces*, 40 (December 1961), 124–131.

23. *Canons of Professional Ethics of the American Bar Association*, Preamble. Another, though overlapping, set of guide lines for lawyers can be found in the oath they are required to take after they pass their written test and character investigation. The following oath is required of those who wish to practice law in the State of Washington. The American Bar Association has commended it as a proper oath.

I do solemnly swear:

I will support the Constitution of the United States and the constitution of the state of . . . ;

I will maintain the respect due to Courts of Justice and judicial officers;

I will not counsel or maintain any suit or proceeding which shall appear to me to be unjust, nor any defense except such as I believe to be honestly debatable under the law of the land;

I will employ for the purpose of maintaining the causes confided to me such means only as are consistent with truth and honor, and will never seek to mislead the Judge or jury by an artifice or false statement of fact or law;

I will abstain from all offensive personality, and advance no fact prejudicial to the honor or reputation of a party or witness, unless required by the justice of the cause with which I am charged;

I will never reject, from any consideration personal to myself, the cause of the defenseless or oppressed, or delay any man's cause for lucre or malice. So help me God.

The canons and oath can be found in several sources including Elliot E. Cheatham, *op. cit.*, Appendix I, p. 543.

24. George Sharswood, *An Essay on Professional Ethics* (Philadelphia: T. & J. W. Johnson & Co., 1860), p. 1. As quoted in Henry S. Drinker, *Legal Ethics* (New York: Columbia University Press, 1953), p. 352.

25. William M. Trumbull, *Materials on the Lawyer's Professional Responsibility* (Englewood Cliffs, N.J.: Prentice-Hall, 1957), p. 348.

26. *Ibid.*, The canons are found throughout his book in the order listed above and are summarized in "Appendix A," p. 373.

27. Drinker, *op. cit.*

28. Frederick B. MacKinnon, "Ethical Problems of Lawyers in Large Law Firms and House Counsel" (Cambridge: Harvard Law School, April 1956, mimeographed).

29. There are, of course, claims and stories about the unethical practice of lawyers in large law firms. Upton Sinclair, in his book *Upton Sinclair Presents William Fox* (Los Angeles: published by the author, 1933), discusses the allegation of William Fox, who maintained that certain lawyers were responsible for his losing his company. Louis Auchincloss, in *The Great World and Timothy Colt* (Boston: Houghton Mifflin, 1956), describes a fictional breach of the code of ethics.

30. Glen McDaniel, "Ethical Problems of Counsel for Big Business: The Burden of Resolving Conflicting Interests," *American Bar Association Journal*, 38 (1952), 205.

31. Henry S. Drinker, "Legal Ethics," *The Annals of the American Academy of Political and Social Science*, 297 (January 1955), 37–45.

32. "Annual Report of the Committee On Grievances," *The Record of the Association of the Bar of the City of New York*, 16 (October 1961), 29, 30.

33. *Ibid.*, pp. 31–32.

34. The constant repetition of professional norms found in the journals published by the bar associations probably constitutes part of the socialization process.

35. Kornhauser, *op. cit.*, p. 86.

36. Only 105,000 of some 250,000 lawyers (approximate figures as of January, 1961) are members of the American Bar Association. The proportion of Wall Street lawyers who are members, then, is exceedingly high. As Everett C. Hughes, et al., note, the power of an association depends upon "the proportion of potential members who actually belong. . . ." See Everett C. Hughes, Helen M. Hughes, and Irwin Deutscher, *Twenty Thousand Nurses Tell Their Story* (Philadelphia: Lippincott, 1958), p. 243. If

this is true and we consider the Wall Street lawyer a special group, the control of the bar association on this elite should be great.

37. Cheatham, *op. cit.*, pp. 79–80.

38. *Ibid.*, p. 82.

39. *Ibid.* As asserted by John H. Wigmore in "All Legislative Rules for Judiciary Procedure are Void Constitutionally," *Illinois Law Review*, 23 (1928), 276.

40. *United States Code Annotated*, Title 28 Rules [Supreme Court], 1962 Cumulative Annual Pocket Part, (Part IV, "Jurisdiction on Appeal"), p. 7.

41. Robert Dubin, in a review of Gouldner's book, *American Sociological Review*, 20 (1955), 120, claims that Gouldner was not really talking about bureaucracy but about bureaucratic rules, for he did not test his typologies against all the criteria Weber thought made up a bureaucracy. In this book, I follow Gouldner's lead for a number of reasons: (1) Since I am comparing the rules found in the law firm with the rules he found in the gypsum factory, it seemed less confusing to continue what had been done than to convert his findings; (2) It is felt that rules are the key to bureaucracy and that they imply other aspects of it; (3) I do discuss in other sections of this book the various criteria generally thought to make up bureaucracy.

42. Alvin W. Gouldner, *Patterns of Industrial Bureaucracy* (New York: The Free Press, 1954).

43. Harold L. Wilensky, *Intellectuals in Labor Unions* (New York: The Free Press, 1956).

44. Alvin W. Gouldner, "Cosmopolitans and Locals: Toward an Analysis of Latent Social Roles—I, II," *Administrative Science Quarterly*, 2 (1957, 1958), 281–306, 444–480.

45. Kornhauser, *op. cit.* See Chap. III, "Professional Controls in Industry."

46. Logan Wilson, *The Academic Man: A Study in the Sociology of a Profession* (New York: Oxford University Press, 1942).

47. Simon Marcson, *The Scientist in American Industry: Some Organization Determinants in Manpower Utilization* (New York: Harper & Row, 1960).

48. Mary E. W. Goss, "Physicians in Bureaucracy: A Case Study of Professional Pressures on Organizational Roles" (unpublished Ph.D. dissertation, Columbia University. 1959), pp. 160–161.

49. Gouldner, *op. cit.*, p. 158.

50. Howard S. Becker, "The Professional Dance Musician and His Audience," *American Journal of Sociology*, 57 (September 1951), 136–144.

TEN

STRAINS AND DILEMMAS

RECENT research concerning professional people who work in large-scale organizations discusses the strains and dilemmas to which they are subjected. The stresses are caused, the various writers[1] on this topic usually say, by the conflict between bureaucratic norms and professional norms which are thought of as contradictory.[2] Francis and Stone sum up the difference between the two principles of organization this way:

> The bureaucratic mode emphasizes the system of organization and the subordination of the individual to it, whereas the professional mode emphasizes the role of the individual and subordinates the system of organization to the individual activity and colleague relations. The bureaucratic principle centers on the relations of persons to one another by means of the system, whereas the professional principle centers on the relation of an individual to his work.[3]

We have seen, and will see further, how a great deal of the conflict engendered from these competing systems has been modified or eliminated in the large law firm. Yet some conflict does exist for most lawyers, although in varying degrees and differently for different categories of attorneys. For these Wall Street lawyers the problem is not as clear-cut as it is for other professional workers. Many of the attorneys discussed in this volume work for other attorneys rather than for nonprofessional employers. However, other reasons for strain, although correlated, exist for our sample (though all of these will not be analyzed). For instance, some feel that group practice of law deviates too much from the ideal professional role; others feel there is a public stigma attached to Wall Street and Big Business.

The Free Professions as Models —

The conflict between bureaucratic needs and professional needs requires a further exploration into the nature of a profession. There are numerous definitions,[4] not all of which take into consideration the various occupations now considered professions. Parsons, for example, separates the applied professions, i.e., medicine and law, from the scientific disciplines such as sociology and chemistry, which are primarily interested in the advancement of knowledge and only secondarily in its application.[5] Hughes talks about the need to get away from the old nineteenth century model of the profession which he feels was based on what medicine and law were supposed to have been; "that is, a profession is conceived as an esoteric art practiced by a closed group of people, each having relations to a number of separate clients, and each collecting his own fees."[6] In other words, not all the definitions include the reality that many professionals work in complex organizations. This means that one of the keystones of a profession—autonomy—must be curtailed, mainly because in the final analysis there is the need to take orders from superiors. Many lawyers think of themselves as members of a "free" profession (nineteenth-century style). Working for an organization makes living up to the old model impossible. This raises the important question of exactly how the Wall Street lawyers deviate from "ideal" professional roles.

Following Hughes' definition of the "free" professions, we see that the lawyer in the large law firm does not meet all the requirements for membership in that category. As soon as he agrees to group practice, the lawyer loses part of his independence; a factor implied as central to free practice. He loses it because he has to depend on others for legal advice and often must take orders from lawyers who are higher up on the hierarchy. For the associate the demarcation is greater than for the partner because the associate is a salaried employee and has little voice in the policy decisions of the firm. In addition, he has less contact with the client and does not collect his own fees. In most large firms the associate is not allowed to bring his own clients into the office. Even when this is permitted, the clients are considered the firm's clients— not the individual's. What this means for the associate is that he must approach the client through a middle man (a partner) and must receive the rewards from the middle man, rather than from the client. This is especially so at the beginning of his career.

The needs of the corporations (and the ever growing complexity of the law with its concomitant specialization) created the large law firms, and it is to these corporate clients that large law offices devote most of their energy. While the corporation is legally an individual, in terms of human relationships it can not be. This means that client contacts for both associates and partners are different from the model, for who is the living client? The person an individual lawyer sees represents only a portion of the client. It is, therefore, hard to determine, despite the fact that some alumni of large law firms are found in important positions in the various corporations, who the client is because he has many heads, and in the relationship between lawyer and client (the corporation) it is difficult to be intimate and confidential. After all, it is usually not the problem of a person which the lawyer is dealing with, but that of the legal entity the person represents.

Another reason for the strains some lawyers feel about large law firm practice has to do with public attitudes. There has been and there still is some stigma attached to the large law firm because of its association with Wall Street. The words Wall Street are still used by some politicians as dirty words and evoke cries against big business.[7] Since many large firms are found in the Wall Street district, some of the stigma attached to big business and to large banking organizations (the large firm's main clients) rubs off on the Wall Street lawyer. To the extent that the general public is interested in the large law firms, reactions to them have been heard which echo some of those uttered by the solo lawyers. Their organizations have been called "law factories," "shops"; their legal staffs have been labeled "stuffed shirts," "yes-men," and "mouthpieces for big business."

Attitudes of Solo Practitioners —

Twenty-seven of the thirty solo lawyers[8] interviewed for this report were vehemently opposed to the lawyer from the large law offices, as seen by these few selected statements: "Why, they are no better than hired hands. They're so specialized they cannot see the entire problem." "One doesn't know what the other is doing. And often a matter slips between them. I should know. I won a case against them." Most of these remarks stem from prejudice, however, and not from direct experience. My observations concerning the antagonistic attitudes held by solo lawyers are more systematically determined by Lortie,[9] who questioned seventy-two Chicago lawyers who had been out of law school for four years. He presented them with factual pictures of different kinds of practice. Only 26 per cent said they would like to be connected with a large law firm.

In England, Carr-Saunders maintains, "Partnership between barristers is forbidden by the etiquette of the Bar," although informal arrangements between them do exist.[10] Partnership between barristers and solicitors is also not allowed. Even recognizable informal arrangements such as an agreement on the part of a barrister to work on all the cases of a particular solicitor for a regulated fee was prohibited. In the United States, as we have seen, partnership between lawyers is allowed, but incorporation is not. However, because of the stigma attached to lawyers in partnership and to the employment of associates, in 1926 Charles A. Boston[11] proposed an addition to the Canons of Ethics which would define the relationship between associates and partners. In part, the suggested rule read:

> Experience has demonstrated that some counsel should be given in respect to the relations between lawyers and their employees, whether registered clerks or other lawyers, or nonprofessional persons. A lawyer's employee who discovers his dishonesty should disclose the fact to the proper disciplinary authorities; such employee is bound both during the employment and thereafter by the

same duty as the lawyer to preserve the client's confidences. A clerk should not accept employment which, by reason of his relations with his client, his employer cannot properly accept; and after the termination of the client's employment, he should refrain from such adverse engagements against the client as the lawyer cannot rightfully accept.

The proposed canon continued to discuss the relationship of the associate and the partner:

The lawyer's employee should observe to his employer and to the client, the principles of fidelity and integrity.

The employee should not be compensated on the basis of the business which he secures for his employer; such method of compensation is a violation of the principles of Canons 27 and 28; nor should he be employed under an agreement measuring his compensation by the amount of the lawyer's compensation or the profits of his professional employment; such measure of compensation is too apt to promote the clerk's solicitation of employment for the lawyer.

THE PROBLEMS OF ASSOCIATES

Associates as Employees —

It is mainly the associate who is caught between professional norms and needs and organizational norms and needs; it is he who has the tendency to be more ambivalent about large group practice as contrasted with the older model of the "free" advocate. These two conflicting situations cause most of the strains associates experience. Perhaps the main source of stress derives from the fact that associate lawyers are employees and are supervised. This means they do not meet one of the criteria of the professional model. Supervision limits their personal responsibility and individual authority. It limits them in terms of the kind of assignments they receive, the client with whom they have to work, the extent to which they can work a matter through on their own. These limitations, the associates feel, are undesirable and some say makes them less professional.[12] A former large law office associate now connected with one of the smaller firms reports:

> At X [large law firm] you feel more like an employee and that your stay there is a temporary thing. Here [small firm] you feel that you are part of it and it is more or less permanent. You feel you are working for yourself. Downtown [large law firm] you feel it is just advanced training. Down there you spend more time on the job and less time at home. In the large firm, you're just behind the scenes. Here, you're right in it. We had a closing [sale of real estate], and I went to it alone. X firm were the other lawyers and they brought two partners and four associates with them. Here we have more responsibility and the clients know you do the work. This leads to your getting other work and gives you independence.

Salaries —

Associates usually work for a fixed salary plus a possible bonus. A few felt their prestige as a professional person was damaged because of it. For most associates salaries are fixed from above. "You don't ask for raises—you wait and receive them." This, and "the lack of tenure makes you feel more like an employee than anything else."

Relation with the Client —

The relationship between the client and the associate is more important to the associate than the fact that the client is the source of the fee. Associates are concerned about not seeing the client. Many feel it is here they lose most by being an employee, and consequently do not feel they are living up to the requirements of the traditional professional.

> I think it is definitely less professional to work for an organization. For example, I don't like the recording of time or being asked where I'm going. I suppose it is necessary; it is probably inevitable with the growth of the firm.
>
> What I'm most concerned about, however, is my lack of contact with the client. I think a professional man should have contact with a client, and should not be an intermediary. They [the client]

have to waste a lot of time getting his [the partner's] opinion. Some partners don't let you see the client.

A few associates say they do not see the right client, at least, not one they would choose:[13]

> There is a significant sacrifice of ordinary professional rights and duties. I have done work I would not have done in private practice. The clients were unreasonable. Or I would not have given a great deal of my time to frivolous or unjust cases. I've seen some middle or junior partners who do not contribute to the firm ask me to do the most piddling little job.

A number of lawyers left the large firms because they could not practice the kind of law they preferred. Others, still with the large firms, thought corporation law too impersonal and complained they were not dealing with significant law. They wanted to go back to private practice where they can deal with "people" and the problems of individuals.

Some bemoaned the fact that while they could argue with a superior about the law, they could not take their argument to the client. One understanding associate reports:

> I have had to do things I thought were not right for the client, but the client is not the individual's client but the firm's client. When the firm fixes policy, that has to be my policy. The firm has to have the personality of an individual but it has to take the responsibility as a firm.

A former associate, now a vice president of a corporation which is a client of one of the large firms, states on the basis of his experience that associates will never give their own opinion when they are in a meeting with partners and the clients. "They become yes-men. I personally felt, when I worked for the law firm, that I could not do this; that it was not professional." Others, mainly those who have left, feel the same way about this organizational necessity. A number of associates were asked, in order to determine whether a dilemma actually existed for them, "If you had to choose between pleasing the client or the partners, which would you decide to please?" One common answer reveals the choice some had to face:

If there was a conflict, the client might lose out, but I haven't had to face that situation yet.

My first responsibility is to the partner and then to the client. Actually, of course, you have a double responsibility.

Strains come for those who feel choosing the partner over the client is not professional. The dilemma for the salaried associate is in deciding which norms to follow; professional norms which mean the client comes first even if the boss [partner] is disturbed, or business norms which in general state the boss is right and must be "obeyed." Obedience to the boss is supposed to help the employee in his drive for promotion.

The Need to Take Orders —

The organizational need to take orders from another lawyer, while accepted and recognized as necessary by most associates, is resented by some as unprofessional. The lawyers refer to the idea that professional people are a body of equals, whereas the employee and the employer are not equals. One irate associate, who admits he is sensitive about taking orders, reports this extreme situation (the firm where this occurred lacked *esprit de corps* and there was dissatisfaction on the part of many associates):

Ten minutes before you [the interviewer] came into the office, a young partner came into my room and said, "Come into my office, while I make the phone call—now." I said I had an appointment in ten minutes. When I got there, the switchboard said you [the interviewer] had come in. I told the partner I had to go. He said, "Sit down." This same partner gave me some work some time ago and I've delayed giving it back to him. One day he's going to call me in and ask where it is. I'll say, "It isn't done yet" and he will say, "What are you going to do—make a career out of it?" I don't like another lawyer telling me what to do and this goes on with great frequency.

There are a number of problems which grow out of being a subordinate in a large firm that were reported to this researcher. Some revolve around the difficulty of becoming a partner. Associates, mainly former or dissatisfied, report that firms will not create new partnerships unless they believe there is a real need. This belief weakens the young associate's hope that he can escape his present situation and eventually become more independent. (Managing partners deny this and report that if a lawyer is excellent, a firm will make him a partner whether or not they have an immediate need for another man.) Some complain they do not know how to go about becoming a partner. One associate observed: "The main problem is what will lead to a partnership. There is no clear-cut method. It is a disadvantage which is inherent in any situation where you work for someone else." The problem is further aggravated by the associate not knowing definitely how he is progressing. Those who feel the strain say that their raises or bonuses are handed to them, not by negotiation, but through the arbitary paternalistic decision of their bosses. Because of this, they do not know exactly when to leave, or if they should leave. They cannot be sure very early in their career with the firm whether they have a good chance for a partnership or not. These frustrations also constantly remind them of their employee status.

Some young lawyers find it difficult to avoid assignments they do not like or do not have the time to do. Because of this they often get caught in the conflicting demands of the various partners. Others report, "It is difficult to know when to bother a partner with legal problems. It is difficult because you have to decide how far to go on your own. You must not go too far."

Some associates report problems of a different sort involving conflict between young lawyers and older secretaries. These secretaries have been with the firm long enough to have taken on some of the power of their senior partners. On occasion they tell a young associate what to do. One associate reports this situation:

> If you are not nice to her, she will give you the business. Sometimes a partner gives you a job that is impossible in terms of time and you may need her help, so you have to be nice to her. I often say that partner "so-and-so" wants this in a hurry. They jump for

the big names. It is a pretty sad state of affairs when a secretary [layman] can tell a lawyer what to do.

The result of this reversal of power heightens an associate's dissatisfaction with being an employee. He feels his professional authority has been corroded.

These strains caused by lack of autonomy or the fear of its loss lead to the dilemma of what to choose: the profession over the organization, the partner over the client, the type of work preferred vs. the type of work assigned, etc. The major dilemma, of course, is whether to stay or not to stay. Most instances of strains and dilemmas reported here were obtained from lawyers who had left the large law offices, who planned to leave, or who were dissatisfied with their firm. As was pointed out in the last chapter, the organization is molded to an extent by the profession —law firm lawyers, if they stay, must accept the rules of the game. This fact modifies these complaints. We will see in the next chapter how the demands of the profession protect most individuals from these strains. In fact, it was easy enough to see which employee lawyers felt the strain the most, which the least, or not at all. Previously, we noted a type of lawyer who was designated as Prince Charming. He is the heir apparent. His success in the firm is almost assured. He and his colleagues, partners, and associates know he will succeed. (Feeling confident he will become a partner, this special lawyer does not mind his employee status. He knows his situation is temporary. It is modified by public recognition of his future position which manifests itself in being given work which is more interesting and which calls for greater responsibility.)

The lawyer on the make is not as certain of his success. He sees that neither the attention nor the assignments he receives from the partners are of the same character as those received by the Prince Charming. The associate on the make expresses his point of view this way: "I still feel independent but protected. I know there is a market for me; if not here, then somewhere else. That may account for the nice treatment I receive." Like the Prince Charming, he too feels he will be a success although not necessarily in his present firm.

A third category of lawyer is composed of those who should

not have accepted jobs in the large firms. They want a different kind of practice, or they have personality problems or they just can't work closely with other lawyers. This type is not happy in the firm and soon leaves. He feels the strains and the dilemmas most acutely. A fourth type is made up of those associates who have little or no chance of being made partners and those permanent associates who have been passed over. These people are most conscious of their status as employees. They cannot, as long as they stay at their present job, be anything but employees. Their position is made more sensitive because other associates consider them failures. For a number of reasons, it is difficult for the permanent associate to leave: his task involves a narrow area of the law (which for some is a cause for strain in itself), which results in trained incapacity; he is well paid; and because he is usually past forty, corporations are reluctant to hire him. We will see, however, that the permanent associate learns to adjust to his job and modify his tensions.

THE PROBLEMS OF PARTNERS

PARTNERS are not as likely as associates to feel the strains caused by the contradictory norms of organization and profession or by the discrepancy between the ideal of the profession and the way they practice it. They are not employees and so are nearer to the traditional "free" profession. While some are supervised, this changes with time. From the beginning a new partner has some say in the running of the firm. Although younger partners complain, "I don't know when you stop being an employee," they do know that they have tenure and feel certain that they will advance up the partnership ladder. In addition, the weeding-out process has eliminated those most predisposed to strains before the partnership stage.

Businessmen or Lawyers? —

Still, partners feel some strains, although seldom that of making a choice between staying with the firm or leaving it. Some say they wish they had taught law or had been a judge; some still feel that when they get older they will go into teaching or politics. One of the largest areas of conflict arises because some partners feel that they no longer are practicing law but are becoming businessmen. This problem seems to have become aggravated with the increase in the size of big business and number of corporations. It is the task of the large firms to tend to the legal problems of these clients. Many partners are asking, "Are we really practicing law?" This question arises on the partner level because some say much of their work involves business decisions. As one partner put it, "We make as many business decisions as decisions about the law." Or, stated a little more vehemently by another partner:

> We are losing the capacity and status of the old profession now that we deal with corporations. I'm sometimes troubled that maybe we are converting a profession into an area of techniques. Now the client doesn't ask what to do; he asks how you do it.

Many lawyers, despite client pressure, refuse to make business decisions if they are able to separate legal advice from business advice. A senior partner states this opinion clearly:

> We should be professional people. The question of business judgment should be left strictly to the client. I never, under any circumstance, volunteer business advice. Unless I'm asked to do so, I don't. It is not the function of a lawyer.

In 1960, Daniel J. McCauley, Jr., the counsel for the Federal Trade Commission, was reported by the *New York Times* to have discussed before the New York State Bar Association the seriousness of lawyers' deep involvement in commercial enterprises. He felt that these lawyers ran the risk of being named defendants when penalties are asked for by Federal regulatory agencies. McCauley said: "They should stick to their legal lasts without always expecting to crawl back into a shell of protective privilege."[14] A few firms have refused to allow their partners to serve as members of their clients' boards of directors and a few more will not accept payment for that service. A partner reports on this subject:

> Our lawyers, generally speaking, do not serve on boards of directors. There is a controversy in legal circles as to whether it is wise for a professional advisor to be a member of a board. The

other point of view is that it is a great help to a board to have general counsel present at all meetings.

Some firms have rules forbidding their lawyers from buying stock in their client's business. They feel if a lawyer is financially involved in a business, he cannot be as objective as he should be. They do not want him to become the businessman. They do not want him to make business decisions. But the client wants him to make the decisions, and the very practice of corporation law occasionally forces him to do so. Also, the lawyers may have to, if they expect to cover the tremendous cost of running a large firm.

Law as a Business —

The problem of whether the practice of law is becoming a business is also an important source of strain for some partners. It is not a new one. In 1916 Jules H. Cohen wrote a book about it, *The Law: Business or Profession?*[15]

Given the size and the overhead of these firms the problem is now probably more serious. Spencer Klaw estimates that overhead can run over $2,500,000 a year, about half of what the firm earns.[16] The quickening trend toward mergers among corporations means that sometimes two or three law firms work on a combined account. These situations create more of a tug of war for business. This striving for the client's work may also be heightened by the increasing amount of physical decentralization of industries. This may mean that, in order to insure its continuity, the law firm— and this is especially true of the new large offices—must go out of its way to please the client. The dilemma occurs when it is thought expedient to please the client by using business techniques— wining, dining, and theater ticket buying. Some lawyers consider this unprofessional.[17]

A partner who has practiced over forty years gives a historical picture of why he thinks law is turning into a business:

We are in the presence of a change in the legal profession, i.e., from a profession to a business. It is partly due to the big city. However, it is true not only for the city but also in less urban areas, because radio and television bring the city to the smaller towns. There is a drive for money not just among the lawyers but among their business clients who pressure the lawyer. There has been a recognition that the difference between the lawyer and the client is that the lawyer merely has a special degree. The lawyer is a businessman now. I have to give a service; I have to pay overhead. When I first started to practice we did not need a cost system. Today the legal publications more and more talk about office management—how to file correctly, how to keep a diary, what labor-saving machines to buy. We're trying to make a business out of a profession—it's due to the spirit of the times. Physicians also have changed. The question is how much money can be made.

With the growth of the law offices we see a concomitant growth of committee work and a formalization of managerial duties. Positions of managing partner, hiring partner, etc., are necessary for the running of the firm. This means, however, that lawyers who want to practice law have to give up part of their practice to take on nonlegal tasks. It may also mean that they reduce their chances of inheriting a large client since they have less chance of working on their legal problems.

The need to run the law firm is only one kind of managerial duty which causes strain. Another is the need to coordinate the various specialties. Senior partners claim they no longer really practice law. Instead they must bring together various aspects of the law. This calls for meetings and more meetings. In some situations they must have the tact of the diplomat because often some partner's advice has to be ignored. A name partner discusses how the practice of law has changed for him:

I'm responsible for organizing the corporate work. I've become more of an executive than a lawyer. I work with ten or fifteen people here every day. When you have a big case, you have to see tax men and other specialists. As you get older, you have less time for law. Law is too complicated now. At one time I could close a deal in one day. Now I have to look up all the possibilities.

Even though partners are nearer to the traditional practitioner than associates, group practice means giving up some autonomy. The client in most firms is considered the firm's client—not the practitioner's. The firm, not the individual, decides whether to take on a matter. The dependence on other specialists limits independent decisions. Some of the older partners despair of these changes.

The growth of the firm bothers some of the older lawyers not only because they may now have a new kind of clientele but because the staff required for these clients is so large that the partners no longer know all the lawyers who work in their firm. This runs contrary to their ideas about the relationship which should exist between professional people. No longer can a senior partner say and mean it: "My door is always open. Anyone can walk in here." Now the more realistic statement is, "Why, at one time I knew everybody here. Now we have three floors of lawyers. There is such a turnover, I really no longer know them all."

Responsibility to Young Lawyers —

The large firms feel that they must train younger lawyers. This is part of the tradition of their profession, but training has become so formalized that it requires time and supervision. It also means that once a man is equipped to do a certain legal task, he is moved to another department to learn other legal jobs. Thus, the immediate needs of the organization may be affected by the needs of the profession. One partner sums it up this way: "Training is another problem. We consider ourselves a training school; yet when we hire people, we hire them for work. When we lose a man, he is an actual loss to us."[18]

Older lawyers feel it their professional responsibility to treat their associate colleagues as equals; to listen to their arguments even though the client is clamoring for his work. "Some of them [associates]," complained one partner, "don't know when to stop arguing. This puts you in a rough spot because you don't want to be rude but you have to finish the matter. You can't take a client for granted, and the major complaint from clients is that you're not getting the work out quickly enough. So eventually you have to stop the dispute." These lawyers are caught between the demands of the profession and the demands of their organization. Most partners, we shall see, find this no dilemma and solve it as in the above illustration, in favor of the client. However, they do it in such a way as not to offend the associate. The partner is after all in the supervisory role. He has final responsibility. He has to assign the work and see that it is completed. He is the boss no matter how nicely he plays his role.

The partners find themselves strained by the conflicts in professional values vs. the organizational values and vs. business values: i.e., how to recruit the best law school graduates without resorting to high pressure "nonprofessional" recruiting techniques; how to treat professional employees according to professional norms without harming the organization; how to avoid becoming part of their client's business for fear of not being able to serve the client properly, thus taking something away from the profession; how to maintain old standards of practice in the face of changing times for fear of going too far from the traditional professional roles and at the same time maintain their high standards of work.

As previously indicated, lawyers who would have the most trouble with group practice do not apply for positions in the larger firms, and those who mistakenly do leave early. Still, for some who stay, a residue of anxiety caused by a multitude of conflicting values remains and must be solved. Otherwise, the strains and dilemmas discussed here grow and affect both the organization and the individual. The major problem of the individual succumbing to the pressures of the bureaucracy and how this is circumvented for most is discussed in the next chapter.

NOTES

1. Among these authors are Simon Marcson, *The Scientist in American Industry: Some Organization Determinants in Manpower Utilizations* (New York: Harper & Row, 1960); William Kornhauser, with the assistance of Warren O. Hagstrom, *Scientists in Industry: Conflict and Accommodation* (Berkeley and Los Angeles: University of California Press, 1962); Peter M. Blau and W. Richard Scott, *Formal Organizations: A Comparative Approach* (San Francisco: Chandler Publishing Co., 1962), pp. 60–74.

2. Robert C. Stone does not agree with the majority. See his "The Sociology of Bureaucracy and Professions," in *Readings in Contemporary American Sociology*, Joseph S. Roucek (Ed.), (Paterson, N.J.: Littlefield, Adams, 1961), pp. 491–506.

3. Roy G. Francis and Robert C. Stone, *Service and Procedure in Bureaucracy* (Minneapolis: The University of Minnesota Press, 1956), p. 157.

4. Here are a few definitions of a profession. As paraphrased from Al-

exander Carr-Saunders and P. A. Wilson, *The Professions* (London: Oxford University Press, 1933), pp. 284–287, a profession is defined as an occupation based on the existence of specialized intellectual techniques, either scientific or institutional, acquired as the result of prolonged training, which creates a sense of responsibility in the supplying of skilled service or advice to others by way of fee or salary and not by profit. W. E. Wickenden, an engineer, lists attributes of a profession which can be found in most definitions. They are: a common body of knowledge, an educational process based on this knowledge, a standard of professional qualifications for admission to a professional group, a standard of conduct, some formal recognition of status generally involving licensing, and a professional association which helps enforce the implied contract between the client and the professional. These are found in Roy Lewis and Angus Maude, *Professional People in England* (Cambridge, Mass.: Harvard University Press, 1953), pp. 55–56. Ernest Greenwood cites five elements which he feels are distinguishing attributes of a profession: systematic theory, authority, community sanction, ethical codes, and a culture. See his "Attributes of a Profession," *Social Work*, 2 (July 1957), 45. Roscoe Pound says a profession is "a group of men pursuing a learned art as a common calling in the spirit of a public service—no less a public service because it may incidentally be a means of livelihood." See his *The Lawyer from Antiquity to Modern Times* (St. Paul, Minn.: West Publishing Company, 1953), pp. 4–10.

5. Talcott Parsons, "Some Problems Confronting Sociology as a Profession," *American Sociological Review*, 24 (August 1959), 547.

6. Everett C. Hughes, "Education for a Profession," in *Seven Questions About the Profession of Librarianship*, Philip Ennis and Howard W. Winger (Eds.) (Chicago: The University of Chicago Press, 1962), p. 39.

7. Burton R. Fisher and Stephen B. Withey polled a national sample of adults to determine their attitudes toward big business. The majority found both good and bad factors connected with big business. However, the more national power a big business was thought to have, the worse it was conceived of as being. (*Big Business as the People See It* [Ann Arbor, Mich.: The Survey Research Center Institute for Social Research, University of Michigan, 1951], pp. ix–x.)

8. The thirty solo lawyers interviewed were not chosen in a way in which we can claim that they are representative. The primary purpose for interviewing them was to obtain their opinions about the Wall Street lawyer which might be of value when questioning large law firm lawyers.

9. Dan C. Lortie, "The Striving Young Lawyer: A Study of Early Career Differentiation in the Chicago Bar" (Ph.D. dissertation, University of Chicago, 1958, microfilmed), p. 95.

10. Carr-Saunders and Wilson, *op. cit.*, p. 11.

11. Charles A. Boston, a past President of the American Bar Association (1930–1931), was both then and previously, as a member of the New

York County Lawyers Association, extremely concerned with the ethics of lawyers.

12. A good deal of the stress felt by these associates, as we shall see in the next chapter, is not due to what actually takes place but rather to what might take place and their negative attitudes toward it.

13. Louis Auchincloss, in *The Great World and Timothy Colt* (Boston: Houghton Mifflin, 1956), writes in detail about such an assignment.

14. *New York Times*, January 28, 1960.

15. Julius H. Cohen, *The Law: Business or Profession?* (New York: The Banks Law Publishing Co., 1916).

16. Spencer Klaw, "The Wall Street Lawyers," *Fortune*, 57 (February 1958), 197.

17. An S.E.C. report discusses the broader problem of the law firm as a professional organization or a business organization. The scramble for remunerative connections, particularly in case of reorganizations, by the more prominent [law] firms specializing in corporation law is enough to make one wonder whether the "professional" attributes of the work of these firms are not open to as much question as the work of bankers, who also on occasion claim for themselves the status of professional practitioners. In this connection, note the following: "Corporate reorganization has long been regarded as one of the most lucrative fields of legal endeavor. . . . In the aggregate, counsel fees frequently constitute the largest single item on the list of reorganization fees. The capacities in which attorneys may serve are numerous. . . . It is not to be wondered, therefore, that these, among the richest stakes in the reorganization, are eagerly sought and that the various legal positions are among the most valuable items of reorganization patronage.

"But there are stakes in addition to direct compensation. Counsel for the company may be desirous of continuing as counsel for the new, or re-organized, company. The value of their professional reputations at times gives them an interest in protecting the management against the assertion of claims based on fraud or mismanagement, for often the acts or omissions upon which such claims will be asserted had in the past received their express approval, or at least their countenance. The same observations are apt with respect to counsel for the bankers. . . .

"The size of the lawyers' bill must frequently be astounding to security holders and others. This cannot be taken to mean that their compensation is always excessive. The importance of the role of lawyers in reorganization is difficult to overemphasize. . . . Nevertheless the vice of the situation remains despite persuasive arguments that particular jobs are well done. . . . Part of this unseemly tendency of the financial bar to demand huge fees may be due to the business cast of law practice of that kind. Part may be due to overspecialization in financial centers with large law offices composed of dozens of lawyers, a huge overhead, and consequent artificial standards of the worth of legal services. In other words, organization for the practice of law on the large scale of mass production has contributed to the alleged necessity of computing legal fees on an overhead rather than on a service basis. Part may be due to the fact that the practice of financial law has been to a great extent monopolized by relatively few firms. This has meant setting monopolistic prices on the legal services of the select financial bar. But whatever may have been the cause, the end result has been that more conservative and modest professional standards have been discarded." S.E.C., *Report on the Study and Investigation . . . of Protective and Reorganization Committees*, Part 1, pp. 866–868. As quoted in Robert Aaron Gordon, *Business Leadership in the Large Corporation* (Berkeley and Los Angeles: University of California Press in cooperation with the Brookings Institution, 1961), pp. 259–260.

18. Not all lawyers argue this way. Some say that training pays off when the men stay, and even if there is a momentary loss created by those who leave, the firm has contributed to the profession and opened its ranks to new men who may be better than those let go.

ELEVEN

THE PROFESSIONAL

ORGANIZATION MAN?

WHYTE postulated in *The Organization Man*[1] that we are witnessing a drastic ideological change in this country, a change from the "Protestant Ethic" to the "Social Ethic." The "Protestant Ethic," Whyte maintained, nurtured independence and nonconformity whereas the "Social Ethic" offers security and group acceptance in return for the renunciation of individuality and initiative. Both ideologies are backed by moral force. The "Protestant Ethic" incorporates the Puritan value system with its emphasis on competition, industry, and self-sacrifice. The moral force behind the "Social Ethic" is the belief that the group can be more productive than the individual—a belief which demands the acceptance of social pressures. Three major propositions make up the "Social Ethic": (1) a belief in the group as the source of creativity; (2) a belief in "belongingness" as the ultimate need of the individual; and (3) a belief that the "belongingness" can be achieved through the application of science.[2]

Not only Whyte, but Mills[3] and Riesman[4] have written about this phenomenon. Robert K. Merton, in his classic article "Bureaucratic Structure and Personality," deals with it in terms of bureaucratic organization. He states: "The bureaucratic structure exerts a constant pressure upon the official to be 'methodical, prudent, disciplined.' "[5] It is generally believed that conformity is necessary if an organization is to be effective. If the bureaucrat is also a specialist, he sees only a portion of the total organizational picture. Unwilling to jeopardize his chances for the rewards which the organization impersonally offers, he is afraid to go beyond his narrow field. The key question in this chapter is whether the lawyer in the large law firm, who has some resemblance to the bureaucrat Merton describes, will allow the demands of the bureaucratic structure in which he works to affect his professional role. Whyte and Mills think that he does. If they are right, this should have serious consequences for the client, especially when a group of professional people are working with the unknown. Many of the Wall Street lawyers face problems in what they call the "grey" area of the law, an area where no one knows positively what the law is. If these lawyers overconform to the bureaucratic structure so that their methodicalness, prudence, and discipline operate in the service of these demands beyond the legitimate needs of the practice of the law, creativity (new ways of looking at and dealing with a matter) will be stifled. This would be detrimental to the best interests of both the client and the legal profession.

Conformity —

The meaning of conformity is not always clear; there seems indeed to be some relationship between the increased use of the word and the difficulty in defining it. The meaning of conformity has been further obscured by the erroneous notion that conformity is a new phenomenon—a product of automation, impersonality, and size of contemporary society. In fact, man has always had to conform. Some degree of conformity is a prerequisite for living in groups, although the degree of conformity necessarily may differ. The same behaviors might be labeled conformity for one person and nonconformity for another, depending on the norms of their respective reference groups.

Other elements enter into any consideration of the word conformity. For example, how important are social factors vs. personality factors for its understanding? Is there meaning in the dichotomy "conformity—nonconformity?" Actually, if one works with both variables, conformity must be placed on a continuum, i.e., degrees of conformity to nonconformity. Because the boundaries are difficult to determine, many students of the subject have attempted to define conformity by breaking it up into a number of types. Marie Jahoda, for example, finds eight patterns.[6] Merton writes of three kinds of conformity: attitudinal, doctrinal, and behavioral.[7]

While these three types of conformity can be found in the kinds of compliance discovered among lawyers, additional patterns are needed. By using these additional categories, which will be described, we can avoid the difficulties involved in the concept nonconformity. Usually, to claim someone is a nonconformist is to say that he is not behaving in accord with some specific norm or set of norms. In reality, however, he may well be registering his own conforming reaction to another set of norms; the beatnik and the bohemian are excellent examples. Perhaps only when the psychology of individuals is considered can the true nonconformist be found. Two types of nonconformists are easily located: the irrational—mentally ill, and those individuals who seem compulsively to specialize in resisting group pressure. Crutchfield calls this counterformity. If you know the individual, this type of behavior is predictable. He writes:

> Here the person is actively opposing the group, being negativistic and hostile toward it, compulsively dissenting from it. The counterformist not only resists having his judgments and actions move toward those of the group, his judgments and actions tend to be repelled by the group.[8]

Such counterformists are difficult to find in the large firms, mainly because they are not recruited in the first place. If one slips through the initial selection process, he is soon weeded out. One might ask about the individual who makes up his own mind and does not allow group pressures to influence him—is he not a nonconformist? Independent judgment is an important factor in the law, but we will see that the large law firms and the type of legal training their lawyers receive sponsor it and make it part of their norms. Independent thinking and the ability to insist upon the right to independent thinking are considered socially correct in large firms.

To explain this and other phenomena to be discussed in this section, three additional patterns of conformity must be examined. These are: (1) Ascribed conformity—in which the individual is born into a culture and accepts and follows its norms. It is usually connected with early socialization and is largely unconscious and internalized. (2) Expedient conformity, as described by Jahoda[9] and Crutchfield. "Here the individual outwardly agrees with the group but remains in inward disagreement."[10] This type of conformity is utilitarian; often, when it occurs in the large law firm, it is designed to help the progress of one's career. If the individual follows the expedient pattern long enough, he may accept it as a correct norm, internalize it, and conform unconsciously. (3) Creative conformity, which has been inferred by Robert Dubin[11] as allowing for independent judgment; here the norms sponsor independence. It is of great importance in understanding why lawyers can conform in some areas of their lives and at the same time remain professionally "free."

AREAS OF CONFORMITY

ONE area of possible conformity—that concerning dress, fashion, etiquette, taste, and residential location—can be listed under the general heading of style of life. Another involves the practice of law and, more specifically, the question of whether associates and beginning partners altered professional opinion because senior members disagreed with them and/or because they considered such alterations expedient.

Conformity of dress and related style of life are the easiest to observe and the one most of the respondents commented on. Forty of the sixty-nine lawyers who mentioned this type of conformity declared it could be found in the manners and dress of their colleagues. The others broadened their comments to include political conformity. Most Wall Street lawyers dress conservatively; their speech and social manners are similar to and compatible with upper-middle- and upper-class training. The majority knew how to behave long before they entered the law firms. As one associate put it:

> Most people in the firm dress alike and talk about the same things. I think the pattern is established back in the law school before they ever see this firm. Boys come here from Harvard, Columbia, and Yale, and a few from Virginia, and you get a per cent who want to go to Wall Street. Those who want to be exposed to corporation practice talk about it and get some notion of what is to be expected. If any adjustment is needed, these men have the proper predisposition to see that it is made.

Where a lawyer chooses to live is also an important indication of conformity. To determine the extent attorneys chose the same residential localities, all the home addresses of all lawyers in four of the large New York law firms where records were available were analyzed. From this information, plus that gathered from the interviews, certain patterns emerged. Twenty-nine per cent of the partners in these firms, for example, list a second "place" in the suburbs. Some were three- and four-place men—the latter have a hunting or fishing lodge far from the city.

Within the usual pattern, the young unmarried associate (though not usually the permanent associate) and the partner live on the fashionable East Side of Manhattan. When a man marries and has children, he moves to the nearby suburbs. As he goes up the hierarchy of the firm, he moves to more appropriate suburbs, until his children go off to school or college or get married. He then moves back to New York's fasionable East Side, often, however, retaining his suburban home and perhaps a summer home, which incidentally is usually not listed in the directories from which much of the data was obtained.

In order to get a clear picture of residential patterns, the addresses of all lawyers from four large New York law firms were analyzed. Of the 90 partners in these firms, 33 (36.7 per cent) live in the more fashionable sections of Manhattan's East Side; 3 (3.3 per cent) live on the West Side; 6 (6.7 per cent) live in what I labeled "Bohemia"—either Greenwich Village or Brooklyn Heights (both areas, however, boast expensive dwellings); 48 (53.3 per cent) live in nearby suburbs. The firms have a total of 202 associates: among these, the residential pattern is slightly different. Thirty-three associates (16.3 per cent) live in the fashionable East Side; 13 (6.4 per cent) live in less fashionable areas of the East Side; 18 (8.9 per cent) live on the West Side; 22 (10.9 per cent) in other boroughs; 26 (12.9 per cent) in "Bohemia"; and 90 (44.6 per cent) live in nearby suburbs.

Much of the conformity seen here is ascribed. Still some of it probably is not, as indicated by the differences in percentages between partners and associates who live in New York City; 78.5 per cent of the partners reside in the fashionable East Side of Manhattan whereas only 29.5 per cent of the associates live in this area. The indications are that lawyers who are not born to the pattern pointed to above either learn the appropriate patterns or are weeded out.

In general while many lawyers know the proper style of life expected by the large law firms, some are lax about it, but contact in the large firms reminds them of the appropriate norms. There are some people, however, who are hired even though they have not been "properly" socialized before they come to the law offices. These attorneys in most instances either conform, are not promoted and become permanent associates, or leave the firm. This is true except for an occasional rare individual who becomes so valuable that the firm overlooks his social nonconformity.

Pressure to conform starts early. A notice in the law library at New York University indicates this pretraining:

> The faculty rule which requires wearing jackets and ties in the library, in the classroom, and at all social functions, has not been changed. Young lawyers in court or in law offices must dress in the conventional manner.
>
> RUSSELL D. NILES
> *Dean*

In fact, pressure to conform to the proper social rules can come from a number of sources, as an anecdote printed in the June 16, 1956, *New Yorker* indicates:

A young lawyer we met in a Pennsylvania Railroad club car the other day told us he was on his way back from Washington, and then related an experience he'd had down there. A junior member of an enormous New York firm called something like, Wicker-wallader, Mushach & Abednego, had received a hurry call from one of his superiors early that morning, asking him to get certain important documents from the office, jump on a plane, and bring them to him at the court—the Supreme Court, where he would be making a plea before the assembled Justices. The young man entered the courtroom, and there a well-dressed guard asked if he was an accredited member of the Supreme Court Bar. He replied that he wasn't—that he was only a member of the New York Bar, delivering some documents to his superior, who needed them for the plea he was about to make. "Well, all right, sir," said the guard, after a pause, "but since you are not wearing a vest, it would be advisable for you to button your jacket."

A partner talked about the pressure the firms put on an erring associate:

If an associate wears brown shoes with a blue suit, a partner who likes him may tell him he's out of step; otherwise he will be left unwarned. If he is not properly presentable, the partners will not send him to their favorite clients; however, we do not stress these things as much as they do for salesmen for Remington Rand. There they tell you to wear a tie clasp. But somewhere, in the give and take, a man learns.

One lawyer who was considered very bright and was doing an important job for a large firm, but was not made a partner, left to become a partner in a smaller office. He felt that his way of dressing was partly to blame for his failure to get promoted.

This subject is something that interests me. I was always a target for my clothing. I did not wear the Wall Street uniform. I dressed a little too flashily. There is a story which goes around Wall Street to the effect that one firm sent out a memo saying that a partner had noticed some people not wearing a hat in the street and even though this was summer, the lack of the hat was a reflection on the firm. Now, nothing is said about these infractions. I was kidded about my dress, but never by a major partner. It was only the junior partners who seemed to be in a vise about clothing.

A young associate in a "social" firm felt there was conformity in large firms. He thought it good and bemoaned the fact that he had gone to a Midwestern private school instead of the more proper eastern schools. He felt he did not fit in properly. He did not wear a hat, and when asked why, since he seemed to me to be over-conforming in other respects, replied: "I have a hat but I feel I'm young enough so that I don't have to wear it all the time. Otherwise, I'm even more conservatively dressed than is necessary. Today I forgot my garters and it sort of upset me. I don't think the firm is that sticky, though."

This associate was conscious of the "importance" not only of his clothes but also of the kinds of people he chose for friends. "When I go out with girls, they come from good eastern colleges. When I went to Harvard I could see that I wasn't really in this group, but I gradually adopted their pattern."

A number of lawyers who were born in the Midwest but trained at eastern law schools found they still had something to learn about eastern, upper-class, social mores, and remarked that they quickly learned by imitation. One reported, for example: "When I first came into the firm, I noticed what the older associates wore, one in particular. I thought he was typical of the successful Wall Street lawyer. I found out where he bought his clothing. In fact, I pretty much patterned myself after him. I may have picked the wrong man because he did not last long."

The factors which mold the individual so that he accepts the dress requirements of his business and professional community also direct his behavior in other areas. Friends have been mentioned, as have the informal rules concerning fraternization between lawyers and secretaries. Questioning on the subject of divorce revealed that while divorce was frowned upon, a number of lawyers had been divorced and suffered no consequences in the firm. However, as one partner put it: "We want no publicity. If an associate gets into a 'messy' social situation, we might well try to get rid of him."

A senior associate recalled, "There was a partner who was involved in a difficult, unpleasant divorce case. He left. I think he was requested to do so. In the law you have to become circumspect." Another associate remembers a different partner who had left a "social" firm under similar circumstances: "He was involved in a messy divorce suit which got into the papers and went up and down the courts, each accusing the other. He may have been forced out. He started his own practice—did exceedingly well. He was brilliant, but eccentric."

How important it is for lawyers to conform to norms outside of their office was not properly determined by this survey. Hearsay evidence is plentiful and the indications are that, if a man can be observed, as well he might be, given the evidence on homogeneity of residential locations, he must obey the rules. Although, as one partner reports: "We would not like our associates to get into a fight with the police, although that has happened and the man is still with us. That would be equivalent to pinching the backsides of senior partners' wives. However, New York is such a big place that everybody is more independent. In New York everybody goes his own way."

Many of the men who leave the large firms are regarded as serious nonconformists. Still, some of those who stay do not seem to be following the norms. Under what heading can these men be classified?

The obvious deviators who stay with the firms must have power or have little client contact. Even then law firms have their own notion of just how much deviation they will tolerate. Mainly among senior partners and permanent associates can one find examples of men who are nonconforming in regard to dress; for example I found them among senior partners, especially the older ones. One senior partner comes to work wearing his tweed suit. Another imitates the academic man, pipe and all, rather than the banker (the law firms' most basic client), who is the model for the Wall Street lawyer. Upton Sinclair, some time ago, described

Colonel Joseph M. Hartfield, one of the senior partners in White & Case, as leading a publicly "bizarre" life filled with race track visits and numerous charming ladies.[12] These men helped build their firms. They found the clients. They ruled, or could rule, with an iron hand. They also can dress the way they please, and this is recognized and accepted.

Those permanent associates who are not socialized into upper-class customs also do not conform to Wall Street standards of dress. Many who have been passed over retain an element of independence by not dressing exactly according to the Wall Street norm. These men have their own norms and follow them. The firms do not press them to change as long as they conform in terms of their job and as long as they do not meet the client. The firm, therefore risks little in the way of reputation and the associate's show of independence in this area does little damage to anyone.

Ideological Conformity —

Conformity of dress and manners is easily recognized unless it should prove contagious. For our purposes, at least, it is superficial, especially so if for most it is ascribed. To help determine whether conformity of ideas (outside of those dealing directly with the law) was also required, and to fill in the continuum of conformity, lawyers were interviewed about their politics and asked situational questions concerning the *New York Post* which is considered not only a "new deal" paper but also by some as a reprehensible tabloid. Lawyers were asked, "Would you bring the *New York Post* into the office?" While some asserted, "I wouldn't hesitate in the least," others felt, "While no one would mind, I don't think it's a good idea." Some were strongly against bringing the *Post* into their law office.

I was going home on the subway with a partner and he asked me, as he was buying his own evening paper, which paper I read. I knew he was a conservative. I said the *Post*—I felt very brave. I sensed a degree of risk in having the *Post* in my hand. But in my office, we have put up some art pictures on the wall. They think we're a little different because of this.

Another associate replied to the question:

> It is a difficult question to answer. I used to read the *Post*. I would not be inclined to bring it to the partners' attention. This firm has a number of Southern partners and this department has three of them—one of them maintains his southern attitudes. I would certainly temper my anti-segregation views in front of him. I have, however, made it clear that I disagree with him, but my position in his presence is stated less strongly than I normally feel.

A senior associate in another firm said that he does bring the *Post* into the office: "But I doubt that others will. I've never seen one around here and I know there are some readers. If you do, people think you're kidding, or that you have a money interest in it, or that you'll see the light when you get older."

Again it must be remembered these men do not normally read the *Post*. As one man said, "I wouldn't be caught dead with it." Yet the fact that so many thought it not politic to bring that paper into the office indicates a pressure to do what is expected.

Political Ideology —

The mores on voting seem to be somewhat different then those which concern the newspapers a lawyer reads. One firm polled its members in a recent national election and found that all but four of the partners had voted Republican, whereas the majority of associates had voted with the Democrats. In keeping with the general mores concerning freedom of the vote, there is no overt pressure on an associate to vote the way the partners do. In fact, associates report that partners go out of their way to allow associates to be independent in their political beliefs. One young lawyer noted that one afternoon twenty associates left the firm to hear a leading Democratic candidate for the Presidency speak. Another associate, speaking about a colleague, reported that he had taken a year off to help run a Democratic campaign and still received part of his salary, although his senior partner was a leading Republican.

Still, it is interesting that most of the partners are Republicans. The question which concerns us is whether associates change their politics as they grow older and become partners, or whether those who are not Republicans are weeded out. The available evidence indicates that slowly but surely the associates take on the values of the partners and their wealthy clients. When lawyers were asked if they could see any change in themselves because of their continued dealings with the wealthy and the conservative, it was not uncommon for a respondent to say he had changed. He was now more concerned with the importance of money and was more conservative.

Independence on Legal Opinions —

Up to this point we have seen some evidence of conformity in areas which involve intellectual ideas and independence of thought; although compliance seems to be less necessary for the Wall Street lawyers in areas which involve intellectual ideas and independence of thought. However, in terms of importance to the client and the legal profession the more significant question still to be answered concerns independence when it comes to matters of the law. One index of independence is seen in the extent to which employee lawyers or younger partners are willing to argue with those in power. Partners and associates agree that this is important and that it is done. Disputatious behavior on the part of an employee in most bureaucratic situations would be considered nonconformity. Disputation on the part of the lawyer in these large firms is conformity. Traditions of the legal profession require it. Law students who attend the major law schools are trained to argue with the professor. The process of socialization continues for those who spend a year as clerks in one of the higher courts before they enter the law offices. It carries over into the law firms. The evidence is clear that judges insist that their clerks express their viewpoints on legal matters. Members of large firms also encourage their juniors to argue with them if the juniors believe themselves to be correct. For these elite lawyers then, dispute is not nonconformity but is, rather creative conformity, for it helps the associate keep his professional independence. The partners are able continuously to sharpen their legal minds, and the client receives the benefits of the free give and take.

Associates do not argue just for the fun of arguing. They feel pretty certain they are correct before they tackle a senior person. Nor is it necessary to argue every point. When they dispute they are serious about it. One associate remarked:

> Yes, I'll argue with a partner because I'm acting in the best interest of the client. I am not talking about bickering. On a lot of points there is a difference of opinion, but that doesn't mean that either choice of action is wrong. Last Saturday I spent some time with a partner. He had one view and I had another. I was doing a major part of the work. I think I may have convinced him that my theory was O.K. too.

Some lawyers thought that *argue* was too strong a word for what they did. A senior associate puts it this way:

> Argument is the wrong word. It's a discussion with the object of arriving at the right solution. In general we agree in judgment because we all went through the same mill. If we think the partner is wrong, we will discuss it with him. If a partner has reached a conclusion and makes it clear that he has, then there is no point to discussing it further with him. At this point, I would stop. The partner I work with has a flexible hand—no absolutism. I suppose in any discussion we may have, it is only at the end that we might disagree.

Tact and Diplomacy —

Whether they argue or discuss, they do it with tact and diplomacy. The young associate, after all, is still a novice. In addition, he has either had previous training in social correctness, or has more recently learned it. An instance of this social correctness occurred while I was interviewing a senior associate. The partner he was working for came into his office and the following conversation occurred:

> *Partner.* [Pointing to a section of a brief] I think I'd leave that out. I'm not quite satisfied with this.
> *Associate.* I put that in because it occurred to me that the client might want it.

Partner. I think perhaps they would; however, you left out the other point I mentioned.

Associate. I didn't think you would want to clutter up the brief and it may no longer be appropriate.

Partner. I think it would.

Associate. Perhaps you haven't seen this latest ruling? May I get it for you?

Partner. No, thank you, I've seen it.

Associate. Perhaps we can discuss this later. Are you free early this afternoon?

Partner. That will be fine.

Who Argues with Whom —

Not all the lawyers in the firm, of course, argue. Generally, men who have been with a law office less than two years hesitate to dispute with partners. Some are afraid and still not sure of themselves. But they do not argue for a number of reasons. The obvious one is that they are still new and are feeling their way. Perhaps as important is the type of work they are asked to do. In many instances their job is only to look up sections of the law. Therefore, they do not see the complete picture and thus are not in the best position to argue. This is especially true if they are working on a "big case" where they are not in a normal partner-associate relationship. Argument here, as on the production line, especially on the lower levels, is neither appropriate nor very valuable. In either event the associate's opinion is not often requested. When it is, it usually concerns his research. Until a member of a firm is sure of an associate, he does not give him as much opportunity to participate as he does the tried lawyers in the office.

The permanent associates are also reluctant to argue. One lawyer, who had been with a large law firm but is now a house counsel, reported: "Most associates would argue, but a lot of older ones avoid these conflicts. Many of them feel that it does not pay to stick their necks out." The older associate's goal is to do his job well and to keep it. He is not trying to get ahead. Generally, he is not working on aspects of the law which need creativity. What is needed and expected from him is to be methodical, disciplined, and prudent—and he lives up to those expectations.

The man on the make does argue; it is expected, and in fact, is one of the ways of getting ahead. A partner confirms this belief: "I've seen many people held up because they will not argue with a partner." An older associate, one just on the verge of partnership, thought that, "if a man didn't argue, he was nuts." The same associate quoted the most senior member in the firm as saying, "What I want you to do is prevent me from making any mistakes of law, fact, or grammar." A senior partner confirmed the importance for the associate of stating his point. "Certainly he will argue, because that is what he is paid for and because he's interested. The lawyer, to get ahead, has to present his side. If he doesn't, and we discover that we have been wrong, he is criticized. He has to do a respectable job."

A partner in one of the larger firms felt that an associate "will never become a partner unless he argues with me. You're paying for his opinions. The only criticism partners make is about the yes-men. The problems we deal with don't have a set answer and you have to have a sounding board for your ideas."

The longer the man on the make stays with the firm and the more responsibility he is given, the closer he comes to areas of legal practice where the law is not definite. The associate who has the initial job of researching the law often knows more about these cases than do the partners (or at least he has read the material more recently). It is his job to bring the law to the partner and to offer interpretations. It is his duty to argue his side with a partner until a decision is made. The yes-men are usually discovered in the long period required before an associate is chosen for partnership. Only the artist at "yessing" may succeed at getting ahead by that method.

Most partners are willing to argue with their associates. They were trained to question; they think it an aid to their own work and part of their contribution to training younger men. On occasion, they set-up situations to encourage dispute. Interview sessions confirmed this impression—for example:

> In a case there is always one boss, but he can't ride roughshod over the others. The associates and I always argue. We do not like the Army way of kissing ass above and kicking ass below. You

have to be careful of the associates—you are so dependent upon them. Those are the guys who have to work until midnight. Law is one deadline after another.

Do associates argue with you? They argue and I listen, and some-times I change my mind. They are supposed to argue but I take the responsibility for the final decision. Mostly, it is not a question of arguing the law in my section. We do little looking up of law. We have to know market economy, questions like what effect will such-and-such have on our competitive ability? On questions like these you get lots of variation of opinion. I may check with a couple of other partners. My assistant, before he sees me, has checked with other associates. This is a two-way street—this busi-ness of using ideas of other people.

For example, when I worked for Judge X, we had a case to decide. I wrote the decision one way. It was unusual. There was no precedent. Another clerk, who is now a judge and my superior, thought my view wrong. We brought it to the judge. He decided that the other man was right. I did not argue. The case was appealed and the court ruled the judge wrong and me right. The judge called me and said: "You were right and you did not have the courage of your conviction." I never forgot that lesson. I'm told now by my senior partners that I ride it too hard. Now I don't want an associate coming in and saying "I think you're wrong" and not knowing why. I ask an associate, "What precedent do you have?" If he doesn't know, I'm unhappy with him. I want him to work it out first, not say he may have overlooked something. I want to know what it is that I've overlooked.

Senior partners probably get less argument from associates than do the other partners, even though they may ask for it. They have less contact with the younger associates and spend more time with clients than any other members of the firm. Work is often siphoned to them through junior partners. On the other side of the coin, some associates do not think it politic to argue with senior partners. However, these same associates report that they try to involve a junior partner in the debate. They feel it is his job (if they can get him to agree with them) to present their point of view to the less accessible older partner. In this way, reluctant associates feel they have done their duty to the client and have kept their professional integrity.

Some kinds of legal work are said not to require as much discussion as other areas of the law. Many who specialize claim that argument is rare because when other lawyers come to them they are asking an expert for advice. A few specify that there is not as much argument in preventive law as there appears to be in other areas. Some feel the amount of discussion differs by department, so that there probably is more argument and debate in the litigation department than in the corporate section. Tax specialists claim disputation occurs in their area also:

> We are working together trying to get a result. What you want in an associate is for him to see the problem. In tax, more than any place else, you can argue, for it is a most fluid field. It has almost a common law of its own. It is a separate system of law which has contact with all other basic systems of law.

Young associates claim that they argue less about tactics than they do about matters of the law because the partners have so much more experience in tactics. Some few have said they would argue on questions of form. In most cases, however, since precedence is so strong, the new man just accepts it. They even accept the personal peculiarities of a partner in this area: "If a partner is used to his comma in one place, I let him have it." The few examples offered which involved dispute about form found the associates either surprised and/or pleased that the partner agreed with them.

Except for the instances previously illustrated, disputatious behavior on the part of lawyers in large firms is expected. It is important, however, for the associate and for the firm, that the associate know when to stop arguing. Eventually, the work has to be completed. It is the partner who usually has final responsibility. If the associate on the matter does not terminate a discussion which has gone on fruitlessly for some time, the partner will have to end it. Essentially what he says is: "We understand each other's position. But someone has to make the decision, and I have the responsibility." A partner, when asked how far an associate can go with his dispute, replied: "He should go to the full extent of expressing his point of view so that he knows that I understand what he thinks is correct. But he will not go to the client." Partners were unanimous in saying associates argue with them. One went so far as to say: "I would feel horrified if he did not raise hell. There comes a time, however, when he has to stop, and good manners are important in any walk of life."

Some partners claim their associates argue too long—that they do not know when to stop. "I've gotten into bitter arguments. There are times when I think he's [associate] stuck to it beyond the point of reason, and I'll tell him so. I suppose, putting myself into the associate's shoes, I might worry about carrying something too far—it would depend upon the partner and the matter." Another partner, speaking of a senior associate, maintained:

> He will argue with me, but knowing when to stop is a question of judgment. The man I'm talking about is capable but he won't stop arguing. He takes up your time. He is knocking at the door [partnership] but I am afraid that his insistence will hold him back. [Why doesn't someone tell him?] I've been tempted to, but it might be misconstrued.

Most associates feel they must stop when a partner says: "I think this is what we should do," or until he says, "I see your point but I think I am correct." In general associates say, "I press my point until I think the partner understands my position."

In most situations where associates and partners work together, it is the junior man who shows the products of his labor to the senior person. The associate then is usually not put in the position of telling the partner that he is wrong or pointing out his mistakes —the reverse in fact is true. This means that usually the subordinate does not have to initiate criticism and thereby avoids what could create a difficult strain on the recognized status structure.

In order to estimate what might happen if the situation were reversed, a situational question was asked of some associates: "You were handling a matter which could not be completed before you left on your vacation. Your partner decided to complete the job himself. When you returned, he sent you a courtesy memo telling you what he had done. You felt, on reading it, that he had made a mistake. What would you do?"

Most associates said that if nothing could be done that would help the client, they would not mention the mistake. Some modified this statement by saying that they would put a "skip memo in the file." The purpose of the memo was to protect the associate if the issue was ever raised; it also served to warn other lawyers who might use the matter as a precedent. This device was probably not employed very often. Some partners maintained that they had not heard of it. However, one senior associate reported:

> I would tell him. I would have been derelict if I didn't—then it is appreciated. It is awfully good to have some one pick holes in it— normally after a full discussion, everybody agrees. There aren't many situations where you are dead opposed. However, if nothing could be done about it, I would either forget it or put a memo in the file just in case it came up again.

Another associate stated, "If I disagreed, I might speak to him. I've never felt around here that I had to write a protective memo."

Still another young lawyer reasons: "It depends on the situation. You have to be careful with anyone so that you are not offensive. I try to criticize in a reasonable way. If you don't, your point may have less chance of getting across."

While the associate is generally willing to defend his own position, he is not quite as willing to initiate an attack on the partner's position. It may be that custom allows the first kind of dispute but custom may also make it expedient not to direct argument at a partner's work. In terms of the situational question, at least, associates seemed far more restrained in their willingness to argue when they were called upon to initiate, as against a situation in which they were attacked.

Autonomy and Assignments —

Professional people in bureaucratic situations seek and fight for autonomy. Both Marcson[13] and Kornhauser write about this with reference to the scientist in industry. Kornhauser calls the theme of autonomy versus integration "the central problem posed by the interdependence of professions and organizations."[14] True, in the situations they discuss, the scientist is working for a businessman, whereas the associate is working for a fellow lawyer. This modifies the problem for us. Still the problem exists. A check on the independence of young lawyers was made through the assignment process and the amount of autonomy the individual had concerning the work he did. Both partners and associates were asked if associates could change assignments they did not like. The evidence is ambiguous. There are men who will never say "no" to an assignment. The permanent associate, true to his policy of expedient conformity, falls into this category, as does the very beginning lawyer. One said, in answer to the question on changing assignments, "If someone says you do it—you do it." Others, however, say they will refuse assignments they do not like, but will do so in various ways that imply varying degrees of independence. For example, some associates plead they are too busy and, therefore, could not do justice to the new assignment. If they are sufficiently experienced, they can manipulate their position and obtain the kind of work they want. They may then in fact be too busy. Some illustrations of associates refusing work on "ethical grounds" are available. "I didn't want to work for that gangster [a particular client] and told the partner so," reported one associate. Another remembered a matter which he refused to work on "because the issues I would be fighting for went against my grain." Only a few actually claimed they had refused assignments because they did not like the work. One senior associate reports: "If I did not like the assignment, I would ask to have it changed unless I thought I was put on the case because of some special talent or knowledge I might have."

Elihu Root, Jr., formerly senior partner in Root-Ballantine and now of counsel in Clearly-Gottlieb, privately printed an old lecture of his for his young colleagues in that firm in which he states what is probably the opinion of most large law firm partners.

A junior ought to assume that while his senior may be a good workman, he is likely to make mistakes, and is sure to have some ideas which are capable of improvement and some which merit complete rejection. The junior ought to be watchful against error on the part of his senior, just as though he himself had sole responsibility for the job, and he ought to be willing, if he sees room for improvement, to speak up boldly and make his point. I cannot overstate to you the sense of security and support and comfort that come from the cooperation of that sort of a junior.

But here we get to the difficult point—it is a matter of balance. Once you have spoken up clearly and made your point and had it listened to, you may be overruled. You may be overruled for reasons with which you find yourself unable to agree. Nevertheless, it is your duty then to reverse your form and concentrate your mind on getting the plan of campaign executed, whether it be litigation or a new development of the flotation process, with the same enthusiasm and loyalty as though you had never had a doubt. This is a hard thing to achieve. But it is an essential element of being valuable in an organization. It involves the distinction between the development of ideas and the formulation of plans— where you need frankness, criticism, lucidity—and the execution of plans and the pushing through of policies once adopted—where you need conformity, loyalty, and enthusiasm. It is a fatal mistake to mix up the two processes.[15]

Partners also offer contradictory evidence. One said: "An associate would not say he did not want to do a certain kind of work." Another offered: "I don't think it happens often that a man must take on a job he doesn't like. It would be very easy for a man to disassociate himself from obnoxious jobs just by making himself unavailable to additional partners." As far as this researcher can tell, the truth of the matter is that it is unusual for an associate to turn down assignments for personal reasons other than that he was too busy. It becomes more and more difficult, the higher the rank of the assigning lawyer. In the few instances reported where associates have asked to be relieved of an assignment, their requests were granted. Generally, or so it was reported, their requests did not have a serious effect on their chances of becoming partners. Their reasons were usually very good and the request was made infrequently. In some cases however, partners say these overtures, while granted, were frowned upon.

Q. Could an associate come to you [partner] and ask for a change in assignment because he did not like a case?

A. He could, but I would not like it. This is an organization and we need him where and when we need him. But a man can still be independent. He can think freely on the matter he is working on.

People have asked for change of assignments. We needed a couple of men to work in the tax department. We asked them if they would. They said yes. I gave one an assignment immediately, but he went to a managing partner and said he did not like tax work. He had only said yes to me because he wanted to be nice.

We thought it peculiar but kept him with the firm anyway.

Q. Can he become a partner?

A. No. He has a history of not getting along.

This does not mean the associate does not have some autonomy over assignments. He does, but he achieves autonomy in a roundabout manner. Mainly, he uses avoidance techniques. Occasionally, in situations where moral values may differ, a partner who knows that an associate will find a certain matter distasteful, gives him the choice of taking an assignment. These factors make refusal to do an assigned job less necessary, and a measure of independence on the part of the associate is maintained.

The various types of conformity and their meaning for autonomy and independence have been discussed. The main questions, however, have not been answered. Are these lawyers methodical, prudent, and disciplined (MPD)? Are they the twins of Whyte's organization man? If so, does this affect adversely their ability to serve the client?

Methodical, Prudent, and Disciplined —

All lawyers have to be "comma and period" lawyers. They take pride in the fact they know the law and practice it in a proper fashion. They have been trained to do this by the elite law schools they attended and by the large law firms which employ them. As one associate put it, "I have always been cautious anyway, and my law school training developed it." And another young lawyer found, "Yes, the law firm makes you methodical. You want the job done right and while the client can't tell if you make an error, another lawyer can."

The law firms sell careful and accurate work. It is part of their packaging. Pressure is put on those lawyers who need it to see that foolish mistakes are not made. If they are made, the lawyer is considered to have poor judgment. The men on the make want to be as accurate as possible because eventually they hope to be made partners. Even if they fall short of this goal, they would like the best recommendation the law firm has to offer. Junior attorneys are under the close supervision of older men. Their work can easily be evaluated by their superiors and these are the same men who distribute the rewards. The permanent associate wants to retain his higher than average paid position (for a lawyer) and he must be MPD to do it. In addition, the clients of these lawyers are more knowledgeable about the law than are most lay people. They can sometimes spot inadequate work. They constitute another conservative force.

All lawyers have to be methodical, prudent, and disciplined. It is in keeping with the needs of their profession. Professional norms call for it. It is taught in the law schools and reinforced in the law firms. Being MPD in this sense is a necessity which has usually been inculcated in the lawyer before he gets to the law firm. If not, he knows it is called for. The conformity seen here is akin to the ascribed conformity perceived earlier in relation to their homogeneity of dress and social manners. The difference in the two situations is that the specific training to avoid errors in the law comes later in life. A young partner sums it up as he points the way to other possibilities:

Yes, we are methodical, disciplined, and prudent. We have to be. We can't afford to make mistakes. It is a trait of a good lawyer. This does not mean that there is a lack of imagination. You can be methodical, disciplined, and prudent and still be courageous and imaginative for the client.

Given the needs of the profession, the question should read: Are Wall Street lawyers MPD beyond the demands of the legal profession? The answer now is yes and no. Some are and some are not. Clues indicating who are and who are not have already been offered. The permanent associate, for example, is certainly considered in this MPD category. An associate on the brink of partnership locates this group: "We have men here who are past fifty who work well but have no imagination or initiative. As of right now there are ten associates who are over the hump, but who are secure."

Twenty-four per cent of the large firm lawyer sample felt that one advantage of the large law office was its offer of security. An associate points this out:

> It is clear that large law firm practice in some ways offers less opportunity to develop than private practice, but private practice is sink or swim. The man who is afraid of private practice will not go into it. So what you find in large law firms are some lawyers who show initiative and some who do not find responsibility congenial, but who are handmaidens to someone else.

The kinds of security are easily seen. The associate does not have to compete with other lawyers in the market place for clients. He is assured of his salary, of his position, or, if he is "let go," of one of similar stature someplace else. He has time to work on his problems. Time means he can afford to be careful about his work and probably increases his chance of coming up with the right answer. He can specialize and feel secure in knowing a small area of the law well. He can depend on the knowledge and criticism of his colleagues and on the wealth of experience found in the office precedent file.

Some lawyers maintain that just the use of these precedent files can deaden initiative and stifle imagination. Most respondents, however, believed the young lawyer should start with these files before he gets too far along in researching a matter. It gives him a head start; some of his work will have been done for him by others. (There is no clear-cut evidence concerning the effect the use of precedent files have on the lawyer.) For example one man stated, "When an associate is pressed, he uses a precedent file. To that extent, as soon as you have an aid available, you use it. Lawyers, after all, are turning out mass-produced products."

On the other hand, another disagreed: "No, precedent files need not affect the lawyer; they should act as a starting point. There is no necessary conformity of thought because of its use unless a man begins to depend on it. That kind of man would conform anyway."

Depression Lawyers —

As previously suggested, there seems to be a relationship between the need for security and expedient conformity. The case histories of respondents who had been with large law firms during the depression indicates this. The story they tell of the need for conformity differs from the testimony of today's large firms. Then (in the 1930's), lawyers did not have the security of knowing they could find another position. Competition to get into the large firms was greater, as was the competition to stay. The picture the depression lawyers painted of large law offices was, indeed, one of a law factory, where the individual counted for little and had to be careful to hold his job. While the evidence on depression lawyers is sketchy, it does suggest the possibility that the present autonomy of lawyers in large law firms is at least in part dependent upon the competitive market for "good" lawyers. In the modern firm the only group consistently displaying a reaction similar to that of the depression lawyer is the permanent associate. The respondents believe that only one other group of lawyers—the house counsel—are more conforming.

Buck-passing —

One index of timidity which ties in with the kind of MPD we are now discussing is "buck-passing." Some buck-passing exists in the large firms. Reports of it, however, were not numerous. There are a number of reasons for this. The obvious buck-passer does not last too long, and the less obvious one is difficult to spot. In fact, it is often difficult to determine what a "buck-passer" is. For instance, is the general corporate practitioner who asks the tax man for his specialized advice passing the buck when he reports in a memorandum to his senior that both he and the tax man have decided on a certain procedure as correct? Is he sharing the possible blame, is he bolstering the confidence of the partner that the correct action is being pursued, or just obtaining the advice of the specialist? A female associate made this statement which she considered buck-passing: "Even if you do come up with a daring idea, you share the risk with the client because you give him the alternatives." These are difficult situations to judge. Some respondents insist, however, that subtle buck-passing does exist. They found it in the unwillingness of some lawyers to give a definite answer where definite answers exist and in the reluctance of some to take difficult jobs where the odds of failure were great. It was also seen in the unwillingness on the part of some lawyers to give advice outside their field as indicated in the "I won't even draw a will" of some legal specialists.

Differential Requirements of the Law —

The law itself has differential requirements. Men who are doing the more routine legal chores involved in blue-sky work or in some phases of real estate and banking law probably have to be more MPD. They are not called on to be particularly imaginative—a requirement for those who deal in the grey area of the law. The point has been made by a number of respondents that there is a correlation between becoming a bureaucratic personality and the department a lawyer works in. A partner in charge of litigation felt:

> Where the law is routine, it is true there is a certain amount of blind obedience to a superior and to the past. In a litigation office, where it is not merely opinion to the client, it is not true. In litigation, you know the result at the end of the case. There is a check on you. It is a much more challenging field.

The kind of work and the number of clients a firm habitually takes care of also may affect the personality of the lawyer. While all firms cover the same fields of law, variation exists among them in terms of emphasis. If an office does a great deal of banking law and very little litigation, its lawyers may tend to become more MPD than lawyers in other firms. If it is an organization with a great many clients, or clients with a great number of small matters, then lawyers are not as pressed by the organization to conform.

Other differentials among firms make for differences in degrees of conformity and MPD. Some offices attract mavericks and goad them into remaining that way. Others have strong leaders who want the firm run their way and leave less leeway for the attorneys who work under them.

A partner in one of the most prestigious firms feels that the degree of conformity a lawyer exhibits depends upon:

> A number of variables such as the kind of individual you work with, the atmosphere of the office, etc. In this firm we have a great deal of informality. We made an effort to get men to call the partners by their first name.
>
> Any man worth his salt will stand up for what he feels—some men are too stubborn. Of course, there are differences because some partners are more informal than others.
>
> I should suppose a young fellow just in is overawed by the partners, but, in my case at least, they get over it. Just the size and importance of the office is impressive.

All lawyers then are MPD, if one defines this within the framework of the structure of law—some, however, more than others. These attorneys become that way because of a variety of reasons previously discussed and shown in a variety of ways. We are primarily interested in overtimidity in the practice of the law. The man on the make cannot be MPD beyond the need of the law if he is to be successful. If his desire for vertical mobility within the firm is to be satisfied, he must argue; he must be independent. One associate put it this way: "The firm is looking for people with initiative and imagination. If a lawyer lacks it, he will quickly be recognized as a second-line man." It is the thesis of this book that elite lawyers are not expedient conformers when it comes to the use of independent judgment and initiative in terms of their legal practice. The legal profession and the law firms sponsor "free thinking." As one partner said, "The firm does not require legal conformity, for you may have to make the bold stand."

Except for the permanent associate and an occasional stray associate, the Wall Street lawyers, then, are not the professional organization man in terms of their practice of the law, although they do generally fit the broad picture of the organization man where style of life is involved, especially in the areas of dress, manner, and choice of residence.

Expedient conformity, thought important for success where nonprofessional styles of life are concerned, is frowned upon where the law is concerned. The needs of the organization are best served by discouraging expedience and encouraging creativity. Because of these professional norms, which the organization absorbs, and a careful recruiting program, the lawyers' independence is possible and the client can receive the benefit of the independent judgment of associate lawyers. This is limited, of course, by the need to meet schedules and to present a solid legal front to the client.

But conformity is present in most aspects of a lawyer's life: In the lawyer on the make we find ascribed conformity in connection with his style of life; in the permanent associate we find expedient conformity in relation to the law; in the elite lawyer we find creative conformity in the practice of the law. The noncomformists have been weeded out. The hope of the law firms, which presently they are fulfilling, is to sponsor a type of conformity that can promote innovation, initiative, and imagination within a system of organized group behavior. It is in this manner that the needs of the clients and the professional posture of the large law firm lawyer may be protected and preserved.

NOTES

1. William H. Whyte, Jr., *The Organization Man* (New York: Simon & Schuster, 1956).
2. *Ibid.*, p. 7.

3. C. Wright Mills, *White Collar* (New York: Oxford University Press, 1951).

4. David Riesman, with Nathan Glazer and Reuel Denney, *The Lonely Crowd* (New Haven: Yale University Press, 1950).

5. Robert K. Merton, "Bureaucratic Structure and Personality," *Social Forces*, 18 (May 1940), 562.

6. Marie Jahoda, "Some Comments on Conformity," Presidential Address, Society for the Psychological Study of Social Issues (Chicago: September 1956, mimeographed). Jahoda's eight patterns, pp. 15, 16, and 17, are summarized here, as they are formally described: (1) Investment, unchanged position, agreement between public and private views; called *independent dissent*. (2) Investment, unchanged position, discrepancy between private and public opinion—implies a person who adheres to his original position, but feels less comfortable with it than he used to; called *undermined independence*. (3) Person who changed his mind as a result of the pressures he experiences, called *independent consent*. (4) Investment, changed position, discrepancy between private and public opinion—implies taking a stand against one's own conviction, publicly a new position is taken; called *compliance*. (5) Implies no investment, no change in position, agreement of public and private views. These people lack the essential ability to respond to environmental influence or in those who reject a stand just because it is demanded by others; called *compulsive resistance*. (6) No investment in the issue, unchanged position, and discrepancy between private and public views; called *expedient resistance*. (7) No investment, position changed, agreement of public and private views; called *conformity*. (8) No investment, changed position, discrepancy between private and public views. With little, if any, investment the position is changed, but conflict results. Person goes along in the direction of the social influence being exerted; called *expedient conformity*.

7. Robert K. Merton, "Social Conformity, Deviation, and Opportunity—Structures: A Comment on the Contributions of Dubin and Cloward," *American Sociological Review*, 24 (April 1959), 177–188. Merton's conformity types simply defined are: attitudinal, which grants legitimacy to institutional values and norms; doctrinal, which expresses attitudes toward others; and behavioral, which is action in accord with values and norms.

8. Richard S. Crutchfield, "Independent Thought in a Conformist World," a study presented in the symposium on "Man and Civilization: Control of the Mind—II" (San Francisco: University of California School of Medicine, January 26–29, 1962, mimeographed), p. 7.

9. Jahoda, *op. cit.*, p. 17.

10. Crutchfield, *op. cit.*, p. 6.

11. Robert Dubin, "Deviant Behavior and Social Structure: Continuities in Social Theory," *American Sociological Review*, 24 (April 1959), 147–164.

12. Upton Sinclair, *Upton Sinclair Presents William Fox* (Los Angeles: published by the author, 1933), p. 146.

13. Simon Marcson, *The Scientist in American Industry: Some Organizational Determinants in Manpower Utilization* (New York: Harper & Row, 1960).

14. William Kornhauser with the assistance of Warren O. Hagstrom, *Scientists in Industry: Conflict and Accommodation* (Berkeley and Los Angeles: University of California Press, 1962), p. 195.

15. Elihu Root, Jr., *Juniors and Seniors* (The Marchbanks Press, 1956, privately printed), pp. 4–5.

TWELVE

REALITIES AND

POSSIBILITIES

CLEARLY, the Wall Street lawyers and their law firms play an important role in our society. Their influence pervades most important social arenas; they have affected the law by their legal innovations and by their ability (implemented by the clients' strong financial position) and determination (when advisable) to appeal decisions more readily and in some instances to bring cases all the way to the United States Supreme Court. The very way they practice law—i.e., in an organizational structure that provides for a division of labor, in which specialists who band together are able to engage in almost unlimited research, allows them to consult easily with men who are especially competent in their specific fields, and on this basis (plus the big assist from their recruitment and development systems which secures and processes an impressive array of talented lawyers) to produce the model brief. This is not an insignificant fact. Riesman says of these briefs that they are "like the anonymous law review note" which many "judges crib from . . . in 'writing' their opinions."[1]

Competition is keen for both the preferred lawyers and the preferred clients. The Wall Street firms easily win this contest. They get more than their share of the best law school graduates and the largest and wealthiest big business clients. This has some importance for the practice of law in areas of the country not represented by large law firms, for other law firms and lawyers, and for the various strata which comprise our society. It means that the wealthy and the powerful have access to the best attorneys and that those not so affluent must be satisfied with what is left.[2] This statement is something of an exaggeration, since the Wall Street firms do not take the best candidates from all the law schools and they do not recruit all the candidates from the preferred schools. And, as Riesman points out, law review graduates (whom the large law firms prefer), do not always make the best attorneys.[3] Still, there is a tremendous concentration of talent in Wall Street. The reputation and excellence of their firms helps perpetuate an imbalance in the distribution of lawyers throughout the country at the same time that this concentration of lawyers helps recruit and retain big business clients.

Some Wall Street lawyers have been labeled members of the "power elite"—a significant element in the "establishment"; it is clear that they are favored advisors to high government and business leaders. In this capacity, as history has shown, they influence business and government decisions and help shape policy for these institutions. Primarily they are advisors to big business and in this capacity they sometimes also serve as its conscience. They provide, as Parsons remarks "a kind of buffer between the illegitimate desires of . . . clients and the social interest."[4] Their main function, however, is to maintain the status quo for their large corporate clients. This they attempt to do, and if speculation is in order (and I believe it is a responsibility of the researcher), they do it in an efficient, quiet, creative, and knowledgeable manner: observers enough to know they are fighting the tides of a shifting economic system; artists enough to advise and provide for cautious change (a position, incidentally, to which many clients object). Thus, these lawyers help give our society continuity. Their cautious use of societal brakes provides the liberal with time and opportunity to seek change in a relatively stable society. The revolutionary is thwarted because the keepers of the status quo do not allow the seeds of deep discontent to flower.

IMPACT ON OWN LAWYERS

ON a more prosaic level, primary data dealing with the impact of the law firms on their own lawyers was previously presented. It need only briefly be summarized here. The excellent post-graduate training provided by many of the large offices mainly teaches the beginning lawyer how to practice business law meticulously—but thus giving the lawyer-in-training a somewhat skewed view of the law. Despite the firm's efforts to the contrary, this produces what Veblen has called "trained incapacity." This incapacity for practicing certain kinds of law increases because the associate in most offices is not encouraged—and usually not allowed—to bring in his own clients. He is therefore excluded from "client-getting" experience; and furthermore, access to greater variation in legal matters and in clients is limited for the associate. He specializes, then, not only in an area of the law but in a type of client as well. These factors also tend to limit the associate's career choice; lack of wide experience and lack of clients makes it very difficult for him to become a solo general practitioner or to practice in a very small law firm. The possibility of making such a choice becomes increasingly remote the longer an associate stays with a large firm. The evidence is conclusive, however, that for those who want to specialize in business law, the training given the young lawyer in the large firm is excellent.

The law firm teaches the associates confidence in themselves if they do not already possess it. They reach this high point of self-assurance because they have the backing of a large, usually old, usually excellent professional organization. The lawyers who stay with these offices know they have been able to keep up with the best and surpass some.

Practically, the large offices set standards for employment, for starting salaries, for dress, and for the practice of law. But more important, they set standards of professional independence. Independent legal opinion is perhaps *the* commodity they offer, and the primary commodity for which they are paid. The client's desire that a firm maintain its autonomy is increased by the growing strength and complexity of business law. As these laws have proliferated and increased in importance, so too have the men and organizations which interpret them. Although the large law offices become more independent with the increase in the importance of business law and the concurrent increase in the quantity of appropriate clients, as Parsons[5] points out, lawyers' independence stems also from the fact that they, in a sense, "represent" the law and must therefore separate themselves from the client. Today, a firm's ability to retain its independence is further strengthened because it has a number of clients, with no one client providing enough income to materially or consciously influence the law office's legal opinion. This was not always true, for at their inception many of these firms depended upon one major client or at best upon a very few important ones; they resembled the legal departments of large corporations and were much more subject to a major client's demands.

The associate who wishes to be successful maintains his intellectual independence with regard to legal practice, with the encouragement of the large firms who must in the end rely upon the steady supply of independent talent willing to reach for responsibility. The problem of the influence of bureaucratization becomes very subtle at this point. The legal organization and professional norms call for independent behavior; while obedience to these forces is technically conformity, it is creative conformity because it sponsors initiative and innovation. On the other hand, the ever-present process of socialization within the firm reinforces social conformity, so that in this area the large law firm law man (though this is not so often true of the founding fathers and the permanent associates) indeed resemble the sociological picture of the conservative organization man.

Impact on Alumni and Other Lawyers —

The alumni of the large firms in turn train other lawyers who work with them, thus passing on, for example, the Cravath method or the Sullivan & Cromwell method. How far this training diffuses has not been determined. Even without the proselytizing of alumni, however, the large law firms serve as models for other lawyers and law offices.

Furthermore, the law firms influence to a large extent the subsequent careers of those attorneys who worked for them. The law offices keep track of their alumni—whether a lawyer's departure was self-chosen or forced upon him—and often recommend them for new positions or send them legal work. Close ties between favored alumni and law firms are continued. This relationship strengthens the influence of the firms as former associates rise to positions of power in the government and in the large corporations. It is impossible here to estimate the degree to which work habits, legal knowledge, and attitudes developed by the law firms carry over and influence alumni in their new jobs. I tend to assume that there is inevitably some carryover and that the firms do leave their mark on their alumni.

In the same fashion, large law offices provide both an internship and a recruiting center for the law schools. Many of the professors who have been practicing attorneys were recruited from the large firms. These teaching alumni would be expected to train men as they themselves have been trained by the Wall Street offices, at least where such training is applicable.

THE IMPACT OF SIZE ON ORGANIZATIONAL STRUCTURE

THAT the size of these Wall Street firms had meaning for our respondents can be seen in their answers to questions concerning the advantages and disadvantages of such firms (see Chapter III). Much of this meaning revolves around the question of how and whether size creates an impersonal atmosphere, and how the impersonal then affects the individual. For example, large firms set up training programs for their young associates not only because the turnover among associates and the competition for recruits make such training a necessity but because the training function which had been fulfilled in smaller offices by greater personal contact between the older lawyer and the younger lawyer no longer is possible.

In most organizational studies, size is considered an important variable, and a number of early writers assumed a correlation between this variable and organizational change.[6] In fact, many writers link size first with bureaucracy and then with overbureaucratization. Nevertheless, despite a great deal of speculation over a long period of time and some research, the relationship between size and change in an organization is not clear. Terrien and Mills for example find that for administrative personnel in California school districts, "the school administrator may expect that the percentage of his organization which is devoted to administrative tasks may rise as his organization grows."[7] But recent studies reported by Blau and Scott[8] indicate that, except for small organizations, increases in size are not necessarily related to rises in administrative personnel. Whether continuing increases in numbers equals continuing increases in rules or in administration is doubtful. Somewhere along a growth continuum the importance of size ceases to be influential; perhaps at this point the complexity of an organization plays a more important part in determining an organization's social structure and degree of bureaucratization. For example, the tendency of new large firms to imitate the older ones may help account for some of the similarities among them. It certainly helps explain why some of the smaller satellite firms have formal organizations which are almost identical to the large firms. Still, size is important, as many sociologists have noted,[9] but to what degree, in what ways, under which circumstances is not yet determined. Size is usually thought to have influence on communication and authority systems and, among other factors, on an increase in the number of regulations needed to improve prediction and social control. In the large law firms rules dealing with housekeeping items, with communication, and other systems of coordination seem to stem from the demands size placed on the organization. All large law firms had a number of structural forms in common; some of them grew out of the requirements inherent in the group practice of law, but others grew out of the need to keep relatively large numbers of people working smoothly together. Some of these rules, although directed at the nonprofessional personnel, affected the professional people as well.

THE IMPACT OF FACTORS OTHER THAN SIZE ON ORGANIZATIONAL STRUCTURE

WHILE common structural forms were found among large law firms, differences were also observed. Since size could be held constant, the differences among these offices had to be ascribed to other variables. Mainly, differences have been traced to the number and size of clients a firm had; that is, the more clients the firm has, and the smaller the client, the greater the tendency for lawyers in the firm to form, except in situations cited above, "small firms" within large firms. When this occurs the practice of law is more personal than in firms of equal size having fewer but larger clients. Large New York offices, which tend to have fewer and larger clients, were more formal and impersonal than large law offices out of New York. The location of a firm also affected its organization, because it affected the recruitment of lawyers and of clients. The histories of both a locality and of a firm are reflected in its organization; some localities, for example "demanded" that lawyers engage in trust work, which in other communities banks would handle. The social norms of a locality may have affected the relationships in a law firm so that impersonal behavior flourished and was sponsored by the norms of the larger community. Age and history clearly made for some distinguishing characteristics.

While no systematic attempt was made in this study to determine how the personality of the various founding fathers or later strong men affected these organizations, most of the histories of these old large law offices indicate that these lawyers had lasting influences on their firms. The part social homogeneity played in the structure of the firm has been suggested; it was thought that because most lawyers came from similar social backgrounds fewer rules were needed to assure social conformity. Most attorneys who stemmed from ethnic[10] groups different from the majority were so similar in social training that their presence at this time seems to make little difference to the structure of the organization.

EXTERNAL INFLUENCES

ALL organizations have in common the need for social control. Much of this need is taken care of by internal bureaucratic procedure. How these procedures affected professional personnel and clashed with professional procedures is central to this volume. That many lawyers in large law firms escaped the reputed consequences (i.e., becoming overmethodical, overprudent, and over-

disciplined) of working in a bureaucratic situation is due in part
to the existence of rules external to the law firms which offered
models of behavior and instruments of social control which mini-
mized "management's" need to inaugurate rules and to enforce
them. All organizations are influenced by factors external to themselves. Witness the demands of the community; of a changing economic environment; of the competition between organizations; and
more specifically, of client/customer demands. As Thompson
points out: "A continuing situation of necessary interaction between an organization and its environment introduces an element
of environmental control into the organization."[11]

All organizations are subject to governmental rules; some are
also subject to union agreements and to other associational regulations. But the professional organization faces a slightly different
set of pressures. Although many organizations employ professional
people in some capacity—as researchers or as consultants, for
example—these professionals are in a sense peripheral to the main
function of the organization, even where they are vital to its
growth. Chemical firms may employ research chemists to develop
new products; nevertheless, the primary function of the firm is
manufacturing and profitably distributing a product. The law firm
represents another kind of organization; here, the function of the
organization is tied directly to the professionals employed by the
firm. In a very real sense, such an organization is marketing the
brains and the specialized knowledge of its professionals, who are
thus central to the function of the firm. This difference—an essential one—to a large extent seems to determine the differences in
degree of external control over the latter kind of organization as
contrasted to the former. The professional organization has not
only the usual external rules and norms to contend with but also
the informal and formal external rules of its professional
employees.

Degrees of the Influence of External Factors —

All professions have rules, but some have them to a greater degree
than others. (Lawyers, for example, have more formal [written]
rules than do physicians.) It is the combination of professional
rules—the formal (which helps make up professional bureaucracy)

and the informal—which together give professional people the opportunity to maintain their professional independence. Each profession probably has a norm peculiarly suitable to helping it maintain this autonomy for its members. In the law it revolves around the right and necessity to dispute (the role of the advocate is traditional, the best law schools support this role, and the large law firms sponsor it). In college teaching it is academic freedom. In each instance it is more likely not to be just one norm, but a series of them—which some might wish to call the mystique of a profession—which helps keep its members autonomous.[12]

Differences among Practitioners —

Not all professions have this mystique to the same degree; how strong it is most probably depends upon the exclusiveness of its competence, its age, and its standing. Differences in the effectiveness of these norms of independence can also be found among the practitioners within a profession. (In fact, behavior varies for the individual—sometimes a person conforms in one situation and not in another.) It has been hypothesized that house counsels are less autonomous than large firm associates, and we have seen in these giant firms differences in the degree of independence between the permanent associate whose work does not call for autonomy or creativity and the associate on the make whose work does call for these ingredients. Gouldner implies that these differences also exist among faculty people.[13] Those who are cosmopolitan are more oriented to their profession and so freer of the college; those who are locals are more oriented to the college and so less free of its domination. Gordon, et. al., find that the type of organization a professional works in influences the amount of independence he has. In a study of 250 research projects in which scientists were engaged, he and his colleagues found that "there is an inverse relationship between the specificity and immediacy of an organization's research goals and the freedom accorded the scientist."[14] In a health agency, therefore, where the goals were specific and immediate, there was also maximal executive authority; scientists in these agencies had less freedom than those in a medical school, where the goals were not so specific and immediate and where there was minimal executive authority.

THE IMPORTANCE OF BEING ELITE

A LINKAGE may also be found between how elite an organization is and its willingness to support the independence of its professional workers. This was seen in the large law firms. Riesman found that in different types of colleges different degrees and meanings of academic freedom could be observed. He noted that in several small teachers colleges the presidents would interpose themselves between the interviewer and the faculty when questions about academic freedom were asked, saying essentially, "We have enough academic freedom here."[15] The more elite the college, the stronger were the insistences about maintaining academic freedom. Harvard then would be expected to have resisted the McCarthy influence most strongly, as indeed it did.

Part of what makes an organization elite is the people it employs. Lawyers in the large firms are generally recognized as elite. While all professionals may be affected by the norms of the profession and the specific ones which help insure independence, it is the elite for whom these norms have the most meaning. The elite help make the rules; they help enforce them; and they have the security to obey them. This security is based first on competence; in the large law firms it may be helped by membership in a social elite (implying an early socialization which tends to make these individuals more independent) as well as membership in the legal elite (which is based on more than competence and which implies greater freedom to choose other employment). Furthermore, these individuals manifest greater concern with and belief in the ideal professional standards which help make the elite autonomous.

SOME GUESSES AS TO THE FUTURE

IT IS difficult to predict the future of the large law firms, although it seems certain that more such offices will appear throughout the country. Much of what will happen depends on how government and business develop. If the trend toward bigness continues, the New York law firms will continue to grow—this in spite of the fact that most attorneys in the mammoth firms (one hundred lawyers or more) feel they have reached or passed their optimum size. Actually, this growth process continues to take place. Between 1957 and 1962 the number of partners in the twenty large New York law firms which have been analyzed from the *Martindale-Hubbell Law Directory* increased by 16 per cent. The investigation of the records for the seventeen large firms out of New York City also reveals an increase (37 per cent between 1951 and 1961) in their membership. Firms which are now only medium in size—as well as some of the smaller ones—will expand as well.

Given the need for the specialist and the related need to coordinate them, even those firms that do not grow will become more like today's large firms, especially if new legal specialties continue to develop. For the large firms it may mean that the scope of a specialty will become increasingly narrow. If the number and scope of specialties increases, it should be expected that the amount of dissensus[16] in an organization should also increase. To offset this, the tendency of the organization then will be to extend its bureaucratic hold over its workers. This tendency, plus the predicted growth of firms considered large at this stage of their development, should make them more bureaucratic. We have in fact seen that this is already happening as a consequence of associates' demands and the increasing difficulty involved in recruitment. The people who control the firms will find themselves further and further away from the lawyers they employ. Time spent on managerial duties will increase, and the number of managerial positions will multiply. Office mechanization of employment records, billing procedures, or cost accounting systems will increase and so will office regulations and an increasing need for discipline on lower level aspects of the job. Even the practice of the law will change (as it is changing in medicine), for machines will be able to "shepardize" a matter (research it) faster and perhaps more thoroughly than a lawyer.

The lawyer-manager who has to see that the organization continues to run smoothly during this growth will probably perform his task more like a manager and less in the tradition of the profession. Conflict between the increased bureaucratic system and the elite lawyer will grow. Some of the same types of trouble industry has with its professional people will also plague the law firms. This trend, however, will be somewhat modified because the image of the legal profession is changing. As the image of the old model of the lawyer as a solo practitioner fades, as it will, problems based on comparisons between the old ideal type and present reality will disappear. The evidence, in fact, indicates that this is already happening. It was common for young firm lawyers to say that they were more professional than their solo colleagues: "How can they present themselves as knowing everything." The popular image of the lawyer will continue to change. The Perry Mason of thirty years from now will not be a solo lawyer but a corporation counsel or a government lawyer.

Competition for the most competent lawyers will continue to grow as government and business press for their share of these attorneys. While government has employed a great many lawyers for some time, industry is just now expanding its demands. The large corporations are and will probably continue to develop their own law departments. A 1959 survey[17] of machinery companies in the United States and Canada found that 47 per cent of the 286 businesses answering the questionnaire had their own law departments. One hundred per cent of the corporations employing 50,000 or more people had their own legal department; for companies employing 10,000 or more, the figure dropped only to 92 per cent. What this seems to mean for the large firms to date is not that they will stop growing (although some think this will happen) but that more of the routine work will be done by house counsel, freeing the large firms for the more exciting legal tasks. As a consequence, the large firms will no longer need as many permanent associates. The reduction in the number of these associates signifies that more of those who are not invited to join the firm will have to leave, thereby giving the law offices a wider choice of attorneys from which to choose their new partners, since more will pass through the firm. Presumably, given the law offices selecting-out process, the competence of partners will continue to grow. (As a corollary, the reduction in the numbers of permanent associates employed by law firms will also blunt the possibility of associates' unionizing, something which may be predicted will happen to lawyers who work in industry and in government—although their protecting organization may not be called a union.) And as discrimination against minority groups disappears, the Wall Street firms will again broaden their possibility of attracting the best legal brains in the country. However, with a less homogeneous social base the Wall Street firms will become less like social clubs and more like organizations whose clear function is to be specialized, impersonal producers of a professional service. (This may produce a need for rules which had been unnecessary because of the social homogeneity of its lawyers.) Social eliteness, then, will be diluted and intellectual eliteness will flourish.

SOME ADDITIONAL RESPONSIBILITIES OF THE BAR ASSOCIATIONS

THE increase in the numbers of lawyers who practice in large firms will mean that the bar must question whether the canons of ethics designed for a different day[18] are adequate for the current and the future practice of the law. The conflict of interest rules are probably no longer viable for the kind of law the lawyer in large firms practices today. Associates and clients need, or will need, new or additional rules to protect them. The bar associations will probably extend their control or attempt at control over lawyers who work in the large firms, for government, and for business. Society may demand that the monopoly of the outstanding legal talent by these organizations be slowed. The bar associations may want to reinstitute the apprenticeship system, where beginning lawyers will be required to spend time in the service of the general public, as for example working for the indigent. In this way all attorneys would see a little more of the law and some who planned to practice with the large firms, the corporations, or the government might change their minds and wish to devote themselves to the individual citizen instead. Certainly some reform[19] of the bar is necessary if only to do away with the inequities in the individual citizen's opportunity for obtaining the kind of legal service the corporations and government now command.

It is of even greater importance that professional people work under the most auspicious conditions possible. More and more, because of the impossibility of digesting the great outpouring of knowledge, it has been found necessary for professionals to specialize and to work in groups. If professional people are to work with others effectively, then bureaucratic systems and professional systems must mesh.

In our society the Wall Street lawyers' special function is to give independent advice in the practice of corporate law—a function they are at the moment fulfilling. Their flexible organization, which is partly based on internal bureaucratic rules and partly on external professional norms and formal professional rules, allows and aids most of its members and professional employees to be autonomous within the limits of group practice. Unlike the scientists in Marcson's[20] study of industrial laboratories, these lawyers do not need new organizing principles in order to accomplish this; in fact, their organizations may well serve as models for other professional work groups and as a reminder to themselves if their organizations should become more bureaucratic. Certainly the model applies to those organizations which deal directly with a client and where professional workers are dominated by other professional people. Because the law firms are successful in sponsoring most of their attorneys' independence, the strains which generally stem from a clash of values between bureaucratic norms and professional norms appear to be very mild; because the firms have been successful in achieving autonomy for their lawyers, the client is in a position to receive the best from his attorneys.

If professional people lose this independence, then it may be predicted that the client in real need is lost, for it is the autonomy of the professional person which sets the stage for his creativity—a required ingredient when dealing with the esoteric, the difficult, and the exceptional.

NOTES

1. David Riesman, "Law and Sociology" in William M. Evan (Ed.), *Law and Sociology* (New York: The Free Press, 1962), pp. 32, 40.

2. On the basis of a study of 207 Detroit area lawyers (none of them members of giant firms, by my definition; the largest law firm in Detroit is composed of 30 lawyers), Ladinsky comes to a similar conclusion. He writes: "*Partly because legal talent from quality law schools has flowed heavily into the large firms for many years, there has been extensive elaboration of legal procedures to handle the problems of corporate enterprises as opposed to those to care for the problems of private citizens. The result has been a high development of corporation protection, often at the ex-*

pense of individual citizens. In addition, areas of law unrelated to the operation of corporate enterprises have not had the same level of creativity devoted to them." Jack Ladinsky, "Careers of Lawyers, Law Practice, and Legal Institutions," *American Sociological Review*, 28 (February 1963), 54.

3. David Riesman, "Law and Sociology," *Stanford Law Review*, 9 (1957), 648.

4. Talcott Parsons, "The Law and Social Control," in William M. Evan (Ed.), *Law and Sociology, op. cit.*, p. 69.

5. *Ibid.*

6. This point is documented in Frederic W. Terrien and Donald L. Mills, "The Effect of Changing Size Upon the Internal Structure of Organizations," *American Sociological Review*, 20 (February 1955), 11.

7. *Ibid.*, p. 13. See also Paul F. Lazarsfeld and Wagner Thielens, Jr., *The Academic Mind* (New York: The Free Press, 1958), pp. 40–43, and Seymour Martin Lipset, Martin A. Trow, and James S. Coleman, *Union Democracy* (New York: The Free Press, 1956), p. 167. These last two footnotes are referred to by Allen H. Barton, *Organizational Measurement and its Bearing on the Study of College Environments* (New York: College Entrance Examining Board, 1961), using the above as examples of the effects of size on conflict in large organizations.

8. Peter M. Blau and W. Richard Scott. *Formal Organizations: A Comparative Approach* (San Francisco: Chandler Publishing, 1962), pp. 226–227.

9. Terrien and Mills, *op. cit.*, p. 11.

10. What part ethnicity of a staff plays in an organization was not determined. The "Jewish" firms studied were different from the old large New York "Anglo-Saxon" law offices and more like the large out-of-town "Anglo-Saxon" firms. This resemblance is probably related to the similarity in clients. Both the Jewish firms and the out-of-town offices have numerous small clients and few large clients.

11. James D. Thompson and William J. McEwen, "Organizational Goals and Environment: Goal-Setting as an Interaction Process," *American Sociological Review*, 23 (February 1958), 24.

12. For example, in law, medicine, and the ministry the right of privileged communication offers the possibility of independence to the practitioner.

13. Alvin W. Gouldner, "Cosmopolitans and Locals: Toward an Analysis of Latent Social Roles—I, II," *Administrative Science Quarterly*, 2 (1957, 1958), 281–306, 444–480 respectively.

14. Gerald Gordon, Sue Marquis, and O. W. Anderson, "Freedom and Control in Four Types of Scientific Settings," *The American Behavioral Scientist*, 6 (December 1962), 43. Differences in scientific types were also found by Donald Pelz and Frank M. Andrews, "Organizational Atmosphere, Motivation, and Research Contribution," *The American Behavioral*

Scientist, 6 (December 1962), 47. They comment: "Five distinct groups of researchers were described, based on data from 552 scientists in 11 research settings. Ph.D.'s in research-oriented laboratories most nearly resembled the stereotype of the 'scientist.' They were highest in influence over person affecting them, motivated from within, willing to take risks, and interested in self-development rather than status. 'Engineers' (non-Ph.D.'s in development-oriented laboratories, and not dominated by Ph.D.'s) had less influence, were more responsive to motivation from supervisors, and were considerably more interested in status advancement. The group of professional 'technicians'—non-Ph.D.'s in laboratories dominated by Ph.D.'s—were lowest in influence, most dependent on supervisors for motivation, most cautious, and most frustrated."

15. David Riesman, "Interviewers, Elites, and Academic Freedom," *Social Problems*, 6 (Fall 1958), 120.

16. It is put this way by Louis Kriesberg. *A Propositional Approach to the Study of Organization* (Chicago: National Opinion Research Center, University of Chicago), p. 6: "The greater the role differentiation within the organization, the greater is the organizational dissensus."

17. Sorrell M. Mathes and F. Clark Thompson, "Organization for Legal Work," 16, The Conference Board Business Record (October 1959).

18. William M. Trumbull, *Materials on the Lawyer's Professional Responsibility* (Englewood Cliffs, N.J.: Prentice-Hall, Inc., 1957). On pages 350–351 the author quotes Philbrick McCoy, Chairman, Special Committee on Canons of Ethics for the American Bar Association in 1956 as reporting: "The original thirty-two Canons of Professional Ethics were designed primarily for courtroom conduct, as was appropriate at the time they were drafted. They were formulated primarily for the lawyer who was in general practice. . . . For example, the present Canons have little to say about the position of the lawyer employed by his "client," such as a house counsel for a large organization. The Canon on partnerships deals primarily with the name of the partnerships. No Canon speaks directly about the problems of the office lawyer in advising his client and in drafting legal papers for him. The Canons do not deal with many of the problems created by the development of specialization nor, except in very general terms, with the problems of a lawyer who practices before administrative agencies or legislative bodies."

19. Some accuse the large law firms of not accepting the responsibility of their leadership by not taking a sufficient interest in the bar as a whole. They claim that this default tends to further separate the various strata of lawyers, making for a fragmented rather than a unified bar, which would have greater influence over all attorneys. See Carlin, who finds it hypocritical that the large firms are not taking effective steps toward reform. The area which he sees as needing special attention is concerned mainly with the quality of training received by the individual practitioner and the type of practice many are "forced" to accept and the unethical manner in

which they find it necessary to practice. Jerome E. Carlin, *Lawyers On Their Own: A Study of Individual Practitioners in Chicago* (New Brunswick, N.J.: Rutgers University Press, 1962), pp. 209–211.

20. Simon Marcson, *The Scientist in American Industry: Some Organizational Determinants in Manpower Utilization* (New York: Harper & Row, 1960), p. 151.

INDEX

INDEX

Abegglen, James C., 111n
academic freedom, 349, 350
Academic Man, The (Wilson), 291n
Academic Marketplace, The (Caplow and McGee), 287n
Academic Mind, The (Lazarsfeld and Thielens), 355n
Acheson, Dean, 9
American Bar Association, 10, 267–8, 272, 308n, 356n
American Jewish Congress, 65
American Lawyer, The (Blaustein, Porter, Duncan), 202n
Anderson, Theodore R., 287n
Andrews, Frank M., 355n
"Anglo-Saxon" firms, 172, 173
and Jewish firms, 173–5
antitrust law, 164, 166, 186
Armstrong, Barbara L., 46, 70n
associates
of middle range, 154–5, 232
and organizational conflict, 294, 296–304
permanent, 156, 231, 232, 330, 338, 352
and relations with partners, 294, 299, 324–9, 330–2
senior, 155–6, 231
Association of the Bar of the City of New York, 10, 22, 33, 172, 272
Auchincloss, Louis, 258, 290n, 309n

Austin, Edwin C., 70n
autonomy, 1–16 *passim*, 345, 349–50, 354
and charisma, 236–7
and creativity, 312, 314, 322, 338, 344
vs. organization life, 292–310 *passim*, 305–7, 345–6

Baker, Botts, Shephard & Coates, 203n
Baltzell, E. Digby, 140n
banks, 174, 185–6, 225, 245n, 294, 337
bar associations, 10, 160, 172, 267, 271–2, 278–9, 353
Barton, Allen H., 355n
Becker, Howard S., 279, 291n
"belongingness," 311
Berle, Jr., Adolphe A., 6, 13, 15n, 202n
Bierstedt, Robert, 235, 247n
"big case," 149, 151, 166, 225, 227–8, 243, 324
birthplace, 118–20
Blatchford, R. M., 114
Blau, Peter M., 289n, 307n, 346, 355n
Blaustein, Albert P., 202n
"blue sky work," 41, 186
bonuses, 81
Boston, Charles A., 295, 308n
Boyden, Albert, 163, 170n

Breed, Abbott & Morgan, 35n, 207, 246n
Bressler, Marvin, 257, 287n
"Brokers' Case," 227–8, 246n
Bromley, Bruce, 8
Brownell, Herbert, 10, 90
"buck-passing," 335–6
"bull pen," 210
bureaucracy, 2–3, 14, 24, 28, 69, 71n, 93, 218, 205–48 *passim*, 249–91 *passim*, 293
  and conformity, 311–40 *passim*
  and hierarchies, 224–8, 279, 293–4
  "mock," 276–85 *passim*
  and power, 234–6, 238, 262
  and professionals, 275–86, 292–310 *passim*, 353
  "punishment-centered," 276–85 *passim*
  "representative," 276–85 *passim*
  and rules, 215–24
  and size, 345–6
Byrne, James, 104

Cadwalader, Wickersham & Taft, 35n, 70n
Cahill, Gordon, Reindel & Ohl, (formerly Cahill, Gordon, Zachary & Reindel), 9, 35n, 43, 207n, 246n
Cahill, John T., 9
Canons of Professional Ethics of the American Bar Association, 267–70, 271–2, 289n, 295, 356n
Caplow, Theodore, 287n
Cardozo, Benjamin Nathan, 274
career patterns, 72–112 *passim*, 116–39 *passim*, 265
  and advancement, 91–3, 99–101
  and failure, 77–8, 85, 231
  and "firing," 81–5, 110
  and tenure, 115, 133–6
  and training, 114–15, 147, 181, 185, 306, 343
Carlin, Jerome E., 109–10, 112n 140n, 141, 167n, 168n, 172, 202n, 356n, 357n
Carr-Saunders, Alexander, 295, 307n–308n
Carter, Walter S., 38, 114
"case," 34n

Case, Clifford P., 8
Cases and Materials on the Legal Profession (Cheatham), 289n
Catholic lawyers, 45, 66
Chadbourne, Parke, Whiteside & Wolff, 35n, 207n, 258
charisma, 236–7
Cheatham, Eliott E., 273, 289n, 291n
Chicago University Law School, 20, 46, 55, 74
civil liberties, 18, 163
Clark, Grenville, 229
Cleary, Gottlieb, Steen & Hamilton (formerly Cleary, Friendly & Hamilton), 34n, 229, 258, 330
client-contact, 97, 98, 165–6, 168n, 174, 185, 200–1, 219, 223, 224, 225–7, 242, 250, 261–2, 265, 294, 297–9, 342, 343
client-team system, 225–7, 242
Cohen, Jules H., 304, 309n
Coleman, James S., 355n
Columbia University Law School, 22, 39, 44, 73, 110, 125, 131, 140n, 181, 182, 191, 198, 204n
compensation, 20–1, 24, 26, 57–8, 81, 92, 172, 184, 297
  and status, 228–32
  and time rates, 20–1, 27
conflicts of interest, 234, 270, 299
conformity, 2–4, 24, 28, 54, 198, 251–2, 258, 263, 312–38 *passim*, 347
  and creativity, 312, 314, 322, 338, 344
  ideological, 320–2
  and legal opinion, 322–3
  in partner-associate relations, 324–9
  pressures producing, 263–4, 316–18
corporation law, 48, 150, 164, 225
Corporation Lawyer: Saint or Sinner? (Levy), 6, 15n
Cotton & Franklin, 9
Cotton, Joseph P., 15n
"counsel," 35n
counterformists, 313
Covington & Burling, 179, 203n, 246n
Cravath Firm and Its Predecessors, The (Swaine), 15n, 35n, 113, 139n, 140n, 169n, 170n

Cravath, Swaine & Moore, 8, 11–12,
    32–33, 34*n*, 46, 78, 113–40 *passim*,
    160–1, 164, 199, 207, 208, 237,
    245*n*, 246*n*
"Cravath Systems," 114–16, 140*n*, 344
creativity, 6–7, 231, 311, 312, 314, 322,
    342
    and conformity, 312, 314, 322, 338,
    344
criminal cases, 150, 166, 271
Cromwell, William Nelson, 6, 11
Crutchfield, Richard S., 313, 314, 339*n*
*Current Research in the Sociology of
    the Legal Profession* (Carlin),
    202*n*

Davis, John W., 236
Davis Polk Wardwell Sunderland &
    Kiendl, 5, 35*n*, 176, 192, 208, 236,
    246*n*
Dean, Arthur, 8, 9–10, 11, 15*n*, 161,
    169*n*, 170*n*
Debevoise, Plimpton, Lyons & Gates,
    192
departmentalization, 195–6, 225–6
    See also segmentation
De Tocqueville, Alexis, 12
Deutsch, Karl W., 288*n*
Deutscher, Irwin, 290*n*
Dewey, Ballantine, Bushby, Palmer &
    Wood (formerly Root, Ballantine,
    Harlan, Bushby & Palmer), 10,
    34*n*, 90, 229, 258, 330
Dewey, Thomas E., 9, 90, 166
diaries, 220–2
Dodge, Emily P., 70*n*, 165, 170*n*
Donnelly, Richard C., 170*n*
Donovan, William J., 9
Donovan Leisure Newton & Irvine, 9,
    35*n*, 54, 87, 143, 176, 246*n*
"door man," 210, 259
Douglas, Paul H., 288*n*
Douglas, William O., 131
Drinker, Henry, 270, 271, 290*n*
Dubin, Robert, 291*n*, 339*n*
Dulles, John Foster, 9
Duncan, Charles T., 202*n*

Eisenhower, Dwight D., 10
elitism, 5, 37–8, 42, 120, 122, 180–1,
    350

Encyclopaedia of the Social Sciences
    (Berle), 202*n*
esprit de corps, 93, 177, 249, 250–1,
    256, 257, 299
Esquire case, 8
Essay on Professional Ethics (Shars-
    wood), 267, 290*n*
Essays in Sociology (Weber), 287*n*
ethics, 18–21, 222–3, 263–4, 266–71,
    288*n*, 289*n*, 290*n*
    See also rules
ethnic (and racial) bias, 37, 44–5, 65–
    7, 174–5
Executive Suite (Hawley), 94
"experts," 153, 155
Export-Import Bank, 12

failures, 77–8, 85, 231
fame, 90, 130–1, 138, 165–6, 235
fees, 213, 293–5, 297, 309*n*
Felix Frankfurter Reminisces (Phil-
    lips), 15*n*
Finletter, Thomas K., 131
"firing," 81–5, 110
Fisch, Edith L., 70*n*
Fisher, Burton R., 308*n*
Formal Organization (Blau and
    Scott), 289*n*, 307*n*
Francis, Roy G., 35*n*, 292, 307*n*
Frankfurter, Felix, 15*n*–16*n*
Fulbright, Crooker, Freeman, Bates &
    Jaworski, 203*n*

Garver, John, 70*n*
"general practice," 150, 204*n*, 225
Gerhart, Eugene C., 246*n*
Gibson, Dunn & Crutcher, 203*n*
Gilpatric, Roswell Leavitt, 11
Goode, William J., 263–4, 289*n*
Gordon, Gerald, 355*n*
Gordon, Robert Aaron, 310*n*
Goss, Mary E. W., 277, 291*n*
Gottlieb, David, 289*n*
Gouldner, Alvin W., 276–85, 291*n*,
    349, 355*n*
government, 160, 164, 179, 181
Great World and Timothy Colt, The
    (Auchincloss), 290*n*, 309*n*
Greenwood, Ernest, 308*n*
Growth of American Law, The
    (Hurst), 15*n*

Hagstrom, Warren O., 14n, 289n, 307n, 340n
Harlan, John Marshall, 10
Harno, Albert J., 168n
Harvard Club, 54
Harvard Law Review, 33, 39, 41, 252–4
Harvard Law School, 38–9, 43, 44, 46, 47, 48, 52, 54, 55, 73, 87, 110, 120, 125, 152, 180–1, 182, 191, 198, 289n
Harvard Law School Alumni Placement Center, 38
Harvard Law School Association of New York, 54
Harvard Law School Placement Information, 69n, 70n
Harvey, John G., 70n
Hatt, Paul, 167n
Hays, Paul R., 131
Henderson, Alexander Iselin, 138–9
hierarchies, 63–4, 224–8, 279, 293–4
"hiring partner," 59–61, 68
Horning, Donald, 34n, 70n, 289n
Horsky, Charles, 179, 203n
"house counsel, " 35n, 74
Hughes, Everett C., 290n, 293, 308n
Hughes, Helen M., 290n
Hughes, Hubbard & Blair, 258
  See also Royall, Koegel & Rogers
Hurst, James Willard, 4, 15n

image-making machinery, 51–4, 68
Indiana University Law School, 55
Individualism, *see* autonomy
Industrial Relations and the Social Order (Moore), 14n
influence, 115–16
insurance companies, 185–6
Intellectuals in Labor Unions (Wilensky), 34n, 291n
Internal Revenue Code, 215
International Law, 48
"internship," 74
Irish lawyers, 140n
  See also ethnic bias
ivy league, 44, 45, 48, 53–4, 65, 73–4, 109, 172
  See also individual schools

Jahoda, Marie, 313, 314, 339n
Jewish College Student, The (Shosteck), 70n
Jewish lawyers, 44–5, 65–7, 71n, 140n
  and firms, 173, 185, 355n
  See also ethnic bias
John William Sterling: A Biographical Sketch (Garver), 70n
Jones, Day, Cockly & Reavis, 203n
Jones, H. Bradley, 246n
"judgment," 260–2, 333
junior partners, 20, 25, 156–7, 183, 229
  and percentage partners, 183–4
Juniors and Seniors (Root), 340n
"junk," 166

Kelley, Drye, Newhall & Maginnes, 35n
Kennedy, John F., 10
Kirkland, Ellis, Hodson, Chaffetz & Masters, 102, 203n
Kirkland, Weymouth, 102
Klaw, Spencer, 30, 34n, 38–9, 69n, 304, 309n
Koegel, Otto E., 38, 69n, 140n, 247n
Kornhauser, William, 14n, 265, 272, 276–7, 289n, 290n, 291n, 307n, 330, 340n
Kriesberg, Louis, 111n, 252, 287n, 356n

labor law, 41, 48, 165, 225
labor unions, 165, 276
Ladinsky, Jack, 354n–355n
Lamb, Horace R., 87
Lasswell, Harold D., 170n
Law: Business or Profession, The (Cohen), 304
Law firms
  as business *vs.* profession, 275–310 *passim*
  differences between, 171–204
  ethnic backgrounds of, 173–5, 185, 355n
  hierarchies within, 224–8, 279, 287n, 293–4
  independence of, 343–4
  location of, 175–6, 178–90 *passim*
  organization of, 182–90, 205–48 *passim*, 346–7
  power of, 234–6, 238, 262

as satellites, 192–5, 199, 201
size of, 190–202, 345–6, 351
work of, 141–70, 185–9
See also bureaucracy; professions;
Wall Street lawyer
*Law Libraries in the United States
and Canada 1960–1961*, 246n
Law for the Lion, A (Auchincloss),
258
"law review" men, 69, 126–7, 143, 175,
249, 252–5, 341
Law and Sociology, 287n
*Lawyer from Antiquity to Modern
Times, The* (Pound), 308n
Lawyers on their Own (Carlin), 140n,
167n, 202n, 357n
Lazarsfeld, Paul F., 355n
Leboef Lamb & Leiby, 87
Legal Education in the United States
(Harno), 168n
Legal Ethics (Drinker), 290n
Levy, Beryl Harold, 6–7, 15n
Lewis, Roy, 308n
lineage, 37, 39–40
Lipset, Seymour Martin, 355n
litigation, 225, 244, 336, 337
Lodge, John, 130–1
Lonely Crowd, The (Riesman *et al.*),
339n
Lord, Day & Lord, 10, 35n, 90
Lortie, Dan C., 204n, 295, 308n
Lumbard, Jr., J. Edward, 9
Lundberg, Ferdinand, 13, 34n

McAllister, Breck, 149, 169n
McArthur, Charles, 111n
McCauley, Jr., Daniel J., 303
McCloy, John J., 11, 137–8
McCoy, Philbrick, 356n
McCutchen, Doyle, Brown & Enersen,
203n
McDaniel, Glen, 271, 290n
McDougal, Myres S., 170n
McEwen, William J., 355n
McGee, Reece J., 287n
MacKinnon, F. B., 270, 290n
Madow, William A., 288n
Making of the President 1960, The
(White), 15n
Malone, Ross L., 70n
management, 115–20, 177, 273, 275

managing clerk, 244–5
managing partner, 238–9
and assigning work, 239–43
Mansfield, Arabella A., 46
Mansfield, Walter R., 54, 87, 143, 153
Marcson, Simon, 14n, 71n, 277, 291n,
307n, 330, 340n, 354, 357n
marriage, 93, 94, 103
Marshall, John, 6
Martin, John W., 34n, 70n, 289n
Martindale-Hubbell Law Directory, 30,
32, 35n, 39, 73n, 108–10, 169n,
175, 179–80, 190–1, 203n, 204n,
207, 233, 351
*Materials on the Lawyer's Professional
Responsibility* (Trumbull), 356n
Mathes, Sorell M., 356n
"matter," 34n
Maude, Angus, 308n
Mayer, Friedlich, Spiess, Tierney,
Brown & Platt, 203n
Mayer, Martin, 5, 10, 15n, 19, 34n, 166,
170n
"Memorandum on Office Practice,"
215–17
Mentschikoff, Soia, 46–7
Merton, Robert K., 2, 14n, 28, 34n,
167n, 258, 263, 288n, 289n, 311–
12, 313, 339n
Methodical, Prudent and Disciplined
(MPD), 2, 332–8 *passim*
Michigan University Law School, 55,
74
middle partners, 158–9, 229–30
middle-range associates, 154–5, 232
Milbank, Tweed, Hadley & McCloy
(formerly Milbank, Tweed, Hope
& Hadley), 35n, 104, 167n
Mills, C. Wright, 5, 12–13, 15n, 202n,
311, 312, 339n
Mills, Donald L., 346, 355n
Moore, Wilbert E., 14n
Morgan, Lewis & Bockius, 203n
Mudge, Stern, Baldwin & Todd, 35n,
90, 207

negligence cases, 150, 271
Negro lawyers, 45
See also ethnic bias
neophytes, 74, 143–7

nepotism, 40, 64, 92–3, 114, 117, 122, 123, 177, 184
"New Clients List," 223
New York County Lawyers Association, 172, 308n–309n
New Yorker, 316
New York Post, 320–1
New York State Bar Association, 303
New York Times, 303, 309n
New York University Law School, 204n, 316
Nixon, Richard M., 90
Nixon, Mudge, Rose, Guthrie & Alexander, 90
noblesse oblige, 270–1
nonconformity, 311–13, 316, 319, 322
"nonpercentage" partners, 183–4, 200

Occupational Mobility in American Business and Industry (Warner and Abegglen), 111n
"of counsels," 35n, 229
office atmosphere, 205–6, 208–10
office hours, 103–4, 218–19
office manager, 244–5
Olds, Irving S., 15n
O'Melveny & Meyers, 203n
opinion letters, 222
Opportunities for Young Lawyers of Illinois, 168n
organization, see bureaucracy; law firms
Organization Man, The (Whyte), 14n, 311
Organizational Measurement and its Bearing on the Study of College Environments (Barton), 355n
Organizational Society, The (Presthus), 287n
overhead, 193, 304
"overtime," 103–4, 218

Parsons, Talcott, 293, 308n, 342, 344, 355n
partners, 31, 91–3, 94, 97–100, 115, 136–9, 183–5, 209–10
    assignment of work by, 243–4
    and associates, 294, 299, 324–9, 330–2
    and hierarchies, 156–60, 228–30
    junior, 20, 25, 156–7, 183, 229

managing, 238–43
and percentages, 183–4, 200
problems of, 302–7
senior, 99, 159–60, 190, 227, 236–8
partnership agreements, 198–9, 210–15 *passim*, 224, 229, 235
Patterns of Industrial Bureaucracy (Gouldner), 291n
Paul, Randolph, 61
Paul, Weiss, Rifkind, Wharton & Garrison, 34n, 35n, 61, 66, 90, 176, 177, 203n, 207
    See also Stevenson, Paul, Rifkind, Wharton & Garrison
Peck, David W., 54
Pelz, Donald, 355n
People ex rel Karlin v. Culkin, 274–5
Peper, Hamilton & Scheetz, 203n
permanent associates, 156, 231, 232, 330, 338, 352
"personal law," 165
personality, 40, 97, 104–8, 114, 336–7
personnel (clerical), 217, 218–22, 224, 228, 247n, 248n, 300–1
Phi Beta Kappa, 126
Philadelphian, The (Powell), 91
Phillips, Harlan B., 15n
Pillsbury, Madison & Sutro, 203n
placement services, 56–7
politics, 9, 321–2
Porter, Charles O., 202n
Pound, Roscoe, 308n
Powell, Richard, 91
power, 234–6, 238, 262
"power elite," 5, 342
Power Elite, The (Mills), 15n
Power without Property (Berle), 15n
Pratter, Harry, 7
preparatory schools, 122–3
Presthus, Robert, 287n
"Prince Charming," 301
Princeton University, 73
professional bureaucracy, 275–86, 292–310 *passim*, 330, 332
    see also bureaucracy; professions
Professional People in England (Lewis and Maude), 308n
professions, 2–3, 64, 77, 80, 96, 250, 257, 263, 307n–308n, 309n
    and bureaucracy, 275–86, 292–310 *passim*, 330, 332–8

codes and controls of, 263–73 *passim*
"free," 14, 293–6
value systems of, 265–6, 276, 279, 283, 293, 349
Professions, The (Carr-Saunders and P. A. Wilson), 307*n*–308*n*
Propositional Approach to the Study of Organization (Kriesberg), 356*n*
Proskauer, Joesph M., 44–5, 70*n*, 159, 169*n*, 175
"Protestant Ethic," 311
public opinion, 278
"public partners," 165–6

"raiding," 9–10
recruitment, 36–71 *passim*
interviewing for, 55–7, 61–3
in Jewish *vs.* Gentile firms, 175
and law schools, 38–55 *passim*
"off-the-street," 60
and small firms, 197–8
Reed, Smith, Shaw & McClay, 203*n*
Remington, William, 163
residences, 315–16
Riesman, David, 43, 69*n*, 70*n*, 178, 203*n*, 252, 287*n*, 311, 339*n*, 341, 342, 354*n*, 355*n*, 356*n*
Root, Jr., Elihu, 229, 330–1, 340*n*
Ropes & Gray, 163, 190, 203*n*
Ropes-Gray 1865–1940 (Boyden), 170*n*
Rostow, Eugene V., 131
Royall, Kenneth C., 90
Royall, Koegel & Rogers, 35*n*, 90, 258 (formerly Royall, Koegel & Caskey and Dwight, Royall, Harris, Koegel & Caskey)
rules, 14, 215–24, 249, 259–75 *passim*, 288*n*, 289*n*, 291*n*
of courts, 272, 273–5
external professional, 264–75, 347–9
informal, 259–62, 265–6, 349
social, 259–64 *passim*

satellite firms, 192–5, 199, 201
Scientist in American Industry, The (Marcson), 14*n*, 71*n*, 291*n*, 307*n*, 340*n*
Scientists in Industry (Kornhauser), 289*n*, 307*n*, 340*n*

Scott, W. Richard, 289*n*, 307*n*, 346, 355*n*
Segment of My Times, A (Proskauer), 70*n*
segmentation, 147–9
See also departmentalization
self-image, 190, 255–6
"semibureaucracy," 277
senior associates, 155–6, 231
senior partners, 20, 25, 31, 99, 159–60, 190, 326
as dictators, 236–8
vs. working partner, 227
Service and Procedure in Bureaucracy (Francis and Stone), 30, 35*n*, 307*n*
Seventy-five Years of Simpson Thacher & Bartlett: 1884–1959, 111*n*
"sex appeal," 234
Seymour, Whitney North, 10
Sharswood, George, 267, 290*n*
Shearman & Sterling (formerly Shearman & Sterling & Wright), 11, 34*n*, 49, 159, 246*n*
Shearman, Thomas G., 49
Shosteck, Robert, 70*n*
Siddal, Roger B., 18, 34*n*, 111*n*–112*n*, 246*n*, 247*n*
Silverman, Samuel J., 23
Simpson Thacher & Bartlett, 8, 9, 10, 34*n*, 43, 78, 79, 92, 111*n*, 207*n*, 245*n*
Sinclair, Upton, 290*n*, 319, 339*n*
Smigel, Erwin O., 34*n*, 70*n*, 289*n*
social background, 14, 37–42 *passim*, 66, 71*n*, 72–4, 97, 102, 117, 121–3, 166, 172, 177, 251, 347
"Social Ethic," 311
"social" firms, 92, 116, 176–8, 319
Social Register, 32, 39–40, 102, 109, 117, 123, 176–7, 191
sociological method, 17–34
solo lawyers, 172–3, 294, 295–6, 308*n*, 343, 351
specialization, 40–2, 48–9, 51–2, 93, 96, 114–15, 119, 136, 149–54, 186, 194–5, 224, 226, 287*n*–288*n*, 295
and buck-passing, 335–6
and status, 233–4
Squire, Sanders & Dempsey, 203*n*

status, 91–2, 184, 209–10, 224–5, 228–34, 262, 284
and age, 232–3
and specialty, 233–4
Sterling, John William, 49
Stevens, Lucia Beth, 111n
Stevenson, Adlai E., 9, 10, 90
Stevenson, Paul, Rifkind, Wharton & Garrison (Washington, D.C.), 207, 246n
in Chicago as Stevenson, Rifkind & Wirtz, 246n
Stone, Harlan Fiske, 166, 170n
Stone, Robert C., 35n, 292, 307n
Sullivan & Cromwell, 10, 11, 35n, 84, 207, 344
Sunderland, Edward S. S., 5
Supreme Count, 7–8, 33, 39, 131, 273–5, 341
Survey of Large Law Firms in the United States, A (Siddal), 34n, 112n, 246n
Swaine, Robert T., 11, 15n, 35n, 113, 116, 130, 132, 164, 165, 169n 170n, 207, 245n

taboos, 18–19, 228
Taft, Henry W., 69n–70n
Tannenbaum, Robert, 288n
tax work, 41, 48, 90–1, 150, 154, 164, 185, 214, 225, 327
Teamplay, 1, 2–4, 24, 28, 54, 115, 174–5, 177, 186, 189, 209, 225–7, 256, 257
See also conformity
Terrien, Frederic W., 346, 355n
Thielens, Jr., Wagner, 355n
Thomas, Dorothy, 70n
Thompson, F. Clark, 356n
Thompson, James D., 355n
Thompson, Victor A., 287n
"tickler" system, 222, 244
Toepher, Louis A., 53
"trappers," 165–6
trial law, 48
Trow, Martin A., 355n
Truman, Harry S, 11
Trumbull, William M., 268, 290n, 356n
Tweed, Harrison, 103, 111n, 150, 167n, 169n

Twenty Thousand Nurses Tell Their Story (Hughes, Hughes and Deutscher), 290n

Uniform Partnership Act, 215
Union Democracy (Lipset, Trow, Coleman), 355n
United States Office of Education Directory, 73
"up-or-out" policy, 44, 64, 67, 68, 80, 127, 182
Upton Sinclair Presents William Fox (Sinclair), 290n, 339n

vacations, 219
Veblen, Thorstein, 343
vertical mobility, 337
Vinson, Elkins, Weems & Searls, 203n
Virginia University Law School, 74, 120, 125, 140n

"Wall Street," 4, 294
Wall Street lawyers:
advancement of, 72–112 *passim*, 116–39
and big business, 4–8, 13, 173, 194, 271, 294
compensation of, 20–1, 24, 26–7, 57–8, 81, 92, 115, 172, 183, 229, 231–2, 259, 297, 309n
and competition, 43–4, 47–8, 51, 55, 57, 58–9, 93–7, 249, 256–8, 287n, 335, 352
and conformity, 311–40 *passim*
education of, 38–55 *passim*, 73–4, 120–6
and large firms, 1–16, 76, 165, 182–3, 224, 293
and organizational conflicts, 292–310 *passim*, 350–1
recruitment of, 36–71 *passim*, 114, 175, 197–8
social background of, 37, 39–40, 44–5, 71n, 72–4, 97, 102, 117, 121–3, 166, 172, 177, 251, 347
training of, 114–15, 147, 181, 185, 306, 343
work of, 141–70, 239–44
Walter S. Carter, Collector of Young Masters (Koegel), 69n, 140n, 247n

Warkov, Seymour, 287*n*
Warner, W. Lloyd, 111*n*
"Washington Correspondents," 207
Washington Lawyer, The (Horsky), 179, 203*n*
Weber, Max, 249, 276, 278, 287*n*
Webster, Bethuel M., 87
Webster, Sheffield & Chrystie, 87
White & Case, 15*n*, 34*n*, 207
White Collar (Mills), 203*n*, 339*n*
White, Theodore H., 15*n*
Who's Who, 32, 109
Whyte, Jr., William H., 14*n*, 311, 312, 332, 338*n*
Wickenden, W. E., 308*n*
Wigmore, John H., 291*n*
Wilensky, Harold L., 34*n*, 111*n*, 276, 291*n*
Wilkie Farr Gallagher Walton & Fitzgibbon (formerly Wilkie Owen Farr Gallagher & Walton), 35*n*
William Nelson Cromwell 1854–1948 (Dean), 15*n*, 169*n*, 170*n*

Willis, Arthur B., 246*n*
Willkie, Wendell, 9
Wilson, Logan, 277, 291*n*
Wilson, P. A., 308*n*
"window man," 210, 259
Winston, Strawn, Smith & Patterson, 203*n*
Winthrop, Stimson, Putnam & Roberts, 35*n*, 163
Withey, Stephen B., 308*n*
women lawyers, 46–7, 68, 69
Women Lawyers in the United States (Thomas), 70*n*
"working partners," 227
Wright, Boykin C., 11, 159
Wright, J. D., 69*n*, 70*n*
Wyzanski, Jr., Charles Edward, 5

Yale Law School, 38, 39, 43, 44, 55, 73, 110, 120, 125, 131, 180–1, 182, 191, 198
Young, Nancy, 47, 70*n*